The Secret Money Market

THE SECRET MONEY MARKET

Inside the Dark World of Tax Evasion, Financial Fraud, Insider Trading, Money Laundering, and Capital Flight

Ingo Walter

HarperBusiness

A Division of HarperCollins*Publishers*

International Standard Book Number: 0-88730-392-7 (cloth)
0-88730-489-3 (paper)

Library of Congress Catalog Card Number: 89-45776

Printed in the United States of America

First published in Great Britain by Allen & Unwin 1985.
First published in *Counterpoint* by Unwin® Paperbacks 1986.
Second edition published by Unwin® Paperbacks, an imprint
of Unwin Hyman Limited, in 1989. © Ingo Walter, 1985, 1986, 1989

90 91 92 93 HC 9 8 7 6 5 4 3 2 1

Contents

Tables, Figures and Exhibits

Tables

Figures

Exhibits

Preface

This book is about global financial flows that nobody is supposed to know about – their size, their nature, their causes, and their effects. It is about the behavior of people who want to keep financial information from others and are willing to pay for it. It is about people, institutions and countries that are happy to handle secret assets and keep the information to themselves, usually for a price. There is demand and there is supply, there are buyers and there are sellers.

Financial secrecy can be considered a business, one that can be analyzed in terms of the economics that underlie *any* business. It forms an industry that produces services people want and are willing to pay for, one that has its own players in a global marketplace. It is a somewhat curious industry, however, in that services are produced that contribute great value to some, yet are perceived as positively bad by others – so that the players are caught in a never-ending series of cat-and-mouse chases.

This book attempts to describe that industry, in all of its economic, political, social and personal dimensions. Consequently, economics forms the basic frame of reference for this book. Concepts of market analysis, macroeconomics, international trade, economic growth and international finance all find application here.

So do war stories and anecdotes. Nobody is anxious to talk about international financial secrecy, and there is little hard evidence available. Almost all first-hand information is confidential. What second-hand information exists depends for its accuracy on those who tell it. Like a jigsaw puzzle with many missing pieces, isolated facts and observations have to be assembled in an effort to discern the structure of the whole.

The first edition of *Secret Money* was published in 1985. In the intervening years, an amazing array of new cases have arisen, ranging from the Marcos story case in the Philippines to the Iran-Contra scandal in the United States, from capital flight and the international debt crisis to the insider trading and money laundering of the mid-1980s. This second edition of *Secret Money* tries to capture these developments and incorporates them into the framework developed in the first edition of the book. Not surprisingly, the 'fit' is quite good.

I am grateful to a number of individuals with whom I have discussed problems of financial secrecy over the years, most of whom don't want to be identified. In addition, I am particularly grateful to Ms Amanda Tealby Lomas, who pulled together the updates for the various chapters and made a very significant contribution to the completion of this edition. Ms Ann Rusolo capably and efficiently handled the often complex word processing. Financial support was provided by the INSEAD International Financial Services Programme in Fontainebleau, France.

INGO WALTER
New York City
September 1988

The Secret Money Market

1

The World of Secret Money

Few aspects of international finance are more fascinating than secrecy. Images flash through the mind of suitcases crammed with currency crossing national boundaries, of close-mouthed couriers slipping easily into and out of airports, hotels and banking offices, of expatriates living handsomely along palm-shaded beaches with no visible means of support, of churning money laundries and quiet slush funds. All find their parallels in the real world. But there are many other, less dramatic but much more important images as well: the tax evader skimming unreported income into an offshore account; the briber shuffling funds to the bribee; the violator of securities laws squirreling away illegal profits; the insecure politician or government official building a retirement fund abroad; the businessman fleeing his creditors; the husband fleeing his wife; the law-abiding citizen fleeing exposure to political or economic risk. All are players in the global financial secrecy game.

International financial secrecy is a subject of enduring and perhaps growing importance for the international economy, one that is well worth exploring. With a little imagination, the conventional tools of economic analysis can yield some useful insights into an otherwise rather murky subject. As we shall see, it is largely a matter of supply and demand.

The demand for financial secrecy

Who needs or desires financial secrecy? Practically everybody. The demand for financial secrecy – meaning non-disclosure of financial information that people are willing to pay for – arises from at least five more or less distinct sets of motivations: personal, business, political, fiscal and criminal. Each has a unique pattern of demand that helps define the overall structure of the global 'market' for financial secrecy.

A personal desire to keep financial affairs confidential may be a purely

1

domestic matter. Surveys reveal an amazing amount of financial secrecy between husbands and wives, perhaps to prevent 'irresponsible' household spending behavior or to avoid unfavorable property settlements in the event of divorce. Parents often keep financial secrets from their children, in the hope of inducing proper motivation and greater effort. Moneyed people withhold financial information from their prospective heirs in the hopes of keeping the vultures at bay. In an employee's dealings with his employer over salary matters, or a shopper's haggling with salesmen over purchases of goods or services, it is usually worthwhile not showing too many financial cards. And there is the matter of personal preference. Individuals feel more or less strongly that personal finances are nobody else's business, that they have a basic 'right' to financial privacy. Nor is it wise to attract thieves, kidnappers, con-artists and other social parasites by unnecessary financial disclosure. Personal financial secrecy usually remains in substantial compliance with the law, and in many countries has been well served by long-standing traditions of banking confidentiality. Indeed, it is often regarded as a cornerstone of personal liberty.

Confidentiality is no less important as an aspect of business affairs. Withholding financial information from competitors, suppliers, creditors and customers is a right that business people assume from the outset. Release of such information is made only in a tightly controlled manner and, where possible, only in a way that benefits that enterprise. As such, financial information is proprietary. It is capitalized in the value of a business to its shareholders. Leakage of financial information could easily erode this value, and so confidentiality and the judicious use of information is generally assumed in business as a critical component of the rules of the game in market-oriented economies. Beyond this, however, people in business may wish to keep financial information from employees, partners, potential acquirers and filers of lawsuits, not to mention the tax man, all the while remaining fully in compliance with the law. Again, standard confidentiality arrangements in national banking and financial systems are usually well suited to meet the need for 'normal' business secrecy.

The kinds of effects the desire for business secrecy can have is illustrated by events on the Tokyo currency exchange. During the mid-1980s, foreign institutions' share of foreign exchange business rose by 50 per cent, to 45 per cent of total trades. This is in part thought to be due to good service and aggressive pricing. But there is undoubtedly another factor, namely a loophole in Japanese foreign exchange regulations. In 1987, the Finance Ministry, worried about the soaring yen, suggested that Japanese bankers cease their speculative sales of dollars. As a result, secrecy-prone corporate traders gravitated to foreign-owned banks. Unlike Japanese institutions, they are not required to report their foreign exchange activities to the Bank of Japan.[1]

There are times when people worry about their exposure to political risk. The owner of a company or a farm worries that a new regime may confiscate his assets. The government official worries about being overthrown, possibly necessitating a hasty exit to save his own life. Ordinary citizens have been wiped out time after time as governments come and go with exciting but often misguided new policies. As the years go by, they develop a deep personal distrust of 'visible' domestic financial and real assets as a reliable store of value. Meanwhile, foreign investors in a country worry about the risks of being aliens, and often seek to submerge themselves as far as possible in the host environment, possibly through the services of local intermediaries or beneficial owners. Because political risk usually extends only to a nation's borders, extraordinary value is placed on 'outside' assets kept under wraps in other, less troublesome political jurisdictions. Yet the ownership of 'outside' assets may itself be viewed at home as evidence of a lack of commitment, a telegraphing of options, and possibly as a crime, thus placing a great premium on secrecy as long as the principal – or people he or she cares about – remains behind.

Then there are the tax evaders. Death and taxes are said to be the only great certainties that face human beings. Around the world people feel that they are unfairly taxed. Some are exposed to high levels of income taxation. Others are hit by confiscatory wealth taxes or death taxes. Still others feel forced by high indirect taxes or wage and price controls to escape into the underground economy, or are encouraged by stiff import duties and other market distortions to enter the contraband business. And there are always those who are simply greedy, for whom the only 'fair' tax is zero.

There are usually ways to avoid taxes legally, for a price. There are also ways to evade taxes – illegally to escape government claims on income or assets. None is entirely risk-free, and all require varying degrees of financial secrecy to work. Once again, 'outside' assets, beyond the reach of the national fiscal authorities, can take on a high value to the tax evader.

Lastly, there are the crooks (we can leave aside for the moment tax evasion and political risk avoidance as examples of out-and-out crookedness). Drugs traffickers not only accumulate huge amounts of cash, but regularly deal in a variety of foreign currencies. So do gun-runners and terrorists, feeding off the political turmoil and insecurities that afflict others. And there is organized and unorganized crime – robbery, burglary, auto theft, illegal gambling, prostitution, loan sharking, protection, extortion and other forms of racketeering. All need ways to stash funds and eliminate paper trails that might be taken as evidence of criminal activity – money needs to disappear and stay that way, reappearing only in freshly laundered form. Bribery and corruption require financial secrecy no less, with slush funds skillfully set up and carefully kept from the public eye.

Whether personal, business, political, fiscal or criminal, the secrecy objective is the same. Yet the secrecy 'products' that are needed, and the willingness to pay for them, are vastly different.

The supply of financial secrecy

As with the demand for secrecy, the supply side forms a rather complex patchwork of intermediaries and assets that yield varying degrees of safety from unwanted disclosure. Supply dimensions can be classified into onshore financial assets, offshore financial assets, and physical assets held either onshore or offshore.

Onshore financial assets include bank deposits and certificates, cashier's checks, equity shares, bonds and notes of public or private issuers. All normally yield 'market' rates of return, yet provide the investor with some degree of protection from unwanted disclosure. Traditional banking practice in most countries provides for confidentiality with respect to unauthorized inquiries, which gives adequate shielding from the prying eyes of many of the institutions and individuals targeted in the 'personal' and 'business' needs for protection from disclosure. Once the law gets involved, however, either in civil, tax or criminal matters, much of this protection is lost.

Under proper legal procedures, the state can force disclosure in the event of divorce proceedings, creditor suits, inheritance matters and tax cases, not to mention criminal actions. Although a certain amount of added protection can be obtained through 'bearer' certificates of various types, this runs the risk of theft, loss or accidental destruction. Onshore beneficial ownership – placing financial assets in the names of friends, associates or family members – can also provide greater protection, assuming the third parties can be trusted and will not themselves face legal trouble as a result. Or 'shell companies' and legitimate business 'fronts' can be used, both to hide financial assets and to launder tainted money. The history of organized crime and fiscal skullduggery worldwide is replete with cat-and-mouse chases of mind-boggling complexity. Sooner or later a rat seems to emerge, confidentiality is blown, and the jig is up. As long as secrecy is sought domestically, governed by a single more or less efficient law-enforcement process and subject to the political whims of the moment, the quality of onshore secrecy 'products' is invariably tainted.

Foreign financial assets may offer a good deal more in this regard, if only because national sovereignty halts at the border, and extraterritorial investigation normally requires disclosure terms carefully and often reciprocally negotiated between governments. Bank deposits may be held abroad in carefully selected countries, outside the political jurisdiction of home authorities, and thus deemed acceptably safe from unwanted disclosure. Foreign equities and debt instruments may provide similar security, yet may be subject to the host country withholding taxes and negotiated disclosure at the request of the home country. Things are a bit easier, of course, when the host country is also a tax haven. Bearer certificates, beneficial ownership and shell companies may provide some added protection, and certainly greatly increase the complexity of the inevitable paper chase. In all cases, the secrecy attributes of the host country – evidenced in its history, traditions and proneness to corruption – are of critical importance.

An alternative to financial secrecy sought in other countries is provided by true 'offshore' assets. These may be held in the form of bank deposits or certificates in Euro-banking or booking centers ranging from New York to London, from Singapore to Panama, from Nassau to Luxembourg. All provide substantial exemption from taxation, although secrecy may be eroded if deposits in offshore branches of home-country banks are involved (or foreign banks that do business domestically), and authorities are able to force disclosure through the domestic entity. Deposits in offshore branches of foreign banks that do not do business domestically may avoid this problem, but could be perceived in some cases as being more risky. All normally deal in large sums, so small-timers may be left out. Another form of offshore assets is provided by Eurobonds, generally available in bearer form, which can be purchased by individuals at retail, either on issuance or in the secondary market. Once again, shell companies and beneficial ownership can be used to further draw the veil of secrecy.

All sellers of financial secrecy products have an important stake in doing their best to limit disclosure as far as possible. Their business depends on it. Any form of discretionary disclosure will damage the value of what they have to sell, perhaps irreparably. Governmental jurisdictions responsible for the secrecy vendors tend to be on much the same wavelength, with the degree of congruence depending on the importance of the secrecy business in generating real economic gains in the form of local employment, income and taxes.

Lastly, there are physical assets kept in the form of collectables, precious metals and stones, other forms of tangible property, or even cash (domestic and foreign), secreted away in walls, mattresses, safe deposit boxes, and holes in the ground. Hoarding is as old as mankind. People in countries ranging from France to India have, over the generations, developed a profound distrust of conventional financial assets as waves of political change, economic mismanagement and social unrest have swept over them. Again, physical assets may also be held offshore, consigned to an individual or an institution to watch over with care. All such assets provide effective secrecy as long as they remain undiscovered, yet may put the owner at risk of theft, fraud, extortion or even bodily injury if information or suspicion leaks out.

Not all assets yielding the desired degree of secrecy are available to everyone, of course. While secreted physical and domestic financial assets are generally usable by anyone, this is not true of many of the more interesting offshore assets that are relatively safe from disclosure. Lack of information and financial sophistication, exchange controls, inertia, fear of getting caught, and size of the necessary transactions are some of the factors that inhibit people's access to the secrecy 'products' available around the world. This leads to considerable market segmentation, which in turn gives rise to both constraints and profit opportunities in the international secrecy business.

The cost of secrecy

As they say, there is no such thing as a free lunch. Like anything else, secrecy has its cost. And the higher the degree of secrecy (the 'quality' of the product), the higher the cost. Nobody expects to pay the same for a Mercedes-Benz and a Hyundai, and people in the market for a Mercedes-Benz are not too likely to seek out the Hyundai showroom or vice versa. What determines the cost of financial secrecy in the international marketplace?

Perhaps appropriately, the cost of secrecy is a bit shadowy, and focuses in large measure on the difference between what sort of return is actually earned on the secreted assets and what *could have been* earned on a comparable portfolio of non-secret assets in the open market. Moreover, non-secret returns generally have to be adjusted for taxes, while secret returns do not. And secret assets may be more risky as well. We thus have an 'opportunity cost', one that comprises at least three differentials: returns, charges and risks.

Everyone knows that assets like gold, domestic or foreign cash and other physical property yield nothing, except for possible capital gains. Neither, ordinarily, do bank checks or demand deposits. And some income-earning assets yield a good deal more than others. The cost of secrecy attributable to return differentials is the gap between returns on the mix of assets actually held in order to achieve the desired degree of secrecy and returns on an optimum mix of assets held by the same individual *if* secrecy were not a consideration. This includes both ordinary asset-related yields and expectations of net capital gains. A numbered foreign account yielding next to nothing (or even having a negative yield), or gold bullion in a foreign bank vault, would seem to involve high-priced secrecy, but a confidential account in a local bank that yields a 'market' rate of interest would not.

Second, charges levied by suppliers of secrecy can add to the cost. Banking fees may be raised for asset-holders known to be driven by the secrecy motive. Transactions may have to be routed in clandestine ways, through narrow markets with wide spreads, via inefficient conduits, all the while picking up transactions costs. Foreign exchange transactions, perhaps repeated several times or involving black markets, may add further costs. People may have to be bribed. Third parties, beneficial owners and shell companies may have to be used to enhance secrecy, all of which costs money. Since many of the counterparties in such transactions know the name of the game well, they may not be shy about pricing their services. Such charges must be added to any yield differential in ascertaining the cost of secrecy.

And then there is the matter of risk. Some assets are clearly a lot more risky than others. Beneficial owners may renege on their pledge. Gold and other physical assets may be highly volatile in price, and subject to theft. Fixed-rate financial instruments and foreign currencies expose the owner to interest-rate and exchange-rate risk. Deposits in potentially shaky banks, and purchases of stocks and bonds expose the owners to default risk. Country risk, in turn, exposes them to the willingness and ability of governments to honor external claims on domestic real or financial assets. And some types of assets that would make possible greater portfolio diversification and earnings stability may simply not be available to the secrecy seeker. The risk differential between a portfolio of assets yielding the desired degree of financial secrecy and an open-market portfolio can thus be defined as an implicit 'cost' to the individual. The greater the person's aversion to risk, the greater will be this perceived cost.

So the real cost of secrecy to an asset-holder with a certain risk-preference profile is the risk-adjusted net differential in returns between an open-market portfolio and one containing the desired dose of financial secrecy. Clearly, different classes of secrecy seekers will face vastly different costs. Even within each class, cost differentials may emerge due to differences in transaction size, sophistication, risk aversion, and the like.

Does it pay to buy financial secrecy? That depends. The cost of secrecy gives half the picture. The other half is based on what may happen if the secrecy cover is blown – what economists call the 'damage function' – and the probability of this actually occurring. Damage can range from execution, exile, prison and political ostracism to confiscation of assets, incremental taxes, social opprobrium and familial tension. Avoidance of damage is, after all, what the secrecy seeker is after, and, since damage usually is a matter of probabilities, his attitude toward the risk of exposure is a critical factor in how this benefit is valued..

How much secrecy should one buy? Simple. Just enough so that the marginal cost of financial secrecy equals its marginal benefit – both sides risk-adjusted, of course. This may sound a bit academic, but it's conceptually correct. It may stretch the imagination to envisage the harried secrecy seeker carefully equating marginal costs and benefits, but he will surely know when he's bought too much (being 'secrecy poor') or too little.

The price of secrecy

When out shopping for secrecy, people thus confront a variety of products, each of which has a price. Some are 'list' prices, paid by everyone regardless of the willingness to pay, while others are individually negotiated. Both are set by the forces of supply and demand in the secrecy market.

List prices such as bank interest rates, bond yields and equity returns are established by broad market forces that extend well beyond seekers of secrecy. The returns involved may well impose an opportunity cost on the secrecy seeker, yet still be higher than what the individual would have sacrificed to achieve the degree of financial secrecy actually obtained. He thus enjoys an unearned benefit we can call a 'secrecy seeker's surplus' (SSS).

Financial products specifically tailored to the secrecy market, like all high-quality items, involve substantially higher opportunity costs and hence smaller SSS. Numbered bank accounts abroad, a jewel among available secrecy products, tend to have correspondingly high opportunity costs. Yet even these are in large part list-priced so that, despite the expense, much of the SSS remains intact.

Not so in the case of custom-tailored secrecy items whose prices are set largely on the basis of bargaining. The secrecy vendor tries to ascertain how much his product is worth, given the apparent motivations of the secrecy seeker. He adjusts his asking price accordingly, and there may be an interval of negotiation before final agreement is reached. He will never, of course, threaten to breach the confidential relationship, since this would seriously and perhaps fatally impair the value of his product. In the final negotiated price, much of the SSS may evaporate – it is drawn off by the vendor.

So supply and demand interact in the market for financial secrecy, just as they do in any other market. A hierarchy of differentiated products exists, each with its own market characteristics. The greater the demand, the higher the price. The more intense the competition among vendors, and the easier the substitutability of secrecy products, the lower the price. The rational secrecy seeker will presumably shop around, insofar as his position is not jeopardized thereby, to fill his basket with an optimum mix of products at a cost that makes the whole exercise worthwhile.

Market structure

If secrecy is a product that can be bought and sold in national and international markets and described in terms like supply, demand, cost and price, then some of the dimensions of the secrecy market itself – in terms of competitive structure, conduct and performance – should also be amenable to rational analysis.

On the demand side, we see highly differentiated characteristics among secrecy seekers, in terms of their willingness and ability to pay. We also see widely divergent secrecy products and vendors, many of whom compete with one another. A few vendors have products with no good substitutes, so that demand for them may well be quite inelastic (insensitive to price) and their sellers are able to command very high prices indeed. Some traditional secrecy products (gold, dummy companies, holes in the ground) are easily available in some places but less so elsewhere. Others have been built up over the generations as secure repositories (Swiss numbered accounts) and can command high premiums. But high premiums also attract competitors, whose entry may alter the structure of the market. It is probably safe to say that higher levels of secrecy involve successively greater degrees of monopoly power in the definition of competitive structure and market organization.

As we shall see, the international market for financial secrecy is perhaps more competitive than might at first appear. Countries see it as in their economic interest to offer secrecy products in competition with one another, and institutional arrangements that threaten to erode some of its value are often fiercely resisted.

Plan of attack

In this book, we shall explore the various facets of secret money as an international economic phenomenon. Chapter 2 outlines the principal secrecy 'products' available in the international marketplace, some of which are quite complex. This clarifies what is being bought and sold, and permits a reasonable definition of the 'market' for financial secrecy in terms of characteristics associated with demand (Chapters 3 to 6) and supply (Chapters 7 and 8). Who are the major players on the demand side, how do they behave, and what are they willing and able to pay for financial secrecy? What kind of vendors have emerged, how do they differentiate and price their services, and how do they relate to their respective governments? These chapters form an illustrative set of real-world cases intended to substitute (albeit imperfectly) for the chronic lack of reliable data in this area.

Chapters 9 and 10 identify and evaluate a variety of measures intended to break the veil of secrecy associated with public policy action to combat corruption, tax evasion, terrorism, drug trafficking, and various other kinds of activities that need financial secrecy to work. They discuss the principal threats to the international market for secret money. Chapter 11 attempts an evaluation of the broader consequences of secret money, and Chapter 12 looks at its future.

Having carefully traced through the available evidence on international financial secrecy, can a coherent theory be devised that fits the facts? Theory is important, after all, in making sense of the whole issue, and in forecasting its future evolution. Annex 1 outlines the principal conceptual aspects of international financial secrecy from an economic perspective. As with much of economics, no matter how useful, the discussion is somewhat arcane. Readers less interested in theory are encouraged to skip to the end of the Annex for a summary of the main conclusions.

Note

1 Ted Holden, 'Look Who's Winning Tokyo's Currency Sweepstakes', *Business Week*, 11 April 1988.

2

What is Secret Money?

It is perhaps best to begin by discussing the 'raw material' of the financial secrecy business – the products that are being bought and sold – as well as the relative importance of clandestine transactions in a broader economic context.

The underground economy

We can define the rationale for the underground economy in terms of transactions that create value, but that are intended to escape something (taxes, revelation of bribes, bureaucratic red tape, exchange controls, criminal prosecution, etc.). It may be convenient to categorize underground economic activities in two ways: (1) transactions to avoid government-imposed impediments to the efficient conduct of business and to evade taxation; and (2) criminal transactions involving drugs, robbery, contract murder, prostitution, racketeering, and the like – basically economically motivated criminal activities. The clandestine cash flows involved may be subdivided into three categories: (a) legally earned income that is undeclared for tax purposes, (b) income in kind, and (c) illegally earned income.[1] Escape means secrecy, and secrecy means that the transactions involved and the economic activity they represent are very difficult to measure – sometimes escaping measurement altogether.

Measurement

There are several ways to attempt measurement of the size of the underground economy.[2] The so-called 'fixed ratio variant' assumes that there is a monetary ratio (currency in circulation divided by gross national product) that, without the underground economy, would probably have remained constant over time, and that there was a 'golden' period in the past when no underground economy existed. The 'golden period' monetary ratio is compared with the monetary ratio at present to estimate the relative change in the share of underground (cash) transactions. It could also be a change resulting in part from inflation.

The 'currency-denomination' variant assumes that the underground economy is associated mainly with the use of bills of certain denominations. The estimate of the size of the underground economy is based on the change in the number of such bills in circulation. For example, in the United States, the proportion of $100 bills has risen from 33 per cent of the value of all notes in circulation in 1977 to 47 per cent in 1987. At least one weakness of this approach is that large-denomination US currency notes are used for transactions and as a store of value in foreign countries. Therefore, the increase in the number of such notes in circulation can be partly attributed to an increase in foreign holdings as well as to domestic underground activities.

The 'currency-equation' variant assumes that underground activities are the direct consequence of high taxes, and that currency is used mainly for carrying out tax-evasion transactions or for storing wealth accumulated out of the reach of the tax man.

Consider changes in the demand for notes and coins relative to the growth in current-account bank deposits. In the United States, the ratio of cash to demand deposits has risen from 25 per cent in 1960 to 60 per cent in the 1980s. Here again, however, factors other than a growth in the underground economy may have played a part – the rise of the automatic cash dispenser, for example, or a shift out of checking and into savings and money-market accounts.

The 'physical input approach' assumes a stable relationship between some physical input into the economy, such as kilowatt hours of electric power, and national output. The difference between the estimated size of the economy, based on such a relationship, and the reported GNP may be attributed to the underground economy.

The 'labor market approach' originated in Italy, where the official rate of labor-force participation has decreased drastically since the late 1950s, while unofficial estimates of labor-force participation rates have been much higher. The difference gives some idea of the relative size of underground economic activity by workers.

The 'gap approach' involves a comparison between income reported in tax returns and income estimated in national income accounts. For the comparison to be meaningful, the national income statistics must be derived from sources other than, and independent of, the income tax authorities.

The 'legal tax potential' approach defines evaded tax as the difference between the legal and the realized tax potentials. This represents the difference between the amount of revenue that would have been raised if all legal tax liability had been paid and the amount of tax actually collected.

In the 'survey approach', information on the income of taxpayers is obtained through a survey. The income determined by the survey is then compared with the reported income in tax returns, thereby estimating the tax non-compliance. Surveys can also highlight interesting discrepancies such as those between what individuals say they earn and what they say they spend. Revealing data on this emerged from the United Kingdom's Family Expenditure Survey – at any level of declared income, the self-employed spend, on average, 10–20 per cent more than employees do.

The 'constant tax ratio' approach applies the ratio of taxes paid to gross domestic product (GDP) of a 'representative' year to the GDP of the year under study, in order to arrive at an estimated tax for that year. This is not really a measurement of *total* tax evasion, but rather a measure of *additional* tax evasion, the level of tax compliance and the quality of tax administration. Another problem is the assumption of a constant tax/GDP ratio, which may not be realistic.

It may also be possible to measure the size of tax evasion by examining tax returns filed during special tax amnesties. Argentina, India and Thailand have offered special tax amnesties more than once in recent history. The US Taxpayer Compliance Measurement Program (TCMP) is an example of the use of a special audit for the same purpose. Unlike regular field audits, TCMPs are line-by-line audits performed by experienced examiners on a nationwide stratified random sample, typically of 50,000 taxpayers. The major weakness is the exclusion of people who fail to file tax returns at all. Not unexpectedly, the TCMP estimate of non-reported income is low.

Finally there is the 'causal approach' which tries to relate all possible causes and effects of the black economy. Countries are ranked according to such factors as their burden of taxes and bureaucracy and their tax morality; these aspects are then set against everything believed to be an indicator of the black economy – the monetary measures discussed above etc. Critics maintain that this approach is tantamount to assuming what it is supposedly measuring.

These different methods tend to produce fairly wide-ranging results. Even the same method can produce a wide scatter in the hands of different economists. Figures on the overall size of countries' underground economies tend therefore to be rather more 'guesstimates' than fully defensible calculations. Table 2.1 presents two estimates, drawn from quite separate surveys, that give some indication of the size of the problem. The two separate methods that were adopted were the currency demand and the causal approaches. The two produced differing figures, but similar placings of countries in relation to one another. The conclusion is that, on average, the underground economy accounts for some 7–10 per cent of GDP in most industrial countries.[3]

Table 2.1   *The size of the black economy as a percentage of GDP*

	Currency-demand approach*		Causal approach	
	1960	1978–80	1960	1978
Austria	2	10	5	9
Belgium	–	21	5	12
Britain	–	7	5	8
Canada	–	11	5	9
Denmark	4	9	4	12
West Germany	2	11	4	9
Finland	–	–	3	8
France	–	7	5	9
Holland	–	–	6	10
Ireland	–	8	2	7
Italy	–	30	4	11
Japan	–	–	2	4
Norway	2	11	4	9
Spain	–	23	3	7
Sweden	2	13	5	13
Switzerland	1	7	1	4
United States	3	5	6	8

*Mid-point of range.
Source: The Economist, 19 September 1987.

It is likely that there would be little in the way of an underground economy without a public sector that, for whatever reason, generates distortions in national markets for goods and services. Figure 2.1 gives an interesting overview of the degree of distortion in various national economies around the world, as related to the rate of measured economic growth. This relationship could well be quite different if the underground economy were included in the measures of economic performance indicated in that analysis.

It thus seems reasonable to argue that the size of underground transactions varies enormously from one country to the next, depending on the structure of incentives and disincentives, past, present and expected in the future.

Causes

The fundamental causes of underground economic activity can be outlined in detail.[4] First and foremost is *taxation*, which in some countries takes over 50 per cent of nominal income. Swiss bankers have a saying, 'There would be no tax havens without tax hells'. Obviously, as the rate of taxation increases, the cost of honesty also increases – honesty with respect not only to income taxation, but also to taxation of wealth, transfers of wealth, value-added, sales, and mandatory social

14

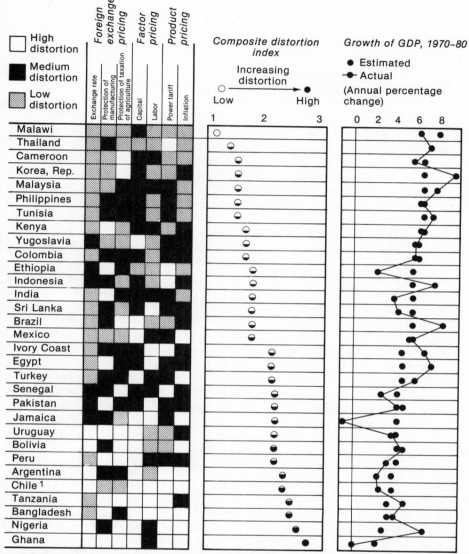

Note: In this figure, countries are listed in order of increasing degree of distortion in prices. In the first section, the color of the squares indicates the degree of distortion in the principal categories of prices. The middle section is a composite index of price distortion for each country: as a country's distortion index increases, the color of the circle changes from gray to black. In the right hand section, the small circles show the actual annual rate of growth of GDP; the large circles are estimates of GDP growth obtained by a regression relating growth to the distortion index.

[1]Price distortions for the decade were heavily influenced by the policies of the Allende regime, which ended in late 1973.

Source: World Bank, Development Report, 1983.

Figure 2.1 Price distortions and economic growth in the 1970s

15

insurance contributions. Expectations of what the government will do with tax receipts also affect the incentive to pay willingly: wasteful government expenditure, consumption and social insurance schemes from which the taxpayer is unlikely ever to benefit broadly in proportion to his or her contribution all sap the incentive to pay taxes. Poor tax administration and inequities in tax burdens may likewise demoralize taxpayers and increase the incentive to escape into the underground economy and create black markets for labor, goods and services, and wealth. Import and export duties may be included as forms of taxation; they lead to smuggling in international trade transactions. Tax evasion always involves financial secrecy, and often transcends national boundaries because of investigative and jurisdictional limits set for revenue authorities. International cooperation in matters of tax evasion obviously exists, but there are plenty of loopholes.

It is interesting to consider the situation regarding taxation in the developed countries in recent years, when the black economy is thought to have mushroomed. Not only have tax rates risen, but the number of people required to pay tax has too. In the United Kingdom, for example, fewer than 4 million workers paid income tax before the Second World War; that figure is today over 20 million. In addition indirect taxation has risen substantially, with VAT payable at all stages of production and distribution. Indirect taxation has been levied on services for the first time; these play an increasing role in an advanced economy and are relatively easy to conceal; they tend to involve a high degree of self-employment. Self-employment accounts for an average of 22 per cent of all employment in OECD countries in retailing, catering and hotels, as opposed to only 6 per cent in manufacturing (see Figure 2.2). The self-employed tend to have greater scope for muddying the tax man's waters than do employees, since they can sometimes understate income and overstate expenses. All this becomes self-perpetuating – the lower the tax revenues received by governments, the more they raise rates, increasing the burden on the honest taxpayer who then has an even greater incentive to join the ranks of the dishonest.

The second cause of underground economic activity is *regulation*, which may involve government efforts to fix prices, wages, returns on capital, exchange rates, etc. Each time a regulation is set, an incentive is created to evade it, along with its symptoms such as queuing, rationing, forced sales, quotas, and the like. In many countries, parallel financial markets (sometimes called 'curb markets') emanate directly from financial controls, as do parallel foreign exchange markets involving currency smuggling and/or over-invoicing and under-invoicing of international trade transactions ('transfer pricing'). All create economic activity that is neither taxed nor recorded in the official statistics.[5]

Third is *prohibition*, usually associated with drugs, guns, prostitution, gambling, protection, usury, and other criminal activity. Most involve

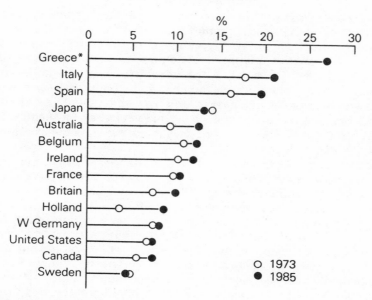

*1973 figure not available.
Source: *The Economist*, 19 September 1987.

Figure 2.2   *Self-employment in selected countries (as a percentage of non-agricultural employment)*

cash transactions that are difficult to trace, and all raise the question whether they add to the value of real output and income in the national economy despite their nefarious nature.

Finally, there is *corruption*, which seems to be endemic among public officials in a large number of countries. Activities include bribes on public procurement contracts, customs clearance, traffic violations, zoning ordinances and building permits, investment licenses, import and foreign exchange permits, allocation of consumption, investment and infrastructure goods that are in short supply, and a host of others. Bribery is always illegal, although it may be part of the national cultural, political and economic system and tolerated with more or less equanimity by society. Actual 'markets' may exist for the right to collect illegal payments and the bureaucratic power to extort them. Corruption that is clearly tolerated probably requires relatively little financial secrecy; big-time corruption, on the other hand, usually involves considerable secrecy. In all cases, corrupt officials run the political risk of a change in regime, which, if malfeasance can be proved and often even if it cannot, may well result in severe social or legal retribution – perhaps death. For this reason the corrupt often demand the highest levels of offshore secrecy, in part to provide for a hasty exit in case of need.

As a generalization, the more intensive the distortions imposed by government on the market economy, and the larger the relative size of the government sector, the greater are the incentives to go underground. In centrally planned economies and many less-developed countries, it may be said that the development of the underground economy derives mainly from the need to sidestep graft- and system-imposed inefficiencies. Underground workers provide services and goods that simply would not be available otherwise. In the developed countries of the West, the emphasis is much more on the avoidance of tax and social obligations.[6]

It has been suggested that the importance of the underground economy to a country follows a U-shaped curve during the process of economic development. It starts at a high level because so much in a typical Third World economy goes unreported and because corruption and government meddling drive so much business underground. It falls as a more liberal and better-organized economic order emerges. Finally it rises again as people demand more from government, but remain unwilling to pay for it, and the natural growth of services and self-employment make concealment of income easier.

The past record of economic distortions plays a role as well, because people get into the habit of doing things off the books – behavior that is often viewed by enforcement agencies as a 'victimless offense', and is sometimes even the source of pride as something of a 'national sport'. Moreover, the past is often a good guide to the future, and may influence expectations about the probable nature and severity of future distortions, thus supporting the precautionary dimension of the underlying incentive structure.

Disincentives include the probability of getting caught, the level of punishment, and the strength of social disapproval associated with tax evasion and other aspects of underground transactions. The disincentive structure may be as complex as the incentive structure, and the two together are highly specific with respect to time and place. For example, among the developed countries, Sweden has a relatively small underground sector, and Italy has a relatively large one. Among the developing countries, Singapore and Hong Kong have relatively small levels of underground activity, and Nigeria and Mexico are characterized by relatively large underground sectors.

Levels of underground activity

In the mid-1970s, the US Internal Revenue Service (IRS) estimated legal-source unreported income in the United States at $31.1 billion, of which unreported interest and dividend income came to $7.5–14.5 billion. Unreported income from illegal-source activities (gambling, prostitution and drugs) amounted to some $30 billion, or 1.7 per cent of the gross national product (GNP). Together, the IRS estimated the size of the US underground economy at about 3.4 per cent of GNP in 1976.[7] These estimates are, however, at variance with others which put the size of the US underground economy at between $176 billion[8] and $330 billion[9] in that year, with the latter representing about 16 per cent of 1976 US GNP. Each uses a different estimation technique. A more recent study places underground transactions at 7.5 per cent of 1981 US GNP, with growth of the underground economy accounting for 0.1–0.4 per cent of US annual economic growth between 1950 and 1981.[10]

By any reckoning, the size of the US underground economy is very substantial indeed. Most observers in the United States today estimate that 2–5 per cent of actual GNP is attributable to criminal activity such as drugs dealing, illegal gambling, and the rackets. In addition, transactions that are not recorded for tax purposes or for purposes of national income accounting have been estimated at anywhere between 5 per cent and 20 per cent of GNP in the mid-1980s.

The high estimates are based on such indicators as currency in circulation, and there is general agreement that the size of cash transactions has been growing in those sectors where it predominates – e.g., transactions of proprietorships and other small-business income. However, these same sectors as a group have been declining in relation to total economic activity, based on such non-financial indicators as employment. So the evidence remains somewhat contradictory.

There have been suggestions that, with recent tax reforms, the incentive for the non-reporting of legal income in the United States will be reduced, and that this will in turn reduce the overall size of the underground economy.[11] While this may have some effect, the phenomenon is unlikely to disappear. Most recent reports would indicate that a reasonable guess of the current size of the US underground economy is $350–$500 billion per year, that is some 10–15 per cent of GNP in 1988, and hence some $90–$100 billion of lost revenue for the government a year.[12]

In Europe, there seems no indication whatsoever of any slowdown in underground activity. Recent estimates suggest that it accounts for roughly 10 per cent of Europe's GNP.[13] Most academic specialists expected that the underground economy, which flourished during the recessions of the 1970s, would die down as legitimate business began to recover in the 1980s. But recent studies in West Germany, the United Kingdom and the Benelux countries show that the underground economy is growing rapidly. It involves people from all walks of life, professionals as well as unskilled laborers and tradesmen, school drop-outs and pensioners, men and women. For one large and growing category of European residents underground work is indeed the only option – hundreds of thousands of clandestine immigrants in France, Italy and West Germany would be liable to expulsion if they tried to get jobs in the legitimate economy. It is thought that in the Sentier district of Paris alone there are more than 200 small tailoring shops where Turks and Yugoslavs work long hours, without job security or government benefits, to supply the French ready-to-wear industry.

The pattern of underground activity differs widely between countries. In Italy and West Germany there exists organized, large-scale, black industrial activity – broad sectors of the heavy metalworking industry in northern West Germany, for example, use a certain amount of illegal and therefore cheap labor. In the United Kingdom, on the other hand, moonlighting appears to be more individually based. Nonetheless, the figures in all cases are quite staggering.

In Italy, some 3 million people are thought to be involved, providing some 20 per cent of goods and services.[14] A 1980 survey found that 54 per cent of all Italian civil servants had a second job, 33 per cent sold goods during office hours, and 27 per cent were doing unofficial work from their desks, such as running consultancies. In Spain, a third of the 21 per cent supposedly unemployed are working illegally; it is thought that more than half of the country's output of textiles and shoes comes from clandestine workshops. In France there are between 0.8 and 1.5 million people involved in the black economy, doing some $8.6 billion in business a year. In West Germany estimates for the size of the black economy range from $16–$30 billion, that is between 5 per cent and 10 per cent of GNP.[15] It is perhaps not surprising when one realizes that a skilled builder there might take home DM12 an hour net of tax, but by the time taxes and social contributions have been added in, his customer would be paying in the region of DM56 per hour – this leaves plenty of room for splitting the difference.

Indeed, the first study of the black economy as a phenomenon was in fact in Italy, long famed for its 'economia sommersa'. Mr Guiseppe De Rita, the President of Censis, an institute for economic and social research, pioneered work on the subject in 1971. He estimated that at that time the underground economy in 'legal' activities amounted to around 20–25 per cent of GDP, with another 10 per cent of GDP representing more nefarious occupations such as drug smuggling. Subsequent estimates have ranged from 10 per cent to 50 per cent of GDP. A 1987 study, in which comparisons of the new national accounts and figures from income tax and VAT returns were made, revealed an overall level of 20 per cent; certain areas of the economy were more prone to the tendency than others – 33 per cent of output in services, for example, with as much as 65 per cent in hotels and catering, was calculated to be underground.[16]

In Eastern Europe too, despite the Gorbachev-inspired market liberalization and crackdown on corruption, the underground economy thrives. In the Soviet Union recent studies indicate that the 'unofficial sector' accounts for over half the country's day-to-day services, a figure that apparently rises to 80 per cent in some rural areas.[17] In Hungary 70 per cent of the population works at least part-time in the hidden economy; and in Bulgaria there's a saying that goes: 'Each worker earns 200 leva a month, spends 400 leva and puts 500 leva in the bank'.

In the developing countries, as we have suggested, the issue probably looms just as large, if not larger. Peru probably has one of the largest underground economies of all, dwarfing estimates for the United States and even much higher ones for Italy. An estimated 60 per cent of Peruvian economic activity is underground. The reason, of course, is taxation, bureaucratic inefficiency, impenetrable regulations, and official corruption. In one experiment, a research institute 'tried to set up a legal government company without easing the way with tips. It took a lawyer and three others 301 days of full-time work, dealing with 11 government agencies, to complete the paperwork – which, when laid end to end, measured 102 feet. (One of the researchers then tried the same experiment in Tampa, Florida and finished it in 3½ hours)'.[18]

In another experiment, a former governor of Peru's central bank investigated how long it took to get permission to set up a small clothing factory – 289 days and 24 requests for bribes. In a more politically sensitive industry it could have taken up to eight years. Small wonder that many people do not bother with the permission and simply run an 'informal' business.[19] Official statistics may list over half of Peru's population as unemployed, but the real world is rather different. Underground business hums along in a variety of sectors, ranging from manufacturing and farming to construction and bus services, and it is estimated that the average Peruvian citizen is about 50 per cent better off than the official statistics indicate – $1,300 in annual income compared to a reported $900. A four-year study found rapidly growing underground economic activity in essentially all goods and services sectors, including at least 85 per cent of garment production, bus assembly, precision tools, and manufacturing of electrical controls.[20]

As yet another example, the Indian government controls about three-fourths of the equity in Indian industry, either through outright government ownership or through shareholdings in private companies. Prime Minister Rajiv Gandhi has tried to improve matters through tax cuts, reductions in import duties, raising limits on industrial capacity and diversification and the removal of some companies and industries from the regulatory net altogether. Yet in reality his government has still to relinquish a single instrument of control. Indian companies have grown comfortably lazy, backed by low-interest loans and subsidies, producing obsolete but expensive products under quotas that guarantee a market regardless of quality or price. Inevitably, black markets have flourished. World Bank economists estimate that India's underground economy could be half the nation's GNP.

An official Indian report puts the figure a little lower, with untaxed money amounting to at least 20 per cent of GDP, with perhaps another 15 per cent generated by smuggling.[21] In 1981 the tax loss was estimated at about 75 per cent of that collected. Whatever the precise figures, there can be no doubt that despite liberalization the use of black money and the level of corruption remain remarkably high.[22] There is still a bewildering web of restrictions, licenses and subsidies, which provides vast opportunities for malfeasance. And any firm benefiting from such complexities can still be expected to channel illicit funds to politicians favorable to their cause.

In Taiwan there is thought to be an underground economy amounting to 20–30 per cent the size of GDP, composed for the most part of small unregistered factories, service businesses and illegal financial markets. The Taiwanese government has resorted to lotteries to attempt to reduce tax evasion. Everyone has a tax number which must be recorded on all invoices and receipts; to encourage legitimate use the government holds lotteries with prizes of up to $67,000 using the receipts as tickets. In Burma, the black economy is said by some to be fully as big as the official economy.

Taiwan's underground economy is estimated to range in size from 25 per cent to 40 per cent of the official GNP figure. A 1987 survey showed that 15–20 per cent of export earnings are uncounted because of double invoicing, that 7–8 per cent of manufacturing output goes undeclared, and that Taiwanese farmers tend never to have a good harvest. In the service sector, prostitution is rife but income is just not declared, while restaurants appear to be thriving but on paper are virtually all loss-making. As for the financial market, the industry is heavily regulated, but numerous small operators are busy providing the services banks and brokers are not – which perhaps explains why Taiwan is one of the world's major customers for Reuters' screens. Currency swaps were illegal but a working currency-swap market existed, and the same is true of commodity futures. Indeed, people are so ingenious that when the Government was perceived as keeping too big a share of the national lottery proceeds, an underground lottery simply sprang up, using the official lottery's numbers.

Not, of course, that all this is particularly helpful as far as managing the economy is concerned. In 1985, income tax provided only 20 per cent of the Government's revenue. Taxes of all kinds only raised 60 per cent of revenues, and by 1987 the figure had fallen to half. Much of the responsibility for the situation lies with the politicians themselves. The state has interfered in all areas of business. It has owned most of the banks, for example, and controls the rest. Collateral equivalent to the size of loan made is the normal requirement. The price of money in the official system is so distorted that lower interest is often paid on long-term deposits than on short-term deposits. And yet, if the figures on the black economy are to be believed, the Taiwanese may well be Asia's second wealthiest people after the Japanese.[23]

One additional factor in all this is the question of the amount of economic value being added unrecorded by people working at home. In terms such as those in Figure 2.3, how does one assign value to the unrecorded jobs carried out at one time or another by most adults in the developed world? As an opportunity cost – i.e., at the individual's wage in the formal economy? Or at the wage that would be paid to a professional in the field to do the job? Whatever one does, it is undoubtedly another important hidden element in the overall economic picture – the average British adult spends some 21 hours a week in paid employment and some 23 in productive activity at home. As such, it is an additional complication in assessing the true state of the economy. To a certain extent the absolute size of this domestic economy, and indeed of the black economy, matter rather less than fluctuations in their size vis-à-vis the official economy. It is when the three are growing or contracting at different rates that the measurement problem is at its most complex.

The existence of a significant underground economy has a number of side-effects that may create problems for economic policymaking. For one thing, actual unemployment rates and inflation rates may be quite different from those that are measured in the national statistics. This may lead to excessively stimulative or contractionary monetary or fiscal policy, not to mention policy related to the balance of payments. Moreover, the underground sector may have a significant effect, both positive and negative, on the level of efficiency of the national economy. For this reason, while measurement of the underground sector may be quite important, direct measurement is nearly always impossible.

Internationalization of underground financial flows

If domestic underground activities are notoriously difficult to identify and to gauge, international secret money flows provide an even greater statistical challenge. The connections, however, are clear. Domestic underground dealings have to be kept hidden by means of cash transactions or 'bearer' financial instruments that cannot be traced. Use of the domestic banking system in this connection is difficult, and the probability of exposure depends on domestic confidentiality rules and traditions – which will almost always lead to exposure in serious cases. International financial secrecy provides a good alternative, with domestic underground goods or services, for example, being paid for by foreign bank transfers from buyer to seller.

International secret money flows have been the focus of attempts at measurement not too different from those aimed at domestic under-

23

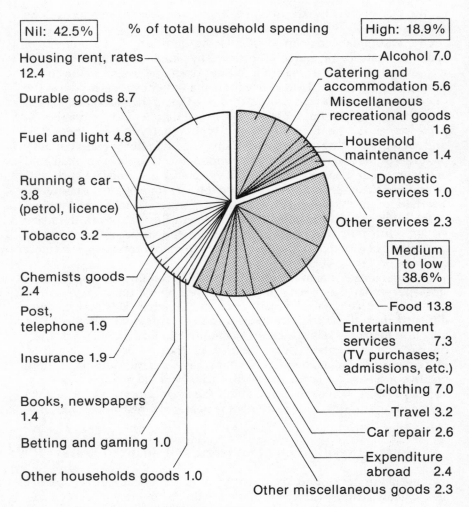

Nil: 42.5%   % of total household spending   High: 18.9%

Housing rent, rates
12.4

Durable goods 8.7

Fuel and light 4.8

Running a car
3.8
(petrol, licence)

Tobacco 3.2

Chemists goods
2.4

Post,
telephone 1.9

Insurance 1.9

Books, newspapers
1.4

Betting and gaming 1.0

Other households goods 1.0

Alcohol 7.0

Catering and
accommodation 5.6

Miscellaneous
recreational goods
1.6

Household
maintenance 1.4

Domestic
services 1.0

Other services 2.3

Medium
to low
38.6%

Food 13.8

Entertainment
services   7.3
(TV purchases;
admissions, etc.)

Clothing 7.0

Travel 3.2

Car repair 2.6

Expenditure
abroad   2.4

Other miscellaneous goods 2.3

Source: *The Economist*, 19 September 1987.

Figure 2.3   *Opportunities for substituting household spending in the official economy with work at home, 1986*

ground economies, and again they are extraordinarily difficult to track. Every once in a while, a customs inspector finds a suitcase or package stuffed with currency. Now and then a government agency or financial institution gets caught making unauthorized or unreported money transfers abroad. The US Internal Revenue Service estimated in 1983 that $20–135 billion in illicit money flows annually from the United States to foreign secrecy havens. Much of this involves drug traffic, but a

Table 2.2   *Summary of global payments balances on current account (recorded and adjusted), 1979–86*

	1979	1980	1981	1982	1983	1984	1985	1986
				(billions of US$)				
Industrial countries								
Recorded	−23	−62	−20	−22	−22	−62	−54	−9
Adjusted	−27	−55	−6	—	−9	−44	−40	−2
Developing countries								
Recorded	6	30	−49	−87	−64	−34	−24	−47
Adjusted	4	33	−40	−70	−54	−21	−12	−44
Total								
Recorded	−17	−32	−69	−109	−86	−96	−79	−57
Adjusted	−22	−19	−42	−63	−58	−58	−44	−39
Other countries	−3	−2	−3	3	3	4	3	1
International organizations	2	3	3	3	3	4	5	5
Total, adjusted*	−22	−18	−42	−57	−52	−50	−36	−34

— Indicates that the figure is zero or that the item does not exist.
Note: For 1979–84 adjustments are based on the *Final Report of the Working Party on the Statistical Discrepancy in World Current Account Balances*; for 1985–6, adjustments are based on preliminary IMF staff estimates.
* Includes adjustments for which no geographical breakdown is available.
Source: IMF, *World Economic Outlook*, Washington, DC, April 1987.

growing share evidently involves tax evasion. In general, no one has even a remote idea of the precise size or direction of global secret money flows, or of the identity of those involved. It is, however, possible to speculate.

For one thing, national statistics that are supposed to keep track of international payments for goods and services simply do not add up. What one country imports, another should export, and if this includes all goods, services and investment income, then the disbursements of one country should equal the receipts of another, so that the 'current-account' statistics in the balance of payments of all the world's countries should add to precisely zero. But, as Table 2.2 and Figure 2.4 show, they do not.

From a rough balance in the world's current accounts during the early 1970s, a deficit of some $20 billion had developed by 1978; by 1982 this figure had reached almost $110 billion; 1986 figures showed a discrepancy of $56 billion.[24] Such discrepancies pose a serious problem – they mean that economic forecasts are based on erroneous information which in turn may lead to the development of inappropriate policies. But how and why do they arise? Unless the world as a whole had a transactions deficit of that magnitude with the man in the moon something is wrong.[25]

Obviously, keeping track of international payments is no easy task,

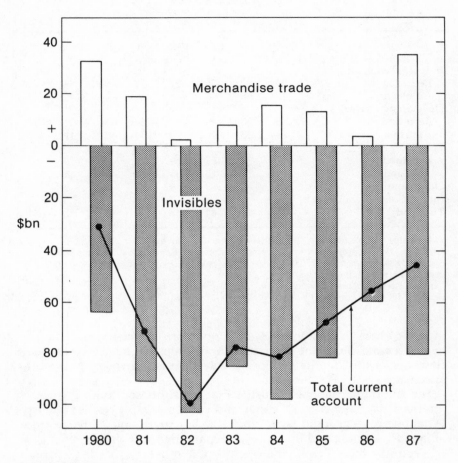

Source: Phillips & Drew; *The Economists*, 20 August 1988.

Figure 2.4   *Discrepancy in world current-account statistics*

and some countries have far better statistical systems than others to
accomplish it. Some countries also misrepresent their numbers. But
there is no reason why the errors on the disbursements side should be
systematically greater than those on the receipts side. Indeed, at least as
far as international trade data are concerned (where balance of

payments disbursements information is collected alongside customs information), it should actually be the other way around. Even allowing for problems related to record-keeping and governments massaging the figures (again biased toward overstating receipts and understating disbursements), much remains to be explained.

Various candidates emerge. Criminal imports (drugs, weapons) are unlikely to be reported to the international trade statisticians. Interest and dividend payments to foreigners tend to be reported by the payer to his government's authorities, but may not be reported by the recipient. Receipts of dividends and interest payments taken into foreign fiduciary accounts are not recorded by the recipient countries in their balance of payments data, since the account holders are not residents. Those who engage in international trade may overstate the value of imports and understate the value of exports in order to avoid taxes or exchange controls, again contributing to current-account deficits in some countries that are not counterbalanced by surpluses in others. Among other major flows that are likely to escape the statisticians are earnings on foreign-owned capital held overseas, and non-remittance of earnings of capital held abroad.

To investigate the factors contributing to the world current account deficit, the IMF set up a working party of international experts in 1984, who presented their report in early 1987. Investment income accounts were identified as a major source of error. The emergence of a large body of 'cross-border assets' or capital held in other countries, appears to have been recognized by most debtor countries but not by creditor countries in their national accounts. Over the period 1977–83, for example, some $300 billion in reported net inflows failed to be registered in the accounts of the countries suffering the outflow. The IMF report broke the overall category of investment income accounts down into several major constituents:

- Direct investment income (the after-tax income from foreign affiliates of multinational companies, as reflected in tax accounts of creditor and host countries) is very difficult to gauge accurately, owing to the complicated structures of the operations involved and the lack of detailed and consistent information from country to country.
- Unrequited official and private transfers are entries covering provisions of goods, cash or services without obligation for repayment (such as development assistance in the official case and remittances by migrant workers in the private case).
- One of the most important categories was shipping and other transportation, where an intricate network of ownership and operating structures muddies the waters. The IMF believes that as much as a third of the world's shipping revenue goes unreported.

- The fastest growing and largest item of discrepancy is portfolio investment income, defined as interest and dividend payments to and from banks and other financial institutions on marketable securities and other financial instruments. This amounted to some $42 billion in 1984, a large proportion of which relates to capital flight.

Offshore centers of course play an important role in all of this. Through secrecy measures they increase the difficulty of assessing international monetary flows. The growth of these centers, combined with the rapid development of highly tailored, often very liquid financial instruments and the increased speed of transactions possible with new technology, have made it ever more difficult to trace the course of the money being traded. As one observer notes: 'Certainly not all the money that shows up in the world current account discrepancy involves secret funds from tax evasion, capital flight and criminal doings. But if even one half is motivated in this way, it is still a very large amount'.[26]

The current account discrepancy that had reached $100 billion in 1982 amounted to only $45 billion in 1987. However, since both contain large offsetting errors that can change dramatically from one year to the next, this was no indication that the statistics had become more accurate or that there had been a decline in the underlying transactions giving rise to these errors. According to a 1988 IMF study, much of the discrepancy is lodged in (presumably unreported) investment income transactions, where credits exceeded debits by $45 billion, partly due to a structural shift from bank lending to securitized forms of financing and the lifting of exchange controls and their reporting requirements by many countries.[27] Other services transactions, which exceed 50 per cent of the combined GNP of the OECD countries, are equally difficult to capture when they enter the channels of international trade. The result is that policy decisions, whether they involve domestic or international targets, are often based on faulty data within which transactions involving financial secrecy are imbedded.

Balance of payments discrepancies can also be identified by looking at the 'errors and omissions' item in individual countries' reported balance of payments statistics. Errors and omissions have increased spectacularly in the United States: over $100 billion during 1979–83. The situation is more serious due to compensating errors. There is no necessary connection between the global current-account deficit and the errors and omissions item in individual countries' balance of payments statistics. Net errors and omissions typically reflect larger errors on a gross basis that happen to be offsetting. Furthermore, the bulk of errors and omissions is believed to represent unreported capital movements.

One implication is that US net borrowing from abroad during the 1980s has been severely understated. An assessment of the 'errors and omissions' item in the US external accounts reveals a 'surplus' of nearly $140 billion between 1978 and mid-1984. The official view is that the bulk of these unrecorded inflows reflects capital inflows. For instance, a study by the Federal Reserve Bank of New York states that errors and omissions are treated as unrecorded private and official capital flows because they appear to fluctuate over time more like capital flows than like current-account transactions. On the assumption that the bulk of the cumulative errors and omissions surplus since 1978 represents capital inflows, US liabilities to foreigners at the end of 1983 were understated by some $120 billion. This would transform the country's stated net creditor status into net debtor at the end of 1983. The implication is that the recorded positive net creditor position of the United States, built up gradually over the entire postwar period, would be reversed in the space of only three years (1983–5). By 1986, US external debt would thus have surpassed that of the whole of Latin America.[28]

Yet another way to try to get at the volume of secret money flows is to follow the external use of national currencies. The Federal Reserve System and other central banks around the world know with a fair degree of precision the amount of national currency outstanding at any given time. Some of that money is in domestic circulation as an active means of payment, and some is hoarded by domestic residents. We noted earlier that a number of economists have attempted to use the relationship of currency outstanding to the total money supply and to economic activity measured at the national and regional level to gauge the size of the national underground economy. For instance, drugs deals, the rackets, organized crime, and tax evasion are all dependent in large part on cash transactions.

In addition, however, domestic currency may be held *outside* the national economy. We know, for example, that foreign countries may from time to time become 'dollarized'. Typically, irresponsible domestic monetary, fiscal and exchange-rate policies, along with exchange controls and other market distortions, rapidly erode confidence in the purchasing power of the national currency, resulting in a growing demand for dollars or other foreign currencies that better retain their value or that can be used to acquire otherwise unobtainable products or services. There are even some countries, such as Panama, where the US dollar is used as the currency and there is no central bank or independent monetary authority.

The demand for foreign money can take various forms, including foreign-currency notes circulating domestically and foreign-currency deposits held either abroad or domestically.[29] Examples include Argentina, Mexico, Israel, Brazil and Poland during the 1980s. Sometimes, even domestic prices are expressed in dollars, as the mismanaged domestic currency loses its meaning as a viable unit of account.

29

It is easy to understand why this should be so when we consider the practical, everyday implications of the types of hyper-inflation such countries have witnessed. During 1985 in Argentina inflation at one point was running at an annual rate of 1,000 per cent and in Bolivia the figure was well over twice that. The result was a desperate rush out of the domestic currency. In Buenos Aires at the height of the crisis, supermarket prices were being changed twice a day; restaurant prices were listed in pencil for speedy adjustment, and real estate agents would not honor a peso price for more than 24 hours. The joke making the rounds during the Israeli inflation of the mid-1980s – 'When in Jerusalem, is it cheaper to take a bus or a taxi? A taxi because you pay at the end' – becomes altogether more understandable. As one Bolivian put it: 'We don't produce anything anymore. We are all currency speculators.'[30]

The implications for countries suffering such currency substitution are profound. It becomes far more difficult for the authorities to control credit and monetary aggregates effectively, and thus to design appropriate monetary policies. This, in turn, means that confidence in the domestic currency continues to fall, making it ever more difficult to re-establish any degree of financial order.[31]

Dollarized economies may play at least two distinct roles in secret money flows. First, the origin of dollars in domestic circulation is, almost by definition, clandestine (except for Liberia and Panama) as holders fail to declare them when they enter the country. Second, such countries represent a 'sink' for hiding and laundering illicit cash transactions that take place elsewhere. It is suggested, for example, that a sizeable part of the drug money generated in the United States finds its way in cash to dollarized economies and, after complex laundry services, emerges with a new image. Large amounts of US currency apparently leave Panama and certain other countries aboard aircraft daily for the United States, to be deposited in US banks in the natural course of interbank transactions, thus enabling the proceeds of illicit transactions to enter the normal channels of payment.

Not only dollars are involved. One popular story has currency leaving France strapped to hang-glider pilots who launch themselves from a French mountain near Geneva and conveniently land in Swiss farm fields on the plain below – to be met by 'clean' accomplices who take the money straight to a local bank.

Secret money vehicles

Even if the vast international flows of secret money are difficult to measure, it is at least possible to pin down the vehicles that are used. As noted in Chapter 1, they range from long-standing traditions of financial confidentiality to schemes of almost diabolical complexity.

The vehicles of financial secrecy are not particularly difficult to identify. Cash is one alternative, but has the disadvantage of zero yield, ease of loss, traceability in large denominations, as well as difficulties and suspicions aroused in large-scale transactions. 'Outside cash' (the currency of other countries) may be considerably more attractive, but suffers from some of the same drawbacks. Gold, silver, stamps and collectables offer an alternative that could provide capital appreciation and desirability, but suffer in the area of security and liquidity as well as frequently low yields and large spreads between 'buy' and 'sell' prices. Bearer instruments such as cashier's checks and money orders can offer a temporary refuge, but also suffer from some of the same disadvantages and are not suitable for long-term holdings. Rather better are bearer bonds, available in some national capital markets and in the Eurobond market, which provide a (secrecy-adjusted) market yield and may be a good long-term alternative – assuming the problem of theft or loss can be taken care of.

From such relatively straightforward 'off the shelf' assets that can yield financial secrecy, we then move to products that directly involve the secrecy seeker with counterparties and hence a relationship of trust.

The privileged relationship between bankers and client goes back at least to ancient Greece, and has sometimes been compared to the Hippocratic oath in medicine, which governs the relationship between physician and patient, and to corresponding privileged ties between client and lawyer that are anchored in law and practice throughout the world. Frederick the Great in 1765 formulated the relationship in a banking regulation as follows:

> We forbid, on pain of royal displeasure, anyone from investigating the banking assets of anyone else. Nor shall bank employees disclose such information to third parties, whether verbally or in writing, on pain of dismissal and criminal prosecution. They must, on accepting employment, solemnly swear that any transactions that come to their attention in the course of their work will be considered the greatest secret that will be carried with them into the grave.[32]

Historically, confidentiality has been an aspect of political freedom and privacy as important in many respects as the freedom of association, religious affiliation and speech.

It is established in the life of a country in a variety of ways. In Italy, for example, it is entrenched through the Banking Act of 1936. In France, secrecy is defined by a broad interpretation of clause 378 of the Penal Code. In Luxembourg the relevant provision is clause 16 of the 1981 Banking Act. West Germany and the United Kingdom regard secrecy as part of the common law. In Austria, which is as strict in this

31

respect, if not stricter, than Switzerland, secrecy is defined in section 2 of the country's 1979 Federal Banking Law.

In totalitarian societies, where the interests of the state override the interests of the individual, the right to financial confidentiality is largely absent. Confidentiality from the state can be achieved only outside the law.

Most countries, however, have reasonable confidentiality safeguards even in tax matters. For example, in 1984 the Netherlands Finance Ministry reached agreement with the Netherlands Bankers' Association to revise a voluntary set of guidelines that had existed since 1948.[33] These guidelines basically protected the right of individuals to financial privacy except when there were clear signs of fraud. However, the enforcement enthusiasm of the tax authorities increasingly breached these guidelines, necessitating a revision. The authorities now have a clearer mandate to pursue suspected tax evaders, but individual privacy safeguards have been strengthened against unreasonable forced disclosure. Similar debates on the 'reasonableness' of government access to private financial information have occurred in West Germany and elsewhere.

Wide differences exist among countries in the degree of confidentiality permitted individual bank accounts under the law in tax matters. As might be expected, Swedish tax authorities are given access to all personal and business financial information, essentially without restriction. The same is true in France, where banks also have to notify the authorities of the account holder's interest earnings for income tax purposes unless he or she agrees to a 40 per cent withholding tax on interest income. The United States likewise provides tax authorities with liberal access to financial records, and all financial institutions are required to provide account holders' social security numbers, with investigative procedures strictly spelled out under the Financial Privacy Act of 1978. Spanish banks must provide fiscal authorities with the names and identification numbers of all account holders, but not specific account information or interest earnings. Danish and United Kingdom disclosure requirements are very similar to those in the United States.

The situation is somewhat more restrictive in West Germany, where tax authorities do not automatically receive account information, and gain access only under specific and relatively restrictive procedural guidelines. The same is true in the Netherlands. In neither case can the authorities go on 'fishing expeditions' in demanding disclosure of account information by banks, in the hope of frightening tax evaders.

Most restrictive in Europe are Austria and Switzerland, where the privileged relationship between banker and client is taken very seriously indeed, and where tax evasion itself is insufficient reason to break banking confidentiality.[34]

Standard domestic banking confidentiality is not, however, a principal secrecy vehicle, except when it is made accessible to foreigners who do not have comparable confidentiality at home. We can also omit domestic cash hoards, collectables and other hidden assets, whose characteristics are fairly obvious, and concentrate our discussion on foreign assets. Exhibit 2.1 lists a sample of US legal cases that have involved international financial secrecy. Scanning them, it is possible to get a rough idea of the range of secrecy products that have in fact emerged.

EXHIBIT 2.1

Sample of US legal cases involving international financial secrecy

VIOLATION OF SECURITIES LAWS

Securities and Exchange Commission v. Certain Unknown Purchasers of the Common Stock or Call Options for the Common Stock of Santa Fe International Corporation (1981); *Securities and Exchange Commission v. Martin* (1982). Gary L. Martin was charged with violations of the Securities and Exchange Act by fraudulently trading in the securities of Santa Fe International Corp. based on 'material non-public information' concerning the acquisition of all of Santa Fe by Kuwait Petroleum Company (KPC), wholly owned by the government of Kuwait. He received the information from a Santa Fe director who had consulted him for tax planning advice. Illegal profits totalled over $1.1 million, at least half of which were secreted in Seattle First National Bank's branch in Zurich, Switzerland. The district court issued an order to 'freeze' the assets pending litigation. Also charged with fraudulent trading based on material non-public information were Faisal Al Massod Al Fuhait, Oil Minister of Kuwait and Chairman of the Board of KPC, and 'certain unknown purchasers of the common stock of Santa Fe', trading through certain designated financial institutions named as nominal defendants, which as of the indictment date had not been identified by the SEC (with the exception of Darius N. Keaton, who agreed to disgorge all profits).

Securities and Exchange Commission v. Banca della Svizzera Italiana (1981). The SEC sought an order to compel disclosure by the Swiss bank of information about its customers suspected of purchasing, on insider information, St Joe Minerals Corporation call options immediately prior to a Seagram Corp. tender offer for St Joe stock. The court required the bank to make disclosure, although Swiss criminal law prohibited the bank from doing so. The court conducted a balancing test, considering (a) vital interests of the nations involved, (b) the extent and nature of hardship that inconsistent enforcement would impose on a person who is to perform conduct, (c) the extent to which the required conduct is to take place on the territory of the other state, (d) the nationality of person who is to perform conduct, and (e) the extent to which enforcement by action of either state can be expected to achieve compliance with that state's rule. The court held that US vital interests were involved in ensuring the integrity of its securities market and the fact that the Swiss government was aware of and expressed no opposition to the litigation warranted disclosure.

SECURITIES FRAUD

Securities and Exchange Commission v. Vesco (1972). Robert L. Vesco, chairman of the board of directors of International Controls Corporation and IOS Ltd, was charged with several counts of securities fraud and misappropriation of hundreds of millions of dollars from US corporations he directed. In a conspiracy which spanned several years and involved several co-conspirators and domestic as well as foreign entities, Vesco caused a fund he directed, the Dollars Fund (DF), to sell approximately $200 million worth of its stock, a portion of this to foreign entities he controlled, and to make investments in his foreign entities without disclosing his interests. The Overseas Development Bank Luxembourg (ODB) and Bahamas Commonwealth Bank (BCB), two banks also controlled by Vesco, were used to hold certain securities he caused DF to purchase, rather than DF's designated custodian of securities, further concealing the misuse of DF's assets. Vesco similarly caused other companies he directed, which had policies of investing predominantly in US securities, to transfer millions of dollars from their US banks to his Bahamas and Luxembourg banks in the form of investments in or high-risk, unprofitable loans to offshore entities he controlled, including several in the Bahamas and Costa Rica, to the severe detriment of these companies' shareholders, in transactions poorly calculated to achieve their investment policies. In order to deceive investors and prospective investors in these defrauded companies, he camouflaged their flagging earnings by evaluating their transactions with his foreign entities in false and misleading ways, not in conformity with general accounting principles. For example, consideration paid by his foreign entities for stock in US corporations frequently took the form of tax indemnification agreements which Vesco would subsequently have reflected in company records at their face value, despite the lack of likelihood of their materialization. The investigation into his activities is still pending, as Vesco remains at large.

United States v. Sindona (1980). Michele Sindona, an Italian financier, was convicted of a conspiracy to defraud American investors and the SEC in connection with the purchase of stock of two US corporations. First National Bank (FNB) and Talcott National Corporation (TNC). Sindona misappropriated $15 million from the general accounts of Banca Privata Finanziaria and Banca Unione, two Italian banks effectively controlled by Sindona, and placed the funds on deposit at the Privat Kredit Bank and Amincor Bank in Zurich, Switzerland. The Swiss banks then secretly transferred the funds to Sindona-owned corporations, which used them to acquire FNB and TNC. Although the Sindona corporations did eventually return the funds to the Italian banks, the transfers never took, nor were intended to take, the form of legitimate loans. In order to conceal the illegal source of the funds used to purchase the stock in the American corporations from American investors, Sindona filed false statements with the SEC, representing that the funds used to acquire FNB and TNC were his own. In 1984, Sindona was extradited to Italy to face separate charges of financial fraud [and was convicted].

TAX FRAUD

United States v. Kilpatrick (1982). William A. Kilpatrick and several co-conspirators, including the Bank of Nova Scotia, were indicted for their participation in fraudulent coal and methanol tax shelters, producing over $122 million in fraudulent tax deductions for investors and yielding $27 million in profits to the defendants. Kilpatrick-owned corporations offered investments in mineral leases producing deductions four times the amount of cash investment, the remaining ¾ of the funds to be met by loans to investors from P&J Coal Company. As P&J did not have the funds for this transaction (necessary for legitimate deductions), defendants opened several bank accounts and formed several corporations in the Cayman Islands to engage in an intricate 'checkswapping' scheme between the Cayman corporations so that a sufficient balance would appear in the accounts of these corporations at any given time. The Bank of Nova Scotia in Cayman processed these checks despite insufficient funds. The defendants also formed limited partnerships offering deductions four times the amounts of initial investments, resulting from deductible payments made by the limited partnership to International Fuel Development Corporation under a contract to conduct 'research and development' into certain methanol processes. Marlborough Investments, Ltd, a Cayman entity, was to meet the balance of the investment for the limited partnerships. As Marlborough also did not have sufficient funds for the loan, they engaged in a similar check-swapping scheme between the Cayman corporations.

TAX EVASION

United States v. Vetco, Inc. (1981). Vetco, International, A.G. (VIAG) was a wholly owned subsidiary of Vetco, Inc., an American corporation manufacturing offshore drilling equipment, charged with tax evasion. The IRS charged that the acquisition of VIAG subjected Vetco to Subpart F of the Internal Revenue Code with respect to reporting VIAG's income. Vetco allegedly avoided this treatment by shipping its products to two Swiss corporations, Weidex, A.G. and Zanora, A.G., which then transferred the goods to VIAG for sale, rather than shipping its products directly to VIAG, thus causing VIAG's income to no longer be 'derived from transactions with a related corporation outside Switzerland'. The IRS issued a summons for production of documents located in Switzerland, which Vetco argued was precluded by the Swiss-US Tax Treaty and not enforceable as a possible violation of Swiss law. The court held that the treaty information exchange provisions were not exclusive, so that summonses were appropriate means of information gathering, and that enforcement of the summons was in order as Vetco had failed to show that Swiss law would in fact be violated or that it had made good faith efforts to comply.

United States v. Hajecate (1982). Thomas M. Hajecate and Thomas H. Hajecate, owners of Uni-Oil, Inc., an oil company, and Lance Eisenberg, their tax attorney, were indicted on several counts of tax evasion. Violations stemmed from a scheme to conceal the Hajecates' interest in a Cayman bank account. To further the conspiracy the defendants filed false tax returns, failed to report financial transactions between persons in the US and foreign institutions to Customs Service, and failed to report transfers of money between the US and the Cayman Islands.

FRAUD

United States v. Carver (1981). Roy R. Carver, vice president of Raytheon Co., a concern that installed Hawk anti-aircraft missile systems in Saudi Arabia; Joseph C. Lemire, a Raytheon executive; Lionel W. Aschuck, chairman of Interconex, Inc., a shipping firm; and John T. Stephens, president of Interconex, were indicted for a conspiracy to defraud the Saudi Arabian government. Carver was charged with conspiring with Interconex executives to add-on inflated costs concealed as freight charges to several hundred units of modular housing purchased by Raytheon for the Saudi project, in return for $1 million in bribes to Carver. Proceeds were paid from secret bank accounts of offshore corporations in Liberia, Switzerland, Liechtenstein, and the Cayman Islands.

New York County v. Firestone (1982). Richard Firestone and Milton Dorison, promoters, were indicted for scheming to defraud over 200 investors of nearly $40 million in a fraudulent coal mining venture. To provide incentives for the investment, defendants arranged loans of 3 times the amount invested, to produce a tax deduction of the entire amount, from Columbus Trust Co., Nassau, Bahamas. Columbus Trust allegedly funneled $31 million through several offshore corporations, then back to Columbus, leaving the impression that legitimate loan transactions actually took place. As the loans were nonexistent and no mining was ever done, the deductions were fraudulent.

BRIBERY

United States v. McDonnell Douglas Corp. (1979). McDonnell Douglas Corporation (MDC) was charged with illegal payoffs to various officials of several government-owned airlines, 'hiking' the quoted prices to cover the sums involved, and later attempting to conceal the bribes through the use of purported 'sales representation contracts' with the same officials or offshore corporations as follows: $500,000 per aircraft to Pakistan International Airlines officials (defendants assisted in transporting funds from California to Swiss bank accounts); $3,250,000 per aircraft to Korean Air Lines officials, concealed through Jetaire, Ltd, a Guernsey Island company, and Sampaquito Investments, Ltd, a Bahamas Company; $2,000,000 to Linea Aeropostal Venzolana officials, concealed through Okemo Ltd and Luciano Chiarini and Associates, Bermuda companies; $600,000 to Air Zaire officials, concealed through Agimex, a Belgian Company.

United States v. McPartlin (1979). In 1971, the Sanitary District of Stickney, Illinois, awarded a sludge transporting contract to the Ingram Corporation after bribery of city officials, including Robert McPartlin. Payments were made in both cash and letters of credit drawn on a Swiss bank. In negotiating two of the letters, the defendants went to a bank in Vaduz, Liechtenstein, to have that bank present the LCs to the Swiss bank concerned.

LABOR RACKETEERING

United States v. Scotto (1980). Anthony Scotto, president of Local 1814 of the International Longshoreman's Association, and Anthony Anastasio, executive vice president, were convicted of labor law violations, tax evasion and accepting illegal payoffs in excess of $250,000. Scotto allegedly received $210,000 over a 3 year period from John W. McGrath Co., a stevedoring firm, in return for his help in reducing fraudulent and exaggerated workmen's compensation claims filed by members of Scotto's local. To keep the illicit payments off the company's books, the money was wired by a Philadelphia bank to Bordier & Cie, a private bank in Geneva, Switzerland, in favor of one C. C. Howard who then had the Swiss bank wire funds back to his account at Brown Brothers Harriman & Co., a private New York Bank. Howard would draw cash from the account to turn back to McGrath, which was then placed in a Chase Manhattan Bank safe deposit box.

MONEY LAUNDERING

United States v. The Great American Bank (1982). The Bank, two Florida corporations and 13 people were indicted for their participation in a money laundering scheme filtering over $96 million in illicit drug profits. Traffickers delivered large sums to the corporations and individuals involved, who then deposited the funds at the Bank, which failed to file accurate currency transaction reports with the Internal Revenue Service, with intent to conceal the illegal source of the money and true identities of the depositors. The Bank subsequently transferred funds to accounts in Zurich, Switzerland (Swiss Bank Corporation), Panama (Banco De Iberamerica), and Lima, Peru (Banco Internacional, Banco de Credito, Bank of Tokyo).

DISCLOSURE

United States v. Bank of Nova Scotia (1981). The bank was held in contempt for failing to comply with a grand jury subpoena to its Miami agent requesting the records of the bank accounts in its Bahamas branch of Robert Twist, Lesser Antilles Trading Company, and Latco Development Corporation. The bank's refusal was premised on potential criminal liability in the Bahamas of bank secrecy laws. The district court engaged in a balancing test considering (a) vital interests of each state, (b) hardship of inconsistent enforcement on the person, (c) extent to which conduct will take place in the other country, (d) person's nationality, (e) extent to which enforcement by either country would achieve compliance with that country's rule. The district court enforced the order, finding (a) US criminal investigatory interests greater than Bahamian secrecy interests, as various exceptions to the secrecy law exist, (b) the Bank made no effort to obtain consent, a Bahamian court order, or a government waiver, (c) disclosure would occur in the US, (d) nationality was insignificant in this case, (e) subpoena enforcement would insure compliance with grand jury's investigatory goal, while exceptions to the laws indicate enforcement is not an unreasonable diversion. The order was affirmed on appeal.

Source: Committee on Governmental Affairs, United States Senate, Permanent Subcommittee on Investigations, *Crime and Secrecy: The Use of Offshore Banks and Companies* (Washington, DC: US Government Printing Office, 1983).

Banks as a group constitute the single most important vehicle in secret money operations. While most bankers do not actively cooperate in highly suspect activities, all find it difficult to distinguish between various types of secrecy seekers, and some prefer to close their eyes to the source of their deposits and thus accept variously tainted funds. Their services may include:

- allowing clients whose funds are not of foreign origin to make investments limited to foreigners;
- acting without power of attorney to allow clients to manage investments, or to transmit funds, on behalf of foreign-registered companies to local companies acting as laundries;
- participating in sequential transactions that fall just under the government reporting thresholds;
- allowing telephone transfers of funds without written authorization and failing to keep a record of such transfers; and
- entering false foreign account number destinations with regard to wire transfers.

Banks can obviously follow careful procedures in vetting new depositors, and failure to exercise due diligence could result in serious costs to the banks themselves. But given the diversity of bank policies and practices, and the minute volume of truly questionable funds as compared to total banking volume, it is unrealistic to expect banks to devote substantial resources to any vetting procedure.

The direct approach

As an example of the direct instruments of international banking secrecy, we can use Swiss deposit accounts.[35] There are two general rules governing the practice of Swiss banking secrecy: first, minor employees of the banks need to be protected from third parties and from themselves and, second, clients need protection from bank employees.

These two rules have caused different internal practices within Swiss banks, and have resulted in different systems of numbered accounts. The contract of bank employment imposes strict adherence to secrecy practices, even when employees leave their jobs. This requirement is both legal and contractual, and is reinforced by an intricate system of numbered accounts and accounts with code names.

There are three different types of accounts generally available: (1) Mr X wants a classic account with banking secrecy but which also allows withdrawal over the counter; (2) Mr X wants a numbered account; or (3) Mr X wants additional protection under an account with another name.

A classic named account   Mr X will have to fill out an 'Agreement for the Opening of an Account or Deposit' and complete his name and address, since the account is not opened primarily for secrecy purposes. Mr X will also need to complete a sample signature card, which will allow the cashier to recognize his signature when he makes a cash withdrawal, which may be made over the counter. If Mr X also wants the bank to manage his account, he will have to sign the 'Special Clauses Completing the Agreement for the Opening of a Current Account and a Deposit.' This classic deposit arrangement is covered by extensive banking secrecy in Switzerland, and insight is strictly limited to investigations of criminal conduct defined as such under Swiss law. All of this may be done by mail.[36]

A numbered account   This is a little harder. It usually requires appearing in person, and may involve presentation of a letter of introduction from an associate who is already a client of the bank or a reference from one's own bank. A few personal questions may be asked including why one seeks secrecy, but the depth of analysis of the answers provided will vary from bank to bank and client to client. Essentially, however, the same forms as for a classic named account must be completed, although this time it is stated on the form that the account is in the name of a number or a series of letters.

Mr X's true signature must still be entered on the agreement. The General Conditions are the same as for a classic named account, with two differences:

- Those banks that consider secrecy seriously will require an agreement that prohibits Mr X from withdrawing cash over the counter. Some banks will permit withdrawals if the number used as a signature corresponds to that on the cashier's record. But additional confidentiality protection of the client from the bank's own cashier is offered by assigning an account manager to follow the client's affairs. The account manager will personally see the client in his office, and if cash is to be withdrawn it is done under the account manager's signature.
- A second agreement is required that is intended to indemnify the bank against any risks arising from the use of this system.

The idea of a numbered or coded account is to permit current trans-actions to be performed by the bank's junior employees, who neverthe-less remain ignorant of the identity of the account holder because it is under a code. The true name of the holder is known by a limited number of people, normally the bank director and the account manager. They are the only ones who have access to the files that give the identity of the account holder. The files are kept in the bank's safe. When the director or account manager wants to see Mr X's file, he must sign a dated card and provide details of the file. In addition, he can examine only one file per visit. There are various internal numbering and control procedures used by Swiss banks, but the goal is always the same – to protect customers' identity from the banks' own employees and to confine knowledge of that identity to a minimum number of individuals.

The bank also moves cautiously when, for example, Mr Y wants to transfer a sum of money to Mr X's account. The bank will take the money and tell Mr Y that Mr X is not a client, but that the money will be accepted subject to investigation. In the meantime, the bank will contact Mr X to determine whether he will accept the transfer. In the absence of instruc-tions from Mr X, the money will be held in suspense or returned to Mr Y. Additional precautions are taken when the bank wants to communicate with Mr X. His bank statements will be sent in plain envelopes, with the recipient's name and address written by hand. In the United States, for example, the tax authorities are prevented from checking any such correspondence, even though they have legitimate suspicion of tax evasion. For this reason, the IRS from time to time has all envelopes arriv-ing from Switzerland photocopied over a fairly extended period, and these are studied by handwriting specialists with the aid of a computer.

An account under a false name   The main advantage of an account under another name is that, even if Mr X is found by his own regulatory authorities to possess a bank statement originating from a Swiss bank, Mr X can always claim that it is not his account, or that he is receiving the statement on behalf of a friend. Further protection (from Mr X's heirs, for example) can be afforded by combining an after-death power of attorney with the use of an open safe in another bank. *The post-mortem power of attorney* gives control over an account to a person whom the individual wishes to benefit from that account, but stipulates that the power will take effect only on the death of the account holder and on presentation of proof of death. The problem with this procedure is preserving proof of the existence of the post-mortem power of attorney so that it is available to the beneficiaries. An open safe at another bank can be used for this purpose.

Alternatives   There are several ways for Mr X to obtain additional protection. For example, a joint account between Mr X and Mrs X may be opened that provides for withdrawal during Mr X's lifetime under the joint signature or Mr X's sole signature. When Mr X dies, Mrs X can operate the account on her sole signature. This is similar in effect to the post-mortem power of attorney. The concept of joint accounts is accepted in most legal jurisdictions. Alternatively, provisions may be made in a will that designate the beneficiaries of the deposits in the account, although there is a potential danger that the provisions of the will do not correspond to the 'testamentary dispositions' provisions of Swiss law.

In either case, the depositor needs to maintain proof of his wishes and assets at the Swiss bank. He now has two choices: he can put the receipt for the deposit and the agreement in a safe deposit box in another bank; or he can put the agreement in a sealed envelope and give it back to the account manager (on Mr X's statement, there would then be another item called 'sealed envelope number 00' and the date when it was deposited).

If a safe deposit box is opened at another bank, then Mr X needs to worry about where to put the key to the deposit box and the post-mortem arrangements. As far as the key is concerned, the Swiss banking system provides Mr X with a solution. He gives the key to the bank where he has his safe deposit box. The bank will then prepare another file and a stiff envelope sealed with wax. The bank and Mr X will then sign jointly. The next step is different among banks. In the most conservative banks, the cashier will want to give Mr X a receipt, which will then require Mr X to open an infinite series of safe deposit boxes to contain the receipts of other banks. Otherwise, Mr X has to rely on his confidence in the Swiss system – he will allow the cashier to keep his receipt for the key in his drawer.

The indirect approach

This description of conventional, direct banking secrecy has used Switzerland as an example. The mechanics of the arrangements differ somewhat from one bank to another, but the general principles are governed by Swiss banking law and tradition. The mechanics in other countries will be somewhat different, and this gives rise to some degree of differentiation in the 'quality' of the secrecy products involved, as discussed in Chapter 8. In particular, the services of intermediaries or beneficial owners may be required in some cases.

Examples can be found in the Bahamas and Singapore. In both cases, secrecy is guaranteed, but the identity of the beneficial owner appears at two points: (1) if the central bank wants to check if the owner is a domestic citizen for exchange-control purposes, and (2) if a trust agreement establishes the true ownership of shares registered in the name of one or more other people with whom the trust deed has been created. To get the maximum degree of banking secrecy under this type of structure, a depositor will use an investment company that is both non-resident and tax-exempt. This company will be free of exchange control, and subject only to an annual flat rate tax regardless of the amount of profit. Filing of accounts with the authorities is not required.

Intermediaries and beneficial owners may also be involved even in the absence of exchange control. Examples in this category include Switzerland and Liechtenstein. The name of the beneficial owner appears in the 'fiduciary' agreement, but nowhere in the records of an official body. There is no central bank check on whether the beneficial owner is a resident or not.

For example, under a classic normal trust created by a 'trust deed', Mr B is entrusted by Mr A with the trust property. Mr B is to hold the property on behalf of Mr C (an individual or a group) for the benefit of Mr C during his lifetime. Rules of trust vary from country to country, but the principles generally remain the same.

An alternative is the 'discretionary trust', under which Mr A empowers the trustee (B) to decide which of the potential beneficiaries will eventually receive the trust property. The British authorities are among those that do not accept this type of trust. In a 'disguised trust', the beneficiary (C) and the trust's originator (A) are the same person, and the trustee (B) is called a 'bare trustee'. If there is a special arrangement between Mr B and Mr A, the lawyer can remain ignorant of it under an 'alternative trust'. Under cross-examination in a court of law, however, this arrangement will not stand up if the question: 'Is your client a possible beneficiary of the trust?' is asked. A more elaborate alternative trust may link the trustee (B) with a group of 'subtrustees' who will decide which group of potential beneficiaries are to receive the trust property. Mr A then has an agreement with the subtrustees that the latter will choose Mr X, who represents Messrs A, A1 and A2. There will also be a letter of renunciation of rights by Messrs A1 and A2 in favor of Mr A. If Mr A has not told the lawyer who set up the trust that he appears in the group represented by Mr X, the lawyer can swear under oath that his client has no direct or indirect beneficial interest in the property. If Mr A eventually replaces this arrangement with a completely anonymous Panama company, he will have still greater anonymity, since Messrs A1 and A2 will not know that Mr A and the owner of the Panama company are actually one and the same person.

Yet another indirect approach involves a 'protector for a virtuous trust'. Under this structure, a 'protector' is appointed who is the real beneficiary of the property – including possibly securities portfolios, real estate and trading companies. The 'protector' never appears as the owner in the strict legal sense, and could himself be replaced by an anonymous Panamanian company. The disadvantages of this arrangement are high set-up and maintenance costs, as well as extreme complexity. Alternatively, Mr A may set up a 'foundation'. This involves a permanent transfer of property, resulting in a legal entity with a name, an object or purpose, and an internal organization to effect the transfer. The true founder, who can also be the beneficiary, enters into a fiduciary agreement with a local lawyer. At this point, his name appears on the document. Again, a major disadvantage of a foundation is its very high maintenance cost.

Shell companies   Anonymous 'shell' companies may be used to provide secrecy in a number of countries. All shares in such companies are issued in bearer form, and no guarantees are required from the administrators. An example of the use of this type of structure involves Panama. The state has no knowledge of who is using these structures. The user does not appear in any written agreement (not even a secret one). Local professionals who form the company under instructions given by a foreign lawyer do not even know the identify of the true owner. Panamanian administrators will give executive powers over the company to Mr _____ (the name is intentionally left blank). In return, the administrators enjoy an annual fee, without having any idea of what use is being made of the shell company or of the authority they have conferred. The user is faced with a choice of whether he should enter his name on the blank executive power, or whether he should use someone else's name. He will have to put his name to a fiduciary agreement if he chooses to use someone else's name.

Offshore captives   A captive bank is an institution that exists purely for the benefit of one physical or legal person, or a group of people. This allows the owner to take advantage of substantial leverage in financing. Suppose A, B and C are companies that belong to Mr X, who also controls captive Bank X, the captive can act to fulfill the financing requirements of the companies. Furthermore, if Bank X is resident in a tax haven, the owner can realize a profit from the interest it charges A, B and C on its loans. While the interest expenses of the subsidiaries are deductible for tax purposes, the interest income of captive Bank X is tax-free in the haven.

Another advantage of a captive bank is its access to the interbank financial markets as well as possibly increased negotiating power with respect to interest rates due to the grouping of the finances of the subsidiaries. Bank X will be charged interest at interbank rates; it then will charge retail rates to A, B and C. The loans extended by the bank and the interest received by it may also be relatively free of exchange control, resulting in a more assured return.

Although the legitimacy of offshore captive banking may not be quite established, the benefits of owning an offshore bank – at a moderate expense of $20,000 or so – are certainly compelling. It can help in protecting the confidentiality of personal business and provide tax concessions under US law. Further, in some nations, where there are no usury laws, the money could be invested or lent at any interest rate.[37]

Some captive banks are set up as offshore institutions, and are therefore excluded from local deposit-taking in the country where they are located. Offshore banks have several advantages. They usually benefit from more flexible regulations and lower reserve requirements compared to banks that take local deposits, since credit created by an offshore bank does not have any effect on the local money supply. The cost of a licence for an offshore bank also tends to be lower, and it does not compete directly with local banks.

The ideal place for a secrecy seeker to form a captive bank is in a country with no meaningful banking regulations whatsoever and where all types of financial activity are allowed. Such banks, which in a number of havens nearly anyone can form for about $5,000 are really ordinary commercial companies that include the word 'bank' in their names. Their value as banks is no more than the paper on which the word 'bank' is written – hence the expression 'paper bank'. The flexibility allowed sometimes has disastrous consequences in the hand of the unscrupulous.

Several conditions are necessary for the successful establishment of an offshore captive bank for purposes of secrecy. One is that it be formed in a tax haven as well as a banking haven that has tight banking secrecy laws. Second, the reserve ratios and the withholding tax on interest should not present too heavy a burden to the bank, and its operations should be completely free of exchange controls. And the true owner of the bank must be able to remain anonymous.

The problem of death

Death is an obvious problem in the secrecy business, because of the tradeoff between secrecy and the assurance that assets will indeed reach a designated beneficiary. It is not easy to make sure that secret property gets into the right hands when the principal dies. Clearly, unless careful provision is made to inform heirs of the whereabouts and avenues for obtaining access to secret assets, they may well be lost. This is obvious in the case of wealth left in holes in the ground. It is less obvious in the case of other high-secrecy assets, particularly offshore, that involve tangled legal contracts, complex and potentially weak trust relationships, and numbered accounts. Upon death, heirs may have great difficulty tracing the assets, establishing ownership, and taking possession. Indeed, under certain circumstances the bargaining power of the heirs could be very weak. The more care the individual takes prior to death to insure an orderly transfer of assets, the greater the potential threat to secrecy through enhanced transparency of the relevant relationships. Failure to lay claim to secret inheritances may mean, of course, that the relevant assets go to the agent (bank, trustee, etc.), to the government, or to unauthorized third parties – or they are simply lost for good.

Under the direct instruments discussed earlier, the heir or executor of the estate would first need to prove his own standing *and* the death of the account holder before establishing any right to information about a secret account. The bank will normally give only current account information, and would oppose any attempt by the inheritors to trace past transactions. The account's current status is generally defined as that existing at the time of the last statement approved by the account holder.

During the account holder's lifetime, he tends to believe that the secrecy provision allows him to make any desired dispositions of his assets. It might not occur to him that his plans could come into conflict with the 'inheritors' reserve' system. In most cases, the bank would follow the depositors' instructions. But when there is a court ruling in favor of 'reserve' inheritors, the banker confronts the problem of whether he is obliged to breach financial secrecy.

In Switzerland, courts tend to consider that the right to bank secrecy passes to the heirs, especially those qualifying as reserve inheritors. However, having a separate Swiss will is dangerous because it might be considered a revocation of an earlier will, and consequently could cause a distribution of inheritance never intended by the depositor. Another problem relates to instructions left with a bank in case of death – that is, whether or not these instructions in fact constitute a will. If the instruction is intended by the depositor as a 'post-mortem' one, it would normally be considered a will in Swiss law, although a bank would still proceed very cautiously in case of death.

When there are indirect secrecy vehicles in the presence of exchange control, there is usually no problem from the point of view of the local authorities for an investment company to be set up – based on the Anglo-Saxon type of tax haven – if the heirs are non-residents. But there will be problems if one or more of the heirs is subject to local exchange controls. To circumvent such difficulties, the beneficiaries have to avoid using a legal entity that would be subject to exchange control. Trust and fiduciary agreements could present as many problems as investment companies. Local judges might not have adequate knowledge to handle the matter, or local law might not recognize the agreements.

Where there is no exchange control, private secrecy-oriented agreements will not encounter such problems, but the same difficulties are found with respect to trust and fiduciary agreements.

Where the owner is a truly anonymous entity, such as a shell company, the difficulties related to the account having been opened directly in the name of the deceased result from administrative subtleties – for example, the problem of how to change the decisions of the administrative council if that power was vested in a person now dead.

An intriguing illustration of the problems heirs may face was revealed in 1986 by the Royal Bank of Scotland.[38] In the late 1960s the bank had received a number of claims relating to the will of Antonio de Segura, a Spanish colonial magistrate in South America, and a deposit supposedly made by him in 1802 with the Royal Bank of Scotland. However, in the absence of any custody receipts or references in the bank's archives, no funds could be traced and the matter was dropped. It nevertheless appeared that de Segura really had existed and that his will was indeed authentic. So what had happened to the $32 million (around $576 million at 1986 values) that he had allegedly bequeathed to the fifth generation of his family? And how did he come to have such a sum anyway?

By 1802, France and Spain had been at war for a decade against Britain. Due to a British naval blockade, no colonial gold bullion had left South America for Spain for five years, and some $48 million was awaiting shipment. The Treaty of Amiens allowed all parties some breathing room, but no sooner had it been signed than Napoleon demanded that the Spanish pay up their war contributions to France. It was clear that the $48 million would soon be on the move. It also seems likely that de Segura was fully aware of the fact. Napoleon's envoy in the matter had been the young Comte Louis Philippe de Segur, and it is difficult to believe that he had no familial connection with de Segura. Though divided by the Pyrenees, both families traced their roots to the Basque country and would doubtless have had contacts with the Guispuscoa Company, a pro-monarchist (and pro-Bourbon) Basque trading organization with a large Caribbean business network.

De Segura appears to have been responsible for the documentation of bullion shipments from Mexico, and it is plausible that he was thus in a position to hijack a large amount of gold for his own ends, especially in view of the administrative chaos reigning at the time in Mexico due to the replacement of the former Viceroy. But why send it to Scotland?

Given the circumstances, de Segura's choices were limited – he could hardly use the Spanish from Havana or the Dutch from Curaçao as accomplices (the Netherlands was under Napoleonic control at the time). The British were the obvious choice, and the Scots particularly so. Not only were they pre-eminent in the Caribbean in trading, shipping and other business but they were well-established as a major banking center.

De Segura's will stated that the bullion was transported aboard a vessel under the dual captaincy of John Doig and John Fanning, and that the deposit with the Royal Bank of Scotland was made through the agency of a banker named Sir Francis Mollison. Doig, who hailed from the great shipping and smuggling town of Montrose on the east coast of

Scotland, and Fanning, from Stonington, Connecticut, were both active in the Caribbean, with access to convenient ports. Sir Francis Mollison, on the other hand, never existed. But there was a distinguished French banker named Comte François Mollien who was well known in British banking circles, and it seems likely that he was the individual identified as Mollison. Interestingly, he belonged to the same Masonic lodge in Paris as the de Segur family.

The cargo supposedly went to the Scottish port of Leith, but none of the port's meticulously kept shipping records and cargo manifests can be found for the years 1795–1805; they were apparently removed to London in 1810 and destroyed in a mysterious fire. A newspaper reference to Fanning's arrival at the end of 1802 was however discovered, so it seems more than possible that the bullion did at least reach Scottish shores even if someone did want the fact hidden. What happened to it?

Not far from Leith lived a poor exile of great political importance, the Comte d'Artois, of the Bourbon line, later crowned Charles X of France. Among his many privileges while in Scotland was complete immunity from investigation by the Commissioners of Customs. Towards the end of 1802 his precarious financial situation was miraculously reversed. The Royalist 'Armée de Conde' mysteriously revived, and the anti-Napoleonic underground everywhere somehow received generous funding. By 1805 Thomas Coutts, 'Sir Francis Mollison's' closest contact in London banking circles, was publicly perceived to be serving as banker to the Bourbons. Small wonder that de Segura's heirs found nothing in the vaults of the Royal Bank of Scotland 160 years later.

Summary

We have seen that ordinary bank accounts provide a certain degree of confidentiality in all countries, but that access to financial information by third parties varies enormously internationally. We have discussed a number of direct and indirect instruments of banking secrecy, which differ significantly in terms of yield, cost, risk and security. In addition, counterparties can serve as trustees, owners of record or shell companies, beneficial owners of asse⁺s, etc. All require that a fiduciary relationship be exercised, which itself carries a risk.

Various secrecy vehicles can, of course, be combined into complex forms and structures, and 'layered' in ways that make them increasingly opaque. Greater complexity usually involves greater cost, but may, at the same time, mean the ability to go after higher yields, or reduced risk through greater diversification, which can more than offset the increased cost.

In the following chapters, we shall discuss the basic characteristics of demand and supply of financial secrecy, and the organization of the market for secret money.

Notes

1 For an up-to-date reference, see 'The Shadow Economy – Grossly Deceptive Product', *The Economist*, 19 September 1987.
2 Somchai Richpuran, 'Measuring Tax Evasion', *Finance and Development*, December 1984.
3 'The Shadow Economy – Grossly Deceptive Product', *op. cit.* (n. 1).
4 Vito Tanzi, *The Underground Economy* (Lexington, Mass.: D. C. Heath, 1982).
5 See Thomas N. Gladwin and Ingo Walter, *Multinationals Under Fire* (New York: John Wiley, 1980).
6 'The Black Economy', *Newsweek*, 30 June 1986.
7 Internal Revenue Service, 'Estimates of Income Unreported on Individual Income Tax Returns', IRS Publication 1103 (9–79).
8 Peter M. Gutmann, 'The Subterranean Economy', *Financial Analysts Journal*, November/ December 1977.
9 Edward L. Feige, 'A New Perspective on a Macroeconomic Phenomenon', mimeo., August 1980.
10 David M. O'Neil, *Growth of the Underground Economy, 1950–1981*. Joint Economic Committee, US Congress (Washington, DC: US Government Printing Office, 1983).
11 Charles N. Stabler, 'The Outlook – Underground Economy May Start Shrinking', *Wall Street Journal*, 25 August 1986.
12 Clare Ansberry, 'Survival Strategy', *Wall Street Journal*, 10 January 1986.
13 'The Black Economy', *Newsweek*, 30 June 1986.
14 Ibid.
15 Rupert Cornwell, 'Virus of the Black Economy is Spreading Fast', *Financial Times*, 16 April 1986.
16 'Lies, Damned Lies and Italy's GDP', *The Economist*, 27 February 1988.
17 Spencer Reiss, Steve Strasser and Joyce Barnathan, 'Moonlighting Soviet Style', *Newsweek*, 30 June 1986.
18 Everett G. Martin, 'Lima's Capitalists Usually are Found in the Underground', *Wall Street Journal*, 16 August 1984.
19 'Peru Economy: Hidden Cash', *New York Times*, 31 October 1983.
20 Ibid. See also 'Why Bankers Should Think Small', *The Economist*, 19 July 1986.
21 'A Looser Corset', *The Economist*, 9 May 1987.
22 Louis Kraar, 'India Bids for Business', *Fortune*, 6 January 1986.
23 'Even Richer Than They Seem', *The Economist*, 19 March 1988.
24 Shuja Nawaz, 'Why the World Current Account Does Not Balance', *Finance and Development*, September 1987.
25 'Some of Our Billions Are Missing', *Fortune*, 13 April 1987.
26 Peter J. Kilburn, 'Global Trade Mystery: A Vanishing $100 Billion', *New York Times*, 30 July 1983. See also Vivian Brownstein, 'The World's Missing Billions', *Fortune*, 22 August 1983.
27 'Economic Statistics: In a Maze of Numbers', *The Economist*, 20 August 1988.
28 Richard Dale, 'Unrecorded Capital Flows: Is the United States Already a Net Debtor?', *The Banker*, December 1984.
29 C. L. Ramirez-Rojas, 'Monetary Substitution in Developing Countries', *Finance and Development*, June 1986.
30 'Chasing the Peso Leaves Argentines Breathless', *Business Week*, 10 June 1985, and Everett G. Martin, 'Precarious Pesos', *Wall Street Journal*, 13 August 1987.
31 C. L. Ramirez-Rojas, *op. cit.* (n. 26).
32 'Reglement der Königlichen Giro- und Lohn-Bank', Kingdom of Prussia (own translation), as quoted in Paul Achleitner, *Das Bankgeheimnis in Österreich, Deutschland und der Schweiz* (Vienna: Österreichisches Forschungsinstitut für Sparkassenwesen, 1981).
33 'Netherlands Bank Secrecy', *The Banker*, February 1984.

34 Paul Achleitner, 'Das Bankgeheimnis in Aussländischen Staaten', *Österreichische Spark-assenzeitung*, 15 October 1981.
35 For practical guides to international financial secrecy, see Mark Skousen, *The Complete Guide to Financial Privacy* (New York: Simon & Schuster, 1983); and Eduard Chambost, *Bank Accounts: A World Guide to Confidentiality* (London: John Wiley, 1983). This discussion of secrecy mechanics is based on Chambost, Chapters 4–8. See also Richard H. Blum, *Offshore Haven Banks, Trusts and Companies* (New York: Praeger Publishers, 1984).
36 Suzanne Woolley, 'Opening a Swiss Account is No Big Secret', *Business Week*, 3 August 1987.
37 Alan Murray, 'We Find It Very Hard to Believe That J. P. Morgan Began This Way', *Wall Street Journal*, 4 April 1985.
38 James Gilhooley, 'Whatever Happened to the Amazing Fortune of Antonio de Segura?' *The Royal Bank of Scotland Review*, no. 151, September 1986.

3

Demand for Secret Money:
Capital Flight, Bribery and
Corruption

There is a broad, worldwide demand for secret assets that differs in intensity and complexion from one country to the next, and over time as well. We can categorize the sources of demand as follows:

- Ordinary business and personal confidentiality motives, totally within the limits of the law, aimed at preventing the erosion of asset values through unwanted disclosure, which may at times necessitate the placement of assets abroad.
- Capital flight, triggered by perceived adverse changes in the economic, political or social environment of countries – or the risk thereof – which could compromise the value of assets or the personal safety of the asset-holder.
- Bribery and corruption, involving funds obtained by corrupt public officials (and sometimes business executives) and placed abroad for security reasons, as well as 'slush funds' maintained by the payers of bribes which must also be kept away from scrutiny by home- or host-country officials.
- Tax evasion, as opposed to (legal) tax avoidance, with taxable earnings not reported to the fiscal authorities and hidden from them in financial repositories abroad. Since tax statutes are often subject to interpretation, a significant gray area often exists here.
- Smuggling and related activities (including evasion of exchange controls) which involve contraband merchandise or financial instruments, the payments for which must be shielded from national authorities, frequently through offshore vehicles.
- Securities law violations, particularly insider trading, which is often undertaken through third parties who may be much more difficult to trace and prosecute if they reside abroad and are able to undertake securities transactions using offshore funds.

50

- Fraud, ranging from self-dealing in banking and finance to outright theft of financial or real assets, the proceeds of which must remain hidden and out of reach of the authorities in order to impede prosecution and recapture.
- Money laundering associated with illegal activities that range from gambling, prostitution, protection rackets and extortion, to gun-running and the narcotics trade, many of which involve cash transactions that must be converted to bankable funds before the proceeds can be spent or invested in legitimate assets.
- Government undercover activities, generally undertaken abroad, which may be aimed at supporting terrorists (or freedom fighters) in other countries, foreign governments or opposition political groups, and other clandestine operations whose legal standing may well be ambiguous but which are considered to be in the national interest. The issues involved are often not too dissimilar from those in money laundering.

In this chapter, we shall review each of the sources of demand for financial secrecy, and in each case try to come up with a sense of the magnitudes involved, as well as the principal policy issues.

Confidentiality

Not much needs to be said about the need to keep personal and business financial matters secret. At a personal level, no laws are broken if an individual decides that an optimum portfolio of assets includes substantial foreign material interests which, in addition perhaps to better diversification and improved flow of returns, shield him from the prying eyes of family or friends. In addition, depending on the country of residence, he or she may be able to avoid taxes and other fiscal levies, again without necessarily running afoul of the law. Moreover, foreign asset managers may well be able to provide better services than those at home.

At a business level, the inherent value of secrecy may convey significant advantages in the marketplace vis-à-vis competitors, customers, suppliers, potential acquirers, investors, and other parties. Certain types of business functions, particularly mergers and acquisitions, depend for their success on a high level of confidentiality and lightning moves designed to catch opponents off-guard.

Confidentiality as a legitimate business need sometimes shades into secrecy that ultimately tests the limits of the law. For example, in an effort to sell a large number of shares in the Hartford Fire and Casualty Company during the 1960s, the International Telephone and Telegraph Corporation (ITT) obtained the assistance of André Meyer of Lazard,

Frères & Co. The deal had to be put over in a highly confidential manner for business reasons, and 'the transaction was a masterpiece of concealment, with its multiple layers of intermediaries and its Liechtenstein companies – all intended to obscure, from the IRS and from other prying eyes, exactly where the wayward ITT stock was going.'[1] In the end, both the IRS and the SEC got involved in investigating the transaction for violations of tax and securities laws, and Lazard, Frères 'had been branded in the public consciousness as the prime mover in a scheme to skirt the law, deceive the IRS and, along the way, line its own pockets and those of a few favored friends.'[2]

Beyond finance, business confidentiality can also shade into secrecy if trade transactions bend the letter or spirit of the law, with potentially adverse consequences for the firm. For example, during hearings concerning the dumping of Japanese TV sets in the US market in the 1970s, evidence emerged that the manufacturers were using secret channels to funnel rebates to US retailers through Swiss accounts, in direct violation of US trade laws.[3]

In 1984, a number of British labor unions availed themselves of international financial secrecy to stash funds offshore with the intent of keeping them out of reach of court judgments levied in civil actions under that country's tough new labor laws. Although the same unions had roundly condemned capital flight in the past, their loss of immunity from civil actions prompted the National Union of Mineworkers (NUM), the National Graphical Association and the Transport & General Workers' Union to use precisely the same financial secrecy routes in order to spirit assets out of the country and out of the reach of the courts. Prior to its longest and most bitter strike, for example, the NUM sold about $11 million in UK government bonds, passing the proceeds through the Isle of Man, as well as banks in Ireland and the United States, to cash and bearer-bond accounts in Switzerland.[4]

In the famous 1984 Flick Scandal in West Germany, secret money was involved no less. It was discovered that an outfit called Europäische Unternehmensberatungsanstalt (European Institute for Business Consulting) in Liechtenstein had issued receipts for payments from dozens of German firms. The funds were then allegedly channeled into the coffers of the Christian Democratic Party in West Germany. Under the law, West German firms are severely limited in the size of political contributions, only a small part of which are tax deductible. Front companies such as Europäische Unternehmensberatungsanstalt issuing phoney invoices for services not rendered, or phoney charities fulfilling the same purpose, thus made possible disallowed political support as well as tax evasion.[5]

Capital flight

There is no generally accepted definition of flight capital, but the term is normally associated with outflows of private capital for speculative purposes or as a result of economic or political uncertainty in the home country.[6]

Defining capital flight

Webster defines 'flight' as 'An act or instance of running away'. To apply this definition to the phenomenon of capital flight requires both the attribution of certain motives to the asset-holder concerned and a frame of reference of the act of flight itself.

Asset-holders in the ordinary course of events engage in constant redeployment in their search for an efficient portfolio – one that maximizes total returns under a given risk constraint. They continuously compare alternative portfolios domestically and internationally, and routinely engage in asset restructuring as risk/return perceptions of individual investment vehicles, currencies and locations change. In any specific instance, the underlying investor motivation may be either returns-driven or risk-driven, depending on which parameter is perceived to have changed. Either one can trigger movement toward or away from a particular asset. Yet use of the term 'flight' is rare indeed in discussions of ordinary portfolio adjustments of this sort. Investors may 'flee' from IBM or General Motors stock, but the word is not often used in this context.

Rather, from the standpoint of the asset-holder it appears that common usage of the term 'capital flight' refers to an unfavorable change in the risk/return profile associated with a portfolio of assets held in a particular *country*, as compared with a portfolio held in other national jurisdictions. This altered profile, in turn, is deemed to be sufficiently inferior to warrant an active redeployment of assets – overcoming normal investor inertia, as well as information costs and transactions costs that can themselves be substantial. In many cases the potential costs include running afoul of the law and risking punishment, or violating an implied social contract. This has a bearing both on the conduits used in achieving asset redeployment and on the process of asset selection. In each case, confidentiality may play a significant role.

Governments normally follow multiple macroeconomic objectives that may include growth, employment, inflation and balance of payments or exchange-rate targets, as well as more specific objectives related to prices of goods and services, income and wealth distribution, economic structure, financing of the public sector, and ownership of the means of production. International flows of direct and portfolio investments under ordinary circumstances are rarely associated with the capital flight phenomenon. Rather, it is when capital transfers by residents conflict with political objectives that the term 'flight' comes into general usage.

Asset redeployment by individuals or institutions in this context threatens attainment of one or more national objectives. It threatens to impose an economic cost on the nation and a political cost on those who hold office. As residents of the country concerned, asset-holders who engage in such behavior are held by the authorities to be in violation of a social contract. This violation may involve illegal conduct, as in the evasion of exchange control regulations. Or it may involve conduct that is deemed immoral or irresponsible, and that could be made illegal in the future. Disclosure of asset redeployment on the part of an individual or institution under such conditions is usually captured under the rubric of capital flight.

Beyond this, flight capital may also involve assets that have themselves been illegally obtained domestically. Assets accumulated through criminal activities such as smuggling, financial fraud, bribery, racketeering and corruption are obvious candidates for capital flight if shifting them abroad yields perceived reductions in the probability of disclosure, asset recapture, and possibly serious legal sanctions applied to the institutions or individuals involved. So are assets that have otherwise been accumulated legally but are involved in tax evasion. Criminal and tax-motivated capital flight obviously depends on the size and character of a nation's underground economy, and will occur even in the absence of ordinary asset-redeployment incentives based on comparative risks and returns. At a minimum it violates fiscal statutes, and may violate a broad range of criminal statutes as well.

Correctly defined, capital flight therefore appears to consist of a subset of international asset redeployments or portfolio adjustments – undertaken in response to significant perceived deterioration in risk/ return profiles associated with assets located in a particular country – that occur in the presence of conflict between the objectives of asset-holders and governments. It may or may not violate the law. It is always considered by the authorities to violate an implied social contract.

Capital flight invariably involves tradeoffs among four sets of factors: expected returns, information and transactions costs, risks, and confidentiality.

Holders of financial assets, broadly defined, are generally thought to be driven by considerations related primarily to the nature of risks and returns. The behavioral characteristics of asset-holders are thoroughly addressed in modern portfolio theory and can easily be adapted to include the international dimension. In the context of capital flight, their behavior may be conditioned as well by confidentiality regarding the size, location, and composition of financial or other assets that comprise a portfolio. Confidentiality clearly has value to the asset-holder

54

whenever disclosure would impose damage upon him or those with whom he identifies. This will be the case for flight capital if it is – or might in the future be – considered illegal or irresponsible, and the asset-holder or his family continues to reside within the country.

If confidentiality has value, then asset-holders engaging in capital flight should be willing to pay for it. They may pay by preferring a portfolio of assets that has lower expected real net returns than one assembled without regard to confidentiality considerations. Or they may pay by assembling a portfolio with higher covariances in expected net real returns among the constituent assets – a more risky portfolio – than if confidentiality were not a consideration. Or some combination of effects of confidentiality on returns and risks may be involved.

Measuring capital flight

Several measures have been employed to measure capital flight. The 'broad measure', includes identified purchases of all foreign assets other than official reserves, plus the 'errors and omissions' line in countries' balance of payments figures. The 'private claims measure' includes only the private sector's acquisitions of external assets, plus errors and omissions. The 'narrow measure' is defined as short-term capital out-flows of the non-bank private sector plus net errors and omissions. The main problem with all these definitions is that they do not allow for the fact that some outflow may correspond to 'normal' portfolio diversifi-cation by domestic residents. And they make the assumption that 'errors and omissions' all represent unrecorded capital flows, which is clearly not the case.[7]

There is thus no satisfactory distinction between reported and unre-ported foreign asset accumulation – an important distinction in any useful definition. It is, after all, not simply the outflow of capital that creates the problem of capital flight, but rather that element which is in some way 'lost' to the country. In other words the alleged 'damage' is done when a government has no knowledge of or returns from (in the form of taxes for example) the foreign assets accumulated by domestic residents. If earnings from such assets remain outside the country or are repatriated through unofficial channels, the foreign income and wealth of domestic residents cannot contribute to the servicing of the country's debt or to the financing of its development programme. One working definition of flight capital might then be stated as the difference between total private capital outflows and that part for which interest income is identified and reported. A similar approach is the 'derived measure', estimated as the difference between the total stock of foreign assets and the capitalized value of the recorded inflow of investment income.

To a large extent, private capital flows that feed the secrecy market are associated with flight capital from countries whose political or economic

Table 3.1   *Estimated net capital flight cumulative flows during 1976–85 and 1986*

	Total* 1976–85	1976–82*	1983–85*	1986†
		(billions of US$)		
Argentina	–26	–27	1	0.7
Bolivia	–1	–1	0	n.a.
Brazil	–10	–1	–7	–1.0
Chile	1	0	1	0.8
Colombia	0	0	0	0.0
Ecuador	–2	–1	–1	–0.2
Mexico	–53	–36	–17	0.9
Peru	–0	1	–1	0.4
Uruguay	–1	–1	–9	n.a.
Venezuela	–30	–25	–6	0.5
Subtotal	–123	–93	–30	n.a.
India	–10	–6	–4	n.a.
Indonesia	–5	–6	1	n.a.
Korea	–12	–6	–6	n.a.
Malaysia	–12	–8	–4	n.a.
Nigeria	–10	–7	–3	1.3
Philippines	–9	–7	–2	1.7
South Africa	–17	–13	–4	n.a.
Thailand	–0	1	–1	n.a.
Subtotal	–75	–52	–23	n.a.
Total for 18 countries	–198	–145	–53	n.a.

* Apparent change in other foreign assets (minus sign indicates increase) through residual capital flows measured as the counterpart of the sum of net direct investment inflows, change in gross external debt, current account balance, and change in selected gross foreign assets. Direct investment and current account data are taken from the reported balance of payments. Debt and asset changes are derived from estimated year-end outstandings in dollar terms.
† Net flows excluding reinvestment of earnings on private sector reinvestment of assets.
Note: Due to rounding, columns and rows may not add.
Source: Morgan Guaranty Trust Company, *World Financial Markets*, March 1986 and March 1987.

circumstances yield an unfavorable risk–reward relationship for asset-holders. From 1976 to 1985, over $200 billion is estimated to have been transferred to offshore assets by residents of developing countries, with $53 billion of that amount moving during the years 1983–5 alone from precisely those countries subject to the greatest difficulties in servicing their external debt, including Mexico, Argentina and Venezuela (see Table 3.1). Table 3.2 provides estimates of liquid asset build-ups, in large part traceable to capital flight, as of 1985. Table 3.3 illustrates how much of an impact capital flight had on the debt of certain developing

Table 3.2   *Identifiable non-bank residents' deposits in foreign banks,
September 1985*

	Total in all foreign banks	Banks in US (billions of US$)	Other foreign banks
Argentina	8.2	4.1	4.1
Bolivia	0.4	n.a.	n.a.
Brazil	8.5	1.7	6.8
Chile	2.2	1.6	0.6
Colombia	1.6	0.7	0.8
Ecuador	1.3	0.7	0.6
Mexico	15.3	11.1	4.2
Peru	1.5	1.0	0.5
Uruguay	2.0	1.2	0.8
Venezuela	12.6	7.1	5.5
Subtotal	54.6	30.3	24.3
India	1.7	0.1	1.6
Indonesia	0.7	0.2	0.5
Korea	0.4	0.2	0.3
Malaysia	1.0	0.0	1.0
Nigeria	1.4	n.a.	n.a.
Philippines	1.1	0.7	0.4
South Africa	1.3	0.0	1.3
Thailand	0.4	0.2	0.2
Subtotal	8.0	1.3	6.7
Total for 18 countries	62.6	31.6	31.0

Source: Morgan Guaranty Trust Company, *World Financial Markets*, March 1986 and March 1987.

countries, as well as the impact repatriation of earnings on capital held abroad could have had on some of these countries' debt service.

Note the wide differences in capital flight patterns among countries, in response to both inter-country differences and variations over time in economic and political outlooks as well as the severity of exchange restrictions and changes in exchange rates. For Mexico, Venezuela and Argentina, capital flight represented between 43 and 96 per cent of the funds borrowed abroad by public and private sector institutions during the period preceding onset of the LDC debt given in 1982.

The problem continued on a grand scale into the mid-1980s. In March 1986 Morgan Guaranty published a report in which it estimated that of the $375 billion added by the ten major Latin American countries to their debts between 1975 and 1985 almost half disappeared in the form of flight capital.[8] Venezuela, for example, added $36 billion to its external debt and evacuated some $41 billion in capital; Argentina borrowed a

Table 3.3 *Impact of capital flight on debt*

	Gross external debt, end-1985		Gross debt as percentage of exports of goods and services*		Earnings on flight capital as percentage of interest payments on external debt
	Actual	Without capital flight†	Actual	Without capital flight†	
	(billions of US$)				
Argentina	50	1	493	16	37
Brazil	106	92	358	322	8
Mexico	97	12	327	61	39
Venezuela	31	−12	190	−55	73
Malaysia	20	4	103	18	n.a.
Nigeria	19	7	161	62	53
Philippines	27	15	327	195	22
South Africa	24	1	131	15	n.a.

* Debt-to-export ratios are based on the average of debt at beginning and end of 1985.
† Assumes that in the absence of capital flight, debt accumulation and related interest payments would have been reduced, and other flows (direct investment, changes in foreign assets of official monetary authorities and banks, and current account transactions other than interest payments) would not have differed from actual.
Source: Morgan Guaranty Trust Company, *World Financial Markets*, March 1986 and March 1987.

further $58 billion, flight capital was estimated at $36 billion.[9] Between 1983 and 1985 alone, according to the Morgan study, Venezuela lost $6 billion, Brazil $7 billion and Mexico $17 billion.[10] A number of the countries took strong exception to these figures. In particular, Mexico said its own estimates suggested a sum closer to $2 billion.[11]

While the exact estimates may be contested, the official Mexican figure seems over-optimistic to say the least. The US Treasury bulletin, for example, showed $11.1 billion of Mexican non-governmental deposits in US banks in 1986, and that did not include deposits held in non-Mexican names or addresses, or other types of investment such as gold, stocks or real estate. Ten years earlier the figure had been only $2 billion.[12]

The IMF's own study using the 'derived measure' method, suggested that for the 1975–85 period total capital flight from the developing countries ran at between $165 billion and $200 billion.[13]

Figures for later years, however, have tended to show some reversal in the trend (see Table 3.1).[14] Overall capital flight from the eight main Latin American debtors appears to have effectively ceased during 1986, with a net financial reflow into those countries of $1.3 billion.[15] While such data give some cause for encouragement, the extent of the reversal should not be overestimated. The returning fund flows are very small when compared with the overall outflows from these same countries in the past decade, all the more so when we remember the likely substantial increase in value (in local-currency terms) that has occurred in the foreign assets acquired through outflows. Much remains to be done before significant capital reflows occur in many of the countries that have suffered from capital flight.[16]

A 1988 study of the capital flight issue concluded that capital flight is essentially impossible to identify with a high degree of statistical precision, and that there is no significant correlation between the available (necessarily inadequate) capital flight measures and indicators of domestic investment or welfare. Nevertheless, it recognized that the problem, though unmeasurable, does exist and is serious for the countries concerned – and that 'solutions' such as capital controls and periodic tax amnesty – are basically ineffective and fail to address the underlying reasons for the problem. According to an Argentine businessman, 'I just throw my tax assessment away every year. I prefer to pay when the government offers a tax amnesty. It's a lot cheaper that way.'[17]

The phenomenon of capital flight is of course not restricted to the major debtor countries of Latin America. Countries such as Lebanon, Israel, France and Italy have been the scene of massive capital flight from time to time.

A 1987 Nigerian government investigation estimated that at the height of the oil boom in 1978, corrupt politicians were transferring $25 million a day abroad.[18] Indeed it seems likely that the involvement of a prestigious London firm, Johnson Matthey Bankers Ltd, in such dealings may have contributed to its demise.[19] Nigerian political figures allegedly moved billions in hard currency out of Nigeria by drawing sterling from Johnson Matthey in the form of loans backed by Nigerian banks against forged bills of lading for imports that never existed.

The Philippines continues to suffer from massive capital flight. In September 1985 visible Filipino deposits with foreign banks amounted to more than 10 per cent of the country's external debt, not to mention hidden sums including the presumed Marcos fortune.[20] Figures for 1986 indicate that a further $1.7 billion fled the country.[21]

In June and July 1987, Belgium (from which some $3 billion a year is thought to slip secretly away to Luxembourg to avoid the highest taxes in Western Europe) briefly became a net importer rather than exporter of capital. The cause? Capital flight – at the rate of $150 million a month – from the Netherlands. The Dutch finance minister had warned that from the beginning of 1988 Dutch banks would be required to give the tax authorities full information on interest earned by clients on their deposits. It has been estimated that about two-thirds of Dutch tax-

Table 3.4 *External debt, capital flight, and capital formation (1974–82)*

Country	Total change in external debt ($ billion)	Total capital flight ($ billion)	Percentage change in gross domestic fixed capital formation
Argentina	32.6	15.3	–36.0
Brazil	93.5	0.2	–20.0
Chile	15.4	–1.9	–34.0
Mexico	82.6	32.7	–27.0
Peru	10.7	1.2	–17.0
Venezuela	27.0	10.8	–23.0

Source: World Bank.

payers normally 'forget' to list their full interest earnings on their tax returns.[22]

Capital flight of course reduces the domestic resources of a country. Table 3.4 illustrates this clearly, showing a significant decline in domestic fixed capital formation for the Latin American countries in question.

It is important to realize that an interrelation exists between the public guaranteeing of debt and private capital flight. Even where governments provide no guarantee, lenders may hold them responsible for the debts of private borrowers in default. The result is that any move by one borrower that increases the possibility of default is perceived by other borrowers as increasing the likelihood of higher tax obligations for them as the government moves to cover the cost of the default – in effect, nationalizing the debt. In order to avoid these higher taxes, borrowers will be inclined to move capital out of the domestic arena, thus making likely even higher demands on funds remaining, which will encourage yet more capital to flee. Similarly, the viability of any private domestic project funded by foreign debt is undermined – the borrower's effort to make a project work will depend on the level of profit that project can provide. This is affected by debt-service obligations and anticipated tax obligations. The potential nationalization of private debt will tend to erode incentives, making default more likely.

This phenomenon has been described as the response of domestic and foreign investors to an asymmetric risk of expropriation. Domestic investors face a higher risk of expropriation so they invest abroad, leaving domestic investment to be financed by foreign funds, with the risk of expropriation related to the level of public guarantee of debt. Using this model, capital flight is seen to be a consequence of a market failure, i.e. the inability to enforce contracts between private agents without public intervention.

Capital flight may have another cause as well – straightforward dishonesty. By placing funds overseas, using secrecy vehicles to avoid detection, borrowers can both escape the obligation to pay taxes to their government and to repay loans to lenders – the funds are simply out of reach. Even if they are traced, lenders will most likely lack the legal ability to attach them or use them as collateral for outstanding debts.

Various solutions have been offered for the problem of capital flight. One is that the tax base of borrowing countries should be extended to include income from private assets abroad. Another is that capital controls should be imposed to prohibit investment overseas. Explicit or implicit government guarantees should be replaced with bankruptcy procedures which would compensate lenders with equity in the assets of private borrowers in default. Lenders could withhold some part of loans to ensure that it is in borrowers' interests to invest domestically. Such suggestions, however, all fail to take account of the ingenuity of those who wish to protect their assets and the difficulty of imposing constraints in practice. In addition, the threat of such actions can in itself trigger a rush for the door. In the final analysis the only foolproof solution is for people to see benefit in investing domestically, for them to have confidence in the home economy.[23]

Capital flight vehicles

The vehicles for capital flight are many. They range from highly sophisticated schemes such as those employed in Nigeria to the very basic method of cramming a suitcase full of currency notes and carrying it across the border. Sources familiar with exchange practices in Brazil, for example, say that couriers frequently take cash to neighbouring Uruguay, which allows free conversion of currencies. Alternatively, a number of travellers regularly buy precious stones or gold in the local currency which they then sell abroad. Smuggling is a popular method elsewhere, as well. It is thought that diamond smuggling, including large amounts passing through the VIP lounge at Luanda airport, costs the Angolan government some $70 million a year.[24] Other tricks of dubious legality consist of borrowing abroad, using a deposit in a local bank as collateral; buying a commodity not subject to a country's export controls, which is then sold or bartered abroad with proceeds staying in an overseas account;[25] or the technology adopted by a number of private companies that involves buying back their own debt in international financial markets at a discount to the amount actually borrowed. Private debtors that qualify for preferential dollars under government schemes thereby make a profit on the difference between the nominal and discounted value of the debt.[26]

Perhaps the most common practice of all involves under-invoicing exports or over-invoicing imports. In the case of the former the foreign

61

purchaser agrees to an invoice showing less than the figure he actually paid. The difference stays in the overseas account of the exporter. In the case of an importer a foreign supplier provides an invoice showing a price higher than was actually paid. Again the difference stays in the overseas account of the importer.[27] Bankers estimate that in Venezuela over-invoicing of imports was running at some $150 million a month early in 1986, while in Malaysia during the period 1976–84 reported exports fell roughly $10 billion short of their FOB value recorded by trading partners, and in Nigeria in 1979 reported oil exports were about $4 billion less than volume and price data implied.

Capital flight – consequences

Flight capital clearly has serious consequences for those countries afflicted. Indeed according to estimates such as those in Table 3.1, few of the Latin American countries would have experienced the severe debt problems they faced in the 1980s if it had not been for capital flight, which essentially represented a vote of no confidence in the economic and political measures designed to cope with their internal and external difficulties. President José Lopes Portillo of Mexico was perhaps missing the point when in 1982 he termed those engaging in capital flight as 'traitors'. Their actions were in many ways a symptom rather than a cause of the country's economic problems at the time.

Capital flight has been much less of a problem in Asia, with the exception of the Philippines and Hong Kong, not because Asians do not seek safe havens and decent real returns on their assets but because national economic and financial policies have consistently carried substantially greater credibility than those in Latin America.

The concerns of asset-holders usually center around overvalued domestic currencies, which make foreign assets such as real estate appear cheap by comparison, and which promise a substantial capital gain in local currency when an exchange-rate correction eventually occurs – as it inevitably will. They also worry about low and sometimes negative domestic real interest rates (nominal rates adjusted for expected inflation), which are kept that way by irresponsible monetary policies. And they worry about the future imposition of exchange controls, tax increases, expropriation and other measures that sometimes cause, and sometimes result from, poor economic management. In short, there develops a profound lack of confidence in the way a country is likely to be run in the foreseeable future, and its implications for real asset values. The result is a rush, sometimes a stampede, for the exit, into assets characterized by higher real returns and lower perceived risk profiles.

One of the implications of this outflow is clearly that, in order to build up foreign-currency deposits abroad, the residents of a country reduce domestic expenditure relative to domestic income. This depresses domestic investment and makes sustained output growth more difficult to achieve.[28] In turn, it may ultimately affect the country's ability to borrow in world markets. As one review of the problem put it: 'When their own residents are unwilling to repatriate capital to invest at home, the debtor countries cannot expect greater willingness from their foreign creditors.' Foreign bankers are becoming a little unwilling to make new loans that may merely finance future capital flight.[29]

It is within this context of a need for the developing countries to 'put their house in order', involving sound economic policies that would inspire confidence in residents and creditors alike, that the Baker Plan should be considered. Set out in 1985 by US Treasury Secretary James Baker, it suggested that further lending should depend on borrowing countries pursuing policies that would improve their economies – to take firm anti-inflation measures, to institute major structural reforms to reduce the role of the state, to liberalize trade, to establish appropriate exchange and interest rates, to arrest further capital flight and indeed draw back some of the billions of dollars held abroad already by their own citizens.[30]

Laudable and relevant though all this is, progress will not come easily. As we have seen, capital flight represents a vote of no confidence by the residents of a country in its economic situation. Although modest progress has been made, the economic plight of many countries is such that a sustained and significant reversal in the capital flight trend remains unlikely.

The most heavily affected region is still Latin America, which has the fastest-growing population within the developing world, more than 360 million people, 41 per cent under the age of 15, with 25–30 per cent unemployed.[31] A number of countries are heavily dependent on the drugs trade for revenue, a state of affairs that itself brings increasing instability and lawlessness. Bolivia saw its revenues from tin and natural gas exports plunge by 70 per cent during 1985. At the same time, repatriated earnings from cocaine traffickers, which account for some 25 per cent of GNP, brought in a desperately needed $660 million – the cocaine trade was in fact thought to be worth $3.8 billion to Bolivian dealers during 1986, but they left the lion's share overseas like everyone else. Inflation spiraled out of control, with the government's revenues covering a mere 15 per cent of its expenditure and a deficit that was nearly 25 per cent of the country's total annual output in 1986.[32]

Bolivia is an extreme example, but it is hardly alone. Colombia supplies some 75 per cent of US cocaine consumption, earning dealers $30 billion annually, of which perhaps $1 billion is repatriated. In Peru, with a GNP of some $16 billion, drugs account for an estimated $800 million in export earnings, more than twice the figure from the legitimate export of copper.[33] Despite incentives including favorable tax and interest rates and an easing in import regulations, President Alan García's government was unsuccessful in halting capital flight. Indeed, although there was an estimated reflow of $0.4 billion in 1986, about $96 million was thought to have left the country between May and August 1987 alone, reducing Peru's net reserves to around $800 million.[34] In an attempt to stem the flow, García announced plans to nationalize the banks, which he said contributed to the flight of capital – once again an example of attacking the symptom rather than the cause.

Against such backgrounds, corruption and violence have become inevitable, and confidence in future development and stability is difficult to muster.

While most flight capital is doubtless linked to perceptions of domestic economic conditions, purely political factors play a role as well. Examples are the aforementioned mass exodus of capital in 1983 from Hong Kong, faced with uncertain prospects under Chinese sovereignty after 1997, and in 1983–4 from the Philippines, faced with economic problems and political uncertainty. According to one account at the time, 'Hong Kong investors are buying up office buildings, supermarkets, restaurants, luxury homes, and condominiums in many US and Canadian cities. "The only safe place for my money is in US dollars, in a US bank, on US soil"', declared one frightened Hong Kong resident.[35]

Private bankers, securities salesmen and real estate agents were quick to take advantage of the capital flight. Real estate operators set up sales offices in Hong Kong, 44 Edge Act (international) units of US banks joined the local banks and 33 foreign banks in Miami to tap into the Latin American market. Foreign businesses set up US subsidiaries in order to facilitate transfer pricing to move capital around exchange controls using intra-firm transactions. The dollar's great strength during this period was doubtless related to capital flight.

In the absence of exchange controls, disclosure requirements and tax regulations, much of the capital flight is, of course, perfectly legal. But even without such barriers, secrecy still plays an important role. Individuals with known foreign assets may be particularly exposed to political reprisals at home. So it may be wise to minimize disclosure in whatever way is best suited to the nature of the individual case.

The unhappy case of Antonio Gebauer

Capital flight figured highly in the case of Antonio Gebauer, a senior New York banker who suddenly resigned in May 1986 from his position with Drexel Burnham Lambert. He had joined DBL from Morgan Guaranty the previous August to help develop a secondary market for Third World bank loans.[36] At the time, he was under investigation for the unauthorized diversion for his own use of over $4.3 million from six private accounts under his management while at Morgan. The peculiar circumstances of his highly successful career seem to have made it too easy to satisfy a keenly developed sense of greed.

A native of Venezuela, Gebauer had played a significant role in building up Morgan's South American business in the 1970s, particularly in Brazil, which during that time was perhaps the most profitable market for commercial lending in the world. The bank had rather neglected the area – Gebauer's own estimates suggested that in 1964 its total outstanding loans to Brazil were of the order of just $50 million; by 1984 they were some $2 billion.

In 1981 Gebauer was appointed Senior Vice-President in charge of Morgan's Latin American business; a year later, he was chosen to act as co-chairman of the advisory committee of US commercial banks set up to attempt to restructure Brazil's $83 billion foreign debt.[37] His contacts in South America, and particularly in Brazil, were at the highest level. His first wife, Fernanda de Souza Queiroz, was the stepdaughter of a leading businessman; her family connections provided the base of a social network that included some of the wealthiest and most powerful people in Latin America. These contacts were not only useful in bringing about deals but also in advising on their quality, an asset Gebauer used to the full, and the bank's loan-loss record in Brazil seemed to bear this out. A key member of the Brazilian-American Chamber of Commerce, of which he was president for a year, he was also an 'honorary citizen' of Brazil. It is understandable, given this background, that Gebauer should have been a natural choice as private banker to a number of his Brazilian friends and contacts. Unfortunately he was not as reliable as they might have hoped. Over a period of seven years he systematically siphoned off funds from six accounts under his care.

To understand how it was possible for Gebauer to accomplish this, the nature of the accounts in question and the consequences for the manner in which they were managed is important. There are indications that all six related to flight capital. None had been declared to the Brazilian authorities, and the movement of the funds overseas had probably violated Brazilian currency laws. All were set up in Panama with a hold-mail arrangement. Except in certain circumstances, it was illegal for Brazilians to hold foreign currency accounts abroad.[38] In this situation, secrecy becomes vitally important, with the result that the client, who must keep a low profile, tends both to grant discretion to the banker to facilitate secret asset management and to forgo receipt of the usual information, such as bank statements. It thus becomes at once easy for the banker to move funds and difficult for the client to monitor them. Gebauer appears to have exploited these factors to the full. His task was made all the easier by the trust Morgan places in its bankers.

It was thus possible for Gebauer to get other employees to issue unauthorized treasurer's checks drawn on his clients' accounts that

65

averaged over $20,000 each, at a rate of 20 to 40 a year from 1976 to 1983. When the withdrawals had been such that the balance in the accounts fell to uncomfortably low levels, or on several occasions to zero, he organized new short-term loans by the bank to replenish the funds. These loans were renewed 46 times with approval from other Morgan officers. When one of the clients became suspicious, Gebauer saw to it that more than 20 false bank statements were prepared.

How was he caught? At times one of his clients would ask, on the basis of a false balance given to him by Gebauer, for a transfer that exceeded the sum actually available. There would then be a mad scramble to cover the shortfall by other transfers or loans. This of course became far more difficult once Gebauer was no longer at Morgan, and in the fall of 1985 the inevitable happened – Gebauer was unable to fill the vacuum quickly enough. The client had to be told that the balance he thought was $3 million was in fact just under $2,900. The game was up. The classic principal–agent problem in the presence of secrecy had run its full course.

At first his attorney argued that the accusations against him revealed a complete lack of understanding of the way business in Latin America was carried out. The point about flight capital and discretionary management was made. This of course only served to add to the scandal, with the Central Bank of Brazil requesting details on the six accounts involved in order to investigate any illegalities – all of which proved to be particularly sensitive given the country's debt problems and vulnerability to capital flight. It was also highly embarrassing for Morgan, a bank known for its solidity and sobriety. Not only had one of its senior officials managed to salt away without notice more than $4 million of clients' funds, but he had taken the funds from offshore accounts, the very existence of which was a delicate matter. Morgan among other banks was exposed heavily to Brazil and at the same time seen as being involved – at least passively – in helping the country's elite invest their wealth elsewhere. Common knowledge, but not the type to be advertised.

Even in view of the discretion argument, the case did not look favorable for Gebauer. He owned a $5.5 million Manhattan cooperative, an apartment in Paris, an East Hampton estate and one third of a Bahia coffee plantation. He had for several years lived a lavish lifestyle, been a regular customer of New York antique shops, rare book agents and art dealers and sent his children to the best schools. Family connections and a senior position in the bank were simply not enough to explain that sort of wealth.

In October 1986, Gebauer pleaded guilty to four felony counts involving bank fraud and tax evasion. He had in effect diverted a total of $8.2 million made up of the $4.3 million from customer accounts, another $1.7 million diverted from other sources and $2.2 million of interest on the misappropriated funds. In February 1987 he was sentenced with the memorable words: 'You are indeed a Lucifer, a fallen angel of the banking world,' to 3½ years in prison and a fine of $100,000. He has in addition to make good the full sum to Morgan and to meet payments of $6.94 million owed to the IRS in unpaid taxes.[39]

Bribery and corruption

The economic and behavioral dimensions of bribery and corruption have been analyzed in some depth.[40] The bribee is generally a government official who has the power to alter his decision from one based purely on merit – to favor one supplier over another, to grant or withhold import permits or foreign exchange licenses, to approve a veterinary certificate or a building permit, not to impose penalties for violations of the law, etc. In the process, the briber passes the costs along to the ultimate customers, who are then exposed to inferior or overpriced goods and services. Bribery almost always injures society, but in many countries it is a way of life, with bribees at various levels often bribing higher-ups to obtain their jobs, and with the ladder of corruption sometimes reaching into the very pinnacles of government.

Technically, questionable payments comprise at least four more or less clearly identifiable categories:

- Bribes: significant payments to officials with decision-making powers to convince them to do their jobs *improperly*;
- Grease: 'facilitating' payments to minor officials to encourage them to do their jobs *properly*;
- Extortion: payments to persons in authority to avoid damage from hostile actions on the part of unions, criminals, utilities, 'renegade' troops, and the like; and
- Political contributions: payments to political parties linked to favors or threats of retribution in case of non-payment.

In many cases, such payments can be routed through 'agent's fees' to independent third parties acting on behalf of the payer.

When confronted with balance of payments difficulties, policymakers frequently resort to the imposition of exchange controls. These invariably give rise to black markets in foreign exchange. Normally, the currency trades at a severe discount on the black market as compared with the official rate. At least three issues are pertinent to measuring the size of the black market in currencies. First, transactions in the black market are unofficial, and thus it is difficult to calculate the size of the volume of those transactions. The money is not accounted for in the legal accounting processes. Second, exchange-rate premiums cannot be legally declared as income. Therefore, what is not used for immediate consumption must become secret money. Third, the entire process gives rise to corruption in government as some groups try to get the scarce foreign currency at the official exchange rate. These bribes must be hidden as well.

Whenever exchange controls exist, secret transfers of funds can be used by those in favored positions, or those able to bribe the authorities, to enrich themselves very substantially indeed. During the 1984 Argentine debt crisis, for example, a scheme was uncovered whereby Argentines with deposits abroad were able to use them as security in a 'self-lending' operation to borrow dollars, which were then repatriated into pesos at highly favorable 'parallel market' exchange rates. Reportedly as much as $10 billion was involved, adding substantially to an already unsustainable volume of external debt, with no productive purpose.

As in the case of bribees, the volume of transactions undertaken by bribers is extremely difficult to estimate. Overseas payments became a major political issue in the United States during the 1970s. Disclosures of well over $1 billion in questionable payments by some 400 US companies under the Securities and Exchange Commission's 'voluntary disclosure' program gave rise to the Foreign Corrupt Practices Act of 1977, which made many such payments by US companies illegal. No comparable disclosures have ever been made by companies based in other countries, many of whose governments take a much more benign attitude toward foreign payoffs. So the need for secrecy in such cases seems to be less critical on the briber's side than it is on the bribee's, who faces possible retribution or claims on a share of the spoils if disclosure occurs.

International financial secrecy is critical for bribery and corruption to work effectively. Payment in domestic (inside) currency is often difficult for the briber and can turn out to be relatively worthless for the bribee – it often won't buy much, and may be difficult to hide in relatively poorly developed financial institutions and markets subject to government scrutiny. Much better to use foreign (outside) slush funds that can be effectively generated (e.g., using phoney invoices for fictitious services), hidden in secret accounts by the payer and then quietly transferred to an equally secret account owned by the bribee.

Bofors

An example of the use of secret money in bribery was the Bofors case in Sweden. It is alleged that in 1986 the Swedish arms manufacturer bribed Indian officials in order to win a major weapons contract.[41] Stockholm's chief prosecutor indicated that up to $47 million was paid into secret Swiss bank accounts to persuade Indian middlemen to land the company a $1.13 billion order for a field artillery system, and he was seeking access to the Swiss bank records in an attempt to determine the identity of the recipients of the funds. This was a crucial step in proving a bribery case under Swedish law, which forbids companies to pay fees to foreign officials to win contracts.

Meanwhile the affair caused quite a stir in India itself, with pronouncements from Opposition figures on corruption within the government. A petition had been placed before the Delhi High Court demanding that two Bofors officials visiting New Delhi be required to surrender documents relating to the matter.

The company denied malpractice, stating that the money paid out constituted no more than legitimate termination fees to agents who had worked on the contract in India.[42]

After five months of inquiry into the case, Stockholm's chief prosecutor came to the conclusion that he could proceed no further and the investigation was stopped. Due to Swiss refusal to grant access to the relevant bank records it was impossible to trace the exact destination of the money paid by Bofors into the Swiss accounts. The parliamentary investigation into the affair continued in New Delhi, with Prime Minister Rajiv Gandhi himself still accused by some opponents of having profited from the deal.

Some $20 million of the alleged $60 million in payoffs have been traced by a joint investigation of Radio Sweden and the Indian newspaper *The Hindu*, indicating that the sum was paid by Bofors to a company linked to the Hinduja brothers, prominent and wealthy Indians whose business transactions have long been mysterious. It is alleged that among other shady deals, they at various times contracted to supply Iran with bomb fuses. The funds were apparently routed through a company registered in Geneva, Moineau SA, owned by the Hinduja brothers.

This was not the first time Bofors' actions have been questioned. Both it and its parent company, Nobel, had previously been the center of scandals concerning shipments of war material illegally diverted to more than a dozen countries including Iran and other Middle Eastern states. Indeed, a 1988 investigation implied that interruption of these shipments directly or indirectly led to the 1986 murder of Prime Minister Olof Palme by agents of the Iran-backed Kurdish Workers Party. Despite some of the toughest export restrictions faced by any weapons manufacturer and a steady stream of lectures by Swedish politicians on the evils of military conflict, Bofors clandestine activities appear to have prospered – apparently the joint work of Bofors executives (many later replaced by Nobel) and middle-level Swedish bureaucrats charged with enforcing the export control regulations.[43]

A Swedish prosecutor indicated in September 1988 that his office had begun legal proceedings against three former directors of Bofors, who allegedly took a cut of up to SKR 5 million (US$ 800,000) from commissions paid by the company to secure weapons contracts in direct violation of Swedish law. Nobel Industries formally admitted that its subsidiary knowingly contravened strict Swedish arms export controls in selling exporting arms in areas of conflict, primarily in the Middle East.[44]

As in this case, 'outside money' paid abroad is often worth far more to the bribee as well as the briber. It may buy merchandise, services or assets not readily available at home, and it can buy security in the form of a foreign retirement nest egg out of the reach of national authorities should the need arise for a hasty exit.

The amounts involved can be staggering indeed. According to one report, $5–7 billion in graft and corruption was collected and subsequently sent abroad by various officials of the elected Nigerian government that was overthrown in 1983. In addition to investments in clandestine financial assets, some unusual safekeeping vehicles turned up, including a solid gold bathtub in the English vacation home of one senior Nigerian official.[45] Comparable amounts have been noted in connection with high government officials in Mexico, Indonesia, the Philippines and various other countries.

Tongsun Park

A much less dramatic scandal involving alleged bribery and corruption came to light in 1977. During the 1960s and 1970s Tongsun Park, a prominent South Korean businessman with an international network of contacts, had played a leading role in Washington society. He entertained the powerful and the wealthy at the exclusive George Town Club, which he helped found and where he was an active member. He made campaign contributions and paid business-consultation fees totalling around $700,000 in the process of serving as agent for South Korea's rice sales, among others. But investigators found that the various payments were far from innocent and Park was indicted for bribery and corruption, much to the embarrassment of the South Korean government. Two years later, the charges were dropped after Park testified against certain members of the House.

Later, one of his South Korean companies collapsed and creditors remained unpaid. In the US, the IRS had outstanding tax claims against him of $6.6 million, plus interest and penalties and attached his salary from Suter's Tavern Inc. which held the real estate of the George Town Club.

Tongsun Park nevertheless continued to thrive. In early 1988 he turned up as 'honest broker' between Panama's General Noriega and a number of influential Washington figures in an attempt, it is thought, to improve the General's image. Meanwhile, he was also active in bringing together prominent Panamanians and Japanese. The US surrenders control of the Panama Canal in 1999 and the Japanese, second largest users of it, want to protect their interests by gaining a stronger commercial foothold in the country. As his friends put it, 'Park's audacity makes him a hard man to put down.'[46]

Dictators and others

The size of secret assets held abroad by political leaders, especially of developing countries, is anyone's guess. Former Nicaraguan dictator Anastasio Somosa is rumoured to have exported at least $500 million before his overthrow in 1979 by the Sandinistas, a substantial portion of which landed in foreign accounts. Emperor Haile Selassie was estimated to have over $15 billion in foreign assets at the time of his death in 1975, including annual deposits in Switzerland of 500kg of gold bullion that eventually strained the storage facilities of a major Swiss bank. President Mobutu Sésé Séko of Zaire is alleged to have placed almost $4 billion in Swiss personal accounts in the 1970s, roughly equivalent to his country's net external borrowings during that decade.[47] According to one observer: 'On the one hand, Mobutu has run out of ways to dodge [the International Monetary Fund's economic] restrictions. But he's also taken a look at his store of wealth abroad and realized that it is enough to take care of himself and his scions for centuries, if not eons.'[48]

When Jean-Claude (Baby Doc) Duvalier and his family fled Haiti in February 1986, the question in Port-au-Prince was how much of his desperately poor country's wealth had he taken with him. Knowledge-able sources suggested between $200 million and $500 million, funds which had been salted away in foreign accounts, since he took office in 1971.[49] The new government in Haiti was trying to recover the assets, and their investigations indicated systematic plundering of public funds by the Duvaliers over the years. 'It appears that they treated Haiti and its public funds as if they were private, personal property . . . You can see a pattern of transfers from government accounts to accounts controlled by the palace and then a day or two later of transfers out of the country.'[50] The Duvaliers claim that heads of state in Haiti had always had certain funds at their disposal for implementing policy, and that all money withdrawn by them had been spent charitably and wisely. The number of six-figure checks to companies with Swiss directors throws some doubt on such claims. The Haitian government investigated Duvalier for embezzlement, and although the Swiss authorities froze his accounts they at least initially provided no information on them, so that tracing and recovering the funds promised to be difficult.

The most staggering example of all, however, must surely be that of Ferdinand and Imelda Marcos, the ex-President and First Lady of the Philippines. When they offered them safe passage out of the country, the US authorities could hardly have envisaged the level of greed that would be demonstrated.

At the end of February 1986, when Mrs Cory Aquino's government came to power, the Marcoses and their entourage were flown out of the Philippines to Hawaii, aboard a US Air Force C-141. Their baggage required a second C-141; it arrived a day later, with 22 crates of goods, including currency and bullion worth several million dollars, the export of which without a licence is against Philippine law.[51]

Customs authorities in Hawaii immediately impounded the goods and, three weeks later, under an income tax treaty requiring the exchange of information relating to tax matters and fraud, the US State Department released full details of the loot.[52] It included $1.2 million of crisp new Philippine pesos; two Philippine bank certificates of deposit valued at $1.8 million; $7.7 million in cash and valuables, including jewelry valued at more than $4 million and a three-foot ivory statue covered in diamonds and other precious stones, believed to be a national treasure. There were also papers indicating assets elsewhere worth millions – one document listed balances totalling $88.7 million in five banks in the United States, Switzerland and the Cayman Islands; handwritten notes indicated that a further $35 million had been deposited but not yet credited.[53] It seemed that the 22 crates were but the tip of the iceberg. As one Philippine official expressed it at the time, the Marcoses had for 20 years been indulging in 'what can only be described as the unprecedented plunder of a nation, something that in terms of magnitude and brazenness defies comparison in our history.'[54]

In an attempt to recover the Marcos loot, Mrs Aquino set up the Presidential Commission on Good Government, a quasi-judicial body with powers to conduct pre-trial investigations, and to sequester 'suspected' Marcos assets until their real ownership is decided by the courts.[55] It had an annual budget of just $2.5 million and relies on a minicomputer and law-school volunteers to keep track of documentary evidence, an estimated 1.8 million items. Nevertheless, after the Marcoses' departure, the Commission swung into frenzied action, starting intensive investigations, both at home and abroad, and hiring legal teams in a number of countries where Marcos was thought to have assets.[56] Papers left behind in Malacañang Palace gave helpful leads. There were 75 file cabinets of documents (not to mention three paper shredders apparently broken through overuse) containing information on Liechtenstein foundations, Netherlands Antilles corporations, Hong Kong moneychangers and coded Swiss accounts; there were statements relating to eight Swiss banks and 15 trusts, two with bond portfolios worth over $25 million, another two with cash of over $115 million and one with blue chip stocks and shares totalling some $65.5 million.[57]

It was estimated that the total salted away by the Marcoses could be in the $5 billion to $10 billion range. It is sobering to realize that such figures represent several times the Philippine national budget, which for 1985 was $3.1 billion. Interesting too is that under the Constitution the annual salary of the President was $4,700,[58] and that at the time the Marcoses fled the country, 70 per cent of Filipinos were living below the Philipino poverty standard, as opposed to 48 per cent in 1965 when Marcos became President.

The Marcoses' wealth was of course held in a variety of assets in a number of countries. The Malacañang papers suggested that large sums were in Switzerland. Estimates for cash held in Swiss accounts begin at a modest $80 million and reach as high as $3 billion.[59] There were also the collections of jewelry and art – one bracelet and earrings set was valued at $1.5 million, only one item among 408 pieces impounded in Hawaii. And there remained another 2,142 items left behind in the palace vaults.

There was also a vast property portfolio. In April 1986 in testimony before the Asian and Pacific Affairs subcommittee, Joseph and Ralph Bernstein, two New York realtors, explained how they managed property for the Marcoses in New York worth over $300 million. In a typical deal, a holding company would be created in, say, the Netherlands Antilles; this in turn would be held by perhaps three firms in Panama, the stock for which would be in bearer form, with no identified owner. Such multiple layers of secrecy afforded significant protection, and eventually made recovery of the assets a highly complex process.[60]

Eventually an injunction was obtained and confirmed by a US Appeals Court blocking the immediate sale of Marcos properties until the position on ownership and source of purchase funds – if the Marcoses are indeed proved to be the owners – is established. The view of one New York lawyer was that 'the US courts have in effect said, "we will recognize the right of foreign people to use the US courts to redress betrayals of public trust by their officials".'[61]

In addition to New York property, the Marcoses appear to have land in Texas worth $1.5 billion, as well as property in the United Kingdom administered through the Cayman Islands and valued at over $4 million.[62]

How did the Marcoses acquire such a fortune? The examples of their corruption as revealed by the Commission's investigations are manifold. There is evidence that at first they simply skimmed money from government institutions in a relatively minor way. But in the early 1970s Marcos declared martial law and thereafter ruled by decree. This made it possible for him, among other things, to award his friends virtual monopolies to handle the country's traditional income-earning exports such as coconuts, bananas and sugar, and thus to take a very significant share of the profits for his personal account.[63]

Indeed an investigation into the sugar industry found 'anomalies' resulting in losses of at least $1.15 billion from 1975 to 1984, anomalies that benefited directly a trading monopoly headed by a close associate.

The inquiry went so far as to say that although drastic decreases in the world sugar price would have in any case had adverse effects on the Philippines sugar industry, these would have been considerably less damaging had it not been for the fraudulent practices of Marcos and his associates.[64]

In a similar case, it was alleged that one of the country's major copper and gold mining concerns had for twelve years been secretly owned by Marcos and his brother-in-law,[65] and that the country's telecommunications monopoly was 40 per cent owned by the ex-President.

In addition to this sort of 'direct participation' in industry and business, it appears that Marcos benefited from the willingness of foreign banks in the 1970s to lend to the Philippines, whose external debt rose from $2 billion to $25 billion during the decade. Marcos was apparently rewarded for facilitating some of the loans with sums of up to 15 per cent of the loan proceeds, retained overseas for his benefit.[66] He is accused too of misappropriating US military aid as well as Japanese war reparations. The latter were for years paid out in the form of big public-works projects – Marcos appears to have collected a commission of 10–15 per cent on each project. Indeed, on a Malacanang summary of one billion yen of road-building contracts with five Japanese companies someone in the palace had printed across the bottom: 'We get 10%.'[67] In another 'commission' case it seems that the US company Westinghouse paid Marcos around $80 million for awarding it a lucrative contract to build the first nuclear power station in the Philippines.[68]

As well as having personal, trust and holding company accounts overseas for their financial gains, the Marcoses operated accounts in fictitious names to provide yet greater secrecy. Records illustrate how a modus operandi evolved from laundering money through friends' accounts to gradually taking over the accounts under an assumed name.[69]

While a great deal has been discovered, far more still remains cloaked in secrecy. There has been some success with the policy of an amnesty for Marcos cronies who surrender assets and provide information. Even so, Mrs Aquino's government still faced very much an uphill battle. In July 1987 the Presidential Commission filed 35 civil lawsuits in Manila against the Marcoses and some 300 associates, seeking $100 billion including damages. It had by that time sequestered 232 corporations and recovered 29 aircraft, $12.5 million worth of Imelda Marcos's jewelry and a significant quantity of currency and real estate in the Philippines. It was also presiding over 23 plantations and 18 television stations. But the lion's share still appeared to be hidden away overseas, and the lawsuits may do little to change that for some time. One of the problems lies in the willingness of others to shield the Marcoses. There was evidence to suggest, for example, that Adnan Khashoggi 'spirited away' for them a certain number of their valuable paintings, not to mention his efforts to claim ownership of their Manhattan properties in order, it was suggested, to later help them dispose of them secretly. 'Khashoggi does this kind of thing for maybe 5 per cent,' said the Commission's US coordinator.[70]

Another problem lies in the country's own constitution. Philippine law requires that a person facing trial on a criminal charge should be present at his arraignment. But Mrs Aquino was not anxious to risk the possibly destabilizing effect of a return by Marcos to the country. If criminal proceedings against the ex-President would thus be rendered invalid, the Swiss in particular would find it far more difficult to release information or surrender assets.

That said, one of the astonishing aspects of the Marcos affair was the level of Swiss cooperation. In March 1986 the Swiss government took the unprecedented step of freezing the accounts and assets of Marcos even before they received the official request to do so from the Philippines. This caused an uproar at the time, since the banks believed that yet one more nail had been hammered into the coffin of Swiss financial secrecy. The move was based on an article of the constitution whereby the federal government is required to safeguard Switzerland's interests internationally. It is revealing in that it indicated a desire on the government's part to avoid being isolated by international public opinion in the matter, a factor that promised to be of continued use to Mrs Aquino's government in the long task ahead. As one Swiss banker put it, 'the political pressure was just too great. None of us are friends of this family.'[71] On 1 July 1987, the Swiss Federal Court ruled that Swiss judicial authorities may assist the Philippines and that banking secrecy over the accounts may be lifted. Still, a long legal battle remained to be fought over whether the Swiss can actually release funds to the Philippine courts before cases pending there are completed.

By August 1988, only about $161.9 million had actually been recovered, less than half in cash, and nothing had been obtained directly from the Marcos family. Moreover, the Good Government Commission – the agency established to track down, sequester and administer the Marcos assets pending legal action – had itself come under the suspicion that it had abused its considerable powers. In response, President Aquino suspended the Commission and began an investigation into its activities, including the affairs of the almost 300 companies under Commission supervision. In retrospect it seemed that, in the hurry to prevent Marcos's money from being spirited abroad after the revolution, the Aquino government had staffed the Commission with a number of individuals who proved to be venal, incompetent or both.

The offshore assets have to a significant extent failed to turn up despite the Commission's efforts. According to one Commission official quoting Swiss legal sources, a 'best educated guess' was that a mere $600–650 million was to be found in Marcos-related Swiss accounts.

These amounts, moreover, are not recoverable until Mr Marcos is convicted of a crime in the Philippines. American real estate valued at $450 million ($100–150 million net of mortgages) would again only be available after legal battles had been fought and won.[72]

Meanwhile Ferdinand Marcos continued to cause trouble. It was revealed that he had during summer 1987 been planning an invasion of the Philippines. A US businessman, posing as an arms dealer, had actually succeeded in taping discussions with the ex-President to that effect. Marcos intended to buy $18 million worth of Stinger missiles, M-16 rifles, tanks, grenade launchers and enough ammunition to equip 10,000 soldiers for three months. This was to be financed on credit backed by $500 million in Swiss accounts and $14 million of gold bullion supposedly hidden in the Philippines. The latter apparently relates to a 'mythical' buried treasure, left by the retreating Japanese at the end of the Second World War.[73]

Notes

1 Carl Reich, *Financier: The Biography of André Meyer* (New York: William Morrow, 1983).
2 Ibid.
3 William H. Davidson, *The Amazing Race* (New York: John Wiley, 1983).
4 'The Unions' Desperate Move to Stash Funds Offshore', *Business Week*, 17 December 1984, p. 50.
5 Peter Gumbel, 'West German Bureaucrat Who Blew Whistle on Flick Scandal Had to Fight His Superiors', *Wall Street Journal*, 27 March 1985.
6 M. S. Khan and N. Ul Haque, 'Capital Flight from Developing Countries', *Finance and Development*, March 1987.
7 'Anything to Declare, Señor?', *The Economist*, 3 October 1987.
8 Morgan Guaranty Trust Company, *World Financial Markets*, March 1986.
9 'Forcing Discreet Money Into the Open', *Euromoney*, 1986.
10 Marlise Simons, 'Tracing the Flight of Latin Capital', *International Herald Tribune*, 9 May 1986.
11 David Gardner, 'Mexico Defends Record on Capital Flight', *Financial Times*, 16 May 1986.
12 Jeff Gerth, 'Flight of Mexican Capital Threatens Debt Plan', *International Herald Tribune*, 6 October 1986.
13 Ibid.
14 Morgan Guaranty Trust Company, *World Financial Markets*, June/July 1987.
15 'Return Flight', *The Economist*, 8 August 1987.
16 Morgan Guaranty Trust Company, *op. cit.* (n. 14).
17 David B. Gordon and Ross Levine, 'The Capital Flight Problem', *International Discussion Papers*, Board of Governors of the Federal Reserve System, April 1988.
18 George B. N. Ayittey, 'The Real Foreign Debt Problem', *Wall Street Journal*, 8 April 1986.
19 'How to Hunt Pink Panthers', *The Economist*, 7 December 1985.
20 'More Credible But How Bankable?', *The Economist*, 1 March 1986.
21 Morgan Guaranty Trust Company, *op. cit.* (n. 14).
22 'Taxy-turvy in Belgium', *The Economist*, 8 August 1987.
23 Jonathan Eaton, 'Public Debt Guarantees and Private Capital Flight', *World Bank Economic Review*, May 1987.
24 George B. N. Ayittey, *op. cit.* (n. 17).
25 Gary Hector, 'Nervous Money Keeps on Fleeing', *Fortune*, 23 December 1985.
26 Keith Grant, 'Latin-American Nations See Progress in Slowing Capital Flight', *International Herald Tribune*, 29 April 1986.

27 J. N. Bhagwati (ed.), *Illegal Transactions in International Trade* (Amsterdam: North Holland, 1981), pp. 148–54. See also J. N. Bhagwati, A. Krueger and C. Wibulswasdi, *Capital Flight from LDCs: A Statistical Analysis* (Amsterdam: North Holland, 1974).
28 C. L. Ramirez-Rojas, 'Monetary Substitution in Developing Countries', *Finance and Development*, June 1986.
29 Donald Lessard and John Williamson, *Capital Flight* (Washington, DC: Institute for International Economics, 1987).
30 Ibid.
31 Leonard Silk, 'Economic Scene – Latin Nations – Capital Flight', *New York Times*, 17 April 1985.
32 Everett G. Martin, 'Precarious Pesos', *Wall Street Journal*, 13 August 1987.
33 'Chasing the Peso leaves Argentines Breathless', *Business Week*, 10 June 1985.
34 'Peru Plans to Nationalize Banks, Other Financial Firms', *Wall Street Journal*, 29 July 1987.
35 'An Exodus of Capital is Sapping the LDC Economies', *Business Week*, 3 October 1983.
36 James B. Stewart and S. Karene Witcher, 'US Attorney Launches an Investigation of Former Banker at Morgan Guaranty', *Wall Street Journal*, 22 May 1986.
37 Daniel Hertzberg and S. Karene Witcher, 'Banker quits Drexel Amid Investigation by Former Employer, Morgan Guaranty', *Wall Street Journal*, 21 May 1986. See also 'Ó Tombo de Tony', *Veja*, 28 May 1986.
38 S. Karene Witcher, 'Brazil is Seeking Morgan Guaranty Account Names', *Wall Street Journal*, 23 May 1986. See also Eric N. Berg, 'Brazil Banking Customs Cited in Morgan Case', *International Herald Tribune*, 24 May 1986. See also 'Capital Scandal', *Fortune*, 23 June 1986.
39 See Peter Truell and William Power, 'Morgan Guaranty Ex-Official Gets 3½ Years in Jail, Fine', *Wall Street Journal*, 3 March 1987. See also James S. Henry, 'Fallen Angel', *Manhattan, Inc.*, April 1987.
40 See Thomas N. Gladwin and Ingo Walter, *Multinationals Under Fire* (New York: John Wiley, 1980), Chapter 5.
41 'Request to Swiss Likely over Bofors', *Financial Times*, 23 July 1987.
42 Marcus W. Brauchli, 'Swedish Prosecutor Investigating Bofors Will Seek Access to Swiss Bank Records', *Wall Street Journal*, 15 September 1987.
43 Pranay Gupte, 'Bomb Fuses for the Ayatollah', *Forbes*, 16 May 1988. Pranay Gupte, 'Who's Got the $60 million?', *Forbes*, 27 June 1988. Gerald Lubenow, 'Swedish Arms Sales: Nothing to Declare?', *Newsweek*, 20 June 1988.
44 'Swedes Suspect 3 in Arms Bribery Scandal', *International Herald Tribune*, 10 September 1988.
45 See *New York Times*, 19 January 1984.
46 Frederick Kempe and Edward T. Pound, 'Tongsun Park Finds an Embattled Client: Panama's Noriega', *New York Times*, 29 January 1988.
47 'Sensible Lotsen', *Der Spiegel*, No. 20, 1984.
48 Lenny Glynn and Peter Koenig, 'The Capital Flight Crisis', *Institutional Investor*, November 1984, p. 304.
49 'Duvalier May Have Amassed a Fortune of $500 Million', *International Herald Tribune*, 19 February 1986.
50 Roger Lowenstein, 'Looking for Loot', *Wall Street Journal*, 2 December 1986. See also 'Docking Baby Doc', *Wall Street Journal*, 17 April 1986.
51 P. Bernard Gwertzman, 'Philippines Moves to Recover Money Marcos Took Out', *New York Times*, 4 March 1986. See also Ellen Goodman, 'Public Service Isn't Meant to be a Rip Off', *International Herald Tribune*, 6 March 1986.
52 'The Elusive Marcos Millions', *The Economist*, 22 March 1986. See also Margaret Studer, 'Swiss Government Freezes Marcos Assets and Accounts', *Wall Street Journal*, 27 March 1986.
53 Joel Brinkley, 'Marcos Papers Detail Assets Worth Millions', *International Herald Tribune*, 20 March 1986.
54 Seth Mydans, 'Rapid Progress on Marcos Assets', *International Herald Tribune*, 3 April 1986.
55 'Marcoses Charged With Embezzlement', *International Herald Tribune*, 17 April 1986.
56 Alain Cass and Samuel Senoren, 'Aquino Team Seizes Assets of Marcos Regime', *Financial Times*, 5 March 1986.

57   June Kronholz, 'Buried Treasure', *Wall Street Journal*, 11 February 1987.
58   Seth Mydans, 'Marcos Wealth is Estimated in Billions', *International Herald Tribune*, 6 March 1986.
59   Richard Lacayo, 'The International Treasure Hunt', *Time*, 21 April 1986. See also Fox Butterfield, 'Marcos Said to Put Millions in Switzerland', *International Herald Tribune*, 15, 16 March 1986.
60   Jeff Gerth, 'Testimony Ties Marcos to New York Property Valued at $300 Million', *International Herald Tribune*, 10 April 1986.
61   Maria Shao, John Templeman, Charles Gaffney, 'Hot on the Trail of the Marcos Billions', *Business Week*, 17 August 1987.
62   'So Far, Two Pesos', *The Economist*, 3 May 1986.
63   James Rupert, 'Revelation of Marcos Shareholding Gives Big Lift to 2 Inquiry Panels', *Wall Street Journal*, 24 March 1986.
64   William Branigin, 'Marcos Tied to $1 Billion Sugar Fraud', *International Herald Tribune*, 29, 30 March 1986.
65   William Branigin, 'Marcos Control of Mining Firm is Alleged', *International Herald Tribune*, 5, 6 April 1986.
66   Ibid.
67   Ibid.
68   Fox Butterfield, 'Marcos Linked to $80 Million', *International Herald Tribune*, 8 March 1986.
69   William Branigin, 'Fictitious Name on Account Helped Pay for Shopping', *International Herald Tribune*, 12 March 1986.
70   Ibid.
71   Margaret Studer, 'Swiss Authorities Seize Marcos Funds, Set Plan to Return Them to the Philippines', *Wall Street Journal*, 19 July 1986. See also Margaret Studer, 'Marcos Blocks Transfer to Philippines of Money Deposited in Zurich Bank', *Wall Street Journal*, 22 July 1986.
72   Raphael Pura, 'Manila Marcos Commission Yields Little', *Asian Wall Street Journal*, 19 August 1988.
73   Ricardo Chavira and Nelly Sindayen, 'Please Speak Into the Microphone', *Time*, 17 July 1987. See also Richard Gourlay, 'On the Trail of Yamashita's Treasure', *Financial Times*, 11 July 1987.

4

Demand for Secret Money: Tax Evasion, Smuggling and Insider Trading

Tax evasion

Governments have laid claim to a large and growing share of the economies of nations, including the developed market economies. Figures 4.1 and 4.2 indicate the relative size of fiscal deficits and public sector debt for the OECD countries in recent years. With high tax burdens in many countries, reinforced by 'bracket creep' (whereby inflation pushes people into successively higher tax brackets under progressive rate structures even in the absence of higher real incomes), the incentive to avoid and evade taxes may have risen significantly in recent years. In some countries of Western Europe, persistently high unemployment may also have been a contributory factor; the sudden drop in standard of living experienced by those suffering redundancy may have encouraged a good number to subsidize social benefit payments – without losing them – by working 'off the books' for cash.[1] This view is not, however, corroborated by a recent OECD study which found that activity in the black economy tends to follow that in the formal economy rather than replace it.[2] And the growing complexity of tax codes and their use for a broad range of political purposes other than raising revenue has added further to the impression of unfairness, gradually undermining tax morality and stimulating the search for escape even among otherwise law-abiding people.

Avoidance vs evasion

Two choices present themselves: avoidance versus evasion; and tax shelters versus tax havens. Avoidance is the legal escape from tax

79

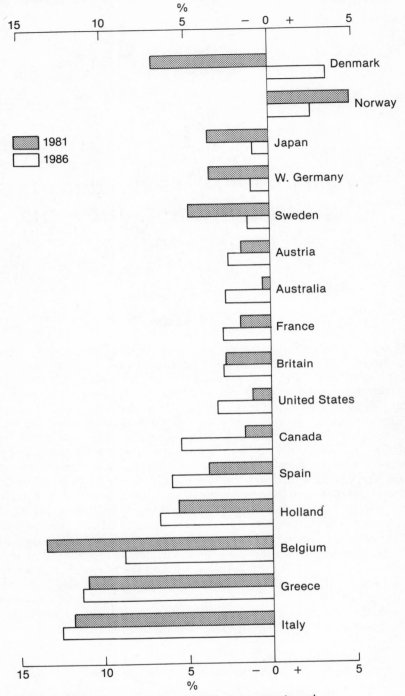

Figures consist of central and local government, and social security funds

Source: OECD.

Figure 4.1 *General government budget balances in selected countries, 1981 and 1986*

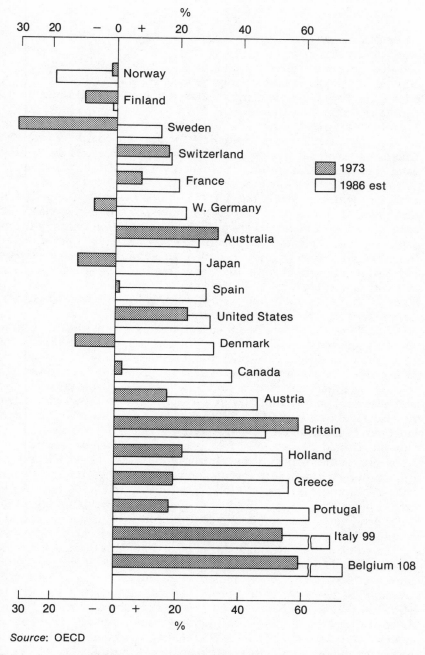

%

| 30 | 20 | − | 0 | + | 20 | | 40 | | 60 | |

Norway

Finland

Sweden

Switzerland

1973

France

1986 est

W. Germany

Australia

Japan

Spain

United States

Denmark

Canada

Austria

Britain

Holland

Greece

Portugal

Italy 99

Belgium 108

| 30 | 20 | − | 0 | + | 20 | 40 | 60 |

%

Source: OECD

Figure 4.2 *Net public debt as a percentage of GNP in selected countries, 1973 and 1986*

81

burdens by means of provisions written into the tax code. Evasion is the illegal non-payment of taxes either by under-declaring income or by over-declaring deductions or exemptions, usually in the face of civil or criminal penalties. The line between the two is of course very fine. Indeed the 'provisions' making avoidance possible can at times be no more than unforeseen anomalies.

An interesting case in point is the situation arising from the different US and UK definitions of 'residency' for a given company. For the Americans a company is resident if it is incorporated in the United States. For the British, residency is wherever the seat of management and control lies. It is thus possible to set up a 'dual-residence' or 'link' subsidiary which is incorporated in the United States, but operated in the United Kingdom. This enables the parent corporation to claim the same 'losses' (to offset profits and so reduce taxes) in both countries simultaneously. The practice appears to be so widespread that when the British Inland Revenue announced plans to amend the terms there was such a storm of protest behind the scenes that the issue was dropped. In fact, with recent changes in Australian tax laws (where residency also depends on management and control) companies with US and Australian subsidiaries may soon join the act.[3]

Tax shelters are generally aimed at avoidance, although they may shade into evasion by taking 'abusive' forms. Tax havens may be legal or illegal, depending on the nationality and residence of the individual and the tax code of the country concerned. We are concerned here only with tax evasion, the associated costs and benefits, the available vehicles, and the chances of getting caught. Tax avoidance gets into the act because the associated cost–benefit profile of legal tax-minimization efforts may well seem to the individual vastly inferior to outright tax evasion.

In the United States, tax avoidance through shelters became big business over the years until tax reforms undertaken in 1986. Oil and gas drilling, livestock, farming, speculation in commodities, energy conservation, equipment leasing, old folks' homes and similar ventures could – if properly structured – produce large-scale tax writeoffs, generate large deductions for charitable contributions, or convert ordinary income into capital gains that were taxed at lower rates. 'Abusive' shelters could artificially inflate the value of donations to charity, falsely identify an asset for business use that was mainly intended for pleasure, claim excessive depreciation or depletion, engage in cross-leasing of automobiles, boats, vacation homes and aircraft, and the like. It was estimated that $8.4 billion was invested in tax shelters in the United States during 1984. As a result, Internal Revenue Service audits of tax shelters were substantially increased in frequency and intensity. The number of shelter cases before the US tax courts multiplied accordingly.

In Canada in 1984, a government attempt to encourage research and development backfired somewhat when it unwittingly produced the perfect tax shelter. The idea was that companies should be allowed to sell their tax benefits to employees, other companies or even members of the public, who could then use them to offset taxable income. But the result was chaos, with provisions designed to ensure a 'legitimate business purpose' proving impossible to enforce. 'There were ... high school dropouts starting R&D companies and selling the losses. Things were completely out of control,' explained a prominent Montreal accountant.[4]

Tax shelters can be costly, however. They tend to involve the services of smart, creative and very well-paid lawyers and accountants. They are often highly promoted and sometimes over-sold, promising far more than they are worth. There is always a chance that a tax shelter project will fail, inflicting sizeable losses on the unwary investor. And there is the possibility that the shelter will ultimately be disallowed by the authorities or that the tax law will be changed. Thus the 'transaction costs' facing the tax avoider and his exposure to loss may be substantial indeed, and may induce him to step over the line into tax evasion.

This is where secrecy comes in. There is no need for financial secrecy in tax avoidance. Indeed, it may well be true that more disclosure is better than less, as long as transactions remain on the right side of the law.

Many of the problems associated with legal tax avoidance are eliminated by tax evasion, which makes it possible for people to deploy their assets far more rationally (provided they don't get caught), and at much lower cost.

A case in point is Argentina, where a complex tax system, internal bank secrecy, poor enforcement, a byzantine court system and non-existent audits, as well as bribery, corruption and periodic tax amnesties, have created 'the second biggest sport after soccer', with a compliance rate of perhaps 50 per cent.

In one Argentine case

[A] clothing retailer in a drab suburb of Buenos Aires. Of every 100 men's suits the retailer sells, 70 are sold without the required sales slip. That makes it impossible for the [tax authorities] to collect the 18% value added tax, included in the price of most goods. Of course, the wholesaler who sold him the 100 units didn't make out sales slips for 70 of them, either. Nor did the fabric merchant account for all the material he sold to the wholesaler. The government thinks the clothing retailer took in the equivalent of $300,000 [in 1983]. But the accountant who helped him prepare his tax returns says the figure excludes, of course, the $400,000 his client spirited away to a Miami bank.[5]

In another Argentine case, an executive intent on evading capital gains tax on a house he sold for $450,000 had a notary public draw up a sales contract for $200,000. The seller avoided tax on the $250,000, the buyer avoided having to account for the same amount of 'black money' he used to buy the house, and the notary received $8,000 in (untaxed) 'lunch money' for his efforts. Tax evasion has become so much part of life that nothing short of top-to-bottom tax reforms, coupled to heavy investment in information systems, auditing and enforcement, will make much of a difference. As one former Argentine tax official noted: 'If you put DDT on ants, they will develop immunity after a couple of generations. No matter what the government puts on us, we Argentines will always find a way to shake the system.'[6]

Naturally, other countries that have value-added taxes are also subject to evasion along similar lines. But computer information systems and tight audits usually make it much less egregious, as do much stiffer penalties than exist in Argentina.

In Italy in 1984, shopowners reported to the tax authorities average annual incomes of $3,579, compared with $5,694 for shop *assistants* and even higher incomes for factory workers. At least 5 million families are involved, and this makes a government crackdown exceedingly sensitive politically. According to one observer: 'There isn't any doubt that tax evasion is rampant. For the three million people either self-employed or in small businesses, evasion has been allowed. It isn't quite written in the statutes, but almost.'[7]

Even in West Germany tax evasion has appeared to be growing, with otherwise law-abiding people 'forgetting' to report income to the tax collector whenever little likelihood exists of getting caught. It is estimated that roughly one-fourth of all securities, valued at perhaps DM40 billion, are hidden from the authorities, with an annual revenue loss of DM1.5 billion. After the collapse of the Herstatt Bank in 1974, taxmen for the first time were able to determine the full extent of evasion through a comprehensive audit of the defunct bank's books. This gave rise to later, controversial 'fishing expeditions'. In one such case, a number of dentists in the Dusseldorf area were found to be buying gold for dental fillings, booking it as a business expense and then reselling it for hidden personal gain.[8]

In the United States, tax compliance has traditionally been high. Whether because of patriotism, a sense of fairness, the need to finance functions of government generally approved of, or fear of criminal or civil prosecution. Americans have on the whole paid a significantly higher share of taxes legally owed than the citizens of most other countries. As a result, the United States relies heavily on the personal income tax, based in large measure on self-reporting and voluntary compliance, while other countries have been forced to resort to import duties, sales and value-added taxes, wealth and death taxes, and other forms of fiscal levies that are more difficult to evade.

All of this changed during the 1970s when inflation pushed taxpayers into ever-higher tax brackets, and the combination in many cases (for example, the average US industrial worker) led to an actual reduction in real disposable income. Heavy capital gains taxes had to be paid on fictitious appreciation attributable only to inflation – in effect partially expropriating private property. The tax code became impossibly complex, and the cost of honest compliance increased dramatically in time, trouble and expense. The Congress riddled the tax code with special provisions, loopholes and benefits aimed at selected interest groups and social engineering, leaving an impression of pervasive inequity. And as stories of tax avoidance and 'evasion' emerge in the media or in rumor-mills, impressions of inequity are amplified.

The result was a significant drop in US tax morality. In 1985, it was estimated that around $100 billion of legally owed taxes were uncollected. Some failed to file tax returns at all. Others filed late. Some were discouraged by the system's complexity. Many who were in a position to do so under-report income. Probably an even greater number overstated their deductions. A 1984 poll revealed that 38 per cent of US taxpayers were believed to cheat on taxes, and that tax evasion is not generally viewed as a serious offense. A law that would have required banks to withhold tax on interest income on savings and other accounts was repealed by Congress under pressure from the banks themselves, in full knowledge that the underlying issue was tax evasion. Tax shelters proliferated, although tax audits declined. Criminal penalties were rare: in 1983, only 1,800 people were prosecuted for tax evasion. In 1985 that number had increased to 2,400; the IRS apparently gained convictions in 90 per cent of cases that went to trial, but even so these figures clearly represented only a tiny minority of wrongdoers. As one former IRS Commissioner has noted: 'If a person is an economic being and figures out the odds, then there is a very high incentive to cheat. That is, of course, putting aside honor, duty and patriotism.'[9]

Most recent figures from IRS studies indicate that as many as 43 per cent of Americans do not pay the full amount of tax they owe. In 1987 this was thought to have cost the IRS about $64 billion. It is obviously not certain whether all were purposely evading tax, but social scientists have estimated that as many as 33 per cent did so. It is hardly surprising in these circumstances that research to understand what motivates people to comply with tax requirements has received considerable attention. The first direct psychological assessment of taxpayers known to have cheated was carried out in the Netherlands, but the researchers indicated that the Dutch evidence was corroborated by findings in the US as well.

The work produced data of importance to economists and policy-makers trying to predict the circumstances which cause tax evasion. It seems that economic models of the problem do not tell the whole story. Assuming purely rational motives for tax evasion – a simple weighing of the expected gain against the risk and cost of punishment – this would mean that in the same economic circumstances every taxpayer would be equally likely or not to evade taxes. In fact, it appears that the personality traits of an individual have a considerable influence on the decision whether or not to engage in tax evasion.

According to the profile suggested by the research, there are several distinctive characteristics to the tax evader. He tends to be of the self-serving type, unconcerned with the social acceptability of his actions and willing to manipulate others for his own ends. He is dissatisfied with the present and pessimistic about the future. His view is that the legal system is unjust, that it therefore does not merit adherence, and in any case 'everyone cheats on taxes – others get away with it, so why not me?' He is likely to be competitive, placing great store on financial success, and likes the thrill of taking a risk.[10]

Other research has found that, quite apart from personality, opportunity plays a role. A 1983 IRS study, for example, found that taxpayers in general reported 94 per cent of their income, but that taxpayers with a greater opportunity to cheat, such as professionals, owners of small businesses and self-employed people, reported only 47 per cent of their income. There is also evidence that the question of paying taxes is one where compartmentalizing one's morals is particularly prevalent. This is the capacity certain people have to be more ethical in some areas than others. Consequently, certain individuals, who do not at all conform to the personality types discussed above, and who in all other respects are fully law-abiding, find it easy to be 'just a little bit immoral' as far as taxes are concerned. Often the two compartments are so well separated in the person's mind that no guilt whatsoever is experienced.[11]

According to one critical review of the IRS's efforts to close tax loopholes,

> ... the weakness of [its] position is that members of the general public are increasingly dissatisfied with the state's presumption that it has the right to deprive the citizen of his wealth ... [It] is quite clear that the avarice of the state in respect of its enormous claims on the private citizen's wealth has been directly connected with the mismanagement of the U.S. public sector's finances ... [T]he public authorities cannot be trusted with the public's money and ... have an incurable tendency to squander it.[12]

Even major sports figures get into the act. On signing a four-year, $4.8 million contract with the Boston Red Sox baseball team in 1985, a 30-year-old relief pitcher came up with one of the more memorable tax-related quotations. Said he: 'I guess I'll have to get one of those Swedish bank accounts.'

Against a background of such loss of faith in and respect for the tax system, new initiatives were clearly needed. Some commentators suggested that the United States should reduce its dependence on personal income tax, and introduce a national consumption tax. They argued that people working off the books would thus pay taxes indirectly whenever they spent, that saving would be encouraged, and that substantial revenue could be raised relatively easily – one estimate suggests that a 1 per cent tax on all consumption expenditure would yield some $20 billion annually.[13]

Whereas such arguments had their merits, they tended to attack symptoms rather than causes. A sounder long-term approach appears to have been an attempt to reinstate a higher degree of tax morality by simplifying the system, rendering it more equitable, and reducing tax levels so that the incentive to avoid payment is itself commensurately reduced. To some extent, the 1986 Reagan-inspired tax reforms tried to move in this direction.

Secrecy may seem like a handy way to evade taxes, but the prospects of civil or criminal penalties are never very far away. Residents of the United States, for example, must indicate each year on their tax returns whether or not they own or have control over a foreign account in excess of $5,000 and, if so, must provide details on a separate form that is likewise filed annually. Since a person's signature on a tax return warrants that the information is true and complete, misrepresentation constitutes an act of perjury and may trigger severe criminal penalties.

Of course, accusations of tax evasion can sometimes be used for political reasons as well. For example, in 1983 the Greek government moved against the Tsatsos family, owners of a successful cement business, who had supported an earlier military regime. Altogether, 13 directors and managers of the company were accused of using questionable payments to foreign subsidiaries to transfer over $100 million illegally out of the country. The action, however, was viewed by some as 'revenge' for the family's earlier political activity and as a way for the government to divert attention from Greece's persistent economic difficulties.[14]

The Marc Rich case

In 1982, the largest tax evasion case in US history came to light. It focused on a highly successful commodities trader, Marc Rich, and a number of his associates.

Three sets of allegations were leveled at Marc Rich. The first concerned evasion of US price controls on crude oil. In a fundamentally flawed program to hold down the price of oil, the United States in 1973 set in place a complicated three-tier pricing structure: 'old' oil, which was already being produced at the time of the first oil-price shock, the price of which was fixed; 'new' oil, which was found thereafter, but whose price was still limited significantly below the market; and 'stripper' oil, produced by small wells at less than 10 barrels per day, which could be sold at the free-market price. The aim was to equalize competitive access to crude oil for refiners and, of course, to ease the oil-price shock to consumers. As with any set of regulations designed to replace market forces, this scheme created enormous built-in incentives for evasion by creating 'daisy chains' of crooked oil dealers intended ultimately to relabel 'old' and 'new' oil as 'stripper' oil, and take the price gap as profit. Marc Rich was accused of being at the center of a daisy chain operation, making well over $100 million in illegal profits. As expected, all such schemes collapsed with the decontrol of crude oil prices early in the Reagan administration, but the accusations of prior wrongdoing remained.

The second allegation against Marc Rich, which is related to the first, was that US profits accumulated in a 'pot' controlled jointly by Marc Rich and the West Texas Marketing Corp. (WTM), from which funds were then drained through a transfer pricing scheme to evade the US corporate profits tax. Oil would be sold at market prices by Marc Rich and Co. AG (Switzerland) to WTM, which would then resell it at substantially lower prices to Rescor, a Panamanian firm owned by Marc Rich. The 'pot' was thus drained by the resulting accounting losses, with Rescor reselling the oil at the free-market price and booking the profits in Panama. All in all, the estimated tax evasion was $48 million, the largest such case in US history.

The third allegation involved trading with the enemy. As part of the US reaction to the events in Teheran in 1977, American firms were prohibited from doing business with Iran. In violation of that ban, the government alleged, Marc Rich's US operations aggressively purchased Iranian crude, which that country's regime was anxious to market, and sold it at high profit in various parts of the world, including the United States.

By October of 1982, a US grand jury investigation was under way into Marc Rich's business affairs, and subpoenas were issued for thousands of documents designed to shed light on them. At the center of the investigation stood Marc Rich himself and Pincus Green, both US citizens and long-time business associates. The specific charges, in addition to tax evasion, eventually included mail and wire fraud, racketeering and conspiracy, in a 51-count indictment handed up by the grand jury. A US associate, Clyde Meltzer, was also charged with 28 counts of tax evasion, racketeering and fraud. The indictments carried penalties ranging from 5 to 20 years in prison and $1,000 to $20,000 in fines, although consecutive sentencing could result in life imprisonment.

Headquarters of Marc Rich & Co. AG, with a 1981 net worth of $200 million, is Zug, Switzerland, a town of 80,000 that lists 8,000 corporate headquarters. Most of these are letter-box companies that benefit from lenient local tax treatment, yet altogether contribute per capita tax revenues that are by far the highest in Switzerland. Each company must have a majority of Swiss directors – Marc Rich & Co. AG had Marc Rich, Pincus Green, and three Zug attorneys.

Three actions were taken by the grand jury and US tax authorities: (1) a subpoena was issued for financial records material to the case, including those in the possession of the Swiss parent company in Zug: (2) a warrant was issued for the attachment of assets of Marc Rich and Pincus Green; and (3) the Internal Revenue Service filed claims for back taxes, interest and penalties amounting to over $100 million.

As expected, Marc Rich & Co. AG refused to comply with the subpoenas, claiming that as a Swiss company it was beyond the reach of US courts. That argument was rejected by the court in view of the enormous amount of business the firm did in the United States, whereupon Marc Rich's attorneys argued that Swiss secrecy laws prohibited compliance, especially inasmuch as none of the offenses involved were considered crimes in Switzerland. The US judge then imposed contempt of court fines of $50,000 per business day on the American subsidiary, Marc Rich International, which were duly paid. In July 1983 the US company was sold to Alexander Hackel, who besides Marc Rich and Pincus Green was the third major shareholder in Marc Rich & Co. AG, and renamed Clarendon. The idea evidently was that, since Marc Rich International no longer existed, the fines imposed by the Judge did not apply. Shortly thereafter, the court froze all of Clarendon's US assets (amounting to over $90 million) and effectively put the company out of business.

Earlier, US prosecutors alleged, about $750 million in assets had been liquidated between March and August of 1983, threatening insolvency and the government's ability to collect back taxes. Even the company's building in Zug was transferred to ownership of the Swiss parent, and during the summer as much as $45 million was shifted to bank accounts in the Cayman Islands and the Bahamas, although it was later returned to the United States under threat of further US legal sanctions. The Clarendon sale potentially added obstruction of justice charges to those already facing Marc Rich and Pincus Green.

In October 1983, the IRS filed an assessment seeking $90 million in back taxes, penalties and interest from 13 of Clarendon's banks. The banks, which had loans estimated at $130 million outstanding to Clarendon, attempted but failed to have the IRS assessment blocked, even though the debt was guaranteed by Marc Rich & Co. AG in Zug. Thereafter, bank financing of Marc Rich's US business became all but impossible, having already become increasingly difficult in the preceding months.

In August 1983 Marc Rich & Co. AG had given in and agreed to submit the requested documents, but, almost immediately following the agreement, US customs agents – evidently acting on a tip – halted Geneva-bound Swissair Flight 111 on the apron at Kennedy Airport in New York and removed several large steamer trunks filled with company documents being taken as checked baggage by a New York paralegal. Marc Rich's attorneys maintained that the documents were being flown to Zug for review and sorting, to ensure that no unrelated confidential information was disclosed. They also noted that other documents had gone to Zug earlier. Unconvinced, the judge told Marc Rich's attorneys that: 'The thinness of the ice on which your client stands is something you must be aware of.'[15]

Meanwhile, the Swiss authorities, apparently fearing that the Marc Rich case, because of its size and visibility, could ultimately blow a large hole in the corporate secrecy veil, went on record denouncing the 'heavy-handed' US tactics and publicly warned Marc Rich & Co. AG of serious violations of Swiss law if it complied with the US court request. Ultimately the Swiss authorities seized what were said to be the requested documents from Marc Rich & Co. AG in Zug.

The Swiss view was, in part, that turning over the documents could reveal proprietory information about companies with which Marc Rich & Co. AG did business, in violation of the Swiss criminal code on 'economic espionage'. Were the United States to follow normal diplomatic channels, the documents would be turned over in due course, it was indicated, but with the names of all third parties deleted.

The US Justice Department took a hard-line approach, even though it was clear that this could alienate the Swiss authorities and jeopardize future cooperation in tax fraud cases. It was only after the Swiss government blocked disclosure by Marc Rich & Co. AG that an effort at cooperation was undertaken. It remained unclear whether the affront to Swiss sovereignty was deliberate or only normal bureaucratic bungling. The Marc Rich case came up after the Swiss had demonstrated greater willingness to cooperate in cases of tax fraud and securities laws violations, and before a scheduled renegotiation of a 1952 bilateral tax treaty. A heavy-handed, prosecutional approach that minimized cooperation and diplomacy seemed to many to be counterproductive in the Marc Rich case and certainly in successful future efforts to curb the role of foreign financial secrecy in the commission of criminal acts in the United States. On the other hand, US prosecutors saw Swiss stonewalling as a potentially critical blow to their case and, as the 'steamer trunk caper' seemed to demonstrate, susceptible to abuse by the accused. The Swiss stakes were very high indeed – especially since confidentiality with respect to third parties was involved – and their actions were entirely predictable, regardless of the merits of the case at hand. But their stakes in continued access to US markets were equally high, and this probably figures heavily in how much pressure the Justice Depart-

90

ment felt it could exert without encountering irreparable damage to bilateral relations.

According to one Swiss official: 'The U.S. has a tendency to consider firms that are controlled by Americans but domiciled in foreign countries to be under U.S. jurisdiction. For us, Marc Rich AG is a Swiss entity under Swiss jurisdiction. That is a fundamental point.'[16]

The US–Swiss confrontation over the Marc Rich documents dragged on through the summer of 1984, even as the $50,000 per day in fines continued. The Swiss position was that the US subpoena was 'confrontational' and an impediment to voluntary and cooperative compliance. The Justice Department's view was that the Swiss had already agreed to comply and that, in any case, it was unclear whether the subpoena could in fact be dropped under US law. A major point of conflict continued to be the role of 'uninvolved third parties' who might be compromised by disclosures related to the Marc Rich case. Under Swiss law, such individuals have the right to object to disclosure; yet materials pertinent to the case would be difficult to separate from those affecting their interests.[17] A note was sent by the Swiss Ministry of Justice to the US authorities in July 1984 indicating that documents would be released in the case of Marc Rich only if the government agreed that he could not be forced to comply with US court orders that violated Swiss sovereignty.

In July 1984, under a 1900 bilateral treaty, the United States filed extradition papers on Marc Rich and Pincus Green to have them stand trial in New York for tax evasion, racketeering and fraud. The Swiss initially refused to accept the documents because they were written in English, noting that the United States only accepts English-language requests. They did accept them about one month later, after translation into German, but noted that the charges on which the September 1984 trial was based were not directly covered by the 1900 extradition treaty, and any affirmative finding by the authorities could still be appealed to the Swiss Supreme Court.

Once again, there was the need to prove that the alleged offense involved commission of a crime under Swiss law. After a warrant was issued for their arrest in 1983, the Swiss consul in New York noted that '. . . it would be "most unlikely" that the Swiss would extradite the commodity traders on the basis of allegations of tax evasion or trading with Iran. The treaty calls for cooperation only in the case of murder, robbery, burglary, counterfeiting, forgery, embezzlement, and breach of trust involving a fiduciary.'[18] However, as one US attorney noted, 'We have every reason to believe, based on their past behavior, that Mr. Rich and Mr. Green will become fugitives from justice. As I understand it, Mr. Rich and Mr. Green are guests of Switzerland. They may become unwelcome guests.'[19] In order to make extradition more difficult, Marc Rich quickly obtained Spanish citizenship and Pincus Green became a Bolivian national, both renouncing their US citizenship – Marc Rich himself having obtained it as a child after fleeing with his family from his native Belgium to escape Nazi persecution.

In mid-October 1984, the case against Marc Rich & Co. AG was settled in New York. The company pleaded guilty to 38 counts of making false statements to federal authorities and two counts of tax evasion. The original charge had involved 51 counts of mail and wire fraud, racketeering, violating federal oil-price controls, and tax evasion. In the settlement, the company paid the government $150 million, forfeited $21 million in court fines already levied plus $24–40 million in future tax benefits, and paid $780,000 in fines and $33,000 in costs – for a total of about $200 million. Clyde Meltzer pleaded guilty to one count of making false statements to the government, and was sentenced to five years on probation and fined $5,000. The government thereupon lifted all restrictions on Marc Rich's US operations, and made possible the payment of $130 million in debt to 14 banks on the part of the parent firm in Switzerland. Marc Rich and Pincus Green still faced fraud, racketeering, tax evasion and other charges, although the likelihood of extradition from Switzerland remained remote. According to the Swiss, all of the particulars in the US extradition request 'are only violations of either currency, economic or fiscal measures, and they aren't extraditable under the US–Swiss treaty of 1900.'[20]

The Marc Rich case was a new milestone in the use of financial secrecy for purposes of tax evasion and other crimes in the country in which business is done. Its importance extended far beyond the case itself, although in some ways the degree of secrecy involved was unique. 'The reason so little is known about international trading companies is that the boundaries between the U.S. and the rest of the world are much less delineated for them. The whole area is so legally foggy and the competition so stiff that it is inherently a very secretive business.'[21] However, the US Commodity Futures Trading Commission (CFTC) has established a set of rules bearing on foreign-based participants in American markets which would ban them if they do not provide adequate information about their trading activity and profits. This in turn, could lead to a disclosure of sensitive competitive information about trading activity both in the United States and abroad.

The sensational Marc Rich case certainly seems to be an exception – and an unnecessary one at that, given the evident trading competence and profitability of the firm even in full compliance with the law.

In fact, Marc Rich and Pincus Green, sheltering in Switzerland with the US charges against them firmly in place, in 1988 still owned one of the biggest commodities trading companies in the world. Marc Rich & Co. AG apparently earned more than $100 million before tax on a trading volume of $12 billion in 1985 and its capital by the end of 1986 stood at $950 million.[22]

Far from being finished in the commodities trading business, in 1988

Marc Rich & Co. AG had offices in 35 countries and a trading volume of more than $13 billion per year, ranking second only to US-based Cargill among the world's diversified commodities trading houses.

In metals markets, Rich is by far the largest, and has been particularly successful in capturing 30 per cent of the world's open market in a tightening market for aluminium by buying up capacity during the early 1980s. A key move, the acquisition of Alcoa's closed Jamaican aluminia plant, was eased by friendships with Jamaican government officials that extended to Rich lending the country $200 million from 1980 to 1985 and reportedly making available to Jamaica's president, Edward Seaga, Rich's private jet.

Rich's courtship of the Soviet metals trading company's London director in the early 1980s bore fruit as Rich captured most of the Soviet Union's external lead and zinc trade later in the decade. When Rich was indicted by the US grand jury in 1983, *Izvestiya* ran a front page story denouncing the US for persecuting such a distinguished businessman. Following an investigation that revealed that the Soviet trading organization had consistently been overcharged by Rich, Rich's monopoly of the Soviet trade dissipated, notwithstanding the $20 million that Rich surrendered to the Soviet Union in 1987 to compensate for the alleged overcharges.

Besides being a respected Swiss resident and pillar of the Zug business community, Rich is one of the largest investors in Spain, the country which has also granted him citizenship and in which he frequently resides.[23]

The case still arouses controversy, with occasional articles in the press alleging further misdeeds. In one case, it seems Marc Rich set up a loan for $21.2 million with a leading Swiss bank, using one of his ships as collateral. But the loan was never drawn down and the suggestion was made that it had merely been a device whereby the bank would supposedly have first claim on the ship should the US authorities try to confiscate it.[24] In another case it was alleged that Rich and Green were trying to manipulate the world aluminium market, and in yet another that in the early 1980s they had been enlisted by the Malaysian government to manipulate the world tin price.[25]

Whatever the truth may be, it is certain that tax evasion in most cases is far less dramatic. The rule in many countries seems to be: 'If there's a reasonable chance that income or capital gains cannot be traced by the authorities, then evasion using secrecy vehicles is fair game.' There are enough tax havens and ways of routing funds to them that, given the continuing evolution of tax hells around the world – marked by confiscatory rates, complexity, inequity, and the high costs of legal avoidance – the use of secret international funds flows for this purpose is bound to grow.

Smuggling

Besides tax evasion, the attempt to bypass other types of government distortions of competitive conditions in free markets is another major source of the demand for secret money. One such distortion is exchange control, whereby governments drive a wedge into foreign exchange transactions by forcing recipients of foreign currencies to surrender receipts to the authorities for local currency at a fixed exchange rate, and by permitting exchange allocations only for specific purposes – again at a fixed rate. Exchange controls invariably foster black markets, in which a 'free' or 'parallel' exchange rate indicates the degree of distortion built into the official rate. Those who are lucky enough to have foreign exchange are much better off keeping it that way (often illegally and hence secretly) and converting what they need into local currency on the black market. Those who require foreign exchange are likewise encouraged to use the black market, even at considerable added expense, to buy what they cannot get official exchange allocations for or to get their money out of the country. There are even instances where such markets are located offshore and hence entirely beyond the control of the domestic authorities. One example of this is the well-developed and extensive 'Hundi' market in the Middle East. This deals in the currencies of a number of countries that have exchange controls and allows expatriate workers to change their foreign earnings for home currencies at competitive rates efficiently and quickly.[26]

Black markets often work (despite periodic government crackdowns) simply by means of smuggled currency (foreign currency in, domestic currency out). They can also work by means of off-market pricing – over-invoicing export transactions or under-invoicing import transactions wherein the foreign partner puts the difference between the agreed price and the invoice price aside in a secret account owned by the domestic partner in the deal. Financial secrecy is necessary for the evasion of exchange control, since discovery of external accounts could destroy future evasion opportunities (or encourage extortion) and subject the individual to severe penalties.

It is generally accepted that the mainstay of the parallel currency markets in a number of the Latin American countries is repatriated drug money. While a large proportion is kept overseas, enough comes back to provide a fair amount of business for the moneychangers. In early 1987, for example, seventeen employees of Colombia's Avianca Airlines were indicted by the US authorities for the illegal transporting over a 15-month period of some $10 million to Colombia. As an attorney on the case said: 'You don't have to be a brain surgeon to figure out why dollars are going back to Bogota.'[27]

In addition to smuggling currencies, people smuggle goods. The flip side of money going to Bogota is of course the goods – cocaine – coming in to the United States. In November 1986, Avianca Airlines had already been fined $4.7 million after 293 pounds of cocaine had been discovered among flower cartons on one of its jets at Miami International Airport.[28] But drugs are a special case, which we shall consider in detail later on.

Conventional smuggling involves evasion of import controls and customs duties by people who purchase goods abroad and sell them domestically at a profit equal to the domestic–foreign price differential less the cost of smuggling. Procurement of contraband normally involves secret accounts and funding channels. Less conventional is export smuggling. This may involve stolen cars or other merchandise, products (especially farm commodities) whose prices are controlled domestically at levels below their foreign prices, and products whose export is restricted for other reasons, such as national security. Again, secret money is usually necessary to carry it out.[29]

Examples abound. In Bolivia, for example, an estimated 15 per cent of the country's gasoline was smuggled out to Brazil in 1985 by state oil-refinery workers, with the help of state railway workers and customs officials. It was a lucrative business since the local gasoline price was fixed at 20 cents a gallon while the Brazilian price was around the $4 level. Similarly, workers at the state tin mines were smuggling out the richest ore in their lunch pails and sending it via a contraband network to Peru. Tin production in Bolivia in 1984 fell from 18,000 to 12,000 tons, while Peru, without a single major tin mine was exporting some 4,000 tons a year. Meanwhile, the owners of private tin mines in Bolivia were smuggling it out under false papers. 'A friend of mine ships it out under an export licence for sulphur,' explained one businessman. 'Then, he buys all the documents from customs so there's no record of the deal.'[30]

Smuggling is virtually a way of life across the borders where Argentina, Brazil and Paraguay meet. 'We get the cream of the crooks from all three countries – drug smugglers, robbers, gamblers, racketeers', explained one young Brazilian police officer.[31] Goods of all types are moved secretly from one country to another depending on which side of the border the exchange rates and bargains are best. The expensive items such as cocaine, gold and computers are shipped from private airstrips; the more mundane cargoes – food, chemicals, electronic equipment – go by boat or car.

It is an ugly environment with violent highway robbery along the Brazilian roads increasingly the order of the day. In the 18 months beginning January 1987, 139 truck drivers were killed by bandits, with 30 more reported missing. Over the same period almost 2,300 trucks were stolen, of which over 200 were traced to Paraguay. While the police say the robbers are Brazilian the truck union leaders blame Paraguay for providing a market. Vehicles are traded there, often at a value in excess of $100,000, for dollars or cocaine. Paraguayan businessmen and landowners have even been known to place orders for the vehicle they want.

95

It is not only trucks, but cars as well that find their illicit way into Paraguay. Legitimate car importers estimate that more than half of the country's registered vehicles have been stolen in Brazil. A vast underground economy has developed for goods of all kinds. Diplomats and economists estimate that 60 per cent of Paraguay's commerce consists of unrecorded or smuggled goods. And the border towns are thriving on it. In Foz do Iguaçu on the Brazilian side, new stores, villas and a casino have sprung up and a $100 million airport is under construction. Although it is said that in Paraguay the smuggling is institutionalized with the political and military forces protecting and possibly even owning the main franchises, the truth is that everyone has a share of the blame. As one long time border resident put it, 'Nobody here can preach. Customs on all three sides are receptive when it comes to bribes.'[32]

Another country with serious smuggling problems is Bangladesh. It is estimated that smuggling costs the government about $350 million a year in lost import duties alone, and that the annual value of illicit trade is broadly equivalent to some 20 per cent of the nation's total import bill. Goods of all kinds flow in – gold, cigarettes, ballpoint pens, wristwatches, sugar, spices, plastics, cotton and synthetic yarn. In some cases imports threaten the very existence of domestic industries – for example, all 80 of Bangladesh's mills face closure, unable to withstand the onslaught of smuggled products from India. In others, the goods coming in actually feed an activity – gold bars flown in from the Middle East supply a now thriving jewelry business. One of the popular methods of bringing in contraband is through the Bay of Bengal. Trawlers from Thailand, often manned by Bengali sailors, load up on fish in the deep waters and then head for Bangkok, where the boats unload the fish and load goods for Bangladesh.[33]

Governments also smuggle, often in order to circumvent sanctions or trade restrictions against their country. South Africa is a classic example. Techniques both for exporting 'unwanted' and for importing 'unwilling' goods are widespread. Country-of-origin labels on textiles are frequently altered. South African citrus fruits are packed in crates marked 'Product of Mozambique'. Steel is routed through Singapore. Many people believe that more sanctions will simply inspire more techniques – although at a price. New regulations are already underway to cloak government and private dealings in oil, gold, uranium, strategic metals and arms in yet deeper secrecy. There was even allegedly a plan for the state-owned South African Airways to repaint its aircraft and lease them to Swaziland as a way around possible overseas bans on landing rights.[34]

The Mueller case

One big-time use of international financial secrecy has been the diversion of sensitive high-technology equipment to the Soviet Union and other Warsaw Pact countries. To a significant extent, the flow of restricted equipment has apparently been channeled through dummy corporations established in Switzerland, Liechtenstein, and elsewhere; it has even involved secret return shipments to the West of defective equipment for servicing. According to reports, several thousand East European 'technology collection' officers are at work in the West under various covers, responsible for assembling precise shopping lists of equipment and components wanted in the East. Orders are then processed, sometimes through dummy corporations and sometimes using unauthorized procedures within legitimate Western European enterprises, through an 'intricate series of post-box companies in Liechtenstein and Switzerland, forged, purchased and misappropriated documents, and great amounts of cash.'[35] The process has continued over decades, only coming under increased pressure in recent years as a result of rather controversial US initiatives. One major conduit, the Hedera Establishment of Liechtenstein, was dissolved in January 1983. 'Under corporate law in Liechtenstein, its papers suggested nothing more about who paid for its multimillion-dollar account other than the two Vaduz lawyers who served as the entire membership of its "administrative" board.'[36]

The use of international financial secrecy in international high-technology smuggling was exposed at least in part in the case of a German named Richard Mueller. For years, the United States had been trying, with mixed success, to keep defense-related high technology out of the hands of the Soviet bloc. Ordinary strategic considerations argued for such a policy, but the issue became far more critical in the late 1970s and 1980s when a massive Soviet military buildup of already numerically superior forces, coupled with rising East–West political tensions, put an increased premium on qualitative weapons-system superiority. The Soviets responded by vastly increasing their technology acquisitions and espionage activities, and the United States sought to tighten leaks wherever it could – often with less than enthusiastic backing from its allies and its own business community. This situation spelled big profits for middlemen who could evade US restrictions using financial secrecy and legal inconsistencies among Western countries. As a West German businessman noted: 'It is not against [American] law to ship U.S. technology to West Germany and it's not against German law for a company then to ship it to Switzerland, and there are no Swiss laws against shipping goods to the Soviet Union.'[37]

Richard Mueller discovered that enormous markups were possible in the trade of restricted technologies early in the game. According to US authorities, Mueller initially operated directly out of California's Silicon Valley, purchasing components and equipment for shipment via more or less clandestine channels to Eastern Europe. Once identified as a major technology smuggler by US agents in 1976, Mueller left the United

States, returned to West Germany and traveled widely on a Swiss passport. The technique was to establish or acquire shell companies in countries that would have legitimate needs for high-tech US equipment, purchase the equipment from US manufacturers that complied with all US export regulations, and then spirit it on to Eastern Europe.

By 1981, Mueller was reportedly clearing over $5 million yearly tax-free, with intensive and open business contracts with the Soviet Union, East Germany, Hungary and Czechoslovakia. His German employees were paid from Swiss accounts, his companies showed no taxable profits in West Germany, and his own earnings presumably remained untaxed in Switzerland. The Mueller organization appeared to function smoothly until 1982, when he purchased control of a more substantial firm, Gerland Heimorgelwerke, a manufacturer of home organs in financial difficulty located near Lübeck. The firm would purchase US electronics equipment, repack and relabel it, and ship it through a series of other Mueller-controlled companies, often by circuitous routes, to Eastern Europe, leaving a complex and highly opaque trail. It also shipped cargoes to West Berlin by road. Some of the cargoes would simply evaporate on the passage through East Germany. The equipment orders placed with the manufacturer '... often displayed unusual features: manufacturers' offers to install the equipment were declined, extra large supplies of spare parts were sought, unusual plugs were demanded, payment was often by unusual channels.'[38] Particularly favored procurement was from Digital Equipment Corporation (DEC), whose VAX series of computers have wide military applications and one of whose former employees was part of the Mueller team.

The Gerland operation closed down in 1982, after some of Mueller's employees reported a night shipment of five truckloads of DEC equipment, on East European vehicles, that was destined for Hungary and the Soviet Union. Mueller thereupon liquidated Gerland and moved his operations to South Africa, where he obtained a residency permit in 1980. A front company, Microelectronics Research Institute (MRI), was set up in Cape Town, controlled by Mueller through two Swiss holding companies and an intermediary South African venture. The whole thing was financed from Switzerland and a well-known South African management consultant was used as a front. On the pretext of establishing a microchip manufacturing operation in South Africa, an export license was obtained from the US Commerce Department for a complete computer-assisted microchip design system, which was fully set up and tested in a converted shoe factory outside Cape Town. These arrangements apparently had the dual purpose of preserving the MRI cover and satisfying the Soviet customer that things worked as they should.

Early in 1983, parts of the facility were dismantled and sent to the Soviet Union via Sweden using Mueller's corporate network and a Swedish accomplice who had rented space in a warehouse near

Stockholm, ostensibly to establish Sweden's first microchip manufacturing facility. On 23 October 1983, the main computers and other gear were shipped from South Africa. After US pressure was exerted on West Germany and Sweden, as well as a chase worthy of James Bond, part of the shipment was intercepted in Hamburg, West Germany, and in Hälsingborg, Sweden. However, substantial amounts of other equipment are suspected to have slipped through the net. Meantime, the Swedish accomplice was arrested on tax and currency violations related to Mueller's payments via Switzerland, and Mueller himself dropped out of sight.

Mueller was described by one US official as the 'most toxic of all' technology bandits. His total take, originally estimated at about $18 million, actually appears to have been much higher. Disclosures by Swiss banks revealed over $100 million in his accounts. Although his network has been dismantled, Mueller escaped unscathed and is now evidently based in Eastern Europe.[39]

An interesting addendum to Soviet attempts to gain access to advanced technology came to light in early 1986. It was reported that in the mid 1970s the Soviet Union had attempted to acquire three banks in northern California and an interest in a fourth, all of which had fairly extensive dealings with a number of high-technology companies. The banks involved were the Peninsula National Bank in Burlingame, the First National Bank of Fresno, the Tahoe National Bank in South Lake Tahoe and the Camino Bank in San Francisco. The attempted purchases were through the holding company of a Singapore businessman. They were only aborted after an initial down payment of $1.8 million when a CIA agent with a banking background, based in Singapore, became suspicious of the lending pattern of a Soviet bank's branch there. The affair highlighted the very grave difficulties involved in discerning the real principal behind any financial transaction where participants wish to remain anonymous.[40]

Violations of securities laws

Rules have been established over the years in many countries to assure orderly, efficient and equitable financial markets. In two respects, however, these rules have been subject to periodic violations: outright fraud and insider trading. Both are generally made possible by international financial secrecy. Securities markets lend themselves particularly well to the abuse of secrecy, precisely because successful dealing legitimately depend on the astute use of non-disclosure of information, and on moving on the basis of available information faster and more decisively than the competition. Fraud is discussed in the next section. Here we shall focus on insider trading.

99

Insider trading in the securities markets is a perennial problem. It involves trading by those in a position to use privileged information about factors affecting the market value of securities before that information is made known to outside investors and the general public. Such information may be acquired directly or by accident, through bribery and reciprocal tip-offs, or through financial espionage and intelligence gathering. Particularly high-stakes financial activities, such as mergers and acquisitions, lend themselves to insider trading. While insider trading in the United States is illegal under the Securities and Exchange Act, there are important gray areas concerning the definition of 'insider' and the circumstances under which particular kinds of behavior could be held illegal and subject to civil or criminal penalties. Moreover, since insider trading seldom involves a paper trail, investigations by agencies such as the US Securities and Exchange Commission (SEC) and obtaining a conviction in a court of law tend to be an arduous and often unsuccessful process.

Because the culprit will often go to some trouble to cover his tracks, the evidence may well be largely circumstantial. For example, a 1982 case involved an office manager for the prestigious New York law firm of Sullivan & Cromwell, who originated tips on a major takeover deal for which the firm was doing the legal work.

Thirteen persons, ranging from New York policemen to brokerage-firm officials, were charged: they were alleged to have made more than $1.2 million in profits on tips passed by the office manager, who was privy to takeover plans of the Sullivan & Cromwell clients.

The SEC subpoenaed telephone records, which showed that one of the traders repeatedly called someone in a Hong Kong hotel in February 1982, just before buying the securities of one of Sullivan & Cromwell's clients. With help from British and Hong Kong law enforcement authorities, SEC officials said, they identified the Hong Kong connection as a vacationing New York brokerage-firm employee.

Hong Kong phone records, in turn, showed that the brokerage employee called the law firm's office manager in Brooklyn shortly before talking to the trader. From the sequence of calls, the SEC alleged that the acquisition tip passed from the office manager through the Hong Kong vacationer and back to the trader in New York.[41]

Pros and cons of insider trading

Some observers argue that insider trading is by no means entirely bad – that, indeed, it improves the efficiency of the capital markets. They view investor mistrust as a fundamental *strength* of open financial markets, in that private initiatives designed to shield investors from the possibility of fraud and malfeasance have created a bulwark that is much stronger than regulation can ever be as the basis for public confidence and constraints on criminal activities. There is little evidence, this view holds, that anyone is hurt by insider trading; indeed, such activities help prices adjust more quickly than they would otherwise.

The positive market-efficiency attributes of insider trading are thus considered to outweigh the unfairness of important information being available to, and acted upon by, a few investors before it becomes known to the general public. Efficient markets, in turn, help insure that shareholders get what they pay for – that their asset values will not be eroded by information not yet released, but that comes to be known later and thus blindsides the investor. Insider information thus may enhance, rather than detract from, fairness. There will always be people with more information than the average; what is important is to spread that information as quickly as possible. More efficiently priced stock, moreover, embodies lower risk. Hence companies should reward employees in part through inside information, on the basis of which they would act and thus trigger share-price movements in the market. Nor is it clear that outsiders lose in proportion to insiders as a result of such behavior. Some outsiders lose and some win; no one knows whether the losers would outnumber the winners, or vice versa, without strict limits on insider trading.[42]

These arguments, while to some extent persuasive and not entirely lacking in merit, have lost some of their force in the recent past. The explosion during 1986 and 1987 in insider trading – or perhaps, more accurately, in its detection – has concentrated attention sharply on the damage done as opposed to the benefits provided. It is argued by many that the 'equity' or 'fairness' costs far outweigh any conceivable efficiency gains. If ordinary investors, including institutions, are going to be excluded from information that benefits the favored few (in terms of capital gains or capital losses avoided), then the integrity of the financial system and the usefulness of market capitalism itself can be called into question politically. It is not just a question of morality; if unchecked insider trading is allowed to undermine investor confidence in the worth of the market, then capital investment will in the long run be harmed. Nobody enjoys being fleeced, and when the sheep become sufficiently numerous and agitated they may end up destroying some very valuable institutions.

This is certainly the view of Gary Lynch, recently head of the SEC, who was quoted as saying that he wishes to pursue insider traders until there is no more run up in share price before the announcement of a tender offer.[43] This may be going a little far, since share movements do not necessarily occur only because of asymmetry of information; asymmetry of *interpretation* also plays its part. And in any case, there will always be those who quite legitimately ferret out more information simply by dint of more or better research. So we come back into those gray areas. An over-aggressive SEC could well impair routine information gathering and distribution, as people hesitate, unsure whether they are committing a crime or just being astute.[44]

Figure 4.3 compares different scenarios in stock prices under alternative disclosure patterns with and without insider trading. Exhibit 4.1 illustrates how financial secrecy serves to make insider trading possible.

EXHIBIT 4.1

Examples of international financial secrecy in cases of insider trading

---

ILLUSTRATION A

Mr X, a hypothetical American citizen, resides in Zurich, Switzerland, and is a member of the Board of Directors of Solar, Inc., a Delaware corporation. On January 15, X learns at a board meeting that an engineer employed by Solar has discovered a practical and inexpensive method for substituting solar energy for gas and oil. The board decides to delay public announcement of the news until final testing has been completed.

Mr X, who at present is not a Solar shareholder, returns to Zurich planning to profit from the anticipated rise in the value of Solar stock. At the time, Solar common stock is selling for $2 per share on the New York Stock Exchange. Mr X is advised by his attorney that, under an earlier US court decision, the news of the discovery is 'material, inside information'. Therefore, Mr X is told, he would be violating the law if he were to trade Solar shares on the basis of this undisclosed information. Moreover, even if he does not purchase the stock until after the news has been disseminated to the public, but then sells the shares within six months of his purchase, he would be required to transfer to the company all profits derived from these transactions. Thus, in order for Mr X to cash in on the expected increase in the value of Solar's shares, he must remain an anonymous investor.

To ensure anonymity, Mr X instructs Geheimnis, a Zurich bank with which he maintains an account, to purchase 50,000 shares of Solar common stock on his behalf. Funds for the purchase are drawn from Mr X's savings account. Geheimnis submits the order to its broker in New York and the transaction is completed. The broker's records indicate that Geheimnis purchased 50,000 shares of Solar on January 20. The identity of the beneficial owner of the shares, Mr X, remains undisclosed.

On February 1, Solar publicly announces its great technological advance. Within one month, the price of Solar common stock soars to $20. On that day, Mr X instructs Geheimnis to sell his 50,000 shares. The transaction is completed; Geheimnis is the seller of record, and Mr X has cleared a gross profit of $900,000.

Meanwhile, the rapid rise in the price of Solar stock has attracted the attention of the SEC. The Commission discovers that less than two weeks before the announcement of the development in solar energy, 50,000 shares of Solar were purchased by Geheimnis. Unlawful insider trading is suspected and Mr X, a

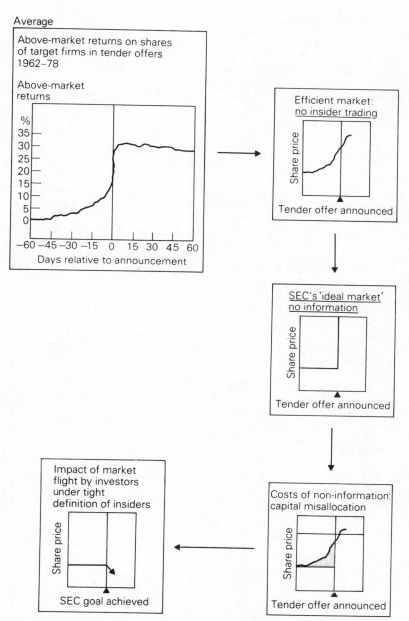

Average

Above-market returns on shares of target firms in tender offers 1962–78

Above-market returns

%
35
30
25
20
15
10
5
0

−60 −45 −30 −15 0 15 30 45 60
Days relative to announcement

Efficient market:
no insider trading

Share price

Tender offer announced

SEC's 'ideal market'
no information

Share price

Tender offer announced

Costs of non-information:
capital misallocation

Share price

Tender offer announced

Impact of market flight by investors under tight definition of insiders

Share price

SEC goal achieved

Source: J. H. Loris, P. Dodd and M. Hamilton Kimpton, *The Stock Market: Theories and Evidence* (Dow Jones-Irwin, 1985); and *New York Times*.

Figure 4.3   *Market price of securities with alternative information*

103

director of Solar residing in Zurich, is a prime suspect. The Commission is presented with a problem. It can subpoena Mr X to testify concerning his transactions in Solar stock. He will undoubtedly refuse to disclose that he purchased and sold the 50,000 shares. On the other hand, if the Commission chooses to subpoena Geheimnis for information pertaining to the account of Mr X, the bank will almost certainly refuse to comply, due to the constraints of Article 47(b) of the Swiss Banking Law and Section 273 of the Swiss Penal Code. Consequently, it is very unlikely that under these circumstances the Commission will be able to gather sufficient evidence to prove that Mr X engaged in unlawful securities transactions.

ILLUSTRATION B

Elastic, Inc. is a Delaware corporation which manufactures rubber bands. In 1976, the corporation issued 500,000 shares of common stock at a par value of $10 per share. The stock is sold in the over-the-counter market. Two years of unsuccessful business has left Elastic close to bankruptcy. The market price of its shares has fallen to $1 by 1 January 1978.

Mr Y, a US resident, maintains an account at Geheimnis Bank in Zurich. He instructs Geheimnis to purchase 25,000 shares of Elastic for his account. The purchase is made in the name of the bank. Mr Y informs investors and brokers, with whom he is acquainted, that he has learned through sources at Elastic that the company will sign a contract with a large Brazilian rubber company. This contract, he explains, will enable Elastic to purchase large quantities of rubber at an extremely favorable price. He suggests that at $1 per share Elastic stock is a 'steal'. Mr Y then orders Geheimnis to purchase 50,000 shares of Elastic. Again, the transaction is made in the name of Geheimnis.

Mr Y's contacts become interested in Elastic as a result of Mr Y's 'tip' and the unusual trading activity in Elastic's stock. Demand for the shares increases and the price begins to rise. Mr Y continues to buy and sell through Geheimnis. The price of Elastic common rises to $25. Mr Y eventually sells all of his shares in Elastic for a large profit. The funds are deposited in his account at Geheimnis. Meanwhile, Mr Y's substantial sales cause the manipulated price at Elastic to crash, and the remaining investors are left with virtually worthless stock. Although Mr Y has violated the Securities Exchange Act of 1933, Swiss bank secrecy would most probably prevent the SEC from ascertaining the principal (i.e. Mr Y) on whose behalf Geheimnis traded Elastic's shares.

ILLUSTRATION C

Suppose XYZ Corporation plans a tender offer for the shares of ABC Corporation. Suppose, further, that either an officer of XYZ or one of its professional consultants misappropriates material non-public information concerning the unannounced tender offer, and places a purchase order for the securities of ABC through a bank in a secrecy jurisdiction. If the transaction had been conducted through a US brokerage firm, the Commission could quickly identify the individual involved. However, because the transaction was effected through a bank in a secrecy jurisdiction, the Commission would be denied access to the information necessary to determine whether a securities law violation had occurred.

Source: Adapted from *International Law and Politics*, Vol. 9, p. 417, and testimony of John M. Fedders, formerly Director, Division of Enforcement, US Securities and Exchange Commission, before the Permanent Subcommittee of Investigations of the Senate Committee on Governmental Affairs, 24 May 1983.

Whatever the merits of the opposing arguments, the fact remains that insider trading is a serious problem. Some people fear that it has already become the rule rather than the exception, and the examples given below lead one to appreciate their concern.

The greatly increased takeover activity of recent years has provided ample opportunity for insider trading practices. In 1979 there were 1,526 recorded mergers and acquisitions, involving around $34 billion; by 1985 that figure had grown to 3,337 deals, involving more than $140 billion.[45] By 1986, takeover activity was close to the $200 billion mark, 20 times its mid-1970s level. In the period 1985–7 80 of the United States' largest corporations have been taken over.[46]

The increasing sophistication and internationalization of markets has also provided greater opportunity for malpractice. The trading of options is a case in point. Options are the right to buy or sell a stock at an agreed-upon price by a certain date. They have proved especially sensitive to insider abuses because they sell for a fraction of the underlying (cash) stock price. The vast leverage available gives even small speculators the chance to parlay hundreds of dollars into hundreds of thousands of dollars overnight. As one commentator explained: 'There are certain exchanges, such as the Pacific, where you trade both the stock and the option, albeit on different floors. The difference between one floor and another is a 30-second run. Using well-positioned traders and some hand signals, if you see something happen in the stock you can trade that option in less than a minute.'[47]

These broad terms had until recently been interpreted in a fairly narrow way, judicially approved by the Supreme Court in 1980 and generally known as the disclose-or-abstain rule. This basically said that an investor in possession of non-public information on a company should either disclose that information before trading in the stock or forgo the transaction. If he did not do so and this was combined with a failure of fiduciary duty by the investor to the shareholders of the corporation in question, then a violation of the insider trading provisions was deemed to have taken to place. However more recently the interpretation has been extended by the lower courts to exclude the fiduciary duty requirement. Under the 'misappropriation rule' information simply has to be obtained from a source with which the accused has a relationship, and there is no need to establish any fiduciary duty between the possessor of the information and investors in the stock.[48] It was under this interpretation that R. Foster Winans, a *Wall Street Journal* reporter, was found guilty in mid-1985, for having leaked advance information about stories to be run in the newspaper's 'Heard on the Street' column.[49]

Whatever the merits of the opposing arguments, the fact remains that insider trading is illegal in most major securities markets, including those in the United States. US insider trading laws are principally set forth in the Securities Act of 1933, which states:

> It shall be unlawful for any person, directly or indirectly, by the use of any means or instrumentality of interstate commerce, or of the mails or of any facility of any national securities exchange: (a) To employ any device, scheme, or artifice to defraud; (b) To make any untrue statements of a material fact or to omit to state a material fact necessary in order to make the statements made, in the light of the circumstances under which they were made, not misleading; or (c) to engage in any act, practice, or course of business which operates or would operate as a fraud or deceit upon any person, in connection with the purchase or sale of any security.

Catching insider traders

Insiders and their cohorts need financial secrecy to cover their tracks, and various secret money channels are in regular use. Indeed, the channels themselves may be used as tip-offs on possible insider activities. For example, a major figure in the Wall Street arbitrage game claimed that he could benefit from insider trading even without being an insider or tippee himself. He carefully observed the stock trading activities of a number of small Swiss banks that he suspected of acting on behalf of Wall Streeters having access to inside information. Any unusual activity could indicate a deal, and he would then himself move immediately in its wake. Since it pays insiders to publicize information after they have taken their own positions, profits can sometimes be made in the short term even if the information ultimately proves to be factually incorrect or exaggerated.

A common securities fraud scheme is thus to effect securities transactions through banks in foreign jurisdictions to avoid disclosure of the purchaser's identity. The authorities' statutory responsibilities cannot adequately be met unless the Securities and Exchange Commission is able successfully to complete an investigation into the alleged misuse of insider information. To do this, account identify of participants and information regarding the transactions in question – such as the reasons for the purchase and/or sale – are vital.

The SEC's investigations of suspicious trading or other securities transactions pointing to insider activities are aided by the various exchanges' own monitoring systems. All securities markets have computers that monitor every trade for price and share volume as it is recorded. Each time a transaction exceeds preset limits for price and volume activity, the computer highlights the trade. If a reasonable explanation cannot be found the information may be drawn to the attention of the SEC which then proceeds along what may be categorized as a twofold approach.

First, trading records of identified brokers and customers involved in the questioned transactions are acquired. Second, sworn testimony is taken. Both avenues are pursued on either a voluntary or subpoena basis. The SEC may subpoena witnesses for testimony and/or the production of relevant books, papers, memoranda, correspondence or other material.

Testimony is used as a fact-gathering method to elicit further information, enabling the SEC to determine whether actual violations have occurred. In most cases, the testimony of customers and representatives of brokerage and financial firms are the most pertinent in the array of evidence sought during the investigations. The identity of the suspected customer is necessary, and information about his transactions are vital to determining and proving a securities law violation.

Of course, the customer may simply refuse to confirm or deny information about suspected transactions. Even this assumes that the SEC has surpassed the first hurdle – obtaining the usual court subpoena enforcement action for the customer's testimony, which is a costly and time-consuming process. The alternative is to request account information from foreign financial institutions, whose officials are likely to refuse, asserting bank secrecy prohibitions.

Despite these obstacles, the SEC has shown itself determined to stamp out insider trading, and has achieved some major results. It was already making inroads into the problem in early 1985. In May of that year it caused quite a stir when Paul Thayer, former chairman of LTV Corporation and a former Deputy Defense Secretary, pleaded guilty to obstruction of justice in an insider trading case and was sentenced to four years imprisonment and a restitution payment of $555,000. He had apparently leaked information on takeover plans by two companies of which he was a director. Although he did not deal himself, associates reaped about $1.5 million from his 'tips'.[50]

The Levine case

However, less than a year later the Thayer case had already paled into insignificance as Wall Street was rocked by a far greater scandal. Never before had such a high-level executive been accused of using so much privileged information for so much personal gain over such a long time.[51] Dennis B. Levine, the 33-year-old managing director in Drexel, Burnham Lambert's mergers and acquisitions department was charged by the SEC with making $12.6 million over a period of 6 years through illegal trading in the stocks and options of 54 companies.[52] He had allegedly used his position as a top merger specialist – at Smith Barney between June 1978 and November 1981, at Lehman Brothers from 1981 to late January 1985, and at Drexel from February 1985 – to benefit from material non-public information concerning actual or proposed tender offers, mergers and leveraged buyouts.[53] In June 1986 he settled with the SEC by surrendering $11.5 million, and was barred from the securities business for life. He also pleaded guilty to criminal charges of securities fraud, perjury, and income tax evasion. In addition, the IRS figured he owed some $8.5 million in tax.[54] He was sentenced to two years in a federal prison.[55]

But how had he done it and how was he caught? On May 27 1980 Levine evidently walked into the offices of Bank Leu International, a subsidiary of one of Switzerland's oldest banks, in Nassau, and opened a trading account with an initial deposit of $125,000. Later in the summer he made further deposits, bringing the sum up to approximately $170,000.[56] Where these initial amounts originated remains a mystery, but a little under six years later the account had been parlayed into over $10 million and Levine had also established accounts in France, Switzerland and two further Caribbean bank-secrecy havens.[57]

His contact at Bank Leu was Bernhard Meier, a Swiss working as a portfolio manager for the Nassau branch. Levine took elaborate precautions – certainly at first – to avoid detection. He never dealt under his own name. His accounts were in the names of two Panamanian companies, Diamond Holdings SA and International Gold Inc. He never allowed the bank to contact him, but would place his orders to buy and sell from pay telephones, often during his lunch hour. On the occasions when he traveled to the Bahamas, he did so under an assumed name and avoided staying overnight. It has even been suggested that he chose Bank Leu as the recipient of his business since it had only fairly recently opened its Bahamanian subsidiary, was keen for business and perhaps less likely to ask awkward questions.[58] Other sources, however, suggest that he chose Bank Leu since his first choice, Pictet & Cie, of Geneva, refused to do business with him.[59]

What went wrong? The fact that he was right too often. It became clear to a number of people that however Levine might be making his investment decisions, he was generally making very good ones. There can be no doubt now that his successes – both at work and for his personal gain – were simply due to an exceptional ability to ferret-out information: concern had been expressed by employers throughout his career at his technical weaknesses in the corporate finance field.

The result, in any case, was a good deal of 'piggy backing' – smaller fry simply copying the big fish's trades for their own account. Meier joined in; allegedly made $152,000 and is still wanted by the SEC. Brian Campbell – the Merrill Lynch broker in New York who executed a number of the trades for Bank Leu – saw a way to make money too. When in May 1985 someone at Merrill Lynch headquarters in New York received an anonymous letter from the Caracas branch accusing certain employees of insider trading, it was only a matter of time before they found that the Venezuelans were following Campbell and that Campbell was following Bank Leu.[60]

Even this information did not mean that the game was necessarily up for Levine, since there was every possibility that the Swiss bank would refuse to reveal the underlying identity of the account holder. To try and protect himself further, however, Levine devised a plan to show that there were sound reasons for all the transactions undertaken, and suggested to the bank that it state that his account had in fact been part of a portfolio on a discretionary basis by the bank itself. He also persuaded Meier and Bruno Pletscher, the general manager in Nassau, to destroy the identity papers with which he had opened his original account, as well as a number of withdrawal receipts.[61] But as time went by Pletscher decided cooperation with the SEC would be a better policy and so, in return for providing information on Levine, negotiated immunity for the bank and all its staff from any US court action.[62] On 9 May 1986, Levine instructed Bank Leu to transfer $10 million from his account to the Cayman Islands. The bank refused and the next day a court order freezing all Levine's assets was obtained. Pletscher, Meier and Jean Pierre Fraysse, managing director in the Bahamas at the time, subsequently all left Bank Leu's employ.

One of the factors that caused most concern in the Levine case was that of the 54 companies Levine traded, 35 were not even clients of his employers. This pointed to accomplices in other firms, and indeed it was not long before a veritable network of contacts was uncovered.[63] The process of discovery was helped a good deal by Levine himself who showed no hesitation in betraying his accomplices. He even tricked them by pretending to telephone from a public telephone box rigged by investigators.

Robert Wilkis, a first vice-president of E. F. Hutton, formerly with Lazard, Frères, was one of those who had apparently traded secrets with Levine. From November 1979, when he made a $70,000 deposit at Crédit Suisse in the Bahamas, to September 1985, he conducted some 50 illegal trades, netting profits of around $3 million. He resigned from Hutton, settled with the SEC for $3.3 million, which represented illicit profits plus penalties, and was debarred from the securities industry for the rest of his life.[64]

Piggy-backers

Ira Sokolow, a vice-president of Shearson Lehman Bros, suffered a similar fate. He had received payments totalling $120,000 from Levine for providing tips on more than 14 takeovers. He settled with the SEC for the $120,000 plus $90,000 in penalties.[65] David Brown, a lawyer and investment banker with Goldman, Sachs & Co. had apparently received $30,000 from Sokolow for information. What was disturbing here was that Brown worked in the mortgage-backed securities area, and thus had no direct connection with mergers and acquisitions. This indicated that he was himself getting information from another source within the firm, which served to highlight the immense difficulties investment banks face in controlling the flow of sensitive information.

Indeed as SEC investigations continued it seemed clear that even the dealings of the 'piggy-backers' were more elaborate and interconnected than originally believed. It seemed highly likely that Meier and Campbell, together with a New York lawyer named Kevin Barry, in fact formed a ring of mutual assistance and information. Several factors point to this. When the Levine affair first broke, Campbell testified to the SEC for three days. However when he was called in for further questioning in June 1987 he refused to respond, invoking the Fifth Amendment. That same month Smith Barney, his employer at the time, pressed for his resignation. Campbell had earlier explained a check for $10,000 received from Meier as a real estate loan but stated that they had no other dealings. However, it transpired that on 13 August 1984 Meier wired from Bank Leu in the Bahamas to Delaware National Bank in Delhi, NY the sum of $5,000. This was credited to the account of one Mark Tuthill, a carpenter who had recently done repair work on properties belonging to Campbell in Delhi.

Campbell's relations with Barry also had a murky quality. The two were co-investors in real estate ventures, the capital for which is apparently provided by a corporation that traded profitably in stocks – strangely in many of the same takeover stocks that Levine traded. The name of the corporation was BCM Management Corporation, which according to Campbell stood for Barry Capital Management but some suggested actually stood for Barry, Campbell, & Meier.

This might well explain some peculiarities in Meier's behavior as well. Although granted immunity, along with the rest of Bank Leu, he nevertheless chose to return to Switzerland rather than testify in the Levine case, thus forfeiting his immunity from prosecution. This seems silly unless he had more to hide – such as an involvement with Campbell and Barry whereby he fed inside information based on Levine's dealings for a share in the real estate ventures.

At about the same time as the Levine case, but apparently unconnected with it, an insider trading ring of five young professionals was uncovered. It centered around Michael David, an associate at the New York law firm of Paul, Weiss, Rifkind, Wharton & Garrison, who participated as counsel in many mergers and acquisitions. He apparently stole information from the firm and passed it on to his associates in six cases over a five-month period from November 1985. The case came to be known as the Yuppie Five.[66]

In August 1988 Michael David and the four accomplices pleaded guilty to charges of fraud, obstruction of justice and conspiracy in return for light sentences – four months in prison, four years probation and $50,000 in fines, and full cooperation with the SEC in its investigation of insider trading. Effectively, David acknowledged that he had obtained confidential information regarding upcoming takeover deals and passed it on to his four co-defendants, Andrew Solomon (a former arbitrage analyst at Marcus Schloss & Co.), Robert Salsbury (a former analyst at Drexel Burnham Lambert Inc.), Morton Shapiro (a former stockbroker at Moseley, Hallgarten, Estabrook & Weeden), and Daniel Silverman (a client of Mr Shapiro's).[67]

Hard on their heels came Alfred Elliott, a partner and takeover lawyer at the Chicago law firm of Schiff Hardin & Waite. The SEC was investigating whether he had used his position as legal adviser to KN Energy Corporation to trade as the company was fighting-off a $216 million takeover bid from T. Boone Picken Jr's Mesa Ltd in early 1986.[68] And so it went on until the greatest shock of all – in November 1986 Ivan Boesky's involvement in insider trading became clear. It was Dennis Levine who evidently fingered him.

The Boesky case

Known by some as 'the king of the modern day traders' Ivan Boesky was an arbitrageur, a man who essentially made his living by taking positions in takeover stocks. As noted, there is nothing illegal about such transactions if the investment decisions taken are based on non-privileged information. And for years Boesky's abilities had been admired with no indication that his success involved any sort of dishonesty. He had made tens of millions through speculation – a survey in the fall of 1986 put his earnings for 1985 at $100 million. But it is clear now that he had no scruples about the nature of the information he used.

In February 1985, Dennis Levine apparently approached him and began to provide one or two useful tips. After a while the two set up a formal agreement whereby Boesky agreed to pay Levine 5 per cent of any profits he made on deals resulting from his tips. Without this arrangement it would have been far more difficult to prove any case against Boesky, but with it he had no chance. Realizing this, he apparently cooperated almost immediately with the government authorities, allowing taping of all his business conversations over a period of six weeks before the story broke, and then pleading guilty to four specific cases of insider trading as well as paying $100 million – which makes the figures associated with the Levine case pale into insignificance. His parting gift to Wall Street? The day before his arrest, knowing the depressing effect it would have on prices, he dumped $400 million worth of stock in the market with the full agreement of the SEC.[69]

Levine's and, subsequently, Boesky's cooperation with the SEC led, in September 1988, to the initiation of court proceedings by the Securities and Exchange Commission against Drexel Burnham Lambert Inc., a major Wall Street investment bank and Boesky's former employer. At the same time, SEC civil and later criminal proceedings were pursued against four Drexel employees including Michael Milken, the head of Drexel's bond operations and originator of the market for high-yield debt securities, the so-called 'junk bonds'. The charges, which include racketeering, include the allegation that Drexel itself, and not just its employees, used Boesky's accounts for its own illegal stock transactions.

For example, the SEC alleged that in one transaction Drexel victimized its client, Wickes Companies, a diversified lumber and building products company, by advising Wickes on its ultimately unsuccessful hostile attempted takeover of National Gypsum Co., another building products company – while Drexel itself purchased the shares of National Gypsum for its own and its employees' accounts. The shares apparently were purchased through companies controlled by Boesky for Drexel and Milken. Drexel's profits from the total transaction, including $1 million in investment banking fees, allegedly amounted to more than $6.6 million. Wickes although supposedly the victim was not dissatisfied with the treatment it received from Drexel's transactions – it made $3 million on its disposal of the National Gypsum shares.[70]

The Vaskevitch case

In March 1987 the SEC charged Nahum Vaskevitch, the head of international mergers in Merrill Lynch's London office, and David Sofer, a leading Israeli businessman, with making more than $4 million in illegal profits from insider trading in 12 deals since October 1984.[71] Vaskevitch apparently only worked directly on one of the bids, but due to his senior position was regularly briefed on all activity within Merrill's mergers and acquisitions department.

The SEC alleged that Vaskevitch passed the privileged information by telephone to Sofer in Jerusalem, who then dealt in the stocks through two Wall Street brokerage firms, MKI Securities and Russo Securities. Profits were shared between the two men, with proceeds passing to Swiss bank accounts in their own names and those of two companies situated in England and Liechtenstein.[72] Their largest single profit apparently came from the acquisition of Pay Less Drug Stores Northwest by K-Mart in 1985, in which they netted $1.19 million.[73] Sofer is thought also to have profited from passing information to two further investors – Fort Worth oilman Louis H. Barnett and Michael J. Jesselson, son of the former chairman of the commodities trading house Philipp Brothers.[74] He reputedly earned another $231,000 in this way.

The case had a number of interesting aspects. First, the authorities were initially alerted by the New York Stock Exchange's computerized Stock Watch system which had detected a suspicious trading pattern in a number of takeover stocks. The SEC then built its case on tracing the trades through brokers' records and the two men's telephone calls. This indicates the SEC's growing success in the field, even in the absence of a direct lead as with the Levine case. In addition, it illustrates the Commission's determination – and ability – to pursue suspects even overseas.

Finally, the case has again revealed an increased willingness on the part of the Swiss to cooperate. The SEC made use of legislation allowing triple penalties, in other words fines equal to three times the alleged illegal profits. This amounted to more than $12 million and in this case it was certain that neither Vaskevitch nor Sofer had a sum anywhere near to that in the United States. It was therefore vital to freeze their Swiss assets before they could salt them away, and a request was consequently made to the Swiss authorities under the mutual assistance treaty existing between Switzerland and the United States on criminal matters. Traditionally, however, the Swiss have refused to act unless criminal charges have actually been brought, but in this case they stated that the United States had provided sufficient information to satisfy them and that it was enough that a criminal investigation was underway.[75]

The Lee case

Yet another insider trading case emerged in the summer of 1988, when a Morgan Stanley & Co. trainee, Stephen Wang, Jr, was accused of passing inside information on pending transactions to a Taiwanese investor, Fred C. Lee, who traded the shares of the companies through accounts in Hong Kong, Switzerland and elsewhere. The SEC asked Swiss authorities to provide information on trades emanating from Switzerland, and possibly freeze Lee's accounts there.[76] Wang was later sentenced to three years in prison.

The Guinness case

Using privileged information to anticipate the price movement of a share has, it seems, become common practice. Less common, and arguably far more damaging to investor confidence, is the manipulation of a share price to achieve particular ends. This practice lay at the heart of the United Kingdom's worst corporate scandal in years – the Guinness affair. It involved the dismissal of its chairman and chief executive, Ernest Saunders, and the Board's request for resignations from two leading directors, American lawyer Thomas J. Ward and Swiss banker Arthur Furer, chairman of Switzerland's Bank Leu.[77]

The malfeasance related to Guinness's bitterly fought bid with rival Argyll Group for the takeover of the Distillers Company. Guinness won the bid, acquiring Distillers for $3.8 billion, but information received in early December 1986 by Britain's Department of Trade and Industry from US investigators dealing with the Boesky case indicated that it had not been a fair fight. It seems likely that somewhere in the region of $38–$40 million[78] was spent by Guinness on a trading operation designed to boost its own share price in the final stages of the bid, and consequently increase the value of its offer to Distillers shareholders. It is suggested that certain investors and institutions were 'encouraged' by Ward and Saunders to buy close to $500 million in Guinness stock.[79] The formation of such 'fan clubs' to invest in a company and thus drive up the price of its stock is illegal.

Deals seem to have involved intermediaries in Zurich, Vienna, the Channel Islands and New York, with a large proportion of the business channeled through Bank Leu.[80]

Bank Leu had been an investor in the company since 1985 when it paid approximately $180 million for a 5 per cent stake. However in April 1986 two of its subsidiaries apparently started buying heavily, bringing total purchases up to 41 million shares. A deposit from Guinness of some $75 million as indemnity against any losses that might be incurred later in selling the shares was paid to the bank's Luxembourg subsidiary. Bank Leu subsequently sold 40 million of the shares – allegedly at roughly what it paid for them – and after some dispute returned the $75 million. It then came under investigation by the Swiss banking authorities for its involvement in the deal.[81]

In its 1988 annual report, the Swiss Banking Commission reprimanded Bank Leu for its role in the affair, stating that it should have notified the authorities of its involvement far more quickly and that it should have exercised greater caution in verifying the legal and business ramifications of the deal.[82]

Large payments were also made to accounts at one of Switzerland's largest private banks, Pictet & Cie, which made the unravelling of the affair all the more difficult, since the Swiss banks are likely to be reticent over details.[83]

Ivan Boesky was apparently one heavy buyer of the shares and it is alleged that in return Guinness invested $100 million in a Boesky partnership. Two leading British companies, Heron International and S & W Berisford, apparently received around $11 million between them for their participation – both have subsequently returned the money to Guinness. Another $3 million went to a Curaçao firm, named Rudani Corp – this was at the request of the official who headed the Morgan Grenfell team advising Guinness and who subsequently resigned from the bank.[84] The largest single payment however – $8.4 million – appears to have been to Marketing & Acquisitions Consultants Ltd, a Jersey concern which had supposedly done work for the company. However the money appears to have passed on to private accounts belonging to Saunders and Ward, and may have been intended for their own use.[85]

The British authorities continued to bring charges against those involved in the Guinness affair. In October 1987 Saunders, already charged with destroying and falsifying Guinness documents, was accused on another 37 criminal counts, including stealing Guinness funds and false accounting. Gerald Ronson, head of the Heron Group, was charged with receiving $9.5 million for buying shares, despite his swift move to return the money when the scandal first developed. Sir Jack Lyons, former adviser to Boston consultants Bain & Co was accused of receiving $5.4 million for gathering investors to the cause. Executives of investment bank Morgan Grenfell and US bank L. F. Rothschild were also linked to the affair.[86]

To cite one final example, early in 1988 investigations began into possible insider trading activity in the shares of Sterling Drug Inc at the time of Hoffmann-La Roche's unsolicited $4.2 billion tender offer for the company.

The week before the offer was made public, a large number of purchases occurred in Sterling's February and May call options. This unusual volume of transactions caught the eye of the SEC, who promptly asked the Swiss authorities to lift banking secrecy restrictions to assist the inquiry. Hoffmann-La Roche agreed to cooperate in the investigations. The principal buyers were Paine Webber Group Inc and Drexel Burnham Lambert Inc, acting on behalf of clients in Switzerland.

Meanwhile, Sterling itself filed a lawsuit against Hoffmann-La Roche for allegedly breaking US insider trading laws, charging that two of the company's finance companies dealt illegally in both stock and options prior to the tender.[87]

Notes

1 Clare Ansberry, 'Survival Strategy', *Wall Street Journal*, 1 October 1986.
2 'The Shadow Economy – Grossly Deceptive Product', *The Economist*, 19 September 1987.
3 Laura Saunders, 'And Then There is Hong Kong', *Forbes*, 23 September 1985.
4 John Hayes, 'Don't Talk to Strangers', *Forbes*, 25 August 1986. See also Allen E. Murray, 'How to Catch Tax Cheaters', *Fortune*, 17 March 1986.
5 Lynda Schuster, 'Argentines Find Tax Avoidance an Untaxing Job', *Wall Street Journal*, 21 August 1984.
6 Ibid., p. 9.
7 'Italian Shopowners Dodge Effort to Curtail Rampant Tax Evasion', *Asian Wall Street Journal*, 28 November 1984, p. 6.
8 'Haertere Gangart', *Der Spiegel*, No. 34, 1984, pp. 68–9.
9 Allen E. Murray, 'Cheating Uncle Sam', *Wall Street Journal*, 10 April 1984.
10 Russell Weigel, Richard Hessing and Henk Ellflers, 'Psychological Profiles of Tax Evaders', *Journal of Personality and Social Psychology*, April 1988.
11 Daniel Goleman, 'The Tax Cheats: Selfish to the Bottom Line', *New York Times*, 11 April 1988.
12 'Tax Havens and Funk Money', *International Currency Review*, Vol. 15, No. 2, pp. 15–35. See also Walter H. Diamond and Dorothy B. Diamond, *Tax Havens of the World* (New York: Matthew Bender, 1984).
13 Allen E. Murray, 'How to Catch Tax Cheaters', *Fortune*, 17 March 1986.
14 'Greeks Join the Chorus', *The Economist*, 1 October 1983.
15 *Newsweek*, 22 August 1983.
16 Felix Kessler, 'Legal Tug of War Over Marc Rich & Co. Centers on Small Swiss Town of Zug', *Wall Street Journal*, 15 November 1983.
17 Dan Baum, 'U.S.–Swiss Accord on Marc Rich Papers is Snarled Over Terms of Pact', *Wall Street Journal*, 3 July 1983.
18 *New York Times*, 20 September 1983.
19 Ibid.
20 'Marc Rich and Firm's Other Top Officer Won't be Extradited to U.S. Swiss Say', *Wall Street Journal*, 13 December 1984, p. 30.
21 *Business Week*, 5 September 1983.
22 Shawn Tully, 'The Lifestyle of Rich, the Infamous', *Fortune*, 22 December 1986.
23 Shawn Tully, 'Why Marc Rich Is Richer than Ever', *Fortune*, 1 August 1988.
24 Richard E. Smith, 'Swiss Court Indicates Banks Must Refuse Some Business', *Wall Street Journal*, 17 October 1985.
25 Allan Dodds Frank and Ralph King, Jr, 'Greed, Inc', *Fortune*, 29 December 1986.
26 'Can South America's Addict Economies Ever Break Free?', *Business Week*, 22 September 1986.
27 Leonard Buder, '17 at Colombian Airline Accused of Large-Scale Money Smuggling', *New York Times*, 10 April 1987.
28 Ibid.
29 Jagdish Bhagwati, 'On the Underinvoicing of Imports', in Jagdish Bhagwati (ed.), *Illegal Transactions in International Trade* (Amsterdam: North Holland, 1981).
30 Everett G. Martin, 'Precarious Pesos', *Wall Street Journal*, 13 August 1986.
31 Marlise Simons, 'The Parallel Economy is Crime, and Crime Pays', *New York Times*, 6 June 1988.
32 Ibid.
33 Reazuddin Ahmed, 'While Bangladesh Struggles, its Smugglers Thrive', *International Herald Tribune*, 26 June 1986.
34 Steve Mufson and Stephanie Cooke, 'Can Pretoria Evade Sanctions? Let us Count the Ways', *Business Week*, 1 September 1986.
35 John Vinocour, 'A Trail of Western Technology is Followed to the KGB's Door', *New York Times*, 25 July 1983.
36 Ibid., p. A6.
37 Steve Mufson and Stephanie Cooke, *op. cit.* (n. 29).

38 Quoted in Joseph Fitchett, 'High-Tech Smuggling Risks are Slight', *International Herald Tribune*, 22 May 1984.
39 Ibid. See also Joseph Fitchett, 'Technology Bandit Led Ring for Russia', *International Herald Tribune*, 5 February 1985.
40 Martin Tolchin, 'Soviet Tried to Buy 3 US Banks', *Wall Street Journal*, 19 February 1986.
41 'Information Greases Mergers, Challenges Courts and Media', *Wall Street Journal*, 2 March 1984.
42 Henry Manne, *Insider Trading and the Stock Market* (New York: John Wiley, 1966).
43 'The SEC's Fight with Itself', *Wall Street Journal*, 19 March 1987.
44 'The Epidemic of Insider Trading', *Business Week*, 29 April 1985.
45 Michael Stone, 'Insiders', *New York Times*, 28 July 1986.
46 Ivan Fallon and Mark Hosenball, 'Secret World of the Inside Stealer', *Sunday Times*, 23 November 1986.
47 Nathaniel C. Nash, 'SEC's New Enforcement Chief', *New York Times*, 5 May 1985.
48 Christopher Stoakes, 'The Insider Trader's Global Guide', *Euromoney*, July 1986.
49 Carol J. Loomis, 'Limited War on White Collar Crime', *Fortune*, 22 July 1985.
50 'The Epidemic of Insider Trading', *Business Week*, 29 April 1985.
51 Gordon M. Henry, 'Dark Clouds over Wall Street', *Time*, 26 May 1986.
52 Scott McMurray and Daniel Hertzberg, 'Drexel Official Accused by SEC of Inside Trades', *Wall Street Journal*, 13 May 1986.
53 Eric N. Berg, 'Dennis Levine: Study in Contradictions', *International Herald Tribune*, 16 May 1986.
54 Gordon M. Henry, 'Circus Time', *Time*, 23 June 1986. See also 'Levine Sues IRS, Asking it to Lift Lien on His Assets', *Wall Street Journal*, 15 July 1986.
55 James B. Stewart, 'Tracing a Scandal', *Wall Street Journal*, 15 July 1987.
56 Michael Stone, 'Insiders', *New York Times*, 28 July 1986.
57 'Court Freezes Banker's Assets in US Insider Trading Case', *International Herald Tribune*, 24 May 1986.
58 Richard Evans, 'Bank Leu – or Pandora's Box', *Euromoney*, April 1987.
59 'Insider Jail', *The Economist*, 10 October 1987.
60 James Sterngold, 'Letter Unravelled Levine Case', *New York Times*, 10 June 1986.
61 Robert J. Cole, 'Witness in US Trading Case Tells of Cover Stories', *New York Times*, 29 May 1986.
62 'Swiss Bank Says SEC Gave It Immunity in US Insider Case', *International Herald Tribune*, 22 May 1986.
63 'Dealers in the Know', *The Economist*, 24 May 1986.
64 'Trading Case in US Ruins Two Careers', *Wall Street Journal*, 3 July 1986. See also John S. DeMott, 'Finger Pointing', *Time*, 14 July 1986.
65 James Sterngold, 'Goldman Aide Tied to Insiders', *New York Times*, 9 July 1986. See also Stanley Penn, 'Levine Case Has Nassau Buzzing Over Bank Leu Unit's Ex-officials', *Wall Street Journal*, 30 May 1986; Susan Dentzer, 'Greed on Wall Street', *Newsweek*, 26 May 1986 and Kenneth Labich, 'The Fast Track Ends for One Baby Boomer', *Fortune*, 9 June 1986.
66 Larry Elkin, 'Levine, 4 Others Plead Guilty in Insider Trading', *International Herald Tribune*, 6 June 1986.
67 Calvin Sims, 'Lawyer Gets 4 Months in Jail for Role in Trading Scheme', *New York Times*, 10 August 1988.
68 Daniel Hertzberg, 'SEC Investigates Schiff Hardin Ex-Partner', *Wall Street Journal*, 30 June 1986.
69 Ivan Fallon and Mark Hosenball, 'Secret World of the Inside Stealer', *Sunday Times*, 23 November 1986.
70 Stephen Labson, 'The US vs Drexel: SEC Action Seen as Just Beginning'; and Scot J. Paltrow, 'In Charges Over One Client: The Gist of a Complex Case', *International Herald Tribune*, 10 September 1988.
71 James B. Stewart and Matthew Winkler, 'Merrill Lynch Aide, Israeli Face Trading Charges', *Wall Street Journal*, 12 March 1987.
72 Stephen Koepp, 'The Insider Scandal Travels Abroad', *Time*, 23 March 1987.
73 James Sterngold, 'Merrill Lynch Official Named in $4 million Insider Scheme', *New York Times*, 12 March 1987.

74 James Sterngold, 'Merrill Dismisses Accused Official', *New York Times*, 13 March 1987.
75 Gary Putka, 'Swiss Freeze Bank Accounts of Defendants in SEC Case', *Wall Street Journal*, 23 March 1987.
76 'SEC Subpoenas Firms' Files, Asks Swiss Aid in Insider Case', *Wall Street Journal*, 29 June 1988.
77 Steve Lohr, 'Guinness Ousts Head in Scandal', *New York Times*, 14 January 1987.
78 Steve Lohr, 'Guinness Thinks Funds Went to Ex-Chairman', *New York Times*, 9 April 1987.
79 Paula Dwyer and Rose Brady, 'The Questions Surrounding Guinness' US Connection', *Business Week*, 27 April 1987.
80 Matthew Winkler, 'Bank Leu is Brushed by Scandals in Its Rush to Expand', *Wall Street Journal*, 26 January 1987.
81 Barbara Toman, 'Bank Leu Sells Embarrassing Guinness Stake', *Asian Wall Street Journal*, 18 May 1987.
82 Paula Dwyer, *op.cit.*
83 Gary Putka, 'Guinness plc Made Secret Payments to Accounts of Swiss Bank Pictet & Cie', *Wall Street Journal*, 26 January 1987.
84 Gary Putka, 'Secret Payment from Guinness Routed to Caribbean Firm by Ex-Grenfell Aide', *Wall Street Journal*, 13 February 1987.
85 Paul Hemp, 'Guinness Alleges Breach of Duty by Former Chief', *Wall Street Journal*, 4 March 1987. See also Nick Kochan and Hugh Pym, *The Guinness Affair: Anatomy of a Scandal* (Christopher Helm Publishers, 1987).
86 Mark Maremont, 'Look Who May Take a Fall in the Guinness Scandal', *Business Week*, 26 October 1987.
87 Elliott D. Lee, 'Swiss Drug Firm Secures Financing for Sterling Bid', *Wall Street Journal*, 14 January 1988.

5

Demand for Secret Money: Fraud

Whereas the use of international fiscal secrecy for insider trading purposes is certainly controversial in terms of its effects on efficiency and equity in financial markets, its use to perpetrate outright financial fraud is a different matter altogether. Charlatans have long used human greed for their own purposes, often with great success. But ultimately the jig is usually up, and it helps at that point to have the loot safely stashed out of reach of victims and law enforcement officials, and to place oneself under the protection of a country that will not honor financial disclosure or extradition requests.

The mid-1980s saw the City of London shaken by serious concern over fraud. There was the case of Johnson Matthey Bankers Ltd (JMB) which had to be rescued by the Bank of England. There was the insurance scandal at Lloyds, where highly irregular activities in the reinsurance market were revealed. Perhaps the most interesting aspect of these kinds of discoveries, however, was the lesson they provided on how attractive a center London was for the international fraudster. The United Kingdom has lagged behind many countries in agreeing to mutual assistance treaties to facilitate the collection of evidence over-seas, the interviewing of witnesses and the capture of criminals. The lack of exchange controls and of regulations on setting up a business are fundamental to its attractions. And then there is the fact that it is a major center of finance, trade and shipping, which means that being based there gives a fraudster a higher level of credibility – all important in the game of international fraud.

The scandals at Lloyds and JMB served to heighten awareness of other nefarious practices giving the authorities cause for concern. In the depressed shipping market, for example, banks' generosity with loans provides ample scope for fraudulent practices. One trick was for shipowners with large bank loans to divert some of their income into secret accounts so as to appear to be making losses and be forced into bankruptcy. Another was for shipowners to take loans against mortgages on their ships but based on inflated insurance values, and then sink the ships. Cargo-based fraud was another common practice. Here foreigners would set up phoney trading operations, and make perhaps two or three good (but small) deliveries to their 'victim' to inspire confidence. Then on the big delivery, when trust had been established, letters of credit would be used, the ship filled with rubbish, and the port authorities induced to hand over the bills of lading needed for the fraudster to cash a draft against his letter of credit. The ship sails; the 'sting' is successfully accomplished, and the crook takes the next flight out.

In September 1988 Euclid, the electronic security transfer network of one of the two principal international clearing houses for bonds, Euroclear, was fraudulently used to effect the transfer of £15 million in securities from Mitsubishi Finance International to Shearson Lehman Hutton. The police were tipped off by Shearson's back office staff, who were puzzled that the transaction should occur over the British August Bank Holiday without Shearson's request. Police in Switzerland seized the culprits when they attempted to withdraw the proceeds of the transfer. Access to the Euclid network was apparently gained by using personal computers, standard telephone lines, and the correct sequence of passwords.[1]

Another type of international fraud which commonly exploits the City's reputation as a supplier of capital, is advance fee or seed-money fraud. In simple form, the victim is often a government of a deeply indebted Third World country. It is persuaded to pay an advance fee to a fraudster with impressive documentation purporting to show that he can arrange a large loan. In more sophisticated versions, banks or large firms are persuaded to participate (by providing some up-front finance) in a scheme, such as a civil engineering project in a Third World country, which then fails to materialize.[2]

Whatever the precise nature of the scam, a common factor characterizes most cases of international fraud – when the perpetrator, victim and scene of the crime are all in different countries, whose problem is it? How does one investigate and prosecute? Who cares? These questions are central to another type of fraud that has become widespread in recent years – the selling of worthless securities over-the-counter by US conmen based in one European country to unwitting investors in another. Freewheeling Amsterdam has been a popular spot for such businesses, known as 'boiler rooms'. A Dutch investigator for Interpol estimates that the half-dozen of the largest North American-run boiler rooms in Amsterdam alone separated Europeans from some $200 million in 1984.

One of the leading practitioners of boiler room skills was perhaps Chartwell Securities, which opened in September 1984 and was closed by a series of police raids ten months later. During its short but lucrative existence it employed 150 telephone salesmen working from a total of five offices in West Germany, Switzerland and Liechtenstein. They are thought to have dealt with some 8,000 clients and to have relieved them of around $30 million.[3]

The J. David & Co. case

Financial secrecy, moreover, is a potent device for drawing-in prospective victims who hope to evade taxes. In 1984, for example, a case came to light in the United States involving abuse of fiduciary relationships in the presence of financial secrecy. J. David & Co. promised investors up to 40 per cent annual returns on their money and complete confidentiality, with records of transactions kept outside the United States. The opportunity attracted large numbers of wealthy investors in California and elsewhere. The investment proceeds were ostensbily to be used for currency trading operations. Much of the money evidently went into the various personal activities of the company's founder, J. David Dominelli, as well as to cover exceedingly high operating costs (six houses, three jet aircraft, over two dozen luxury automobiles).[4] Little apparently went into actual trading activities, certainly not in the volume that could conceivably have yielded the kinds of returns promised to investors. Despite suspicions of fraud, the nature of the interbank foreign exchange market made it impossible to substantiate or refute earnings claims made by the company, and transactions were routed through offshore points such as Guernsey and the Caribbean island of Montserrat.

Records kept by J. David and Co. appear to have been either sloppy or non-existent, with tax identification numbers often missing – indicating at least inferentially the intent of many of the firm's prominent clients to evade US federal and state taxes. Few people appear to have withdrawn their funds, while those who did may have been paid largely out of investments by others. The whole scheme began to unravel in the fall of 1983, when J. David's obligations began falling past due, various other signs of trouble began to emerge, and Dominelli began to scramble to cover withdrawals. Checks bounced with increasing frequency, suits began to be filed by investors, and at an early stage in the investigation only $600,000 in liquid assets could be located to cover over $150 million in liabilities.

Dominelli eventually escaped to Montserrat, where he had set up a captive shell bank for secrecy purposes. From there he flew to Antigua, where he was arrested and extradited to the United States to face the music. Suspicions arose that the affair did indeed involve an elaborate Ponzi scheme – in which existing investors are paid off out of the proceeds of subsequent investments, to the extent that they withdraw their funds – or that Dominelli lost large amounts in actual foreign exchange speculation and in efforts to cover those losses. For the rather unsophisticated but greedy investors for whom a promise of a 40 per cent annual return and the chance to evade taxes seemed too good to be true, it was. Still, indications were that large numbers of investors, lured by the dual prospects of high returns and tax evasion, would rather walk away from their losses than risk disclosure of their financial affairs in court proceedings.

Then there was the case of Edward Markowitz, a financial promoter who peddled tax shelters to investors. These supposedly involved legitimate dealings in the secondary government securities market and in forward contracts for precious metals – both unregulated, over the counter markets. However, it turned out that many of the deals were fictitious and based on fraudulent documents. Some of these trades were with mysterious Cayman Islands companies, and his associates '... were unable to learn anything about the financial strength of the Caribbean entities with which Mr. Markowitz traded, or even who their owners were'.[5] In the end, he was brought up on tax fraud charges ($445 million), pleaded guilty to a number of them, and cooperated with the authorities in their investigations.

The Chase-Colombia case

International financial secrecy can thus be used as bait in fraudulent financial dealings, as well as a way to protect the spoils by making money disappear. An interesting case in the latter category occurred in May 1983. Chase Manhattan Bank and Manufacturers Hanover Trust Company of New York had made a loan to the Colombian government in the amount of $47.2 million, for the purchase of equipment and supplies by Colombian military and police authorities. Some of the loan had already been drawn-down, but most of what was left in the Colombian current account at Chase's London office ($13.5 million) was ordered transferred to an account at the Morgan Guaranty Trust Company in New York, an account that in turn belonged to the Zurich branch of Bank Hapoalim, a major Israeli financial institution. The ultimate owner of the account was apparently Robert Russell, a Texan who often acts as a middleman for banks in arms and other sensitive deals.

Chase maintained that it followed accepted principles in transferring the money on instructions telexed from Bogota bearing the name of the Finance Ministry's director of public credit and the telex number of Colombia's central bank. The Colombians argued that no record of any such telexed instructions could be found in Bogota, and in any event the transfer should not have been made without a disbursement order from Chase's own Bogota representative. Moreover, normal telex security precautions evidently were seriously flawed, and there were misspellings and other procedural errors. Whether Chase checked the inconsistencies is not known, but a religious holiday in Colombia in any case would have prevented immediate verification.

The Colombian government accused Chase of mismanagement in what was clearly a case of highly sophisticated bank robbery, and just as clearly an 'inside job'. Where did the money end up? Russell testified that in late 1982 he had been approached by a Colombian military contact and asked to act as a middleman in a deal to buy 'German arms' for Argentina. Two weeks after the $13.5 million entered his account he allowed a Colombian called Colonel Lara to transfer $12.7 million, with the balance staying as commission. The $12.7 million went to the Panama branch of Bank Leumi, another Israeli bank – and there the trail ends in the mists of Panamanian secrecy. Domestic Colombian investigations into the case were accompanied by several suspicious deaths of people with information about the affair.[6]

Insurance fraud

A particularly unpleasant form of fraud has been on the increase in recent years, murder for insurance. Life policies are taken out on a relation or a business associate. The unsuspecting insured person is then quietly 'removed' and the beneficiary claims the cash from the insurance company. 'What was once unusual is now routine', explains one vice-president of a leading insurance company. 'We had 30 homicide cases last year in which beneficiaries are suspect. Five years earlier we didn't have more than ten or eleven.'[7]

Why? There seem to be several contributory factors. First, the stakes are now higher. Policies of $100,000 to $500,000 are commonplace, whereas at the beginning of the decade, the norm was more like $15,000 to $20,000, a significant increase in real terms. Second, insurance is more easily obtainable. Many policies are simply mass-marketed by direct mail. When a claim is made, investigations can be cursory. Third, companies tend to accept the information provided by the claimant unless the sums involved are very large. In addition, the insurance company risks potentially heavy legal costs if it contests the claim. The beneficiary may sue for payment, plus punitive damages on the ground that without criminal charges of wrongdoing the refusal to pay has damaged his reputation. 'For the insurance company, it's an economic decision. When attorneys' fees begin to approximate the amount of the claim, the insurance company often decides to pay it.'[8]

Individual case details can make unnerving reading. In 1982, Craig

123

Young was found shot to death on a road near Houston. Mr Young had been president and sole stockholder of a Montana company, Container Finance Mining Co. It seems Container Finance was no more than a shell set up by a friend, Jack Dickie, and secretly controlled by him. Dickie had offered Young the presidency on incorporation, and the company had then purchased mining claims for some $2.5 million on promissory notes signed by Young. Dickie advised the taking out of a 'key-man' life insurance policy to cover this liability, advice Young duly followed. What he did not know was that the company from which the claims had been bought, Vanguard World Holdings, was a Panamanian shell corporation controlled by Dickie. So when Young died, the $3 million insurance proceeds paid to his estate were required to pay off the promissory notes, thus filling the coffers of Vanguard World Holding. In October 1987, Dickie was found guilty of procuring Craig Young's murder in order to collect the insurance.

In another case in Minneapolis, 56-year-old May Wilson, an ex-nurse, honorably discharged from the Air Force on full medical disability in 1968 and subsequently hospitalized on a number of occasions for both physical and mental reasons, was found dead with two stab-like wounds in her neck in the basement of a building leased by her half-brother, Leonard J. Richards. Her life was insured to the tune of some $3.5 million through 30 policies. It was discovered that she had entrusted her financial affairs to Richards, who had set up the insurance with the beneficiaries being nonprofit trusts and charities established and run by him. When one of the companies refused to pay, Richards sued, only to lose in the civil court, where a jury found that he had had Miss Wilson killed. No criminal charges were brought at the time, but the Minneapolis prosecutor began an investigation.

Then there is the story of Linda Von Bergen. A Florida savings-bank manager, she carried $5.2 million of insurance cover with her husband as beneficiary. In May 1986, she drowned while on a fishing trip with her husband off the coast of Puerto Rico. Apparently the captain of the vessel had been instructed to go far from shore, even though he had warned that the fishing was poor. Another passenger on the trip testified that Mrs Von Bergen had stumbled into him and they had both gone overboard; he had tried to save her but failed. Plausible, except that another witness stated in probate court that he had been offered $100,000 by Mr Von Bergen in 1985 to kill his wife on a cruise ship in a way that would make the death appear accidental.

Shortly after the incident, Mrs Von Bergen's father sued the husband, accusing him of having taken out substantial policies on his daughter's life just prior to her demise. Before a judge could rule, however, the parties settled. The suit was dropped, and Mr Von Bergen transferred his rights as beneficiary to her father.[9]

124

The Blay-Miezah case

There is the extraordinary case of John Ackah Blay-Miezah, a 46-year-old Ghanaian. The Philadelphia District Attorney issued an indictment filed against him in March 1986, charging that over the past 15 years he swindled investors out of some $100 million. Many of his clients were Americans, with a significant proportion from Philadelphia, where he was helped in his dealings by one Robert Ellis – now serving five years in prison for his part in the case. Blay-Miezah himself lives on a Ghanaian diplomatic passport in London. He was arrested in Ghana at the time of the Philadelphia indictment but was later released.

The subject of concern was a Cayman Islands registered charity, the Oman Ghana Trust Fund – a fabrication according to the cynical, a potential goldmine in the eyes of the believers. Blay-Miezah's story was that Ghana's first prime minister, Kwame Nkrumah, set up the $20 billion fund because he did not trust the politicians of the day. Gold and diamonds were said to have been smuggled out with Blay-Miezah's help, the proceeds to be salted away in European bank accounts, and used when the time was right for Ghana's economic development. On his death in 1972, Nkrumah left a deed naming Blay-Miezah sole trustee of the secret accounts. But before the money can be released, a number of specific conditions must be met. For example, Blay-Miezah must hold a valid Ghanaian diplomatic passport, number 000065, he must be a member of the Ghanaian government and own 200 square miles of land in the Nzima region of the country, none of which ever quite seemed to materialize.

In the meantime, of course, funds were needed to help unravel the Trust and secure the eventual release of the assets – which is where the trusting investor comes in. He puts up cash and in exchange receives Oman Ghana Trust Fund notes, guaranteeing returns of 1,000 per cent or more.

Blay-Miezah's past record would provide little comfort to the investor. He was first imprisoned in Ghana for two years in the mid-1960s, an embarrassing fact given his supposed intimacy with Nkrumah, although he has indicated that the prime minister was unaware of the matter. In 1972, he spent a year in Pennsylvania's Graterford prison for fraudulently representing himself as a Ghanaian diplomat. In 1979 he was back in jail in Ghana for fraudulently claiming to have obtained degrees from the University of Pennsylvania.

Yet he had followers who remained unshaken, believing implicitly his current claims that the funds are about to be liberated. 'It's not the fraud you think it is', said one.[10]

The Ballestero case

In 1980 and 1981 eight banks, led by Banque Keyser Ullman en Suisse SA, made loans totalling approximately $45 million to four Liechtenstein companies, controlled by a Spanish businessman, Jaime Ballestero Aquilar. Ballestero, described as a 'worldwide entrepreneur', had previously gained 68 per cent ownership of Safco, the largest fruit exporter in Chile at that time. The $45 million was in part to provide fresh capital for the company and in part to finance the development of a holiday complex, 'Shangri-La', on the Spanish island of Minorca.

Collateral for the loan was provided by the deposit of precious stones owned by Ballestero, and valued by a Belgian appraiser, Franz-Maurice Verbruggen, at some $90 million. This valuation was corroborated by a Swiss gemologist and a professor of mineralogy at the University of Mainz in West Germany. As an additional safeguard, insurance policies were set up in London to repay the loans in case of default. All seemed well.

However, in November 1981 Safco filed for bankruptcy and liquidation. By early 1982 work had still not begun on 'Shangri-La' and it was becoming obvious that the loans were not good. Nor was the collateral. The gems appeared to be worth no more than 5 per cent or 10 per cent of their stated value. Allegations of a highly sophisticated fraud were made, and investigations began.

It turned out that Verbruggen's name had appeared in connection with other cases where banks had sustained major losses on loans with gems serving as collateral. It also seems that the British broker, Albert Roy Lee, who set up the insurance package, worked for Vesed International Ltd, an insurance firm in Cardiff, Wales, of which Ballestero was the major shareholder and sole director. In the meantime Keyser Ullman, which had extended $16 million of the $45 million in question, was in serious difficulty and was sold and reorganized by the Swiss banking regulators.

The whole affair set off a bitter dispute between the banks and insurers. The banks claimed that they were not liable since fraud was involved – losses due to fraud are typically excluded from insurance policies of the type in question.[11]

The Heiwa Sogo case

In the summer of 1985 information began to appear on a major banking scandal in Japan. Heiwa Sogo, a leading mutual savings bank, was alleged to have made improper loans to the tune of ¥190 billion since 1982. The precise charges involved loans to a property company totalling ¥11.6 billion to buy forestry land valued at ¥3.6 billion; ¥4.1

billion in order to buy a folding screen valued at ¥300 million and ¥1.5 billion to buy an uninhabited island worth ¥500 million.

The aspect that caused the most concern, however, was the fact that neither the Finance Ministry nor the Bank of Japan had drawn attention to the irregularities in their 1983 and 1984 reports. Records were apparently faked to mislead the regulators, but there is also the suggestion that political pressure was perhaps exerted on Ministry officials. Heiwa was rescued by Sumitomo Bank.[12]

The Galanis case

Cases of gullibility and greed abound. Take John Peter Galanis, who appears to have been involved in a variety of fraudulent practices since 1970. In 1985 he set up a scheme to develop a stretch of Atlantic City's boardwalk. Some 1,200 individual investors were persuaded to contribute, attracted by the tax benefits promised. Tax-advantaged limited partnerships of about $100,000 each were established, offering at least 2–1 tax write-offs from real estate depreciation and mortgage interest deductions. Around $60 million flooded in, of that amount $35 million simply disappeared, probably into offshore accounts in the Netherlands Antilles. The balance appears to have found its way to Atlantic City, but not all necessarily into the building project, which in any case soon folded with the Galanis-controlled syndicator of the scheme filing for bankruptcy.[13] In another example Henry Gherman, who from 1979 to 1988 defrauded some 150 doctors of at least US$20 million through bogus investment funds and pension plans, withdrew $4.4 million, mostly in 100 dollar bills, from his account at a branch of Commercebank in Miami and fled the country in early August 1988, before the FBI was able to arrest him.[14]

The Pedley case

In the early 1980s many Americans opened dollar accounts in Mexico to take advantage of the high interest rates there. In 1982, the Mexican government in effect froze these accounts in pesos, stating that henceforth they could only be reconverted at the official (disadvantageous) rate.

Investors caught in this position became prime targets for a scheme set up by a California family who established a bank that offered to convert Mexican pesos to dollar-denominated instruments, such as certificates of deposit. The scheme was equally attractive to Mexican residents wishing to circumvent currency exchange restrictions. However, the instruments in question turned out to be worth far less than promised, as did the collateral backing them. The Pedley family were subsequently charged with mail and wire fraud, interstate transportation of stolen property, and racketeering.[15]

The DeLorean case

Another case of alleged fraud that hit the headlines in the mid-1980s, possibly because of the flamboyant character of the central figure, was the DeLorean affair. One of the major charges was that John DeLorean had improperly used $8.9 million of DeLorean Motors Co. funds to improve his lifestyle and to buy Logan Manufacturing Co. in Utah, a manufacturer of snow-grooming equipment for ski slopes. The money was allegedly siphoned off through a Swiss bank account in the name of GPD Services Inc., a Panamanian company with a Geneva address, which ostensibly was doing research and development work for the DeLorean car. It is suggested however that the money moved on to DeLorean's personal account in the United States. Among the plaintiffs in the case are 90 of the 140 wealthy Americans who invested in a DeLorean research and development tax shelter, creditors of DeLorean Motors, and the British government, which provided much of the finance for the Belfast plant.

An interesting aspect of the case is the blame being placed on the company's auditors, Arthur Andersen. It is alleged that the firm knew, or at least had good reason to suspect, that all was not well, and plaintiffs have therefore laid part of the responsibility for their losses at Andersen's door. This approach is indicative of an increasing trend to hold accountants significantly responsible for malpractice at a company which they have audited and given a clean bill of health.[16] Perhaps as a reaction to this, the American Institute of Certified Public Accountants has formed a National Commission on Management Fraud to address the problem of why businessmen go astray and what the accountancy profession might do to improve matters.[17]

The Mao case

In 1985 the Hong Kong authorities found John Mao guilty of five years of fraudulent financial practices which had taken a severe toll on the island's banking community. Between 1977 and 1982, Mao had run an elaborate check-kiting scheme which netted some $153 million. It involved acquiring cash advances from one bank against uncleared checks from a second. By writing checks faster than banks could clear them, he received what amounted to an unauthorized interest-free loan.

These transactions were a major contributory factor in the failure of the Hang Lung Bank, which the government rescued in 1983 at unspecified cost. They also are thought to have led to the fall of Dollar Credit and Financing Ltd in 1982, which in turn triggered collapsed among other local deposit-taking companies.

Having unravelled Mao's involvement, the authorities turned their attention to the banks with which he dealt. Prominent amongst them was Citibank, whose assistance to Mao proved highly embarrassing.[18]

The Mediobanca case

After four years of investigation, criminal charges were brought in May 1988 against nine executives of the Milan-based Mediobanca. Italy's leading merchant bank was on the point of privatization when the affair became public.

The charges related to an 'occult fund', as the Italians termed it, amounting to some Lire 24 billion. Undisclosed to shareholders, it was used secretly to offer incentives to Mediobanca executives and to provide important clients with particularly attractive deposit rates.

Of the men involved, three were the bankers who in the late 1970s and early 1980s ran the state banks constituting Mediobanca's major shareholders. One of them subsequently became Mediobanca's chairman.

Also charged was the bank's honorary chairman, Enrico Cuccia, who founded the institution in 1946 and had been closely associated with its workings ever since. Mr Cuccia had been investigated though not prosecuted before for alleged involvement in a 1970s embezzlement scheme.[19]

The Polo case

The founder and head of a New York money management firm, Private Asset Management Group Inc (PAM), which handled funds primarily for Europeans and Latin Americans seeking non-taxable investments, was sued by his clients for the misappropriation of some $110–130 million. It was alleged that Roberto C. Polo, a high-living and prominent figure in New York and European social and art collecting circles, diverted the funds to his own accounts in order to support his extravagant lifestyle. The majority of the assets came via personal holding companies based in the Cayman Islands for investment in bank time deposits.

Rostuca Holdings was a typical case. It opened an account with PAM in January 1984, and for the next two and a half years its 'trust and confidence in Polo grew stronger'.[20]

As early as May 1984, Mr Polo's former office manager, Mrs Ramona

Colon, suspected that all was not as it should be. Apparently at around the same time as Polo bought an impressive town house in New York City, he had transferred from his clients' deposits a sum roughly equivalent to the purchase price. This went to an account named ITKA at Crédit Suisse in the Bahamas, which Mrs Colon believed was Polo's own personal account. She began to fear that the financial statements being sent to clients were fraudulent, and that their deposits in fact no longer existed. Her fears were increased when her boss began a 'major cleanup' of client files, taking shopping bags full of them home with him and demanding the erasure of all the deposit computer records. When Mrs Colon challenged Polo, her duties were curtailed. In May 1986 the firm's operations were transferred to Geneva.

By fall 1987, even the clients were becoming nervous, wondering how Polo could possibly afford the way of living he had adopted. In December of that year his town house was emptied and his wife and daughter moved to his Paris apartment. It was not long before rumors started to circulate that the Polos were in financial difficulty – rumors apparently substantiated by the sale of jewelry and auction of paintings. Clients began to ask to withdraw their money, but no funds were forthcoming. They sued.

By that time, Polo himself was thought to be in France, having been spotted at a Parisian auction house. Lawyers sought legal help in Geneva to track him down – he was believed to hold Swiss citizenship. Although the suit in New York was a civil one, the Swiss authorities issued an arrest warrant since they considered his behavior might have been criminal on financial-fraud grounds. The French police attempted to serve the warrant, but Polo escaped. His whereabouts remained unknown. In the meantime, his Paris apartment had been seized, a New York state court granted a temporary restraining order barring him from disposal of assets and the Swiss PAM operation was apparently being liquidated.

Euroscam

Equity Management Services, Falcontrust Financial Ltd and Pruden-trust Financial SA of Switzerland, Ketter Investment Finanz AG of Liechtenstein, and a host of other respectable-sounding companies formed a network of what was exposed in 1988 as being the largest single international securities fraud enterprise so far uncovered. Direct, sophisticated sales tactics by professional, polished salesmen representing the enterprise's various firms in some 20 countries and using glossy, well-written investment newsletters with such titles as *Strategy for Investors*, *Swiss Analyst* and *Invest News* defrauded over 5,000 investors of as much as $250 million during 1987–8. The international 'boiler

130

room' enterprise was centered in Switzerland and targeting European middle level investors, but also stretched out to Asia, the Middle East, South Africa and South America. Its mastermind appears to have been Thomas F. Quinn, a former US stockbroker with a long record of securities laws violations.

The tactics varied. Some investors would be ensnared by urgings that they make investments in blue chip stocks. Then, when they began using the enterprises's services, they would be persuaded to buy more speculative shares. Sometimes investors received no share certificates, but did receive a steady flow of optimistic reports designed to allay their suspicions. False share price information was distributed on falsified Over the Counter (OTC) 'pink sheets', and, on occasion, investors were urged to buy shares of companies that had already ceased trading. Those who tried to withdraw their funds were often unable to do so. They were either told that their company had gone bankrupt or would discover that their broker had mysteriously disappeared. The enterprise also duped clients into making investments in 'blind pools', investment trusts where their funds were to be invested at the discretion of the trust's management. In practice, the trust might make no investments at all. By sending out a constant stream of investment reports, they would entice the investors to maintain their positions.

In an unprecedented coordinated investigation of securities laws violations involving Interpol, Swiss, French and West German authorities, 18 arrests were made at the end of July 1988 which included a Briton, and a Swiss, and Quinn himself at his villa outside Cannes. The Swiss authorities sought and received US cooperation in their investigation of various OTC firms. There was doubt, however, that the enterprise was in fact out of business. Shortly after the arrests, investors received letters from Equity Management Services, postmarked Hong Kong.

Funds involving the Euroscam were channeled through Swiss banks, which have been cooperating with the investigation. The investigation, which was in its early stages at the end of 1988, revealed a level of sophistication reminiscent of organized crime. The organization itself may indeed have been started as a method of laundering criminal funds. As one investigator observed, 'If you buy shares with dirty money, selling them to pigeons allows you to have clean money.'[21]

Bank fraud – Central National Bank of New York

It has been found that in a significant proportion of bank failures, criminal activity by insiders has played a role in the institution's problems.[22] Central National Bank of New York seems to have been a case in point. It was declared insolvent on 11 September 1987. Three weeks later its owner, Jackie Finkelstain, was accused of diverting $31.5 million from the bank to his own Swiss bank accounts. He was charged with siphoning off customers' funds, using repurchase agreements supposedly backed by Argentine bonds.

Even before Finkelstain was involved, the bank appears to have had some shady dealings. It embarked on risky South American loans and other activities, including, apparently, participation in the Buenos Aires currency black market. In 1981 its major stockholder, Al Kevelson, was removed as chairman after a conviction for income-tax fraud. It was at that point that Finkelstain, who had begun his career in construction and made a fortune in real estate, moved in. He, and Gustavo Andrew Deutsch bought Central for $20.50 a share, twice its book value.

The US authorities kept the bank under special scrutiny, but losses kept mounting despite the surveillance. In 1985, Deutsch pulled out. In 1986 Finkelstain tried to dispose of his interest, but there were no takers. Central's steady deterioration continued until its final collapse. The issue has raised questions about the ability of regulators to cope with problem banks engaged in international transactions even when the warning signs are clear.

Precious stones and jewelry-related fraud

For over 60 years secrecy has played a vital role in Belgium's important diamond-trading industry. Although the sale of diamonds inside Belgium is not subject to tax, dealers are nevertheless supposed to declare their stones at the border and to state proceeds from sales abroad for income tax purposes. However, there has been a tendency for the authorities to 'turn a blind eye' to these requirements, with the result that Antwerp has over the years become the most important diamond-trading center in the world, doing an estimated $7 billion a year in business, (about 6 per cent of Belgium's gross national product) and employing some 30,000 people in 1987. Secrecy in the business is vital since many buyers come from countries where strict currency-exchange and income-tax controls render 'open' trading impossible or unprofitable.[23] This arrangement was severely disrupted in January 1986, however when the authorities, as part of a minor investigation into a gold dealer, stumbled across the biggest tax fraud case in modern Belgian history.

It appeared that Roger Kirschen & Co., a prominent Antwerp currency trader, had been acting as an illegal clearing house for money earned from unreported diamond dealing. As much as $20 million in unpaid taxes and as many as 800 diamond merchants were thought to be involved. Understandably, the investigation sent waves of panic through the market and for a while sales plummeted. Confidence has to some extent been restored with the authorities' subsequent 'low-key' approach of pressing for fines rather than criminal proceedings, but the whole affair has undoubtedly reduced the attractions of Antwerp for dealers and clients alike.[24]

Another case involving the jewelry business came to light in mid-1987 with the collapse of the prestigious French jewelers, Jacques and Pierre Chaumet. Their bankruptcy took everyone by surprise. Purveyors of gems to royalty, aristocracy, high society and the rich since 1780, they were considered the epitome of respectability. In Chaumet's last published financial statement they had declared profits of FF31.8 million ($5.2 million) on sales of FF674 million. Pillars of the French Establishment, the sons of Marcel Chaumet and Henriette Monet, a sister of the Impressionist Master, they were indicted in June 1987 and charged with bankruptcy, breach of trust and fraud.

It appears that the brothers ran two very distinct operations. There was the official business of selling fine jewels, and there was what one banker has described as 'a very private backroom operation', conducted outside France, with peripheral companies trading precious stones. It is thought that this second facet of the business went dramatically wrong creating an 'off balance sheet hole' of anywhere between FF1 billion and FF2 billion. There may have been other factors contributing to the company's difficulties as well – the collapse of the diamond price in the early 1980s, a dwindling of petrodollar-rich Middle Eastern customers, as the oil price fell, and a costly investment in a shop in New York. But these troubles alone are apparently insufficient to explain it all. The Chaumets were almost certainly involved in the shady and secretive world of hidden jewelry transactions which make possible international tax evasion and capital flight.

As their difficulties increased, the brothers' attempts to extricate themselves from financial ruin became increasingly desperate. In frantic bids to obtain loans, they sold off or offered as collateral gems they did not own. And in the final months they even produced fake receivables (unpaid bills from customers) in an attempt to appear more financially healthy than they actually were and increase their ability to borrow. In 1987 the police were faced with the task of trying to unravel the tangle – a task all the harder because operations stretched to countries that included Switzerland and Panama.[25]

The E. F. Hutton case

In May 1985 E. F. Hutton, at that time the fifth largest brokerage firm in the United States, pleaded guilty to an elaborate fraud, which, through manipulation of the check clearing system, allowed it use of as much as $250 million a day interest free. At the expense of some 400 of the banks it dealt with, Hutton is thought to have earned up to $8 million in extra income in the period in question, between July 1980 and February 1982. The scheme resembled a check-kiting system whereby a series of checks, without funds behind them, are written one after another, each to cover the previous one. Hutton's policy was in fact simply to write checks for far larger amounts than it had in bank balances, and in addition it shuffled funds between its own branch, regional and head offices as well as between numerous small banks in order to facilitate the operation.

The firm eventually agreed to pay criminal fines of $2 million, plus $750,000 court costs, and to pay restitution of up to $8 million to the defrauded banks.[26] However, because of the complexity of the scheme it seemed unlikely that all the banks involved would claim restitution. In order to do so, they would have been required to perform expensive computations of overdrafts. In addition, there was some concern that a claim against E. F. Hutton could endanger business relations with the firm, a risk small banks might have preferred not to take.

Whether the check-kiting scandal was the direct cause or a contributory factor, E. F. Hutton's prestige and profitability slumped. In 1986, the company's results showed a net loss of $90.3 million at a time when other brokerages were prospering. From a high in January 1987 of $447/8 the company's stock fell as low as $11 after the October 1987 market crash. By the end of the year the parent company of the tenth largest US retail brokerage was actively seeking a buyer – a move that was to end 83 years of independence through a takeover by Shearson Lehman. The company had offered $1.6 billion twelve months earlier but the price it finally paid (after the stock market crash) was just $1 billion.[27]

The ZZZZ Best case

One of the major US cases of business fraud came to light in 1987. ZZZZ Best, a carpet and drapery cleaning business, was set up in 1981 by a Los Angeles student, Barry Minkow. Six years later, when Minkow had just turned 21, it was a $200 million empire and Minkow was the toast of Wall Street.[28] He talked of building ZZZZ Best into the General Motors of carpet cleaning, and then running for President of the United States. At their peak, ZZZZ Best shares stood at $18.375; three months later they had dropped to less than $1.00.[29] Minkow had resigned, claiming poor health, and the company was at the center of a fraud scandal.

The SEC carried out a wide-ranging investigation into a whole variety of transgressions – phoney receivables, bogus financial results, organised crime connections, stock manipulation, to mention but a few. The new management of the company sued Minkow for fraudulently removing, in the month before he left, more than $3 million from ZZZZ

Best accounts, as well as having over the years diverted $18 million to a firm owned by an associate, for nonexistent 'insurance restoration' work.

The Los Angeles Police Department suspected the company was used for laundering organized-crime drug money, and search warrants for the premises were issued – a charge that was perhaps the most surprising one, since Minkow had campaigned vociferously against drug abuse, adopting the slogan: 'My act's clean, how's yours?'

The first outward signs of irregularities were reports that in 1985 ZZZZ Best had used customers' credit card numbers to run up at least $72,000 in inflated charges; the same thing happened to the tune of $91,000 the following year at a flower shop owned by the company's chief operating officer. Minkow blamed both overcharges on unscrupulous subcontractors and an employee, and repaid all the customers. Later it appeared that these transactions were in fact the thin end of the wedge.

In June 1985, ZZZZ Best, apparently already in financial difficulties, had borrowed money at a rate of 2 per cent to 5 per cent a week from Jack M. Catain Jr, a reputed mobster and loan shark. It appears also that Catain began to take a hand in 'organizing' the company, as well as taking up to 50 per cent of profits on business funded by his loans. Then there was Maurice Rind, who was brought in as 'financial adviser', a securities specialist with previous convictions for mail fraud and forgery. And there were joint ventures on 'restoration work' contracts which had never been awarded with a Mr Victor, also known as Robert Viggiano, convicted in 1973 of grand larceny in connection with a robbery that also established links to the head of one of New York's Mafia families.

The Los Angeles Police Department believed that, through contacts such as these, ZZZZ Best formed part of a conspiracy to use legitimate businesses in the Los Angeles area to launder the proceeds from illegal narcotics sales.

Hundreds of cases of secrecy-related financial fraud such as these have come to light over the years, but certainly the story of the decade (perhaps of the century) was the Banco Ambrosiano case.

Banco Ambrosiano

On 18 June 1982, the body of Roberto Calvi – chairman and president of Banco Ambrosiano, a major prestigious bank headquartered in Milan – was discovered hanging from scaffolding under Blackfriars Bridge in London. Calvi was often called 'God's Banker' in the press because of his close association with the Vatican. About $1.3 billion of his bank's funds were soon found to be missing, most of it evidently extended as loans to a handful of Panamanian and Liechtenstein shell companies owned directly or indirectly by the Vatican's own bank, the Instituto per le Opere di Religione (IOR). None of the missing assets have been recovered.[30]

The IOR is perhaps best seen as an offshore merchant bank in the heart of Italy serving the Roman Catholic Church. The Vatican is a sovereign state, not subject to exchange controls or border checks. Money deposited in an IOR account could be sent anywhere in the world. From Michele Sindona, the financier who declared bankruptcy in 1974 and was convicted in the United States of fraud and perjury in 1980, Calvi learned the means to exploit the opportunities offered by the system.

Italian legislation, framed to prevent repetition of the financial disasters of the 1930s, prevents banks from buying non-banking interests, and vice versa. The way to get around this legislation was to establish foreign shell companies, preferably in tax havens where local scrutiny is lax. These foreign shell companies could then make the prohibited investments. Ownership of a bank offered the perfect means to activate the system. Bank funds could be appropriated and, through the 'fiduciary' or trustee accounts, exported out of Italy to the shell companies abroad, owned either by the initiator himself or by his associates. The funds could then be used to carry out financial operations that would normally be illegal back in Italy or elsewhere.

Speculative assets, once bought, might subsequently be moved around a network of companies at ever-higher prices, creating 'profits' for further speculation. If the price of the underlying Italian assets seemed deficient, one's own bank could step in, pushing up the value of the shares in question by buying on the relatively thin Milan market. This brought the further advantage that one could then more easily pass the shares on to innocent third parties at an inflated price. The initiator would always retain majority control, usually concealed in the offshore labyrinth.

Roberto Calvi's elaborate and complex scheme was possible only with the consent of the IOR, which was either knowingly or unknowingly involved. The IOR was an ideal, much-respected, candidate for the role of fiduciary, or trustee. To get the IOR interested in Calvi's pursuits, the Banco Ambrosiano paid unusually high interest rates on its IOR deposits. Calvi would transfer funds, or the shares of a company, to the IOR. According to the instructions received, the IOR would either hold the assets in Calvi's name, or pass them on to a specified recipient, usually outside Italy. In addition, the IOR's well-respected secrecy and offshore status made discovery of what was taking place particularly difficult for the Italian authorities.

Archbishop Paul Marcinkus, chairman of the IOR since 1971, disclaimed any responsibility for Calvi's manipulation. The IOR maintained that Calvi had taken it for a colossal ride. Its sins, if any, were those of naivety and inexperience. The question nevertheless remains: where does negligence and naivety end and collusion begin? The truth about the Vatican bank's relations with Calvi will probably never be known. Was the IOR acting on its own interest? Was Ambrosiano acting on behalf of the IOR? Was the IOR behind Ambrosiano, which in turn was behind the IOR?

The relationship between Calvi and Marcinkus dated from August 1971, if not earlier, when Marcinkus joined the board of the newly formed Cisalpine Overseas in Nassau, Bahamas. Cisalpine Overseas marked the beginning of Calvi's scheme to buy up control of Banco Ambrosiano itself, and Bahamian financial secrecy laws played a critical role. A subsidiary in the Bahamas not only fitted Calvi's image as an internationally minded banker, but it would also later permit him to conduct his most sensitive business safely away from the prying eyes of the Italian financial authorities. With Marcinkus, as director, the Vatican had an original shareholding of 2½ per cent in the Nassau operation, which later rose to 8 per cent.

Banco Ambrosiano's first foreign acquisition actually occurred in the early 1960s, when it bought Banca del Gottardo, just across the border in Lugano, Switzerland. Besides Cisalpine, a second firm, Suprafin, was established in Milan in November 1971, controlled by a Luxembourg holding company called Anli. Suprafin would deal in Ambrosiano's shares, and smooth out fluctuations in the stock price.

The fall of Michele Sindona, as well as rumors about Calvi, resulted from two separate investigations of Banco Ambrosiano by the Banca d'Italia (the central bank of Italy) between 1971 and 1973. This caused massive selling of Ambrosiano's shares. Suprafin bought shares to support the price, and gradually began gaining control of Ambrosiano. Most of the shares purchased were sent to an entity called Ulricor in Vaduz, Liechtenstein, supposedly owned by the IOR. All in all, Suprafin sent abroad 15.4 per cent of Banco Ambrosiano's outstanding shares. The recipients were shell companies, like Ulricor, consisting of no more than an entry in a lawyer's books. But all of them were in one way or another managed by Calvi and his banks. The stock purchase placed with Suprafin had come first from Banca del Gottardo, and later from Cisalpine Overseas.

In 1974 and 1975, more shell companies were set up. Besides Ulricor in Vaduz, there were Sapi, Rekofinanz, Sektorinvest, Finkus and Sansinvest. There were more distant shells in Panama, where registered companies did not even have to provide accounts, including La Fidèle and Finprogram.

Calvi evidently worked in close collaboration with the Vatican bank throughout. Besides the IOR's probable ownership of Ulricor, the Banca del Gottardo in November 1974 set up another Panamanian company,

United Trading Corporation, in the name of the IOR. The United Trading Corporation established various nominees, two of them in Liechtenstein, which later purchased full ownership of Suprafin.

It now appears that United Trading was in fact the recipient of a number of loans over the years for which the IOR acted as intermediary. In one case, the Lima unit of Banco Ambrosiano, (set up in 1979) deposited with the Vatican bank approximately $130 million. The IOR proceeded to lend an identical amount with identical maturity to United Trading, taking an interest rate turn of $\frac{1}{16}$ per cent for its trouble. When the deposits matured, however, and the Lima unit asked for repayment, the IOR declined, saying that the money was in fact owed by United Trading. This omitted the fact that it effectively controlled United Trading. The money was never repaid or traced.[31]

Besides buying control of his own bank, Calvi had his eyes set on gaining control of a newspaper as well. The purchase of *Corriere della Sera* by the Rizzoli publishing group presented Calvi with an opportunity. Rizzoli bought *Corriere* (the newspaper had been owned by the Crespi family, the oil magnate Angelo Moratti, and the Agnelli family, which controls Fiat) in July 1974 for 44 billion lira. But *Corriere* lost 12 billion lira in the first year. Roberto Calvi provided Rizzoli with much of the needed purchase price and gradually gained control as capital was added to cover the paper's financial losses. In the summer of 1977, Rizzoli's capital was increased from 5 to 25.5 billion lira to keep pace with the paper's growing debt. The funds used by Rizzoli to subscribe the increased capital were put up by Banco Ambrosiano as collateral for the loan. Later, this majority interest appears to have been passed on by Calvi to the IOR. On the surface however, the entire sum was put up by the Rizzoli family and they retained a 91 per cent share of the newspaper group.

The so-called '159' law, passed in April 1976, signified the beginning of Calvi's troubles, and eventually led to his downfall. This law turned illegal export of currency from a simple 'administrative' offense into a criminal one. Its effect on Calvi was to make it harder to operate an offshore company with impunity. Previously, if a foreign debt became a serious concern, the possibility existed of settling it by remitting lira from Italy. After April 1976, that safety valve was largely removed. Foreign debts could now only be paid off by contracting new ones abroad. Most often, the debt was denominated in US dollars, which continued to rise against the Italian lira throughout the period.

Because the law was made retroactive, Calvi's failure to describe the nature of his dealings to the Italian authorities laid the groundwork for the impending investigations and the criminal charges to come. The first was his involvement in the November 1975 purchase by La Centrale, a holding company once owned by Michele Sindona, of 1.1 million shares in Toro, an insurance company. It was later revealed that the Toro shares in question were in effect already owned by La Centrale. The transaction was merely a re-import of shares into Italy, and an illegal export of currency representing the difference between their value on the Milan market and the price actually paid – some 23 billion lira.

A second factor that eventually brought about Calvi's demise was the 1978 Bank of Italy investigation of Banco Ambrosiano. 'Not at all satisfactory' was the verdict of the 12-man task force after a 7-month investigation. It was confirmed that Banco Ambrosiano had put together a foreign network that allowed it to shift large sums without scrutiny by Italian authorities. The report also identified the chain of command within Ambrosiano itself, from Milan through the Banca del Gottardo in Lugano to the key – Cisalpine Overseas in Nassau. By then, Cisalpine had borrowed more than $200 million from Banco Ambrosiano. On the other side of its balance sheet were $183 million of assets, described only as unspecified 'financings'. And on the board of Cisalpine sat not only Calvi, but Archbishop Paul Marcinkus, chairman of the IOR, which was also found by investigators to be the owner of Suprafin, the mysterious buyers of 15 per cent of Banco Ambrosiano's shares between 1974 and 1977 – shares that had in turn been dispatched, on buying orders placed by Cisalpine through Banca del Gottardo, to the group of Liechtenstein and Panamanian companies.

What the inspectors could not prove was that various foreign entities were the property of either Banco Ambrosiano or the IOR. But they had their suspicions. The mysterious growth of $183 million in assets in Nassau might be connected with the massive purchase of Ambrosiano's shares. That is, Banco Ambrosiano had lent the money to Cisalpine to buy control of itself. Their report also remarked that 'it cannot be excluded' that the Liechtenstein and Panamanian companies were part of the Ambrosiano group. Although the Vatican bank said it had a shareholding of only 1.37 per cent in Banco Ambrosiano, it 'could not be excluded' that it owned more through Panamanian companies that had bought large blocks of stock, with instructions from Cisalpine on whose board sat the chairman of the IOR himself. The report also noted that 32 per cent of Ambrosiano's capital was in the hands of 22 large shareholders, all of them in one way or another 'friendly' to Ambrosiano. The inspectors needed to prove that Calvi and the IOR were behind these offshore companies. Besides the suspect illegal offshore activities allegedly undertaken by Calvi, the inspectors also found further breaches of Italian banking law and severe organizational shortcomings, and that Ambrosiano was severely undercapitalized.

Calvi was alarmed by the central bank's findings, but evidently had his contingency plan well thought out. In September of 1977, Ambrosiano's Luxembourg subsidiary, Banco Ambrosiano Holding (BAH), set up a new bank called Ambrosiano Group Banco Commercial in Managua, Nicaragua. During 1978 and 1979, a good part of the unspecified 'financings' by Cisalpine was transferred to the books of the new bank, which was run from Nassau by Cisalpine. Besides exemption from tax, the bank was the only one not to be nationalized by the Nicaraguan government – which is perhaps indicative of the amount of money Calvi spent to buy political support in furtherance of his scheme.

In October 1979, Calvi again transferred his business, this time from Managua to Lima, Peru, where he established the Banco Ambrosiano Andino. Filippo Leoni became the first chairman of the bank, and his deputy was Giacomo Botta, both trusted lieutenants from Ambrosiano's international group in Milan. Decisions were taken in Milan and conveyed through Banca del Gottardo or Cisalpine in Nassau. From late 1979 on, most of the loans extended to the Panama and Liechtenstein companies were transferred to Lima.

Between 1977 and 1980, a new group of companies (17 altogether), usually with a nominal capital of $10,000 each, were formed in Panama and Liechtenstein. They were registered through resident agents but were owned by Manic SA of Luxembourg, formed in 1971 under the nominal ownership of the IOR. The main purpose of these companies was to finance the other Panamanian and Liechtenstein companies owned by Manic, which in turn owned Banco Ambrosiano shares. Physically, the shares never left Milan, but were on deposit with Ambrosiano itself. These companies were also to serve as repositories for other Calvi activities, evidently including funds that were channeled to the secret and highly controversial P2 Masonic lodge, in which he appears to have been active.

In 1979, Ambrosiano was forced to increase its capital from 20 billion to 30 billion lira. If Calvi were to retain control and avoid the risk of a drop in Ambrosiano's share price, the shell companies in Panama and Liechtenstein would have to undertake more borrowings. Calvi's plight thus continued to worsen. In June 1980, the construction group of Mario Genghini declared bankruptcy, defaulting on a total debt of 450 billion lira, one-third of which represented borrowings from Ambrosiano. A few days later, Italian authorities finally concluded that La Centrale's purchase of Toro in 1975 was in fact an illegal export of currency. The magistrate demanded that Calvi surrender his passport. In late 1980, Calvi purchased 20 per cent of the Artoc Bank and Trust Company (based in Nassau) through Banco Ambrosiano Overseas (formerly Cisalpine). The main attraction was the prospect of rich new financial contacts in the Arab world.

New Italian financial regulations were passed in January 1981 that further complicated Calvi's life. These regulations frowned upon Italian banks' ownership of foreign holding companies that were not them-selves banks, and warned that such an interest could be permitted only under two conditions: (a) that they could be properly scrutinized by the

Banca d'Italia, and (b) that they were operated in countries with a proper system of banking supervision.

In the spring of 1981, Calvi was confronted with yet another challenge. The Milan stock market's regulatory authority forced Calvi to quote Banco Ambrosiano shares on the open market. Ambrosiano had always been quoted on the over-the-counter market, which was subject to fewer regulatory controls, where financial disclosure of consolidated accounts were not obligatory, and where trading only occurred once a week, allowing Ambrosiano to control trading in its own shares easily and cheaply.

In May 1981, Calvi was imprisoned on a charge of illegal currency exports. Calvi's family pressed Archbishop Marcinkus to admit involvement of the IOR, but he refused to come forward although the ultimate owners of the companies in Panama and Liechtenstein would have been the IOR by virtue of its ownership of Manic SA and United Trading Corporation. However, proof could only be obtained through Banca del Gottardo, which was bound by Swiss secrecy.

While in prison, Calvi instructed two emissaries to go to the head office of Banca del Gottardo, where they ascertained that shell companies owned by Manic SA and United Trading Corporation altogether owed Ambrosiano's Latin American affiliates over $900 million. The main asset used to secure these borrowings was a large block of shares in Banco Ambrosiano itself. Thus, the IOR was the owner not just of its declared 1.6 per cent, but of at least a further 10.2 per cent of Ambrosiano stock. On paper, the IOR thus controlled Banco Ambrosiano.

The trial of Robert Calvi lasted two months. He was sentenced to four years in prison and a fine of 16 billion lira. His lawyer appealed the conviction. Calvi was released on bail and surrendered his passport. The appeal was expected to be heard on 21 June 1982.

In August 1981, the Bank of Italy demanded full disclosure of Ambrosiano's overseas affiliates and a list of all of its stockholders owning 10,000 shares or more. In desperation, Calvi requested from the IOR 'letters of comfort' confirming ownership of the nominee companies in Panama and Luxembourg, to which funds had been lent, on two conditions: that the letters would entail no legal liability and that the financial tangle would be resolved by June of 1982. The IOR did indeed provide two comfort letters to the Ambrosiano Group Banco Commercial in Managua, Nicaragua, and Banco Andino in Lima, Peru. Two months later, the Vatican sent more letters to Managua and Lima, providing new figures and confirming that it would not dispose of the Panamian shell companies 'without your prior written approval'. Calvi was told that he, and not the IOR, should unscramble the financial mess that he had created. Ambrosiano's 'Vatican connection' had turned from a blessing into a curse.

The Vatican has always claimed that the letters were issued by the

141

bank in a fiduciary role and did not represent proof of management responsibility. Their purpose, it has been asserted, was to try to prevent the piling-up of further debt by the companies involved. Yet a letter from IOR officials to Calvi in October 1981 names him 'attorney in fact' for those same companies, which raised the question of how the IOR could possibly give such authority if it was not itself the owner.[32]

Calvi tried to avoid impending disaster by inviting Carlo de Benedetti, chief executive of Olivetti, to be deputy chairman of Banco Ambrosiano. De Benedetti paid 50 billion lira for 1 million shares in the bank. With 2 per cent of its capital, he would be Ambrosiano's largest single declared Italian shareholder. Calvi's motive might have been to polish Ambrosiano's image both at home and abroad and to encourage foreign banks to resume lending to Ambrosiano. The arrangement was, however, terminated after three months during which de Benedetti encountered 'a wall of rubber' everywhere he turned. It seemed that unidentified forces were manipulating Calvi, and were signaling that de Benedetti's presence at Ambrosiano was intolerable. De Benedetti received calls at home threatening his life and his family. In the style of the Mafia, his children were referred to as his 'little jewels'.

In January of 1982, the procedure for having Ambrosiano listed in Milan's main stock market was initiated and Calvi, having resisted for several months, agreed that Ambrosiano stock should be quoted as soon as possible. The first list of Ambrosiano's main shareholders would also be disclosed at that time. In February, the Bank of Italy stepped up its demand for comprehensive information on every aspect of Ambrosiano's foreign activities. In addition, copies of the minutes of board meetings had to be sent to the central bank, and it vetoed the proposed merger between Ambrosiano Overseas and Artoc to create a single Bahamas bank with a deposit of $1 billion.

In May 1982, the Bank of Italy sent a letter to Calvi which stated that the documents thus far submitted by Banco Ambrosiano showed that the group's lending to 'unspecified third parties' exceeded $1.4 billion. This exposure was abnormally high, and was concentrated in only three banks: Banco Andino in Lima, Ambrosiano Group Banco Commercial in Managua, and Ambrosiano Overseas. Of the total, more than $650 million was provided directly by Ambrosiano Overseas and Banco Ambrosiano Holding of Luxembourg. The latter had given its guarantee for a further $300 million in loans.

A week later, Calvi tried to persuade the IOR to acknowledge its responsibility for the debt, but Archbishop Marcinkus replied flatly that there was nothing to be done. On 11 June 1982 Calvi left for Trieste, then proceeded to Klagenfurt, Austria, and finally to London, traveling with a false passport bearing the name 'Gian Roberto Calvini'. The next morning, the news broke that Calvi had disappeared. Ambrosiano's shares fell by over 15 per cent on Monday, 14 June. Three days later,

Italy's leading financial newspaper published the Bank of Italy's letter of 31 May to Calvi. It was to be the last day of trading in Ambrosiano shares – the stock price was half of that one-and-a-half months earlier, when Ambrosiano shares were first quoted on the main market.

On 16 June, an inventory was taken of the IOR's assets held in Panama:

- 5.2 million shares in Banco Ambrosiano (10.4 per cent of its capital);
- 5.5 per cent of La Centrale, held in the name of two Liechtenstein entities called Zwillfin and Chatoseu;
- 6 per cent of Banca del Gottardo;
- 5,500 shares in Suprafin;
- 2 million shares in Vianini;
- 189,000 shares in Rizzoli;
- 300 shares in Ambrosiano Overseas Nassau;
- 520 shares (52 per cent) of Sorrisi e Canzoni TV.

These were funded by a total of $1,287 million in debt.

Ambrosiano officials argued that the bank had to liquidate at least some of the loans immediately, but IOR spokesmen insisted that the debts were not theirs. A final scheme was put together. It called for the sale of Banca del Gottardo and other assets for $250 million. The IOR was to raise $1 billion through an international loan with maturity of six–seven years. When the loan came due, the IOR would repay it by selling the 5.2 million Banco Ambrosiano shares. On the following day, Marcinkus demanded a firm promise that the Vatican could not meet the interest payments of roughly $100–150 million a year or accept the foreign exchange risk involved. On the same day, the board of Ambrosiano was dissolved. It was explained that the Panamanian and Luxembourg companies controlled by the IOR owed Ambrosiano's foreign subsidiaries, especially Banco Andino, almost $1.1 billion, while IOR owed them $100 million directly.

On 19 June, Roberto Calvi's body was found in London.

On 2 July, a meeting was held between Archbishop Marcinkus and Bank of Italy commissioners. Marcinkus continued to deny responsibility. The IOR was not generous with information, and it was assumed that Marcinkus managed to convince the Vatican Chief of Staff, Cardinal Casaroli, and the Pope that the IOR had been deceived by Calvi.

The Bank of Italy ceased assisting Ambrosiano's overseas affiliates in meeting their debts, a decision based on the 'Basle Concordat' among central banks of 1975. The Corcordat only obliges a central bank to come to the aid of banks in its own territory or their branches, for which it has regulatory and supervisory authority. It does not oblige a central bank to act as 'lender of the last resort' for bank *subsidiaries* located abroad. In this case, subsidiaries such as Banco Ambrosiano Holding (Luxembourg) and their appendages would not fall under the central bank's agreed responsibilities. The Bank of Italy commissioners also hoped that this uncompromising policy would exert pressure on the IOR, since they realized full well that they were otherwise powerless to act against that institution, representing a foreign bank on foreign soil. Banco Ambrosiano Holding (Luxembourg) collapsed immediately, and the Bank of Italy set about the difficult task of reconstruction of the Nuovo Banco Ambrosiano back home.

In July 1982, the IOR announced the appointment of its own 'three wise men' to examine relations between the IOR and Banco Ambrosiano. The three investigators made clear that the IOR disowned not only the indirect borrowings through Panama 'covered' by the letters of comfort, but the direct ones as well. Although the IOR continued to insist on its innocence in events leading to Banco Ambrosiano's collapse, the Pope made an effort to help the Italian government in coming up with resources to repay Ambrosiano's domestic creditors. In November 1982, he told President Sandro Pertini of Italy of his intention to make 1983 a Holy Year – a surprising decision both because of the short notice and because it was only eight years since the last Holy Year. The secular significance of the decision was that there would be substantial expansion of travel to Rome, and consequently in tourist expenditures which would benefit the Italian economy – an elegant and indirect way to redeem the IOR's 'debt' to Ambrosiano and Roberto Calvi.

In February 1984, Pope John Paul II authorized a 'good will payment' of $230 million by the Vatican to help compensate banks for losses suffered when Banco Ambrosiano Holding (Luxembourg) failed. This payment would be part of a settlement of the $450 million in claims filed by 88 non-Italian banks against the Italian government liquidators. The rest of the money was supposed to come from the sale of Banco Ambrosiano's assets, including Banca del Gottardo in Lugano, Switzerland, which was valued at $100–130 million. Some would also come from funds that were recovered from various Swiss bank accounts controlled by the associates of Roberto Calvi. The Vatican insisted that this represented a voluntary payment, and was not in any way an acknowledgement that it was at fault. Wide-ranging speculation about where the unrecovered $1.3 billion ultimately went ran the gamut from international arms trading and the 'Bulgarian connection' to a major secret struggle between East and West and the financing of Solidarity in Poland.

The final settlement was signed on 25 May 1984 in Geneva, among over 50 representatives of Ambrosiano's creditor institutions, the Bank's liquidators and the Vatican. The principal sum of the settlement was about $539 million, allocated as follows:

- $406 million to Banco Ambrosiano Holding's creditors, of which $152 million was paid by the IOR, $144 million from Ambrosiano's sale of its shareholding in Banca del Gottardo to the Sumitomo Bank of Japan, and $110 million from other Banco Ambrosiano Holding assets that retained value;

- $85 million to creditors of Banco Ambrosiano SPA, Milan, involving $50 million from the IOR and $35 million from the sale of back-to-back deposits in Latin American banks at a discount (a $40 million IOR deposit in escrow was available to make up deficiencies in assets covering payments to creditors of the parent bank);
- $8 million to be paid by the IOR to creditors of Ambrosiano's Nassau affiliate.

At the same time, the IOR agreed to surrender to the creditors an assortment of 'bearer shares' in its possession. These included 500 shares in United Trading, forming the entire share capital; 5,499,000 of the 5.5 million shares of a Luxembourg company, Zitropo Holding SA; 44,944 shares of the 50,000 shares of Manic SA and 53,300 shares, or 23 per cent of those outstanding, of Banco Ambrosiano Holding SA, the Luxembourg affiliate – indicating a far higher degree of control on IOR's part than it has ever admitted.

All claims against the bank's successor, Nuovo Banco Ambrosiano, were dropped, and the settlement represented a loss to creditors of roughly one-third of their claims against Banco Ambrosiano and its affiliates. All further claims against the IOR were likewise dropped.

The IOR reiterated its stand that its overall payment of about $44 million was made voluntarily 'in recognition of moral involvement'. However, it seems that the Vatican was pressured into accepting this obligation by the Italian authorities and by a writ that had been prepared by the creditors for use against the IOR itself – an unprecedented action. The funds were raised by selling about $160 million of Vatican property and investments in debt and equity securities, and there were rumors that the balance was being raised through a bank loan in the United States. In April 1985 the IOR sold its 51 per cent stake in the Banco di Roma per la Svizzera to the Chase Manhattan Bank of New York for about $100 million.

The Vatican has persistently disclaimed any responsibility for Calvi's machinations, maintaining that it had been used and misled. However, by February 1987, investigating magistrates in Milan believed they had enough information to justify the issue of warrants for the arrest of Archbishop Marcinkus and two other senior IOR officials on charges of being accessories to fraudulent bankruptcy.[33] For five months the three sheltered within the walls of the Vatican – as noted earlier, a sovereign state without an extradition treaty with Italy – claiming immunity under the Lateran Treaty, a bilateral accord between the Holy See and the Vatican State dating back to 1929. Prosecutors argued that this was invalid, since the Vatican Bank engaged in international activities beyond the Vatican walls. But in July 1987 the case was thrown out by the Court of Cassation, Italy's highest court concerned with criminal matters, holding that the aforementioned treaty between Italy and the Vatican prohibits Italian interference in Vatican affairs.[34] The decision was appealed, but was upheld by the Italian Constitutional Court in June 1988.[35] Although it still seemed clear that the IOR was deeply involved in the affair, it was virtually certain that any case specifically against Marcinkus will not be pursued.

While the financial nightmare had apparently been cleared up, the mystery of Roberto Calvi's death – whether suicide or murder – lingered. His financial dealings, particularly his links to the P2 Masonic lodge and its notorious underground political manipulations in Italy, continued to raise suspicions of foul play. Indeed, the story took on new life when a man named Licio Gelli was arrested in Geneva during 1982 while attempting to withdraw $120 million from a numbered account with the Union Bank of Switzerland. The account had been set up by Calvi, and the arrest brought to light a long association between the two men, as well as Gelli's own unusual past.

From humble origins in Tuscany, Gelli, an early supporter of Mussolini, rose to become grand master of the P2 Masonic lodge, whose membership of 923 included at least three former Italian cabinet ministers, senior officials in the secret service and the military, judges, police chiefs, civil servants, and bankers. Gelli himself evidently developed a significant international pharmaceutical and weapons business, which brought him into contact with Juan Perón in Argentina and which in turn reinforced his influence in Italy. He allegedly amassed a number of confidential state documents, which were used to blackmail and cajole reluctant participants in his own and P2's causes. Among those influenced was Roberto Calvi, with Gelli protecting Banco Ambrosiano from the early investigations by the Bank of Italy that would have exposed its problems far sooner than they ultimately came to light. On 17 March 1981, a police raid on Gelli's villa near Arrezzo produced a raft of documents that, among other things, helped expose Calvi's fraud, and an arrest order was issued for Gelli on charges of extortion and sedition. Gelli fled the country, probably to South America, only to reappear later in Geneva traveling on a forged Argentine passport.

Gelli's arrest in Geneva triggered an extradition request from Italy. For nine months he was held at the high-security Champ Dollon prison, while receiving various visitors and associates from the old days. Shortly before his extradition was to take place, Gelli escaped by bribing a warden with SFr 20,000.

Accounts of the ease of his escape strain credibility, and it is generally assumed that people in high places – in government, financial institutions, and organized crime – feared nothing more than the possibility of Gelli's testimony in Italy. Such testimony might have answered a number of questions about the Banco Ambrosiano affair and the death of Roberto Calvi. Following Gelli's escape, Calvi's son, Carlo, was quoted as saying: 'It goes a long way towards backing my belief that the people who were capable of freeing Gelli were certainly capable of murdering my father.'[36]

There may at last be a chance to discover how valid such suspicions were. After four years of living as a fugitive, reportedly mostly in Latin America, Gelli gave himself up to the Swiss authorities in Geneva on 22 September 1987. He was accompanied by his son and four lawyers, who claimed that he was in need of medical treatment for a heart condition. As yet it is only possible to speculate as to the reasons for his surrender.

Several suggestions have been put forward. Some think that he had indeed decided to settle a few political scores by returning for trial in Italy. However by giving himself up in Switzerland he in effect delayed his eventual extradition to Italy, since he now faced Swiss charges of bribery in relation to his prison escape and these will have to be heard before he can leave the country. Meantime, he could only be extradited to face trial in Italy on the charges set out in the original extradition request, i.e. for fraud, defamation and bankruptcy. Since that time, however, far more serious charges have arisen against him in Italy including involvement in the 1980 bomb attack on Bologna railway station in which 35 people died. A new request would have to be made to address specifically these new charges.[37]

While still unable to get their hands on Gelli himself, the Italian authorities were assiduously pursuing the money held by him in Swiss banks. This amounted to some SFr120 million ($68 million). Asked why he had not returned directly to Italy, Gelli replied, 'People are assassinated in Italian prisons.'[38]

Three months after his reappearance, Gelli received a three-month suspended sentence from the Swiss for his bribery of the Champ-Dollon prison guard. By suspending the term, the judges made possible his extradition to Italy, and this in fact occurred in mid-February 1988. Due to the terms of extradition, however, he only faced trial for the crimes specifically cited in the order, namely fraudulent bankruptcy, fraud, swindling and false denunciation.[39]

The Banco Ambrosiano fallout continued to spread, with a loss of perhaps $300 million facing the government of Peru. That country's Banco de la Nación had acted as middleman on some $235 million in transfers to the Banco Ambrosiano affiliate in Lima, and the collapse brought suits by foreign banks against Banco de la Nación. The suits made it difficult for the bank to operate abroad, increasing Peru's already serious international financial problems.

One of the leading characters in the Banco Ambrosiano affair, Francesco Pazienza, was arrested by customs authorities in New York in March 1985 and held for extradition to Italy. Pazienza had been sought since 1982 to face charges of fraud and misappropriation of funds in connection with setting up dummy companies for Banco Ambrosiano and the $1.3 billion still unaccounted for in the case. He was also sought in connection with his presence in London a few days before the death of Roberto Calvi, who had hired him to help pull Ambrosiano out of the mess in which it found itself and to keep the Italian authorities at bay. Pazienza was apparently well-connected in Italy, including high-level links to the intelligence service and the Mafia.[40]

Another of the important figures involved, Michele Sindona, met a mysterious end. Having served four years of a 25-year prison sentence in the United States for fraud, he was extradited to Italy in September 1984. In March 1985 he was convicted of fraud, and in March 1986 of contracting for the murder of Giorgio Ambrosoli (who had been appointed by the Bank of Italy to liquidate Sindona's Banca Privata Italiana). Four days later Sindona was dead from cyanide poisoning. Whether suicide or murder was involved will remain a mystery, but Italian politicians and journalists were unanimous in their opinion that Sindona held just too much embarrassing information.[41]

Notes

1 Alan Cane, 'Shearson Staff Vigilance Thwarted Fraud Attempt', *Financial Times*, 23 September 1988.
2 Clive Wolman, 'The Crime That Can Span a Host of Countries', *Financial Times*, 14 April 1986.
3 David Henry, 'America's Hottest Export – Funny Money Stocks', *Forbes*, 23 September 1985.
4 Frederick M. Muir, 'Can Investors Get Any of $150 Million Back from J. David & Co.?', *Wall Street Journal*, 21 March 1984.
5 Arnold H. Lubasch, 'Promoter is Guilty in $445 Million Tax Fraud', *New York Times*, 26 April 1985. See also 'House of Cards', *Wall Street Journal*, 29 October 1984.
6 'Colombia Battling Chase Over Missing Money', *New York Times*, 15 November 1983. See also 'The Chase is on for a Telex from Bogota', *The Economist*, 13 April 1985.
7 Stanley Penn, 'Deadly Policies', *Wall Street Journal*, 4 January 1988.
8 Ibid.
9 Ibid.
10 Richard Morais, 'He Gave Off That Kind Of Aura', *Forbes*, 8 February 1988.
11 Anthony M. DeStefano, Daniel Hertzberg and Gary Putka, 'False Glitter', *Wall Street Journal*, 20 August 1985.
12 'Bankers in the Dock', *The Economist*, 19 July 1986.
13 Allan Dodds Frank, 'You Can't Keep a Smart Crook Down', *Forbes*, 29 December 1986.
14 George Volsky, 'Millions Swindled from US Doctors', *International Herald Tribune*, 6 September 1988.
15 David Wessel, 'US Accuses 5 of Using Bank to Defraud Holders of Pesos', *International Herald Tribune*, 5 March 1986.
16 Judith Cummings, 'DeLorean's Auditors Under Fire', *International Herald Tribune*, 27 March 1986.
17 Carol J. Loomis, 'Limited War on White Collar Crime', *Fortune*, 22 July 1985.
18 Jesse Wong, 'Hong Kong Kiting Probe Looks at Citibank', *Wall Street Journal*, 13 May 1986.
19 Alan Friedman, 'Milan Bank Executives Charged Over 10 Million Secret Fund', *Financial Times*, 15 May 1988.

20 Stanley Penn, 'Blemished Picture', *Wall Street Journal*, 26 May 1988. See also Carol Vogel, 'Financier's Absence Deepens $130 Million Mystery', *New York Times*, 27 May 1988.
21 John Templeton and Frank Comes, 'Euroscam: A Stock Scandal Mushrooms', *Business Week*, 22 August 1988. See also William Dullforce, 'Charges in $150 Million Fraud Case', *Financial Times*, 4 August 1988; Ferdinand Protzman, 'Too Good to Be True: A 20 Nation Scam', *International Herald Tribune*, 20 August 1988; Thomas Kamm, 'Shell Game', *Wall Street Journal*, 2 September 1988; Steven Greenhouse, 'Swiss Ask SEC for Help in Stock Inquiry', *New York Times*, 18 August 1988.
22 Frederic A. Miller, Richard Kessler and Jefferson Ryser, 'Closely Watched Banks: One That Got Away', *Business Week*, 19 October 1987.
23 Bill Hewitt and David Fouquet, 'A Diamond in the Rough', *Newsweek*, 24 February 1986.
24 Peter Maass, 'Buyers Are Returning to Antwerp', *New York Times*, 10 July 1986.
25 Thomas Kamm, 'Lost Luster', *Wall Street Journal*, 10 July 1987.
26 Nathaniel C. Nash, 'E. F. Hutton Guilty in Bank Fraud; Penalties Could Top $10 Million', *New York Times*, 3 May 1985. See also James Sterngold, 'Hutton Moves Resulted in Interest Free Loans', *New York Times*, 3 May 1985 and Andy Pasztor, 'Only About 50 Banks Seek Restitution From E F Hutton for Illegal Overdrafts', *Wall Street Journal*, 3 June 1987.
27 'Humbled Hutton', *Time*, 12 February 1987.
28 Philip Elmer-DeWitt, 'ZZZZ Best May Be ZZZZ Worst', *Time*, 20 July 1987.
29 Daniel Akst, 'Fallen Star', *Wall Street Journal*, 10 July 1987.
30 For a detailed discussion, see Rupert Cornwell, *God's Bankers* (London: Victor Gollancz, 1983).
31 'Still Cash in Calvi's Cache', *Euromoney*, February 1986.
32 Laura Colby, 'Vatican Bank Played A Central Role in Fall of Banco Ambrosiano', *Wall Street Journal*, 27 April 1987. See also Alan Friedman, 'Ambrosiano Settlement Signed by Bankers', *Financial Times*, 26 May 1984.
33 John Tagliabue, 'Vatican Prelate Said to Face Arrest in Milan Bank Collapse', *New York Times*, 26 February 1987.
34 'Court Blocks Arrest of Vatican Banker', *Chicago Tribune*, 18 July 1987.
35 'Court Forbids Prosecution of 3 Vatican Aides', *International Herald Tribune*, 9 June 1988.
36 As quoted in *The Sunday Times*, 14 April 1983, p. 11.
37 Thomas W. Netter, 'Italian Wanted in Bank Collapse and Bombing Gives Up in Geneva', *New York Times*, 22 September 1987.
38 William Dullforce, 'Swiss Court Sentences Gelli for Bribery', *Financial Times*, 23 December 1987.
39 'Switzerland Hands Over Gelli to Italy', *International Herald Tribune*, 18 February 1988.
40 E. J. Dionne, 'New Hope for Clues in Italian Scandals', *New York Times*, 25 March 1985.
41 E. J. Dionne, Jr., 'Sindona Dies of Poisoning; Dose's Origin Unknown', *International Herald Tribune*, 24 March 1986.

6

Demand for Secret Money: Money laundering and undercover activities

Money laundering

Within the overall structure of demand for international financial secrecy, the laundering of money has probably experienced the most rapid growth. Laundered funds are, by definition, ill-gotten gains. And there are a lot of them. The President's Commission on Organized Crime concluded in March 1986 that organized crime is cheating the United States of more than $18 billion a year in taxes and costing more than 400,000 jobs. The Commission found, for example, that at least four outlaw motorcycle gangs had evolved into fully organized crime groups with chapters reaching into Europe and Australia. Self-perpetuating gangs had also established themselves in US prisons, and ethnic criminal societies abound. Wharton Econometric Forecasting Associates Inc. estimated that 1986 net income from organized crime activities was about $46.6 billion and that gross receipts amounted to $65.7 billion.[1]

The need to use money laundries has been necessary for US crooks at least since 1931, when the Internal Revenue Service put Al Capone behind bars for tax evasion. Whereas direct evidence of criminal activity may be very difficult to enter in a court of law, tax evasion cases may be comparatively easier to prosecute. For this reason, money laundries have become big business, involving bank employees, executives, lawyers, accountants and other professionals at all levels. According to one US attorney, government agents running an undercover drug operation '. . . are getting solicited with all kinds of offers from business and professional people willing to provide them with false documents to give them an apparently legitimate source of income or to avoid taxes.'[2]

The essence of laundering is not simply to hide the proceeds of illegal activities, but also to render them re-usable for legitimate purposes. The

150

use of shell companies with money deposited in overseas banks and recycled into the system through speculative currency or commodity option transactions is one of many methods employed.

In the 1985 Hearings on the Current Problem of Money Laundering before the Subcommittee on Crime, one witness explained that laundering was now

> an extremely lucrative criminal enterprise in its own right. Treasury's investigations uncovered members of an emerging criminal class – professional money launderers who aid and abet other criminals through financial activities. These individuals hardly fit the stereotype of an underworld criminal. They are accountants, attorneys, money brokers, and members of other legitimate professions. They need not become involved with the underlying criminal activity except to conceal and transfer the proceeds that result from it. They are drawn to their illicit activity for the same reason that drug trafficking attracts new criminals to replace those who are convicted and imprisoned – greed. Money laundering, for them, is an easy route to almost limitless wealth.[3]

Secret money and the drug trade

Traditionally associated with organized crime involved in the rackets, protection, prostitution, extortion, illegal gambling, and so on, the real growth in laundering in recent years has come from drug trafficking.

1988 estimates suggest that annual gross revenues generated by all narcotics sales in the US were somewhere between $60 and $120 billion. Of that amount, some $20 billion was believed to be transferred abroad to pay expenses. Of the remaining $40–100 billion, around half was believed to be transferred out of the US for investment elsewhere, with the other half remaining in the country for investment in a range of legitimate instruments and businesses.[4] In 1987, US courts seized cash and assets worth over $500 million belonging to drug traffickers.[5]

Other statistics indicate that the flow of cocaine, for example, has essentially doubled during 1981–7. The Drug Enforcement Administration maintained that in 1981 somewhere between 33 and 60 metric tons of the drug entered the country, and rose to around 80 tons in 1987, some 80 per cent of that passing through Colombia. The price faced by about 5 million cocaine addicts and many more casual users during this period fell commensurately, from $40,000 per kilo in 1981 to $15,000 in 1987, and according to some estimates as low as $8–10,000 in Miami.[6]

The drug trade today could well be described as a multinational commodity business with a fast-moving top management, a widespread distribution network and relatively price-insensitive customers. Its global sales could be as high as $500 billion a year. In the United States, there are some 20 million marijuana smokers, almost 6 million cocaine users and half a million heroin addicts.

The volume of international currency movements arising out of drug trafficking appears to be enormous. A recent estimate for the United States puts the figure at $70 billion, which would place it in the top rank among US imports of goods and services. Other surveys provide figures just as staggering. In 1986 the Congressional Select Committee on Narcotics Abuse & Control estimated that the US retail market for illegal drugs was in the area of $120 billion. The US Drug Enforcement Administration produced a smaller figure of between $50 and $80 billion – still very significant. Reports suggest that the US market involves some 500,000 heroin addicts, nearly 6 million cocaine users and literally millions of marijuana smokers.[7] Drug profits for 1985 have been put as high as $25 billion, or more than the net earnings of the United States' eight biggest corporations.[8] Colombia's gross exports of narcotics (mainly marijuana and cocaine) have been estimated at $30 billion, helping that country's bilateral trade surplus with the United States to rise from $500 million in 1974 to over $3 billion in 1983.

With this sort of money involved, small wonder that laundering is big business. According to the head of smuggling investigations at the US Customs Service, 'We see narcotics organizations now being set up like major corporations, with an operational arm to move the drugs and a financial arm to handle the money.'[9] The two arms tend to be kept quite separate with quite 'different' people working in each. This was emphasized by 'Mario', another witness giving testimony during the Hearings:

> I am a Colombian national ... I'm what they consider college-educated, as most of the money launderers are – different from the drug dealers, which are two identities completely apart. The drug dealers of Colombia, and I think from every part of the world, tend to have a low education, while the money launderers in general are well educated, well dressed, mainly in order to fit into the business world here in the States.[10]

Colombia

The plight of Colombia is clearly illustrative of just how complicated and difficult the underlying drug problem is. Colombia's economy is not as dependent as that of certain of its neighbors, especially Bolivia, on the drug trade. Indeed, in some ways the country might almost be considered a Latin American economic success story. GDP has grown every year throughout the 1980s; in 1987, despite a 40 per cent fall in the world price for coffee, the country's most important legal export, economic growth was still 5.6 per cent in real terms, although inflation was running at 24 per cent. Urban unemployment in 1987 was down to 10 per cent. Payments on both principal and interest on a foreign debt of $15.7 billion were on schedule, and net reserves stood at $3.4 billion. Private sector investment for 1987 was up by 10 per cent.

Much of this sterling performance was due to conservative financial management including restrained public spending and a strong private sector – only 13 per cent of GDP is in state hands – as well as the traditional strength of Colombian agriculture, which provides 23 per cent of GDP and fresh cut flowers as well as coffee generating important foreign revenue.

But these figures do not tell the whole story, and the contribution of the drug trade to economic performance cannot be ignored. In the late 1970s, cocaine replaced marijuana as Colombia's principal illegal export. The country is thought to have no more than 25,000 hectares planted in coca, as compared with Bolivia's 50,000 or Peru's 100,000. Its dominance lies not as a grower but as a processor and trafficker. Estimates suggest that upwards of 200 tons of processed cocaine leave Colombia annually. There is significant uncertainty as to what value in 'narco-dollars' this actually represents to the country. The early 1980s' figures of $6–9 billion a year are thought to be a reasonable average for drug exports, helping that country's bilateral trade surplus with the United States to rise from $500 million in 1974 to over $3 billion in 1983. But in the late 1980s, with lower drug prices, estimates have fallen to around the $4 billion mark. [11]

Much of the profit, of course, remains abroad, and of that which is repatriated, only $900 million to $1.5 billion is believed to find its way back into the central bank. That nevertheless is a sizeable contribution to foreign exchange earnings, and it has its effect, not least in terms of boosting private sector confidence by making foreign exchange easily and cheaply available. [12]

The most powerful and wealthy cocaine lords in the world are considered to be the members of the 'Medellin Cartel', named after Colombia's industrial center, a city of 1.5 million in the Andes. One of their number, Carlos Lehder, was sentenced in 1988 by a Florida court to life imprisonment with no prospects for parole for his activities as the 'king of cocaine transport'. But other leading members remain free. There is Pablo Escobar, who reputedly started life as a car thief. Gonzalo Rodriguez Gacha, originally Escobar's associate and now a senior member in his own right, handles routes to the Los Angeles area. The Ochoa family controls the distribution network out of Miami – father Fabio, known as a smuggler of Scotch whisky and television sets, is believed to have pioneered the business in the mid-70s at the instigation of Escobar, but has since passed the work on to his sons. [13]

It was thought by some that Lehder's conviction might seriously damage the Medellin cartel, but drug specialists suggested that this is unlikely. The group is not a unified force with political objectives – as has been suggested – but a loose-knit coalition of criminal groups working together on drug ventures as it suits and offering mutual assistance against common enemies. It appears that the drug barons first banded seriously together in November 1981, when Ochoa's daughter Marta was kidnapped by leftist guerrillas demanding a $1 million ransom to finance their revolution. The Ochoas called a meeting of the leading 223 cocaine traders in Medellin, all of whom realized that they too were vulnerable to such attacks due to their immense wealth. They formed an organization, 'Death to Kidnappers', and set about putting the name into practice. By February 1981, Ochoa's daughter had been released and the drug barons realized that co-operation could also mean improved profits and safety in their drug dealings.

Despite its loose-knit structure, the cartel is a very effective operation. By 1984 the annual income for the Medellin groups was estimated to be $1.5 billion. Together with the smaller cartel in Cali, a city to the south, they are reputed to account for the production and shipment of some 60–70 per cent of Colombia's cocaine. There is a certain level of organization, with different divisions attending to specific duties. The financial division, for example, is responsible for collecting revenues, making investments and of course laundering proceeds. An 'enforcement' division takes charge of bribes, guards, and hit men. But the group does not appear to mastermind every move of its members.

The traffickers protect themselves in several ways. A system of subcontractors is used throughout from the buying of coca paste in Peru and Bolivia to the distribution of the cocaine on the streets of North America. Each contractor takes liability for his share of the process from the time he gets involved. The police have tapes, for example of Escobar informing buyers that once the plane takes off from Colombia, the cocaine is their responsibility. Each shipment tends to contain cocaine from various cartel members so that none is wiped out if a load is seized.

The influence of the drug barons in Colombia is immense. They have the means and the will to use either violence or corruption to achieve their ends – or to put it their way 'plomo o plata' (lead or silver). Throughout the 1980s they assassinated scores of opponents, including the country's attorney general, 57 judges and 2 cabinet officers. They have established alliances with at least two of Colombia's guerrilla armies, have used their wealth to 'befriend' contacts on both sides of the Nicaraguan civil war, and have relationships with military, political and criminal leaders in Panama, Honduras, Belize, Mexico and the Bahamas. Escobar even had himself elected to the Colombian Congress in 1982 as an alternate member. As a 'politician' he has been mainly concerned with lobbies against extradition laws for suspected criminals to the US.

On the economic front, their influence is perhaps equally significant. Cocaine is estimated to be Colombia's major export – some $4 billion a year at wholesale prices. Without drug profits to help Medellin's economy it is thought that unemployment would almost double to around 25 per cent. To put it in context, according to one Colombian politician, 'just imagine if the US had a Mafia richer than the Federal budget.'[14]

The Medellin cartel is both ruthless and versatile. In 1982, the members agreed to build a huge cocaine-processing complex in the jungle. Known as Tranquilandia (quiet village) it contained 19 labs, had 3 airstrips, was spread over a 35 mile radius, and produced more than 7,000 pounds of the drugs each month. In March 1984, Colombian police raided the plant, destroying it and nearly 14 tons of cocaine. The response? Within two months the country's justice minister was murdered and arrangements had been made for processing to continue elsewhere.

When the US Coast Guard cracked down on air shipments from the Bahamas in 1979, the drug runners showed themselves to be just as flexible. They dropped cocaine into international waters to be picked up by speedboats. The US wholesalers took the risk related to seawater seepage. As the expensive powdered cocaine peaked as a 'luxury' drug for the well-to-do, new and cheaper cocaine in the form of 'crack' was introduced and, at $5–15 a dose, it spread the drug to the streets. In Latin America, fresh demand was created among youth by packaging crude cocaine with marijuana or tobacco in a highly addictive cigarette called 'bazuco'.

The only level on which the Colombian drug barons seem seriously vulnerable is on the handling and laundering of their financial gains. While the Panama banking system was still functioning well, that country was a primary haven. Government officials apparently made sure that their planes of bills were met at Torrijos International Airport and the money escorted by military guard to banks. The 1987 and 1988 disturbances created a brief crisis, but new homes for the cash can still be found. Paraguay, for example, appears to be playing an increasingly important role, aided by lax government controls.

Participants in swap transactions of developing-country debt have been concerned that some of the schemes which allow foreign companies to exchange hard-currency sovereign debt for domestic equity in those countries are an invitation to abuse by money launderers. This is especially so because the traders have neither the incentive nor the obligation to investigate thoroughly offers to purchase discounted developing country debt. The fact that Colombia's leading drug baron reportedly offered to repay a major part of that country's foreign debt in return for immunity from extradition to the United States suggests that their concerns are well founded.[15]

Against such a background, it is easy to see why Colombia's battle against the drug trade may appear less than whole-hearted. But it is trying. The authorities say they have, with US help, intercepted $1.5 billion in drugs, chemical stocks and arms. It has been suggested that up to 30 per cent of cocaine is intercepted at some point. The government has boosted public spending in poor rural areas, and has provided subsidies for other crops to persuade peasants to abandon growing coca. Following the brutal murder in early 1988 of the attorney general, it announced all-out war on the drug barons.

But where the choice offered to politicians, judges and policemen fighting the drug cartel is often between riches and violent death the struggle is all uphill. When corruption fails, fear may do the job.

Asia

The heroin trade in Asia originates mainly in the southeast, in the Golden Triangle, a remote mountainous area where the borders of Burma, Thailand and Laos converge. Burma alone is believed to have exported 65 metric tons of heroin in 1987. The business is unlike the Latin American trade in that no cartels dominate it. Instead, a number of warlord adventurers each have a stake. The most powerful is reputed to be Khun Sa, who claims that he is a revolutionary, not a trafficker. He reportedly has 5,000 men under arms plus a 10,000 man support group, and has, on a number of occasions, offered to phase out his drug trading in exchange for economic aid of $300 million annually for eight years.

Heroin is a lucrative business. A batch of opium costing $170 in northern Burma yields $2 million or more in American and European cities after relatively cheap processing and dilution.

The normal route is by horse and donkey caravan from Burma to refineries along the border with Thailand or in Laos. From here the processed product mostly crosses into Thailand, and continues either concealed in legitimate exports, such as furniture or textiles, or with couriers, known as mules, traveling by commercial aircraft. They often proceed to the US via Japan or Taiwan, since passengers from these countries tend to raise less suspicion with Customs.

Thailand is officially attempting to stop its significant involvement, but lacks the resources and the will. Corruption has taken its toll – payoffs are apparently so rewarding along the country's drug routes that crooked policemen bribe their superiors to assign them there. In addition, Thai law makes the job almost impossible for honest officials by stating that only those caught red-handed with drugs can be prosecuted, thereby insulating the kingpins of the trade. Even if the Thai route could be effectively closed and the Golden Triangle crops eradicated, plenty of opium remains to fill the gap in Iran and Afghanistan.

The Asian dealers have an easier time than their Latin American counterparts as far as money laundering is concerned. Much of it passes through Hong Kong, which imposes no restrictions on currency movement and where bank secrecy is very effective. The other major conduit involves a maze of financial transactions among ethnic Chinese, whose extended families run gold shops, trading firms and foreign exchange dealerships throughout Southeast Asia. The cash is hard to trace since it rarely moves – a dealer can deposit money in a Hong Kong gold shop, for example, and collect a voucher enabling him to pick up the sum in Bangkok. The Chinese community is also increasingly involved directly in drug trafficking.[16]

Problems of concealment

Broadly speaking, then, laundering is all about concealing the illicit origins of criminal money in order that it may re-enter the 'mainstream' of funds and be made available for re-use.

To understand the problem that this causes drugs dealers, for example, one must consider the nature of their ill-gotten gains. Drugs are sold for payment in the form of 'street money', millions of small-denomination bills resulting from a multitude of street sales. Currency in small bills is, of course, far bulkier and heavier than money in large bills. For instance $1 million in $20 bills weighs 110 pounds, in $100 bills just 22 pounds.[17] So the criminal is faced with an initial, very practical problem – how to shift the enormous sums he has made without causing suspicion. One of the first objectives of any operation laundering drugs earnings is therefore 'to reduce the volume and weight of illicit narcotics profits for easier manipulation or transportation out of the United States.'[18] This task is made considerably more complicated by the Bank Secrecy Act reporting requirements – these are discussed in some depth in Chapter 8.

The general stipulation is that any cash transaction of over $10,000 must be reported to the authorities. These needs and constraints have given rise to the 'smurf', a courier who spends his or her time visiting banks throughout the United States, engaging in transactions small enough to avoid the reporting requirement, the aim of which is to reduce the money into manageable and negotiable form. This involves the purchase of cashier's checks that do not name the payee. These may then be exchanged a number of times in Latin America, Europe or the United States itself to cover a variety of drugs-related or weapons-related transactions, for example. Or they may be transported overseas for cashing or deposit in a secrecy haven, often in the past via Panama.[19] The funds tied up in the cashier's checks, of course, earn no interest for the holder and represent 'float' to the issuing bank, which, in addition, may charge a fee of 1–3 per cent for the service. In a 1983 Senate staff study, 24 Florida banks had over 3 per cent of their deposits outstanding

157

in cashier's checks, generally regarded as a sure sign of money laundering.

For the most part, smurfs have tended to be young, presentably dressed Latins, who will not be out of place in a bank anywhere in the United States.[20] Because tellers have become more suspicious of transactions just under the $10,000 reporting limit, the size of the launderers' deposits has declined steadily, to $7,000 or even $5,000. The smurfs have proved to be remarkably prolific: 'On a good day, working in teams, they can do 30, even 40 transactions at $5,000 to $7,000 a shot,' commented an FBI agent.[21] Most smurfs operate in cities where banks have short lines at teller's windows. Hence, New York City is out because it would take too much time to buy the cashier's checks. Money laundering evidently remains hottest in Jacksonville, San Francisco, El Paso, Los Angeles, Nashville, Philadelphia and San Antonio.[22]

Money laundering is a complex and diverse business. There is no one method for 'washing the cash', and no single destination once it is clean. Apart from the smurfing, for example, there are other ways in which small bills can be amalgamated into more manageable instruments. A popular trick has been to take cash to a gambling casino, exchange it for chips, gamble for a while and then turn in the chips for large bills. In one casino in Atlantic City, one launderer brought in $1,187,450 in small bills, the volume of which was 5.75 cubic feet and weighed 280 pounds. After losing around $300,000 he withdrew $800,000 in $100 bills. The new volume was a mere 0.33 cubic foot and weighed 16 pounds.[23]

The routes the more 'manageable' partially laundered cash will follow, and the requirements for it, differ substantially as well. In some cases the criminal will want the money to remain in dollars for use within the United States, in others he may want it stashed away in an offshore haven, in yet others he may want a proportion in the local currency of the country in which he operates. According to one of the statements submitted to the Congressional hearings:

> These launderers carry on a number of activities at one time. They arrange for the deposit of illicit cash into domestic financial institutions; arrange for the transportation or delivery of currency into or out of the U.S.; they may buy U.S. dollars in exchange for Colombian pesos; buy pesos in exchange for dollars; buy and sell both Colombian banking instruments as well as U.S. cashier's checks, personal checks or corporate checks; manipulate U.S. domestic narcotics profits from one U.S. bank account to another; arrange for disguised wire transfers of funds from the U.S. to relatively secure havens such as Panama, the Cayman Islands and Switzerland; set up sham foreign corporations ... sometimes all these things are happening at the same time.[24]

The only important thing is that the money is made suitable to feed back into the system in 'legitimate' ways. And the indications are that, despite the efforts of the authorities and a certain amount of success on their part, vast quantities of cash are indeed slipping back into the mainstream. It is illuminating, for example, that during 1985 net purchases of US equities by Latin American and Caribbean investors jumped 250 per cent over the previous year's level to $1.7 billion, while investments in US Treasury bonds and notes tripled to $4.3 billion. Not all is obviously drugs-related, but it strains credulity to suggest that drugs money is not at least a significant factor.

The problem is of course not only focused in the United States. It is worldwide. While Latin and North American cocaine and marijuana traffickers tend to prefer Panama and the Caribbean havens, Asian heroin dealers have financing networks operating through international banks in Pakistan, Hong Kong, Bahrain and Dubai. But the purpose is always the same.

Some of the methods used by the launderers can be especially ingenious. For example, in Puerto Rico it was discovered that lottery tickets were being used to dodge government efforts to track the flow of drug money. Some winners were willing to sell their ticket on the black market for a premium, which drug smugglers were happy to pay because they were thus provided with a legitimate source for at least part of their income.[25]

The 'casas de cambio' (foreign exchange houses) which sprang up along the United States–Mexico border in 1982 provide another way for laundering ill-gotten gains. The casas were born of the 1982 Mexican financial crisis when Mexican banks were nationalized, dollar deposits frozen and the peso devalued. Pesos poured into the US casas to be exchanged for dollars, it was reported. US customs authorities estimate that for the $1 billion reported as flowing through the exchange center of San Ysidro each year, a further $1 billion slips through secretly. Initially the United States allowed the border exchange houses to operate virtually free of regulation, but with the apparent narcotics connection, both federal and state authorities tightened their surveillance.[26]

In another case, during July 1987 President Alan García of Peru announced proposals to close the country's parallel-market exchange houses and henceforth allow only the banks to deal in dollars. His reason was that they were 'contributing to capital flight and fuelling inflation because they were being used by drug traffickers to launder or disguise proceeds of drug sales.'[27]

In 1986, a report from Colombia's Comptroller General's Office, the independent department that audits government finances, stated that funds 'of dubious origin' helped raise by 58.5 per cent the volume of US dollars entering the central bank in 1985. Figure 6.1 gives an indication of the numbers involved. Again, not all the funds necessarily relate to

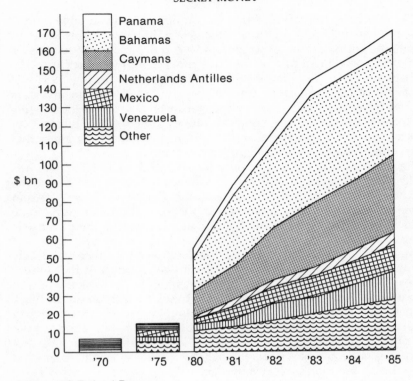

Source: US Federal Reserve

Figure 6.1   *US bank liabilities to Latin America and the Caribbean, 1970, 1975, 1980–5*

the drug trade – earnings, for example, from coffee exports in violation of export quotas must also be included. But the figures nevertheless arouse suspicion. No questions are asked at the foreign exchange window (known as 'la ventanilla siniestra' – the [sinister] window) at the Banco de la Republica in Bogata and there is no limit to the amount that can be exchanged. In 1985 the quantity of dollars changed by individuals purporting to be tourists rose by 147 per cent from 1984 levels, and yet the number of tourists visiting the country was only 12 per cent higher than the year before.[28]

Another method of money laundering that appears to be popular with Colombian drug barons is the use of fraudulent commercial invoices. Drug money in the United States will be used to purchase a letter of credit for ostensible importation from Colombia, for instance of coffee. False invoices are prepared for this supposedly legitimate commercial transaction. Then all that is needed is to present the invoices at the bank in Colombia and the letter of credit will assure payment. In other cases, genuine purchases are made: 'We saw [in South Florida] . . . checks that, say, were the result of a money laundering activity [being] used to purchase Remington typewriters in a large volume, which only meant one thing: that it was for export, and it was going to be sold, for instance, in San Andreas Island in Colombia.'[29]

Some even more unusual ways of moving the money around have come to light. In May 1985 it was reported that customs agents at Miami airport had found nearly $30 million of drugs money hidden in all sorts of ways – in baggage, televisions, cans of deodorant, even tennis balls.[30] One customs agent had one or two other unusual examples to add to Congressional hearings on the subject:

Put the teddy bear up there. This one is my favorite seizure of all time. We were going to start giving awards for most clever mode of transportation. This was in some people's luggage . . . the teddy bear had $150,000 in there. It was mostly twenties . . . Michael, put up the candy wrappers. This came in number two for our awards. It was only $57,000 rolled up in candy but it shows you the extent to which these people are now going.[31]

The size of the cash hauls can be staggering:

Federal agents stopped a Learjet as it taxied for takeoff from Fort Lauderdale (Florida), bound for Panama. They confiscated nearly $5.5 million in cash. A subsequent search of the home of one of the passengers yielded 62 pounds of cocaine valued at $18.5 million, 15 weapons, including a submachine gun, and $40,000 in counterfeit bills.[32]

Take the case of Eduardo Orozco Prada, who deposited over $150 million in cash with about 18 banks and foreign exchange firms, mostly in New York, for transfers to Panama, the Cayman Islands, the Bahamas, and in various accounts distributed around the United States. Most of the money apparently was from drug trafficking. The laundry operation also involved Orozco's interests in small business in a variety of countries in Europe, the Middle East and Latin America, as well as major currency exchange businesses in Colombia and several other countries in the region. Described as a '. . . well educated, sophisticated, highly intelligent professional, with all the trappings of a legitimate businessman',[33] Orozco enjoyed the support of many legitimate business people and senior-level Colombian politicians.

Once established in New York, Orozco set up a company called Cirex International at 120 Wall Street, which in retrospect was clearly a money laundering operation. Over a four-month period, he placed $2.3 million in cash deposits with a Swiss bank until it refused to take any more, and subsequently with the Marine Midland Bank & Trust Company and the Irving Trust Company, both in New York. The cash evidently came from his own exchange houses in Colombia, either via Miami or via Panama using couriers and occasionally planes of the Colombian Air Force – on average about $3 million monthly. Cash transport was difficult and risky, but necessary to avoid FBI surveillance of South Florida banks and to avoid the cash-deposit fees charged by some of them. The deposits were then transferred after varying periods of time to accounts in other banks by wire, and were thus effectively laundered.

Apparently the laundering operations were highly sensitive to the investigative activities of the federal authorities. In 1980 and 1982, Orozco was doing substantial business with the currency exchange house of Deak-Perera in the name of Interdual, a Panamanian affiliate, and Dial Securities. Unlike other laundry operations that find ways to avoid filing currency transactions reports, Orozco's transactions were always in compliance with the law, yet difficult or impossible to trace because he used other people's names and never made a cash deposit himself. Intermediaries were evidently paid 25 cents per $100 cash deposit, with possible further payments to bankers to see that funds were transferred without delay. By mid-1981 his deposits at Deak-Perera were running at $10–12 million a month and were beginning to attract an unusual amount of attention.

In his search for yet another bank, Orozco fell into a Drug Enforcement Agency trap. Subsequent fund movements through third parties were tracked – mostly deposits of $10 and $20 bills, totaling $15 million over an 18-month time span. Tape-recorded conversations confirmed that most of it was drugs-related money, with a 3 per cent laundry commission probably earned by Orozco and possibly large additional gains from acting as a principal in the drugs trade itself – yet he never physically came into contact with the drugs. In 1983 Orozco was found guilty of drug law violation and sentenced to one year in prison and a $1 million fine; he was immediately released on $2 million bail pending appeal.[34]

Money laundering also played an important part in the 1984 'pizza connection' case, a multimillion-dollar Sicilian-run heroin operation that used pizza parlors as fronts in various parts of the United States well outside the established crime centers, and employed orders for various pizza ingredients as codes for narcotics trafficking. Funds were mainly transferred through Swiss accounts, and law enforcement officials became suspicious when one of the central figures was moving far more money than was justified by his bakery in New York.[35] According to a US attorney:

He was, for a guy in the bakery business, depositing a tremendous amount of cash [representing] a highly sophisticated means of investment and money laundering. Multimillions of dollars were transferred from the United States to Switzerland and Italy for payments of past and future heroin shipments, and for investment in legitimate and illegitimate enterprises there.[36]

An additional point of interest in the case is the illustration it provides of how costly laundering can be to the criminals involved. Some $13.45 million of the funds were passed through the brokerage firm of E. F. Hutton (see Chapter 8). Hutton accepted numerous deposits of small bills which were then used for commodity trading. Of this some $10.5 million was apparently lost in precious metals trades. In other words, the drugs barons ended up gambling away $10.5 million in order to legitimize less than $3 million, which amounted to a laundering fee of 75 per cent.[37]

Over a period of eight years a Cuban-born American citizen, Ramon Milan-Rodriguez, allegedly converted more than $1 billion in illicit drugs profits into seemingly legitimate investments for his clients. They included everything from Learjets to apartment complexes. His case is considered to be the biggest one-man international money-laundering scheme in American history. Normally, cash was flown to Panama for deposit in anonymous accounts, and then fed back into the system through offshore companies in havens such as the Netherlands Antilles. In one particular investment proposal discovered in Milan-Rodriguez's files, the money passed through Panama, the Antilles and Liechtenstein before returning to the United States for investment in 'minority-owned' businesses in Miami designed to help the investors 'enhance their stature in the community'. And there was the added advantage that the businesses would have 4–1 leverage from US minority business development loans, through the Small Business Administration.[38]

Ramon-Milan Rodriguez's money laundering schemes landed him with a 43-year prison term. Testifying before a Senate Foreign Relations Committee panel in early 1988, he explained how he had worked, among others, for the Medellin drug cartel, arranging currency shipments from the US to Panama and in some cases funneling them back to the US through a maze of foreign entities. He evidently managed as much as $11 billion in this way, purchasing real estate, securities, and bank deposits.

At times he was buying certificates of deposit for $100–200 million, using several leading banks including Citibank, Bank of America and First National Bank of Boston. According to Milan-Rodriguez, such banks had 'special representatives for people like me.' The banks in question denied any irregularities. Although banks are required to report large cash transactions, this does not apply where funds are deposited from abroad by wire, as was the case here. As Robert Serino, general counsel for the comptroller of the currency put it, 'If you physically get the money out of the US you can do almost anything you want with it.'[39]

Where there are drug profits to be made, the Mafia is never far away. The Venezuela-based Cuntrera-Caruana family, headed by Sicilian-born Pasquale Cuntrera and Alfonso Caruana and linked by marriage as well as 'business' has been under close investigation by the Canadian and Italian authorities. It is believed to be a leading supplier of heroin to the US market, acting through bases in Britain, Canada, Switzerland, Venezuela and Sicily. Members have allegedly hauled millions of drug dollars across the Canadian border from the US for laundering. At least $35 million is thought to have passed through one branch of Montreal City & District Bank and two other Montreal banks, en route mainly for accounts at Swiss banks such as Crédit Suisse and Union Bank of Switzerland. It is fairly easy to smuggle currency from the US to Canada since border controls between the two countries are quite relaxed. There is no requirement in Canada for banks to report large cash deposits.

The Cuntrera-Caruanas would apparently 'test' banks with small cash deposits to see if they were receptive, favoring in particular those where there was an Italian manager. Montreal's City & District Dollard des Ormeaux branch fitted the bill. Its manager, Aldo Tucci, a Sicilian immigrant, accepted a cash deposit of $1.1 million in January 1981 and, when challenged by the bank's head office said the funds came from Venezuelan oil and casino profits. Head office transferred him at that point.

The Cuntrera-Caruanas have built a business empire which includes interests in tourism, real estate and agriculture. They are thought to have connections with both of Venezuela's main political parties. There have been setbacks, however. In 1985, British and Canadian police seized a $300 million shipment of Thai heroin packed into hollowed-out tops of teak tables, shipped through London to Montreal on its way to New York. Gerlando Caruana, Alfonso's brother, is serving 20 years in a Canadian prison for his part in that affair. In 1987, Canadian police seized a large consignment of hashish in Newfoundland, arresting at the same time Vito Rizzuto, the son of one of the family's leading associates. In February of 1988 his father was arrested in Venezuela on charges of conspiring to ship cocaine. And the Italian authorities were seeking to extradite Pasquale Cuntrera himself on charges of drug trafficking and membership of the Mafia. Venezuela's constitution, however, forbids extradition of its citizens for any reason.[40]

There is some optimism that the Mafia is on the run, with US officials contending that since 1980 the Mafia share of the New York City heroin market has shrunk by more than half, to less than 30 per cent. However, the Italian authorities are not so confident. Italians have compared the Mafia to an octopus, not only because of its tentacles but because of its ability to regenerate an injured limb.

Both the Milan-Rodriguez and Cuntrera-Caruana cases indicate just how difficult is the task facing those combating money laundering in a highly international and financially sophisticated world. With wire transfers and other interbank transactions and an unregulated $1 trillion Eurodollar market available to all comers, good and bad money soon mingle. As one Scotland Yard official put it, 'Electronic funds transfer has done for money laundering what the washing machine did for clothes washing.'[41]

Another example of a drug runner attempting to launder his proceeds and win for himself a legitimate lifestyle is the case of Jose Leonardo Contreras Subias, alias Joe Guillen. Contreras, considered one of the top ten traffickers in Mexico and suspected of involvement in the 1985 torture-killing of a US drug agent, jumped bail in 1980 in Los Angeles, where he faced charges relating to cocaine distribution. It is known that he ended up in Atoka, Oklahoma, under an assumed name, posing as a wealthy rancher. Townspeople were somewhat suspicious, given the conflicting accounts 'Guillen' gave of his past, and were even more wary when his 'right hand man', Elbert Johnson, who only a year earlier had been too poor to buy a pair of shoes, put up a 50 per cent cash payment on 2,800 acres of his boss's land.

Contreras concentrated on winning friends and securing a place in the community. He bought land from ranchers facing bankruptcy; he hired 30 ranch hands at $1,000 per month in a county where unemployment was at 15 per cent; he spent over $4,000 a month in local stores for cattle feed; bought trucks and farm equipment from nearby dealers and made generous gifts to the City Manager, not to mention unspecified payments to the County Sheriff. Before too long his cover was established and Guillen 'belonged'.

Things began to unravel in summer 1987. It was discovered that Johnson was growing marijuana. He was convicted and sentenced to 12 years in prison. In the course of the investigation, it was found that his farm and Contreras' ranch shared a mailing address. In April 1988, the FBI arrested Contreras on the 1980 drug charges in Salt Lake City, where he was buying a $500,000 home. It was revealed that he had been laundering drug proceeds by funneling funds from Mexico through US banks for real estate purchases in Oklahoma and Texas. In May 1988, federal authorities seized all of Contreras' Oklahoma properties on the grounds that they had been funded by drug money.

The whole affair seemed chilling to many. As a DEA agent explained, 'For years these guys have taken control of towns and businesses in Mexico. Now they're trying to do it here. Our job is going to be much more difficult if they can manipulate whole economies.'[42]

Money laundering has attracted large numbers of otherwise respectable people who evidently see nothing wrong in being accomplices to crime. Take the case of Richard McConnell, a former trial attorney in the

US Justice Department's Tax Division from 1967 until 1971, and subsequently in private practice in Alexandria, Virginia. On behalf of a client named Julian Penell, McConnell used his firm's escrow accounts to deposit large sums of cash, which were withdrawn after short periods and paid to newly established US corporations or trusts set up in the Cayman Islands. In this way, over $30 million of Penell funds were moved during a seven-year period without filing federal currency reports. These funds, it turned out, came from marijuana and hashish operations in which 20 people, including Penell, were charged and later convicted. McConnell, charged under a racketeering statute, claimed he was 'used', and that the Cayman trusts were intended to help Penell's heirs (his age at the time was 38) avoid estate taxes in the United States. He, too, was convicted, along with another lawyer in the case.[43]

Lawyers appear confident of using their privileged relationships with clients to shield themselves from prosecution in such cases. Bankers can hide behind dense layers of bureaucracy and blame misconduct on lower-level employees. But once the activity becomes large and greed gets the better of caution, defenses may fall by the wayside. Another lawyer, Nathan Markowitz, previously an SEC attorney, paid the officers of a Los Angeles bank to take in large cash deposits without the required federal currency reports, funds that were subsequently wired to Bermuda trust accounts controlled by Liberian companies and re-lent to US corporations established for his clients. The loans, as laundered funds, were used for payment of salaries, pensions and other expenses. In a tape-recorded conversation offered in evidence by the government, Markowitz offered drug-related services directly on imports from South America: 'I can give you buys, if you have to buy it down there . . . I can give the airstrips. I can give you guys that, press it, package it. I can give you the street [dealers] . . . I've done it for those people for years.'[44] Unfortunately for Markowitz, IRS undercover agents were on to him and his career came to an abrupt end. A couple of months after search warrants had been served on his office and those of the bank branches he had used, he inquired about the possibility of cooperation with the government. A week later, on 3 April 1981, his bullet-riddled body, with over $50,000 in cash in his pockets, was found in a Los Angeles parking garage. Even for lawyers, the laundry business can be hazardous to health.[45]

In the United States, money laundering activities have clearly been concentrated in Florida, where forgery, bad checks, credit card fraud and highly questionable banking practices are by-products of clandestine cash flows and a go-go environment that has attracted 'scoundrels' from all over the world. A report of the US Comptroller of the Currency confirmed that Florida can lay undisputed claim to having by far the largest number of bank crimes in the United States. An estimated 75 per cent of narcotics enters the United States through Florida (perhaps as much as $50 billion annually) with net contributions to the Florida economy of over $10 billion a year – all in cash, which is either counted by high-speed machines or simply weighed (300 lbs of $20 bills = $3.6 million). Latin couriers have regularly deposited shopping bags full of small denomination bills in smaller Florida banks, commonly known as 'Coin-O-Washers'. On one occasion, '. . . the teller questioned a shopping bag woman about the source of her money, which reeked of fish. She dropped the bag and ran, leaving $200,000 behind.'[46] Estimated violations of federal currency reporting requirements in Florida ran to the tune of $3.2 billion in 1981 alone. Another revealing statistic comes from the Federal Reserve Board. Of the Fed's 12 districts only 2 – Atlanta and San Francisco – show large dollar surpluses on their books. Federal investigators have suggested that drug proceeds could account for much of that excess. Of the total surplus, some 60 per cent, or $6 billion, was on deposit in the Atlanta Fed's Miami branch alone. Of that sum, approximately $1.3 billion came directly from Panama's Banco Nacional.[47]

Miami was also the scene for the first discovered case in the United States of a drugs smuggler actually acquiring control of a financial institution. In May 1985 Ray L. Corona and his father Rafael L. Corona, the suspended Chairman and Managing Director respectively of Sunshine State Bank, were accused of helping one José Antonio Fernandez, a convicted drug smuggler, and a partner to buy control of the bank. The Coronas arranged for Fernandez to buy the stake through a nominee and later when Fernandez became a federal fugitive, actually bought it from him themselves. There was no charge that the bank had in fact been used to launder money, though it had at one stage provided $250,000 for a deal in marijuana.[48]

The South Florida drugs and money laundering business has also given rise to enormous demand for legal services, including 25 or so top drugs lawyers who practice mostly in Miami and defend individuals accused of narcotics-related crimes. In 1982 the federal court in Miami handled more cases than the federal courts in Boston, New York, Philadelphia, Chicago and Washington, DC combined. Business for the lawyers began to pick up in the mid-1970s, when the narcotics business was increasingly taken over by Colombians, and kidnapping, murder and related offenses were added to drugs charges, smuggling and money laundering – at one point the Miami morgue had to rent a refrigerator truck to handle the overflow. Legal defense in such cases is highly lucrative, visible and creative, sometimes involving constitutional issues argued before the US Supreme Court. It is also dangerous if the client is promised too much or the lawyer is not performing up to expectations – in 1980 Miami attorney George Gold was gunned down in a still unsolved case, possibly by one of the Colombian hit men who are available for only $500 a contract (plus expenses).

This mixture of high risk/high reward is fully evident in the case of Carlos Lehder, the alleged Colombian drug kingpin, convicted of drugs dealing in 1988. Lawyers were talking of a base fee for simply walking into court of $500,000. Additional indictments, extensive pre-trial investigations and other work evidently raised the bill past the $3 million mark. But Lehder was generally viewed as dangerous and unpredictable – the Colombian government had linked him with the murder of the Colombian minister of justice as well as the 1985 attack on the Colombian Supreme Court in which 97 people, including 11 justices, were killed. As one lawyer put it: 'There's no way of knowing how he might react to a legal strategy, or to a loss.'

An added element of risk has been introduced to the equation in recent months from another source. The 1986 Anti-Drug Abuse Act contains a provision expanding the definition of money laundering to include knowingly accepting money from someone who made it illegally. This could mean that drugs-defense lawyers might face forced forfeiture of their fees, or even prosecution for having accepted them in the first place.

Legal tactics rarely produce an acquittal, but endless technical and procedural motions to suppress evidence or wear down the opposition often pay off. A client of Miami attorney Joel Hirschhorn '...was arrested after an airplane loaded with hundreds of pounds of cocaine touched down at a rural Florida airport at 3 a.m. and taxied to his car. He was charged with conspiring to import cocaine. His first trial ended with a hung jury. The jury in the second trial found him guilty. Mr. Hirschhorn then persuaded the judge to set the verdict aside on grounds of insufficient evidence.' In another case, '...a Miami prosecutor recalls watching Mr. Hirschhorn move a jury to tears over a murderer. It was an airtight case, he says, but he began to worry when the jury was crying, the defendant was crying, and Joel was crying.'[49] That case nevertheless ended in a conviction.

There has been some indication that, due to the strength of the anti-drugs crackdown in Florida, some business has moved to California. The state has a tradition of virtually anonymous banking, attributable to a large, expanding and historically mobile population. In addition, it has experienced strong economic performance and a generally booming real estate market for many years, with the result that 'new' money is not considered exceptional. The area is a major international trading center, with powerful links on both a geographic and cultural level with Latin America. This combination of factors makes it an attractive place for money launderers, a theory borne out, it would seem, by the data. Between 1980 and 1983, major cash transactions reported in compliance with the Bank Secrecy Law requirements rose by 60 per cent from $13 billion to nearly $21 billion. In 1980 the banks of California reported a $300 million cash deficit; two years later they had between them a surplus in cash of $1 billion. Interestingly as well, the two most egregious examples of violations of the reporting requirements (see Chapter 8) occurred with two Californian-based institutions, Crocker Bank and Bank of America. In the words of John K. Van De Kamp, Attorney General of the state, 'There is a kind of leukemia of illicit money in the financial bloodstream of California.'[50]

A fascinating look into the financial aspects of drugs trafficking emerged in early 1984 in connection with a Bahamian Royal Commission inquiry into official corruption. High officials in the government were accused of receiving bribes of over $100,000 a month in order to 'overlook' an elaborate drugs smuggling base complete with aircraft hangars and maintenance facilities, helicopters, speedboats and armed guards. Although the charges were vehemently denied, it seemed unlikely that they were entirely groundless in a country that is highly dependent on the drug trade and related financial flows.

Indeed, with the magnitude of funds involved, the problem of corruption is a very real one. The governments of the drugs producers in Latin American face an almost impossible task. In early 1984, for example, two drugs dealers evidently offered Colombia's Attorney General $2 billion to help the government bolster the country's reserves – in exchange for a government pledge to allow them to return from self-imposed exile in Panama. On a smaller scale, the going rate for a police commander in Chapare (Bolivia's largest drugs producing region) to ignore the three-day process of stomping, processing and loading coca was $25,000 in 1987 – a large sum of money by most people's standards but a fortune in South America. The 36-year-old major who headed surveillance in the region at the time earned less than $500 a month. Even senior politicians and judges were suspected of links with the drugs trade – it was widely believed in La Paz that orders from near the top level of government expressly forbade the destruction of certain airstrips in the northern jungle regularly used by dealers.[51]

A similar picture emerged in Mexico, the leading single-country source of heroin and marijuana entering the United States and a leading point of transfer for cocaine. Mexico's share of the US heroin market peaked in the mid 1970s (after the 'French connection' case was broken and a narcotics agreement was signed with Turkey) at 90 per cent. As a result of Mexican anti-drugs work it then fell to as low as 20 per cent by 1978, but has climbed again steadily since that time, to around 46 per cent in 1988. Mexico also supplies around 40 per cent of the marijuana for the United States and some 30 per cent of United States-bound cocaine passes across its borders.

It is not surprising that, with stakes so high, criminals are determined to ply their trade, and attempts to combat them are fraught with danger. In February 1985, a US Drug Enforcement Administration agent,

Enrique Camarena Salazar, and his Mexican pilot, Alfredo Zavala, were abducted, tortured and murdered by a drugs smuggling ring. The DEA alleged that this was carried out with the assistance of former and present Mexican police officials who had been corrupted. The affair caused an uproar in the United States, and the Mexican authorities showed signs of trying to bring to justice those responsible. However, although 67 people were jailed and hundreds fired, the kingpins remained for the most part unscathed. Indeed the DEA's most wanted man in Mexico, Miguel Felix Gallardo, still walked free in 1988, with the Mexicans saying they had no idea where he was, even when he was spotted at a party. It appeared as if too many paid-off officials stood to lose if he was arrested.[52]

In the United States itself, drug enforcement efforts are hampered by the corrupting influence of the enormous amounts of money involved. In testimony during the Congressional hearings, for example, attorney Robert J. Perry explained how on one important case, known as the Grandmother Mafia case, there had been five separate instances of corruption. These had included an IRS agent participating in the armed robbery of one of the suspects to the tune of $700,000 and a DEA employee being persuaded to infiltrate the DEA's computer system in order to provide information on one of the undercover agents for the crooks.

In 1983 and 1984, the President's Commission on Organized Crime held hearings throughout the United States, and naturally developed a strong interest in money-laundering channels. Acting on the suspicion that the Deak-Pereira Company, a major foreign exchange dealer, had laundered over $100 million since 1969, an effort was made to obtain testimony from the firm's chairman, Nicholas L. Deak. He refused to testify, and the Commission had no subpoena powers at the time. Some organized crime members did testify, however, and disclaimed any knowledge of money-laundering activity. For example, 70-year-old Aladena (Jimmy the Weasel) Fratianno of Los Angeles said he knew little – organized crime chiefs 'don't keep no records' but instead 'rely on front men they can trust'.[53] Nevertheless, Commission investigators turned up a number of money-laundering cases by big-time criminals, including $95.7 million brought by one individual to a Manhattan Deak-Pereira office in May 1981 in the form of small denomination currency notes packed in cardboard boxes.

The activities of fugitive US swindler Robert Vesco appear to have been made possible by secret money flows as well, in connection with an alleged drug-running and trade sanctions-busting business jointly operated with the Cuban Intelligence Service.

Vesco helps arrange for shipments of heroin, cocaine and marijuana from South America to Cuba, has it transferred to smaller boats and planes there, and delivered to the U.S. and Canada. The money is laundered through offshore banks, and the Castro government is said to get payments per large boatload of drugs. Vesco also helps Castro get American goods, which the U.S. prohibits selling to Cuba. In exchange, [he] gets safe harbor in the workers paradise, living quarters at a yacht club and in a beach house near Havana, and his profit.[54]

International undercover activities

Governments need regular financial channels to implement foreign policy, some of which must necessarily be kept secret. National policy may dictate the financial support of a friendly government abroad, yet the existence of that support may be an embarrassment (or worse) to its recipient. Alternatively, national policy may require financial support of groups seeking to promote change in another country or even to overthrow the established government of a sovereign state with whom the home country may or may not have diplomatic relations. Intelligence services need money to finance their activities and to pay local operatives around the world. In all such cases the financial transactions involved, which may be highly complex and involve multiple currencies and intermediaries, must be kept from the public eye. Geopolitics and regional conflagrations, superpowers and surrogates, purchases of embargoed weapons and salaries of mercenaries, financial resources of dissident groups – the need for secret money covers a broad range of players and games.

The FLN case

An interesting case that wound its way through the 1960s and 1970s in Switzerland involved Algeria.[55] In the course of less than ten years, and through a labyrinth of facts and legal proceedings, a war chest of approximately 40 million Swiss francs that was built up by the Algerian National Liberation Front (FLN) evaporated.

In June 1962, the FLN created a provisional political bureau to operate until a government was appointed by a proper assembly. Mr X was Secretary General of the provisional bureau, with full responsibility for the FLN's finances. In October 1962, Mr X opened an account in his own name with the Banque Commerciale Arabe SA (BCA) in Geneva. By signing the agreement with the bank, Mr X acknowledged that the legal relationship between himself and the bank would be governed by Swiss law. In addition to opening an account, Mr X also signed the account agreement twice – as the person solely authorized to dispose of the account, and also as the person in whose name the account was held.

In April 1963, Mr X resigned from the position of FLN Secretary General, but indicated a willingness to retain his financial responsibilities. In September 1963 the new Algerian constitution was adopted, and the FLN's finances became the property of the Algerian Republic. Mr Y became the new Secretary General of the FLN. He subsequently sent a letter to BCA in Geneva, notifying the bank that he would now be the 'sole person legally entitled to dispose of the funds and revenues of the FLN'. In March 1964, Mr X changed the account opened in his name with BCA to a numbered account – BP 510. He also asked to have all correspondence retained at the bank. A new FLN political bureau was formed in April 1964, which no longer included Mr X. Instead Mr Z was given responsibility for finance.

On 12 June 1964, Zouhair Mardam Bey, the administrator of BCA, met with Mr Z and agreed that some account details should be altered. Between 18 June and 1 July 1964, Mr X withdrew 99.6 per cent of the funds in his account at BCA. Curiously, starting on 22 June 1964, four numbered accounts related to the case were opened at BCA by one or more unknown clients. On 6 July 1964, Messrs Y and Z sued Mr X and the BCA administrator for a breach of trust. A civil sequestration order was placed on account BP 510, and two days later the civil order was replaced by a criminal one. In November, the court ordered Zouhair Mardam Bey to hand over the files relating to the four numbered accounts. The latter, standing on Swiss banking secrecy, refused to comply with the court order. He also refused to cooperate with any investigation that would prove the existence of these accounts even if the anonymity of the account holders would be respected. Mr X was assassinated in Madrid on 3 January 1967.

In February 1971, the Swiss Court of First Instance ruled that the defendants in the case should pay the Algerian Republic the sum of SFr 39,246,851.80 with interest at 5 per cent from July 1964. The court determined that the FLN alone was the depositor and that Mr X acted only as a representative. The repayment to Mr X was viewed as the bank's error. The defendants appealed to the Court of Justice of the Canton of Geneva. In June 1973, this court confirmed the judgement of the Court of First Instance. In July 1974, the Swiss Federal Court annulled the decision of the Court of Justice and rejected the demands of the Algerian Republic.

Three key questions were asked by the Federal Court in arriving at its verdict: (1) Was Mr X the account holder, or was he acting on behalf of the FLN under the terms of agreements that the bank should have observed? (2) Given that the bank was not unaware that the money really belonged to the FLN, was it able to accept instructions from Mr X? and (3) Should the existence of a dispute between Mr X and the FLN have led the bank to oppose Mr X's instructions?

There is a legal device in Swiss law known as the 'third party open account'. This states that the person represented (in this case the true owner of the money – the FLN) has no claims against the bank. If the bank was unaware of Mr X's political problems, it could not, and should not, have refused to follow his instructions. Under the Swiss law, Mr X had full power over the funds involved, and could use or alter the account as he wished. The purpose of the meeting between Mr Z and the BCA administrator on 12 June 1964 should have been taken as a verbal revocation of Mr X's power. If a civil or criminal sequestration order were used, proceedings against Mr X would have been possible. Although both civil and criminal sequestration orders were used in this case, Mr X withdrew the money before they became effective. The Federal Court therefore found that BCA was not only able to return the deposits to Mr X, but was also obliged to do so.

The Nugan Hand case

A rather different case involved the now-defunct Australia-based banking group, Nugan Hand. In its heyday, over $1 billion reportedly passed through Nugan Hand each year.[56] Bank executives were evidently engaged in major weapons shipments to certain forces engaged in the Angola civil war, sale of a US intelligence vessel to Iran, extensive dealings with heroin syndicates, and related deals. Suspicions also emerged that Nugan Hand was heavily involved with clandestine dealings for the CIA – suspicions reinforced by the number of ex-CIA and US military officials who were employed by the firm or who had extensive dealings with it. Rear Admiral Earl Yates, for example, who had been in charge of all US strategic naval planning from California to the Persian Gulf, was a top executive. The bank's US attorney was ex-CIA director William Colby. And it later transpired that such Iran-Contra figures as Richard Secord had played a part in the bank's affairs.

The Nugan Hand group collapsed (with losses of over $50 million to depositors) shortly after its chairman, Frank Nugan, was found shot dead in his car on a deserted Australian road in 1980 – an apparent suicide. His partner Michael Hand, a highly decorated former Green Beret and CIA contract agent himself, fled the country.[57]

The IRA case

In February 1985, the government of Ireland seized a Bank of Ireland account valued at $1.65 million, allegedly containing IRA money obtained through bank robberies, kidnappings and death threats, as well as donations from IRA sympathizers in North America. There were reports that the IRA intended to use the funds to complete a large international arms deal. Fearing that the funds would be transferred outside the Republic's jurisdiction, an emergency law was enacted to permit the Dublin government to seize the funds. The money allegedly traveled from Ireland to Switzerland and then back to Ireland. If the funds remained unclaimed for six months, they would revert to the Irish state. Sinn Fein, the political wing of the IRA, denied that the account contained IRA money. More generally, it was feared that the seizure would cause a fresh round of bank robberies, kidnappings and extortion demands designed to replenish the IRA resources.

Testimony by former IRA members, during a 1983 Brooklyn gunrunning trial, also confirmed that the IRA regularly moves secret money between the US and Ireland. Since 1970, the Irish Northern Aid Committee of New York City (NORAID) has channeled $2–3 million – collected in the humble surroundings of Irish pubs and testimonial dinners – through An Cumman Cabhrach, a relief organization in Dublin. The testimony revealed that most of the funds found their way into the hands of the IRA, and that at least half of the money was sent back to the United States to purchase weapons.[58]

The PLO case

The Palestine Liberation Organization is estimated to have total assets in various forms of between $2 billion and $14 billion. Whatever the exact figure, it is certain that the PLO controls a large and diversified international financial empire, the details of which are predictably veiled in secrecy. At its head has been Yasser Arafat, leader of both the PLO and Fatah, the largest of the eight commando units grouped under the PLO. Funds come from Arab oil states and taxes on the pay of Palestinians in Arab countries. Fatah apparently has a separate secret budget, business operations and cash that, it is rumored, are used to cover PLO deficits resulting in part from the decline in oil prices.

PLO assets finance a variety of activities – from attacks on Israeli-occupied territory to welfare payments to Palestinians on the West Bank and Gaza Strip and in refugee camps elsewhere in the Middle East; from the funding of hospitals and universities to the running of its own news agency and its diplomatic offices in 90 countries. It also seems that a certain amount of money is judiciously spent to buy loyalty and influence. Between mid-1985 and late 1986 some $200 million appears to have been deposited in Tunisian banks as a favor to the government of Tunisia, where the PLO has its headquarters. A loan of $100 million was allegedly made to Iraq, the site of a major PLO military command post. And it has been suggested that $200 million passed to Lebanese President Amin Gemayel at one stage in exchange for Lebanese passports for Palestinians. There are even allegations that, when political strains between Jordan and the PLO were particularly high, Arafat moved $700 million out of the Arab Bank in Amman.[59]

The Abu Nidal terrorist group, long established in Syria, Lebanon and

174

Libya, apparently also ran a major undercover organization in Warsaw between 1979 and 1986. In return for an agreement that the group would carry out no attacks on Polish soil, the Polish government was reputed to have offered a number of scholarships at Polish schools to members of the group, as well as permitting the establishment of a 'front' operation, SAS Trade & Investment Co. This enterprise, thought to have been the center of a network of Abu Nidal companies with offices in Europe and using a branch of a West European bank to channel funds between them, acted as an export–import dealer in a variety of goods. These were often arms destined for Arab nations. The deals not only provided weapons for the Middle East, but earned badly needed foreign currency for Poland and healthy profits for Abu Nidal with which to buy arms. In one deal, some 4,000 Kalashnikov rifles were apparently shipped from East Germany through Poland to Libya for $500,000. In another, 115 British Enfield anti-riot weapons, en route for Africa according to the documents prepared by SAS, were diverted at Rotterdam, with 100 going to East Germany and the remaining 15 to Abu Nidal.[60]

A recent report suggests that Saudi Arabia has been deeply involved in such secret 'donations' for almost twenty years. It has made use of its oil wealth to make clandestine contributions to countries where it feels it has a particular political, regional or religious interest, generally seeking to oppose communism and promote stability in Muslim countries. Whilst Saudi and American interests do not always coincide (for example, in the case of Israel) the Saudis appear also to have endeavored on the whole to serve the interests of the United States.

In certain cases they have apparently helped finance US foreign policy when funds for such policy have not – for one reason or another – been approved by Congress. Saudi's secret contributions to the Nicaraguan rebels were disclosed during the Iran-Contra hearings. But there are other examples as well. It seems likely, for instance, that Saudi money was used to circumvent the Congressional ban on American aid to Jonas Savimbi's rebel forces fighting the Marxist government in Angola.

At the request of the US ambassador to Mogadishu, the Saudis provided substantial funds to the government of Somalia in the late 1970s, thus helping to reduce that country's dependence on the Soviet Union. In 1977, they financed an airlift of Moroccan troops to Zaire to assist the administration of Mobuto Sésé Séko. In 1979, Saudi money helped the government of North Yemen repel invasion from South Yemen. And they cooperated with Washington to aid the anti-Soviet guerrillas in Afghanistan.[61]

Irangate

Perhaps the most startling example this decade of international under-cover activity involving secret money is the Iran-Contra affair, which came to light at the end of 1986. Long before the clandestine activities involving White House officials were revealed, however, significant quantities of weapons had been quietly shipped to Khomeini's regime from sources all over the world.

After November 1979, when US hostages were seized, US arms shipments to Iran were embargoed. The ban included more than $200 million of US military supplies purchased during the Shah's regime but never delivered. A number of other Western nations also introduced embargoes. Since that time the Iranians have been desperate to build up their armaments, which are suffering depletion through the war with Iraq. However, since the arsenal upon which they were building was procured in the 1970s by the Shah from the United States and the United Kingdom their task was not easy. They were forced into the shadowy world of arms smugglers to acquire what they needed, spending up to $4 billion a year and often paying two or three times the going rate because of the middlemen involved.

The middlemen themselves are brokers and dealers who conceal their connection with Iran behind a maze of corporations and offshore banks. When buying from American suppliers, the broker typically represents an Iranian shipment as a legal arms transaction with a friendly nation. The State Department does require an arms exporter to certify that the weapons are going to a 'legitimate' recipient, but false 'end-user' certificates are apparently easy to obtain in return for payoffs to officials in friendly foreign nations. The arms are then shipped to the destination on the forged certificate, and from there they proceed to the Mideast, often through the offices of Danish ship brokers who have a long tradition of arms shipping.

As well as acquiring arms 'direct' from the United States in this way, Iran has also followed a policy of buying from countries having surplus US stocks. There is a State Department ban on such resales, but a number of countries seem to have managed to upgrade their military equipment with new supplies from the United States while selling on their obsolete weapons to arms dealers. In such cases the middlemen are often agents posing as arms dealers to conceal the government-to-government deal. It is believed that much of Iran's arms procurement is centered in London. Western intelligence sources suggest that the headquarters of the National Iranian Oil Co. there also houses the Logistics Support Centre, which, it is estimated, deals with some 70 per cent of all illicit Iranian arms purchases.[62]

It was into this network of secrecy and greed, corruption and bribery that a small group of White House officials entered in 1985. Many questions about their actions remain unanswered, but the general details of the story have been pieced together. The undercover methods used seem to have stemmed from three main considerations: (1) the arms sales they were undertaking were against stated US policy and

176

thus required the utmost secrecy; (2) the relationship between the participants was highly sensitive politically; and (3) the disposition of the proceeds involved actions in direct contravention of Congressional ruling.[63] The men involved sought to avoid both accountability for their actions and strictures imposed upon them by regulation.

Although the exact circumstances in which it began remain unclear, a behind-the-scenes rapprochement between the United States and Iran started to take form in Spring or Summer 1985. It was hardly one of mutual trust or friendship. Rather the two sides were simply persuaded to talk to one another with a view to the benefits each might glean from improved relations. Instrumental in this change was Manucher Ghorbanifar, a 'refugee' Iranian businessman who nevertheless maintained high level contacts in Iran and was quoted as saying, 'I had brokered many business deals, I wondered whether I could broker a diplomatic deal as well'.[64] The skeptic might well query to what degree Ghorbanifar was genuinely motivated by such high ideals, and how much was a question of having a healthy eye for commercial gain. Whatever the real driving force behind his actions, however, he discussed his ideas with Adnan Khashoggi, a Saudi Arabian businessman, reputed to be one of the richest men in the world. The latter apprently saw enormous profit potential in a United States–Iran rapprochement, and the two men began working toward that goal. Again reports differ, but it seems likely that at this stage Khashoggi asked the Israelis to act as diplomatic broker.

Predictably, it was not long before the Iranians asked for weapons. The Israelis had useful experience to offer in this field. Its government-owned arms industry depends heavily on foreign sales to defray research and development expenses. Indeed, military sales account for a quarter to a third of Israel's industrial exports. However, many potential customers are countries that have no diplomatic relations with Israel. As a result, the Israeli government has become skilled in using private citizens to set up deals that cannot be made openly, which is exactly what was needed in the circumstances.

But what was driving US officials into undercover arms deals with Iran? After all the investigations, it still appears that the major motivating factor – at least at the outset – was to secure the release of the American hostages still held. Making a profit, which could be diverted to use in other undercover activities, certainly played a part, and indeed as time went on and hope of real progress on the hostage front diminished, it seems to have played an ever more important part. But the predominant consideration must have been the hostages.

The first shipment was in August 1985. At that stage the arms sold came from Israeli supplies, which, it was agreed, would be replenished by the United States.[65] The deal on the Israeli side was managed primarily by Yaaccov Nimrodi, a former Israeli intelligence agent who had established extensive contacts in Iran during his ten years as military attaché in Tehran. Ghorbanifar acted for the Iranians, and Khashoggi provided the finance. Since the Iranians refused to pay for the arms in advance, and since no one was going to part with them without payment, a 'guarantor' – for a fee – was needed. For the first deal Khashoggi put up $1 million in August and then a further $4 million in September. His payments to the Israelis and the Americans, and Ghorbanifar's payments on behalf of the Iranians to him, passed through Swiss accounts. Iran received 500 TOW anti-tank missiles, and in return in September the American hostage, the Reverend Benjamin Weir, was released.

It is thought that the value of the 500 TOW anti-tank missiles was in fact only $3.5 million; there was thus a substantial profit available, even after allowing for middlemen commissions. The treatment of these funds, it is believed, set the pattern for later transactions. They were scooped off under the auspices of certain American officials, most notably Lieutenant Colonel Oliver L. North, and his associates, Major General Richard V. Secord and his business partner, Albert Hakim, into Swiss bank accounts, whence they were later siphoned off for use in other undercover activities, in particular to support the rebels (Contras) in Nicaragua.

The next shipment took place in early 1986. This time Israel acted only as a transfer point, with the arms coming now directly from American stocks at the Pentagon. Some 2008 TOW missiles were apparently sold by the latter to the CIA for $12 million. At the same time, North was working out a $30 million sale price from Tehran. It is now believed that the US Army charged the CIA an improperly low price for the missiles in order to facilitate the generation of profits for the 'secret undercover slush fund'.[66] Whether that is the case or not, the same scheme was followed, with Khashoggi raising some $12 million to provide the 'float', which was paid into one of the accounts under North's control in the name of Lake Resources. The exact sources of this money, and the $15 million he advanced to Lake Resources for the next shipment in May 1986 are unknown. However, two Canadian businessmen, Donald Fraser and Ernest Miller, with whom Khashoggi had already had substantial dealings, appear to have contributed considerably. The May 1986 shipment was reputedly an unfortunate affair for Khashoggi and Ghorbanifar. Both say they were left deeply out of pocket, since the Iranians repaid only $5 million of the advance. Thereafter the two men, who had seemed in any case to be experiencing some cash flow difficulties for the earlier transaction in 1986, fell out of the picture. Two further shipments, in the Summer and Fall of that year, were made before the game was up, but it is not known how they were financed.

In all these transactions – the arms deals with Iran and the disposition of the profits arising from them – a complex network of accounts was used to conceal the source and destination of the money involved. A picture has emerged of a tight web of dummy companies stretching from the Swiss cities of Geneva and Fribourg to Panama and the Cayman Islands.[67] The exact nature of the links between the companies and accounts and the precise role played by the people involved are as yet hard to define, but some connections have come to light.

Lake Resources, mentioned above, was apparently set up in May 1985 as a Panamanian corporation. The board chairman of the company was one Suzanne Hefti, an accountant in the Swiss firm of Auditing and Fiduciary Services – Audifi SA. Audifi's headquarters in Fribourg also housed a Swiss affiliate of the Stanford Technology Trading Group International, the Californian-based company controlled by Albert Hakim (see above). The Fribourg affiliate of Stanford was in turn headed by Jean de Senarclens, who was also the chairman of a Geneva-based fiduciary company, CSF SA.[68] CSF was linked to both ends of the Iran-Contra dealings, and appears to have coordinated bank transfers. It is believed that some $18 million from the Iran arms sales was paid into CSF's Cayman Islands account, and that funds from a Bermuda subsidiary of the firm was transferred to Panama to pay for the purchase of planes for the Contras.[69] It seems that funds went first to Albon Values, a Panamanian corporation in which CSF employees were principals, and thence to Amalgamated Commercial Enterprises, the Panamanian shell corporation used by Southern Air Transport, a Miami-based freight carrier instrumental in arms shipments to the Mideast as well as Contra resupply operations.[70]

Although the Iran arms sales were the starting point of the Congressional inquiries, and dominated them in their early stages, it gradually became apparent that funding for the Contras involved more than skimming off the profits from weapons sale to the Iranians.[71] Under the Boland Amendment US funding of the Contras was banned from October 1984 to 1985.[72] However this did not deter North and his associates from running secret accounts to do expressly that. Some sources say that from 1984 through 1986 as much as $50 million was raised covertly for the Contras. The Iran profits probably accounted in the end for less than $10 million. There were two other major sources of funding. One was private US donations, the other money from friendly foreign governments. Most prominent amongst the latter was Saudi Arabia, where estimates for aid range from $23 million[73] to $30 million.

Nevertheless, the Contras indicated that they received nowhere near the total of funds purportedly raised for them. It seems likely that all along the way substantial sums of money were being skimmed off for kickbacks and commissions. Indeed in Iran it has long been traditional for the purchaser to pocket 5 per cent on arms deals and it is unlikely that the custom has died out.[74] It also seems unlikely that at the Nicaraguan end some such payment did not exist. As well as these factors, there are

179

suggestions that North may have found the power involved with his slush fund just too attractive and that funds may also have gone to other causes he considered 'worthy' – political campaigns in the United States, intelligence activities in Angola, Afghanistan, Ethiopia, even the purchase of a ship with a radio transmitter to beam propaganda messages into Libya.[75] 'It became irresistible to Ollie. He had the means at his right hand to solve problems and it was so easy. He was trying to short-circuit but sometimes in the big world you can't do that.'[76]

And then there is the question of accounting practices and slips. To the great embarrassment of all concerned it was discovered that although the Sultan of Brunei had made a most generous contribution of $10 million in August 1986, nobody could find it. It transpired that when instructions had been given to him of the number of the Swiss bank account to which he should send it, two figures had been transposed and the money had duly ended up in the account of a Swiss business-man. Not one to miss an opportunity, the individual in question had transferred it to another bank within days – he was expecting $10 million from the sale of a ship. Unimpressed by this startling coincidence the Sultan of Brunei asked for his cash back plus interest.[77]

Tracking the course of funds has been made all the more difficult by the levels of intricate financial secrecy employed. It has been further complicated by the fact that not all the accounts used still exist. Lake Resources, for example, was dissolved as a company in November 1986.[78] However, quite early on the Geneva branch of Crédit Suisse agreed to freeze the assets of two of the accounts thought to have been managed by North, and to hold them, and any others involving North, Secord or Hakim under 'heightened surveillance'.[79] Towards the end of December 1986, the US Justice Department asked the Swiss to freeze the accounts relating to seven more individuals – Khashoggi, Ghorbanifar, the Canadians Fraser and Miller, de Senarclens, Willard I. Zucker (manager of CSF), and Roy M. Furmack, a former business associate of the late CIA chief, William J. Casey.[80] The Americans also sought access to the records of the accounts.

In February 1987 the American request extended to information on CSF.[81] Under Swiss law, the account holder may appeal any such access and through most of 1987 investigations were blocked as the Swiss courts waited to hear appeals.[82] The first real breakthrough came on 20 August when Switzerland's Supreme Court turned down the appeals of Secord, Hakim and Ghorbanifar, ruling that the US independent counsel, Lawrence Walsh should be allowed to see the relevant records.[83]

Hakim and Ghorbanifar immediately lodged a further appeal, but this too was rejected[84] and in mid-September 1987 documents began to trickle through.[85] Another month passed; no new appeals were lodged; on 4 November 1987 the Swiss turned over thousands of pages of records, reflecting transactions involving bank accounts linked to 20 companies and individuals, including not only Secord, Hakim and Ghorbanifar, but North as well.[86]

The public hearings on the Iran-Contra affair ran throughout the summer of 1987. But even after 250 hours of testimony from 29 witnesses, the examination of a quarter of a million pages of documents and the release of 1,059 official exhibits, the full details of how it all could ever have been allowed to happen remain a mystery.[87] In the closing speeches of the panel it was difficult even to find a consensus of opinion on the gravity of the offences involved. House Select Committee Vice-Chairman Dick Cheney was inclined to play the matter down, remarking: 'We've heard talk of a grave constitutional crisis, listened to expressions of moral indignation and outrage and even been treated to talk about a coup in the White House, a junta run by a lieutenant colonel and an admiral. My own personal view is that there has been far too much apocalyptic rhetoric about these events, most of it unjustified. If there ever was a crisis, which I doubt, it ended before these committees were established.' Senate Select Committee Vice-Chairman Warren H. Rudman took a sterner view, pointing out that: 'These actions and the attitudes they represent are antithetical to our democratic system of government. They cannot be justified by passion [or] patriotism...' Senate Select Committee Chairman Daniel K. Inouye was also shocked by the revelations, remarking that: 'The story has now been told ... I see it as a chilling story ... of deceit and duplicity and the arrogant disregard of the rule of law. It is a story of withholding vital information from the American people, from the Congress ... It is a story of how a great nation betrayed the principles which have made it great.'[88]

Summary

The examples cited in this and the preceding three chapters should suffice to convey an impression of the level of complexity imbedded in the demand for secret money. Tax evasion is almost a mortal sin in some countries, severely punishable in others, and a national pastime in still others, while the incentives to evade are equally varied. Capital flight is no less complex in terms of its motivation and consequences facing individuals and countries alike. Neither tax evasion nor capital flight is likely to wither away as economic incentives, ingenuity and human nature continue to clash with the machinations of politicians frustrated by authority that stops at the national border. Both require secrecy that provides effective shelter from taxation under the law of sovereign states abroad, shelter that is likely to remain durable.

Bribery and corruption, fraud, the drug trade and other criminal uses of international financial secrecy likewise have their own unique demand patterns, which attract often vigorous law-enforcement attention and considerably greater cooperation among countries. Yet they continue to thrive. The levels of secrecy they require command a high price, and, where such demand emerges, supply cannot be far behind. Still, while the direct perpetrators are often hardened criminals who raise major law-enforcement challenges for the authorities, the money launderers are quite different in how they do business and in their attitudes toward risk, and this may provide an effective indirect route for the application of pressure on the criminals.

Each class of secrecy customer demands, and is willing to pay for, a unique class of secrecy products that carry different price tags. The characteristics of suppliers of these products will be explored in Chapter 7.

Notes

1 George Lardner, Jr, 'New Mobs Change Organized Crime', *International Herald Tribune*, 3 April 1986.
2 Robert E. Taylor, 'Laundry Service', *Wall Street Journal*, 25 July 1983.
3 'Current Problem of Money Laundering' April 16, June 13, July 24, September 12 1985, US Senate, Committee on Government Affairs, Hearings (1985), Serial No. 109.
4 Jeff Gerth, 'Vast Flow of Cash Threatens Currency, Banks and Economies', *New York Times*, 11 April 1988.
5 'Cleaning up Dirty Money Laundering', *The Economist*, 20 August 1988.
6 Ed Magnuson, 'Tears of Rage', *Time*, 14 March 1988. See also James M. Perry, 'Drugs is a Big Campaign Issue Only for Jackson, But It's a Hot One That Could Backfire on Bush', *Wall Street Journal*, 21 March 1988; and 'Colombia – the Drug Economy', *The Economist*, 2 April 1988.
7 William Branigin, 'Mexican Anti-Drug Campaign Failing to Stem Flow Into US', *Washington Post*, 4 August 1987.
8 Allan Dodds Frank, 'See No Evil', *Forbes*, 6 October 1986.
9 Ibid.
10 Subcommittee on Crime, Committee on the Judiciary, US House of Representatives, 99th Congress, *Current Problems of Money Laundering* (Washington, DC: US Government Printing Office, 1985.)
11 'Colombia – The Drug Economy', *The Economist*, 2 April 1988.
12 Jeff Gerth, *op. cit.* (n. 4).
13 Robert Graham, 'Guerillas Fail to Dent Colombian Economy', *Financial Times*, 23 February 1988.
14 Ibid.
15 'Cleaning up Dirty Money Laundering', *The Economist*, 20 August 1988.
16 Louis Kraar, 'The Drug Trade', *Fortune*, 20 June 1988.
17 Committee on the Judiciary, *op. cit.* (n. 10), p. 310.
18 Ibid.
19 Gary Cohn, 'These Smurfs Aren't Blue, But Some Have Reasons to be Sad', *Wall Street Journal*, 11 July 1985. See also Committee on the Judiciary, *op. cit.* (n. 10), p. 17.
20 Gary Cohn, ibid.
21 Ibid., p. 15.
22 Committee on the Judiciary, *op. cit.* (n. 10), pp. 127–51.
23 Ibid., pp. 255–6.
24 Ibid., p. 305.
25 'Laundering Schemes Traced to Puerto Rico', *New York Times*, 9 June 1985.
26 Dianna Solis, 'Shady Exchanges', *Wall Street Journal*, 19 July 1986.

27 'Peru Plans to Nationalize Banks, Other Financial Firms', *Wall Street Journal*, 29 July 1987.
28 Andres Oppenheimer, 'In Colombia, It's No Problem to Launder Loot', *Miami Herald*, 11 March 1986.
29 Allan Dodds Frank, 'New Hub for Old Web', *Forbes*, 7 April 1986.
30 *International Herald Tribune*, 21 May 1986. See also 'Curbing the Bombay Kerb', *The Economist*, 22 March 1986.
31 Committee on the Judiciary, *op. cit.* (n. 10), p. 301.
32 Shirley Hobbs Scheibla, 'Where Hot Money Hides', *Barrons*, 11 July 1983.
33 Ibid. See also 'Chasing the Peso Leaves Argentines Breathless', *Business Week*, 10 June 1985.
34 James Cook, 'Everybody's Favorite Laundry Man', *Forbes*, 5 December 1983.
35 'An American Connection', *Newsweek*, 15 October 1984.
36 'Mafia Portrait: Aging Leaders and New Competitors', *New York Times*, 4 October 1984, p. B12.
37 Allan Dodds Frank, *op. cit.* (n. 29).
38 Ibid.
39 Robert E. Taylor, 'Ex-Smuggler Tells of Huge Drug Profits Laundered, Placed at Major US Banks', *Wall Street Journal*, 12 February 1988.
40 William C. Symonds *et al.*, 'The Sicilian Mafia is Still Going Strong', *Business Week*, 18 April 1988.
41 Jeff Gerth, *op. cit.* (n. 4).
42 Kevin Kelly, 'The Oklahoma Town That Drug Money Bought', *Business Week*, 23 May 1988.
43 Robert E. Taylor, *op. cit.* (n. 2).
44 Ibid.
45 Committee on the Judiciary, *op. cit.* (n. 10), pp. 92–3.
46 Penny Lernoux, 'The Seamy Side of Florida Banking', *New York Times*, 5 February 1984.
47 Ibid.
48 Martha Brannigan, 'Bankers Face Trial Today for Aiding Smugglers in Getting Control of Bank', *Wall Street Journal*, 5 August 1985.
49 Thomas E. Ricks, 'Drug Lawyer', *Wall Street Journal*, 25 June 1983. See also Thomas E. Ricks and Martha Brannigan, 'Drug Lawyers View Carlos Lehder Case With a Mixture of Lust and Trepidation', *Wall Street Journal*, 10 February 1987.
50 Committee on the Judiciary, *op. cit.* (n. 10), pp. 407, 416.
51 Jeffrey Ryser and Bill Javetski, 'Can South America's Addict Economies Ever Break Free?', *Business Week*, 22 September 1986.
52 William Branigin, 'Mexican Anti-Drug Campaign Failing to Stem Flow Into US', *Washington Post*, 4 August 1987.
53 Selwyn Raab, 'Financier Declines to Testify in Cash-Laundering Inquiry', *New York Times*, 15 March 1984.
54 'Partners in Crime', *Forbes*, 25 September 1984, p. 42. See also Thomas N. Gladwin and Ingo Walter, *Multinationals Under Fire* (New York: John Wiley, 1980), Chapter 7.
55 See Eduard Chambost, *Bank Accounts: A World Guide to Confidentiality* (New York: John Wiley, 1983), Chapter 9. See also Richard H. Blum, *Offshore Haven Banks, Trusts and Companies* (New York: Praeger, 1984).
56 Jonathan Kwitney, 'Nugan Hand Acted in Covert Operations of U.S. Government', *Wall Street Journal*, 21 August 1983.
57 Jonathan Friedland, 'Banking Scandal Down Under', *Institutional Investor*, November 1987. See also Jonathan Kwitney, *The Crimes of Patriots* (New York: W. W. Norton, 1987).
58 'IRA Funds Seized', *New York Times*, 18 February 1985.
59 Barbara Rosewicz and Gerald F. Seib, 'Big Business', *Wall Street Journal*, 22 July 1986.
60 William M. Carley, 'Terrorist Group Has Financial Operation at Warsaw Company', *Wall Street Journal*, 16 October 1987.
61 Steven V. Roberts, 'Secret Saudi Funding Aids US Policy Goals', *International Herald Tribune*, 22 June 1987.
62 Stanley Penn, 'Illicit Trade', *Wall Street Journal*, 5 September 1986. See also John J. Fialka, 'War Center'. *Wall Street Journal*, 30 January 1987.

SECRET MONEY

63 Jeff Gerth, 'The Iran Money Flow: Tracing the Complex Steps', *Wall Street Journal*, 15 December 1986.
64 George J. Church, 'The Murky World of Weapons Dealers', *Time*, 19 January 1987.
65 'Khashoggi Reportedly Made $250,000 in Deal', *New York Times*, 15 December 1986.
66 Tim Carrington and Andy Pasztor, 'Weinberger Says Army Apparently Set Improper Price for CIA on Iran Missiles', *Wall Street Journal*, 7 January 1987.
67 David Rogers, 'Contras Helped Fund Military Activities With Panamanian Firms' Bank Accounts', *Wall Street Journal*, 5 March 1987.
68 John Tagliabue, 'Companies in Switzerland Appear to Have Been Fronts', *New York Times*, 15 December 1986.
69 John Tagliabue, 'Swiss Company Calls Dealings Legal', *New York Times*, 2 December 1986.
70 David Rogers, 'Panama Records Show Strong Link Between Swiss Firm, Airlift to Contras', *Wall Street Journal*, 30 January 1987.
71 Walter S. Mossberg, 'Trail of Money from the Iran-Contra Arms Sales Remains Murky Despite 6 Months of Investigation', *Wall Street Journal*, 5 May 1987.
72 Charles R. Babcock, 'Anti-Libya Plan Tied to Iran Slush Fund', *International Herald Tribune*, 20 May 1987.
73 Fox Butterfield, 'Courier for North Tells of Carrying Cash for Contras', *New York Times*, 15 May 1987.
74 Andy Pasztor and Edward T. Pound, 'Iranian Officials May Have Gotten Kickbacks on US Arms Sales Via Inflated-Price Scheme', *Wall Street Journal*, 5 March 1987.
75 'North Reportedly Aided a Political Action Group', *New York Times*, 15 December 1986. See also Walter S. Mossberg, 'Most of Iran-Contra Affair Remains a Mystery, Including Israel's Role, Arms-Sales Suspension', *Wall Street Journal*, 7 January 1987.
76 Charles R. Babcock, *op. cit.* (n. 72).
77 Fox Butterfield, 'North's $10 Million Mistake: Sultan's Gift Lost in a Mixup', *New York Times*, 14 May 1987. See also Thomas Netter, 'Sultan Asks for Return of Contra Cash, Interest', *International Herald Tribune*, 13 June 1987.
78 John Tagliabue, 'Accounts at Bank Frozen by Swiss', *New York Times*, 16 December 1986.
79 John Tagliabue, 'Swiss Account Linked to Arms Deal is Frozen', *New York Times*, 8 December 1986.
80 John Tagliabue, 'US Gives Swiss 7 Names in Inquiry in Iran Affair', *New York Times*, 20 December 1986. See also John Tagliabue, 'Swiss to Freeze Iran Arms Accounts', *New York Times*, 31 December 1986.
81 Thomas W. Netter, 'US Seeks More Information from Swiss on the Iran Affair', *New York Times*, 26 February 1987.
82 Scot J. Paltrow, 'Iran-Contra Inquiry Could be Delayed by Bids to Block Access to Swiss Accounts', *Wall Street Journal*, 21 January 1987.
83 'Iran-Contra Prosecutor May See Bank Records, Swiss Court Rules', *Asian Wall Street Journal*, 22 August 1987.
84 'Swiss to Provide Records of Contra Aid Accounts', *New York Times*, 1 November 1987.
85 Philip Shenon, 'Swiss May Open Files Tied to Iran Case', *New York Times*, 17 September 1987.
86 Philip Shenon, 'Swiss Bank Records in Iran-Contra Case Are Released to US', *New York Times*, 4 November 1987.
87 Haynes Johnson, 'Three Months of Hearings Fail to Crack the Case', *Washington Post*, 4 August 1987.
88 'North's Courier Handed Funds to Contras', *Wall Street Journal*, 20 May 1987.

7

Supply of Secret Money

In the financial secrecy business, demand creates its own supply. People have always hidden wealth – from their neighbors, from thieves, from their rulers. Mattresses, caves, loose bricks in basement walls, hollow tree trunks and holes in the ground have provided financial secrecy services for centuries.

With the advent of sovereign states, and the ability to transfer financial resources between them, came the possibility for secrecy seekers to solicit protection offshore. The principle of sovereignty of states insures that foreigners will have limited insight, strictly controlled by domestic law and policy; anything more is politically unacceptable. So the likelihood of disclosure to private parties in the asset-holder's home country is minimal, while disclosure to home-government authorities in civil and criminal cases is a matter for intergovernmental negotiation and treaties. Since countries differ widely in their political and economic systems, and in their interpretation of what constitutes unacceptable behavior (within their own borders and abroad), there is ample opportunity for the provision of financial secrecy in the international environment.

While it is clear that national sovereignty is the foundation of international secrecy, it is equally clear that some countries are well known as secrecy 'havens' whereas others are not. Some are quite willing to accommodate investigations by foreign governments, whereas others fiercely resist them. And some actively solicit the secrecy business. Why? The answers are found in international differences in law and policy, and in perceptions of economic costs and benefits.

Elements of supply

Some countries have more onerous tax systems than others, perhaps because of a strong social aversion to differences among people in income and wealth, or because of a powerful preference for the state over the private sector in the allocation of resources. The tax system is used as a vehicle for implementing such policies, and taxes drive a wedge between risk and return, between effort and reward as faced by individuals in society as a whole. Symmetry may exist at the level of society, but it is certainly lacking at the level of the individual.

The feeling in many countries is that their governments cannot be held responsible for the consequences of the taxation systems of others. And if they stand to benefit in the process of simply safeguarding their own sovereignty, so much the better. So tax investigations launched in one country may well be received in others with a singular lack of sympathy or cooperation, unless two countries have comparable tax arrangements or other forms of reciprocity and have negotiated mutual financial insight.

The use of tax havens is certainly nothing new. In ancient Athens merchants would detour 20 miles to avoid a 2 per cent tax on imports and exports. And in the United States havens were in use as early as 1721 when the colonies shifted their trade to Latin America to avoid paying duties imposed by England. Nowadays tax havens abound in virtually all parts of the world. A 1981 report prepared for the IRS named six characteristics besides minimal taxes that distinguished the tax haven: existence of stringent bank secrecy rules; importance of banking to the country's economy; availability of communications and transportation facilities; lack of currency controls; active solicitation of financial business; and (usually) the absence of tax treaties.[1]

Table 7.1 provides a listing of countries regarded as tax havens by the US Commissioner of Internal Revenue. Given the global reach of the US tax system as far as its own citizens are concerned, this listing is likely to be quite comprehensive.

Going beyond tax matters, countries that supply financial secrecy in criminal cases have a somewhat more difficult time justifying their actions on grounds of national sovereignty. As we have seen in Chapter 6, the criminal dimensions run from securities law violations and fraud to the rackets, gunrunning and the drugs trade. However, a crime may not be considered a crime unless it is committed on the territory of the host country, which makes financial disclosure associated with criminal offenses committed abroad difficult to justify under virtually any circumstances. An alternative position is that disclosure is warranted *only* if a crime committed abroad is also defined as a crime in the host country. Here a case has to be made that the appropriate domestic due process and the associated legal tests are satisfied, which may not be easy in many instances and impossible in cases such as bribery and corruption, exchange control avoidance, securities law violations and antitrust infringements. Of course, arm-twisting can be exercised if the country where the crime has been committed has sufficient bargaining leverage. Host countries have on occasion been known to bend their own rules.

186

Table 7.1 *List of countries or territories regarded as tax havens*

Caribbean and South Atlantic	Europe, Middle East, Africa
Antigua	Austria
Bahamas	Bahrain
Barbados	Channel Islands
Belize	Gibraltar
Bermuda	Isle of Man
British Virgin Islands	Liberia
Cayman Islands	Liechtenstein
Costa Rica	Luxembourg
Falkland Islands	Monaco
Grenada	Netherlands
Montserrat	Switzerland
Anguilla	
Netherlands Antilles	*Asia-Pacific*
Nevis	Cook Islands
Panama	Guam
St Kitts	Hong Kong
St Lucia	Maldives
St Vincent	Nauru
Turks and Caicos Islands	Vanuatu
Uruguay	Singapore
	Tonga

Source: Letter from Roscoe L. Egger, US Commissioner of Internal Revenue, to Sen. William V. Roth, Jr, 2 November 1981. Tax havens are defined as having little or no income tax and high levels of banking and commercial secrecy.

Patterns of secrecy supply

Secrecy is basically supplied by countries in two ways. One is domestic bank secrecy laws, which bar insight by national and foreign authorities alike. The other is blocking statutes, which effectively prevent the disclosure, copying, inspection or removal of documents located in the host country in compliance with orders by foreign authorities. Moreover, legal depositions may not be taken on national territory in connection with judicial proceedings being undertaken abroad. A variety of countries other than those usually identified as tax or secrecy havens have comprehensive blocking statutes to guard their sovereignty from the extraterritorial reach of foreign authorities. These include the United Kingdom, France, South Africa, West Germany, Australia, Norway and Canada.

Beyond the 'passive' supply of international financial secrecy by simply enforcing national laws and regulations, a number of countries have become very active sellers of secrecy services. Why? Predictably it is largely a matter of economics.

187

Countries with very small, open economies have often embraced the financial secrecy business as a way of promoting economic development. With some notable exceptions, these countries tend to be geographically isolated, with narrow production bases concentrated on a few major commodities, usually destined for export. This tends to make them vulnerable to adverse climatic conditions or international market developments. It also limits their ability to produce efficiently for the domestic market, invest in adequate infrastructure, attract foreign direct investment, and gain access to a diversified mix of export markets and import suppliers. Such economies face extremely restricted choices in mapping out a viable development strategy, choices that generally focus on geographic location, weather conditions, and human resources. Tourism is one example of an industry that such countries often turn to in the search for economic development.

Efforts to become a financial center can take two forms. One is to become a 'functional' center, where transactions are actually undertaken and value-added is created in the design and delivery of financial services. Examples of functional centers include Geneva, Zurich, London, Singapore, Bahrain, and Hong Kong. The other is to become a 'booking' center, where transactions are recorded but the value-added is actually created elsewhere. Examples in this category include the Bahamas, Cayman Islands, Seychelles, and Vanuatu. In order to attract financial booking business, one prerequisite is a highly favorable tax climate alongside a benign regulatory and supervisory environment. Clearly, strict financial secrecy or blocking statutes can play an important part in determining a country's attractiveness as a financial booking center. The benefits include induced employment, fiscal contributions, and positive linkage effects to firms and industries that service the financial sector. Unfortunately, the size of these benefits in most cases appears to be quite small.[2] However, if the marginal cost of creating a favorable secrecy environment is equally small, the number of such centers is bound to remain significant and may grow.

Of particular interest is the supply of financial secrecy for criminal purposes, which characterizes some (but not all) of the major vendors. According to one US study,

Africa, Central America and the Caribbean Islands are the areas most vulnerable to involvement in politically corrupt or direct criminal matters where suitable control is not exercised by headquarters [of US banks]. Of these three regions, the Caribbean Islands are characterized as the most vulnerable in the world. That appraisal conforms ... to our impression of gross inadequacies, improper influence, and reported criminal involvement in the Caribbean involving some banks, local officials, assorted travelling highwaymen, narcotics traffickers and the like.

Headquarters standards vary depending on the company and the homeland's central bank. Variations occur within the same banking company among its branches in offshore locations. For example, in the Caribbean, one major Canadian international bank has a consistent reputation for encouraging dirty money. One shell branch of a UK bank in the Bahamas is held suspect for its own manager's discretionary tolerance in accepting questionable funds. In the Caymans or Panama, the majority of banks are said to accept suitcase currency.[3]

One relatively new example is Vanuatu, a tiny Southwest Pacific island nation, formerly the joint French–British colony of New Hebrides. With a population of 125,000 scattered across some 80 islands, Vanuatu has attempted to promote itself as a financial center by selling political stability, the lack of exchange controls, the absence of estate, death and income taxes, adequate communications, and limited financial disclosure. Lately it has made a special effort to attract capital from Southeast Asia, the Caribbean, and especially Hong Kong by allowing shareholders of registered companies to remain anonymous, with no requirements for character references or checking of Interpol criminal suspect lists. Annual financial audits are optional, as are notifications of ownership changes as long as the enterprise does not conduct business in Vanuatu itself. This does not apply, however, for banks, insurance companies, trust companies, and securities dealers.

Or take the Kingdom of Tonga, which passed an offshore banking act in 1985 providing for *pangike fakapulipuli* (secret banking) and thus joined Vanuatu, Nauru and the Marshall Islands as a Pacific haven located about 2,000 miles east of Australia. Tonga has only 270 square miles of territory and a population of 87,000, and its finance minister was quoted as envisaging offshore banking as 'the fastest and easiest means, even surpassing tourism' to enhance its foreign exchange earnings.[4]

Many of the countries that sell financial secrecy can be described more or less in these same terms. Secrecy is simply good business in an environment where alternative routes to economic growth are severely limited. This applies to a much lesser extent, of course, to countries like Switzerland and Austria, although the underlying economic incentives are much the same. To illustrate, we can briefly survey the patterns of secrecy in a number of countries around the world.

Switzerland

Financial secrecy in Switzerland is an outgrowth of that country's long tradition of personal and individual privacy – a tradition that dates back at least as far as the age of feudalism. The legal foundation of Swiss bank secrecy is based on the personal rights established in the Swiss Consti-

189

tution, the Civil Code and the Code of Obligations, supplemented by provisions in the Criminal Code. There is, in addition, the Banking Law of 1934, which was enacted partly in response to the financial crises of the early 1930s, but also as an attempt to deal with the Nazis' investigations into Jewish accounts in Switzerland. It provided for severe criminal penalties for violators of disclosure prohibitions, and made Swiss secrecy laws among the toughest anywhere. However, the Banking Law of 1934 did not include a definition of bank secrecy. Instead of narrowly defining secrecy by legal statute, definition is left to custom and practice, and to judicial discretion.

The origins of Swiss federal laws to protect the silence of bankers themselves can be traced to 1916, although utmost discretion on the part of the Swiss banking community vis-à-vis foreign authorities extends much further – certainly to capital flight associated with the Edict of Nantes and the French Revolution. In the 1930s, Swiss bankers were insisting that their privileged relationship to clients should be on a par with that of clergymen, physicians and lawyers. The 1934 law basically accepts this view by making it a federal crime to breach the confidential relationship between client and banker. Such action, willful or negligent, on the part of any present or former bank employee is subject to a fine of up to SFr 50,000 and imprisonment of up to six months. Those who induce such action, or attempt to do so, face a fine of up to SFr 30,000. Revision of the Swiss Banking Law in 1982 dropped this last provision, and eliminated negligence as a basis for prosecution of bank employees under the law. It is worthwhile pointing out that there has been no negligence case brought before the Swiss courts in decades. 'Inducements' related to political or economic espionage are covered under other sections of the Swiss penal code. It is interesting to note that, whereas violations of professional secrecy by lawyers or doctors, for example, are only prosecuted if the injured party specifically requests that they should be, violations of banking secrecy are prosecuted ex officio by law.[5]

Specifically, Article 47 of the Swiss Banking Law provides that:

1. Whoever divulges a secret entrusted to him in his capacity as officer, employee, mandatory, liquidator or commissioner of a bank, as a representative of the Banking Commission, officer or employee of a recognized auditing company, or whoever tries to induce others to violate professional secrecy, shall be punished by a prison term not to exceed six months or by a fine not exceeding 50,000 francs.
2. If the act has been committed by negligence, the penalty shall be a fine not exceeding 30,000 francs.
3. The violation of professional secrecy remains punishable even after termination of the official or employment relationship or the exercise of the profession.

4. Federal and cantonal regulation concerning the obligation to testify and to furnish information to a government authority shall remain reserved;

Moreover, Article 273 of the Swiss Penal Code provides, in part:

Whoever makes available a manufacturing or business secret to a foreign governmental agency or a foreign organization or private enterprise to an agent of any of them, shall be subject to imprisonment and in grave cases to imprisonment in a penitentiary. The imprisonment may be combined with a fine.

Unless waived by the client, or by the application of a treaty, these provisions had until recently been strictly enforced, even against disclosure requests by foreign law-enforcement agencies.

Moreover, Swiss authorities took a very dim view of any kind of unauthorized disclosure of business information, even when 'whistle blowing' was clearly in line with the country's own international commitments and obligations. Take the case of Stanley Adams, a former executive with Hoffman-La Roche, the Swiss pharmaceutical firm. As manager of Roche's international vitamins operations, Adams discovered an array of company tax-avoidance schemes involving transfer pricing, as well as price-fixing arrangements in EEC countries that were in direct violation of the Community's competition law – to which Roche was accountable under a 1972 Swiss–EEC trade agreement. Based upon Adams' disclosure, Roche was indicted and convicted in a court action brought by the Community's antitrust division. Once his disclosures came to light, Adams himself was jailed in Switzerland for industrial espionage. Informed that her husband faced 20 years' imprisonment, his wife committed suicide while he was being held without formal charges. The EEC eventually provided bail, and Adams fled first to Italy and then to the United Kingdom. In Switzerland, according to Adams, 'whatever affects big business affects the state'.[6]

A 1984 example of the sensitivity of the Swiss system to possible disclosure involved the Wozchod Handelsbank, the Soviet Union's principal gold-trading vehicle, operating in Zurich. The bank's chief trader and foreign currency dealer (a Swiss) was accused of fraudulent activities that cost the bank anywhere between $36 million and $350 million in losses, eventually resulting in the bank's liquidation and its replacement in Zurich by a branch of the Soviet Foreign Trade Bank. He was dismissed and charged with criminal mismanagement. However, given the size of the fraudulent operations it was clear that a number of the bank's other employees were involved as well. All were fired, but the matter of potential disclosure was considered so sensitive that no criminal charges were brought against them.

Since the body of laws covering secrecy is rather loosely defined, Swiss banks and their employees generally exercise extraordinary caution, and do not release information unless explicitly required by judicial act. Moreover, Swiss secrecy laws apply not only to bank–outsider relationships, but also to bank–government and bank–bank relationships. For example, the acknowledgement of the *existence* of an account is a direct violation of the law, even if it is between employees of two different banks.

However, while Swiss bankers still pride themselves on the provision of financial secrecy, things are no longer quite as they once were. Secrecy still has a major role to play, but in recent years chinks have appeared in the armor. The freezing of the Marcos and Duvalier accounts, for example, would hardly have happened in earlier times. Indeed, efforts to reach Swiss-managed assets of fallen dictators had failed miserably in the past – Ethiopia was firmly rebuffed in the 1970s when it sought possession of the funds of the deposed Emperor Haile Selassie, and Iran fared no better in its claims to the wealth of the Shah.[7] Bank Leu's cooperation in the Levine case was yet another indication that Swiss bank secrecy is no longer inviolate. Swiss bankers will insist that each incident is a special case, but there is undoubtedly a general and perceptible trend towards greater flexibility on secrecy matters.[8]

In part, this is due to the changing nature of world financial markets – a point to which we return later – and in part (as shown in the Marcos case) evidence of the growing importance of public opinion. With involvement not only in these cases, but with a host of others including Banco Ambrosiano, Irangate and Guinness, Switzerland has suffered a surfeit of adverse publicity.[9] As a result there appears to be a gentle reshaping of attitudes, a growing awareness that the opaque nature of Swiss banking can have weaknesses as well as strengths. The first major sign was perhaps as early as April 1977, when the Chiasso Affair came to light.

The Chiasso branch of Crédit Suisse failed in its fiduciary responsibilities. Instead of investing clients' funds in the Euromarket with top-tier financial institutions, the manager of the branch lent heavily to an Italian wine and food group, whose profits were quickly eroded by high interest rates and depreciation of the lira. The resultant losses were covered by Crédit Suisse itself, backstopped by the other two major Swiss banks. This case nevertheless pointed up the 'moral hazard' to which each of them was exposed by virtue of the degree of secrecy embodied in the system.

The question was how to enhance the safety of Swiss banking without sacrificing the attributes, including secrecy, that give it strength. The outcome was a *Vereinbarung* (gentlemen's agreement), which signaled a tightening of control over banking operations and an end to simple self-discipline as the major guiding force in Swiss bank treatment of customers. In addition to a passport, depositors interested in a Swiss account today should be prepared for a fairly exhaustive series of interviews. At Union Bank of Switzerland, for instance, there is an initial screening followed by a lengthy chat with an investment counselor who will seem to be evaluating the depositor's investment philosophy, but will also be trying to find out whether there are reasons for concern about his legitimacy.[10]

Moreover, the Federal Banking Commission has increased the number of bank audits, instituted a wider range of monitoring activities, and issued guidelines on how banks are to manage fiduciary funds.

In addition, in 1977 the Convention of Diligence (*Sorgfaltspflicht*) was signed by all the major Swiss banks, and by the Swiss National Bank and the Swiss Bankers' Association. It prohibits signatories from doing business without knowledge of the identity of the counterparty – whether such business involves accepting cash or securities deposits, fiduciary activities, or the use of safe-deposit boxes. Only banks, and not the bankers themselves, can be punished under the Convention, with fines up to SFr 10 million. Alleged violations are brought before a three-man committee that meets in Lausanne, and that can impose fines of up to SFr 10 million. These fines are paid over to charity, and the cases heard by the committee are not made public. As of 1983, 30 cases had been brought under the Convention, with the largest fine being SFr 500,000.[11] A proposal has been made to extend the fines to bankers as well. The Swiss banks fought the Convention vehemently prior to its post-Chiasso enactment in 1977, but subsequently have used it as a major justification for not deeming additional legislation to be necessary, representing it in effect as a certificate of morality.

Nevertheless, the same 1977 Chiasso scandal induced the small Swiss Social Democratic party to introduce a formal *Bankeninitiative* (bank initiative) which would have, through referendum: (1) lifted bank secrecy in certain tax evasion cases, whether at home or abroad, and in evasion of exchange controls; (2) broadened disclosure in bank financial statements, which would also be extended to hidden reserves, and allowed discussions of these statements in parliament; (3) limited bank ownership and control of non-banking enterprises; and (4) instituted insurance for savings deposits. Under the *Bankeninitiative*, foreign fiscal authorities would have been permitted to examine Swiss bank records in cases of tax evasion and currency violations.

The Social Democrats had been calling for reforms in the Swiss banking law for more than a decade, but did not receive significant public support until the Chiasso affair, followed coincidentally by the rapid and economically damaging appreciation of the Swiss franc. In the aftermath of the scandal, the party leadership argued that the franc was chronically overvalued because of secrecy-seeking capital inflows, and that the country had become a haven for the ill-gotten gains of corrupt public officials, criminals and tax evaders from all over the world. Although the Swiss population appeared to accept only part of this argument, public confidence in the banking industry did seem to be called into question.

The Social Democrats' *Initiative* was opposed by both the government and the Swiss parliament, but was nevertheless scheduled to be put to a referendum vote in the summer of 1984. No previous Social Democrat initiative has passed since 1917, although many of the ideas embodied in them have eventually found their way into law.

In June 1984, after over five years of discussion, Swiss voters rejected the *Bankeninitiative* by a 3–1 margin. To some extent the *Initiative* had been pre-empted by the tightening of regulatory and supervisory controls over Swiss banks, and by the banks' leading role in bailing out domestic recession- and competition-plagued industries such as watch-making. But besides that, a major exportable service was clearly at stake, one the average Swiss was not about to let slip away.

The Swiss banks mounted a massive public relations campaign, variously estimated to have cost around SFr 15 million, to defeat the effort – including such tactics as comic books aimed at preschoolers to convince them of the value of Swiss banks. Even knowing that not more than half of Swiss voters usually turn out for referendums and then usually vote 'no', the banks wanted to achieve at least a 60 per cent vote against the proposal to prevent the issue coming up again in the near future. Their arguments included the suggestion that erosion of secrecy would limit human rights, increase unemployment, trigger a crash in the stock market, and threaten the prevailing low Swiss interest rates on home mortgages. The banks maintained that they had no interest in retaining 'dirty money', variously estimated during the campaign as comprising SFr 8–100 billion – not including funds attributable to tax evasion, capital flight, evasion of exchange controls, and other motivations that are not considered illegal in Switzerland. They also maintained that a significant tightening-up of the Swiss banking system, including disclosure of more detailed financial information to the Swiss National Bank and the implementation of a self-financed deposit insurance scheme to cover savings and salary deposits, was already under consideration before the *Initiative* was put on the agenda.[12]

Following the defeat of the referendum, the chairman of Crédit Suisse was quoted as saying that the banks' opponents had actually '. . . rendered a valuable service not only to the Swiss banking industry, but to the whole economy and to the future of our country.' Bankers' expectations appeared to be that substantially greater inflows of funds would result, including those of institutional investors seeking 'to be safe from indiscretion and surreptitious or malicious prying', and an uncharacteristically competitive battle seemed to be heating up among the major Swiss banks for institutional business.[13]

For their part, the Social Democrats continued to press their case even in defeat, fearing that the outcome of the referendum would be considered a license for Swiss banks to promote tax evasion and flight capital around the world.

One suggestion was that on its expiry at the end of September 1984 the Convention of Diligence agreed between the Swiss National Bank and the Swiss Bankers' Association should be included in a revision of the 1934 Banking Law. In the event, the Agreement was renewed, but with certain major amendments. The Swiss National Bank announced its unwillingness to be involved for a further term, stating that regulatory functions were not its responsibility and proposing therefore that the Banking Commission take a more active role. This it did, and the modified version of the agreement was signed on 23 March 1987[14] and came into effect on 1 October 1987. Under the revised terms, the loophole whereby lawyers and accountants could open accounts for unidentified clients has been closed. Any fiduciary agent must now sign a statement that he handles business for the client and is not merely providing a front for someone else.[15] Also included is a further change to the limit for client identification to the bank on substantial withdrawals or deposits, down from SFr 500,000 to SFr 10,000.[16]

An interesting alternative explanation for the *Bankeninitiative* emerged as well. It goes as follows: contrary to popular impression, the Swiss themselves are fairly heavily taxed, especially on earned income (salaries and wages) and on wealth – a particularly sensitive issue when yields on assets denominated in Swiss francs have generally been very low. Consequently, many Swiss are themselves tax evaders through the country's own system of banking secrecy. Those supporting the Social Democrats' initiative were really after their own countrymen rather than the foreigners or the bankers. This is why the initiative received as much support as it did. Otherwise, the theory goes, to shoot oneself in the foot through a concerted attack against a major export industry makes no sense.

Given the nature of Swiss personal banking, people choose to deposit funds in Swiss banks for several reasons, some having nothing at all to do with secrecy laws:

- the well-known competence and integrity of Swiss bankers and their standing in the international banking community;
- the 'financial supermarket' nature of the broad range of services that Swiss banks can provide for a client;
- the ability of the depositors to place liquid assets in Swiss francs or other currencies as a hedge against inflation and currency fluctuations;
- the freedom from exchange controls, government regulations and interference in banking activities; and
- virtually unparalleled political stability.

195

Swiss banks may execute transactions on the basis of telephone instructions and, unlike some other banks, can offer a broad range of trust, investment and related services. Swiss accounts can be opened by mail, although the establishment of a relationship through personal contact or formal introduction appears to be more common. Swiss banks maintain that they do undertake background checks in cases where questions arise, but the frequency or depth of such checks is unknown.

Despite the bad publicity from its involvement in affairs such as Chiasso, Levine and Guinness, Swiss banking has on the whole maintained a reasonable track record of careful and prudent management, perhaps at some cost to short-term earnings. For example, Swiss banks stayed more clear than some of their competitors of the international debt crisis of the early 1980s by limiting exposure in developing countries, concentrating on short-term trade financing and loans guaranteed by the Swiss government. In part, their cautious behavior may have been attributed more to strict capital ratios than to self-discipline, and in 1984 the Swiss banking authorities imposed on them the requirement to disclose their international exposures semi-annually on a consolidated basis by domicile of the borrower and guarantor (if any). Additional data also has to be provided on international assets and liabilities with respect to both banks and non-banks, as well as on their foreign exchange operations and forward commitments.

From the point of view of secrecy seekers, the Swiss image may benefit as well from the elaborate precautions the country has taken for the possibility of nuclear war. The objective is to provide a modern nuclear fallout shelter for every resident of Switzerland, in cities, towns, villages, even farms, by the year 2000. Since 1970, Switzerland has spent over $2.5 billion on its shelter program, far more than any other country on a per capita basis, and all new homes (including vacation chalets) must have fallout shelters. The government pays half the cost. A large standing military, mandatory conscription, and high level of civil defense preparedness completes the Swiss readiness effort.[17] The idea is to give Swiss residents a better than average chance of survival in the event of nuclear war, which perhaps not coincidentally bolsters Switzerland's image as a safe haven for outsiders' funds. What would be left of the real assets backing Swiss deposits in the event of catastrophe is of course open to question. On the other hand, large numbers of depositors certainly would no longer be around to collect.

Even given the 'lapses' and changes, secrecy and secrecy laws still provide an enormous additional incentive for people to place funds with Swiss banks. The use of numbered accounts, *Aktiengesellschaften* (stock companies), personal holding companies and 'base' companies are a few of the available vehicles. And the location of Switzerland itself, with outstanding transportation and communication facilities, makes it easy to shift funds into and out of the country without attracting undue attention. Much of the business remains in the hands of the 'Big Three' – Union Bank of Switzerland, Swiss Bank Corporation, Crédit Suisse – although numerous smaller players obtain a respectable share. Competition among them appears to be 'gentlemanly'.

According to one account, Switzerland therefore remains an expensive alternative for tax avoidance or other less-than-hard-core secrecy seekers and those who simply want ordinary banking services. 'All banks – including foreign-owned ones – operate a complicated price cartel. For example, a Swiss bank takes a 0.5 per cent cut on any deposit it makes for a client with another bank; it would take a minimum £1,300 fee (plus dealing costs) for buying L100,000 worth of British equities for a client. By the time other extras charged by the cartel are included, running a portfolio from Switzerland could cost over 2 per cent a year – against 1–1.5 per cent in London.'[18] Consequently, clients not driven by secrecy may seek alternatives. According to one attorney, 'All my clients have made their money under the eye of the taxman, so why pay extra to hide it?'[19]

The Liechtenstein link

There is a close connection in the supply of financial secrecy between Switzerland and Liechtenstein, a small principality of 65 square miles with a population of 22,000 permanent residents. Bank secrecy in Liechtenstein rests on the Company Law, enacted in 1926. This allows for the formation of several kinds of corporations such as the *Aktiengesellschaft*, the *Stiftung* (family foundation), the *Anstalt* (establishment) and various kinds of trusts. Most such forms of corporate organization are openly referred to as 'dummy' or 'paper' corporations, used to hold or transfer assets while at the same time protecting them from tax liabilities.

The *Anstalt* is the most popular form of corporate association and is unique to Liechtenstein. These are non-share corporations, which have a limited liability and initial capitalization of at least SFr 20,000. Once the corporation is formed, the capital can be immediately repatriated to the owners. Many *Anstalten* can be set up in Switzerland by a Swiss banker, who arranges the formalities through a Liechtenstein banker or lawyer. They are always listed in the Public Register, but this does not require disclosure of the name of the *Anstalt*'s owner. Only the Swiss banker, and possibly the lawyer in Liechtenstein, know the owner's true identity. In addition to the bank and legal fees, a tax of only $\frac{1}{10}$ per cent of the initial capitalization is levied in Liechtenstein. This Liechtenstein–Switzerland connection or relationship is often described as the best and possibly the cheapest means of securing privacy and anonymity for an international investor.

If the figures are anything to go by, it is certainly very popular.

197

Deposits into Switzerland from Liechtenstein in 1982, for example, were running at around $5 billion, a fourfold increase from 1978.[20] And it may be that as Switzerland is coerced into further concessions on the secrecy front, the additional level of privacy provided by the Liechtenstein channel will become ever more important.

With a population of 27,000, Liechtenstein had between 25,000 and 50,000 letter box companies in 1988, which contributed up to one third of national income.

Crown Prince Hans Adam (who acceded in 1984 as Liechtenstein's fifth ruler in 125 years) is fully aware of the vital role bank secrecy plays in his country's prosperity. His family bank is now one of Europe's fastest growing banks. Between 1980 and 1985, assets under management grew threefold to an estimated $7 billion.[21] He appears determined to bring his family bank into world markets. With the help of the bank's chairman, Swedish-born Christian Norgren, lured from Frankfurt's Deutsch-Skandinavische Bank in 1981, expansion has occurred at a considerable rate, and the bank is represented in Frankfurt, London, Zurich, New York and Hong Kong. In 1986 it went public, raising $140 million through an issue of non-voting stock in Zurich and Frankfurt. The following year it bought the respected New York investment-counseling firm of Trainer Wrotham, as well as helping launch a $70 million US real estate management venture with the British company, Grosvenor Estates.

A major part of its business is investment management for private clients, concentrating on those worth more than $5 million. Some 70 per cent of the $1 billion managed by Trainer Wrotham is in private accounts, and a Californian branch was opened to cater for the needs of the wealthy in Silicon Valley. Liechtenstein has more stringent secrecy laws than Switzerland and the Prince himself describes his country as a 'tax oasis'. Still, he appears to realize that the bank cannot rely on tax avoidance alone, and that investment performance is paramount for success on a global scale. Investment policy nevertheless continues to emphasize caution and conservatism, with the result that accounts run by the Liechtenstein office lost less than 10 per cent in the October crash of 1987.

The Prince also seems aware of the danger of the bank overstretching through excessively rapid growth, and of failing to establish any corporate identity. He has taken steps to avoid these problems, such as the establishment of a Swiss holding company. In the meantime, business seems to be thriving. Between 1982 and 1987, assets under management more than doubled to $4 billion, and capital increased four times to $420 million.[22]

Product differentiation is reflected in the saying 'If you want a real Swiss bank account, come to Liechtenstein'. The country does not have a withholding tax on investment income as imposed by the Swiss, and opening a numbered account is reportedly simple. Asked by a reporter whether he could open such an account, the director of a Liechtenstein bank said, 'Only after we've seen your passport and got your address.' Asked about laundering of money through Liechtenstein, he replied, 'I personally look at all transfers of SFr 10 million and above. We don't want criminal money here.'[23]

Costs

'If you've got $10,000 or $20,000 go to Citibank,' one Swiss banker has noted. 'We can't help you and you can't help us.' While the major Swiss banks say they do not have a formal minimum for opening a numbered account, most discourage deposits under $50,000 and interest develops only well into six figures. Minimum deposits in Swiss accounts can be substantial.[24]

Current accounts bear no interest at all. Deposit accounts bear very low interest rates. Withdrawals under many types of accounts often require notice, are possible only with limited frequency, and sometimes involve withdrawal penalties. Obviously, exchange-rate expectations must be taken into account in comparing returns, as well as the likelihood of future interest-rate changes. Swiss deposits are also subject to an interest withholding tax of 35 per cent, of which 30 per cent will be rebated if the account holder is not a Swiss resident.

In 1986, banks in Switzerland had SFr 848 billion ($520 billion) on their balance sheets, of which SFr 260 billion was foreign-owned. In addition, they had SFr 187 billion in fiduciary accounts. Private banks are not required to publish balance sheets if they do not advertise their services, although they are required to report annually to the Swiss National Bank.

The figures on the size of fiduciary accounts in general are highly suspect, and may in fact be much larger. Some suggestions have put the total figure for foreign investors' funds managed by Swiss banks as high as SFr 1.6 trillion.[25] An estimated two-thirds of these are concentrated in the five major banks, UBS, Swiss Bank Corporation, Crédit Suisse, Swiss Volksbank and Bank Leu, with the rest spread among 104 foreign-owned banks and 24 specially designated private banks.[26]

Economic significance of banking

Overall, Swiss banks retain a very strong competitive position in international private banking – there are more bank branches than dentists, one for every 1,250 of the population, as compared with one for 6,000 in the United States. This has resulted from time to time in massive capital inflows, far out of proportion to the size and performance of the

Swiss economy. A large part of these inflows is placed directly in foreign and offshore financial markets, with the Swiss banks acting as financial intermediaries for their clients.

The Swiss financial sector employs 111,400 people (1986), about 3 per cent of the working population, and generates tax revenues of over SFr 6 billion. The net income from its activities (SFr 15 billion in 1986), makes possible a current account surplus on the country's balance of payments broadly equivalent to 4 per cent of GDP.[27]

Portfolio management activities contribute positively to the Swiss economy in several ways, including the increased leverage in world financial markets by Swiss banks. In 1984, the assets of the top 71 banks in Switzerland were valued at $200 billion, more than twice the Swiss gross national product. Commissions on portfolio management accounts supplement income derived from traditional lending and securities business. Bank fees are earned on fiduciary, discretionary and non-discretionary accounts, in addition to ancillary fees for brokerage commissions, cable transfers and other services that are normally for the account of clients. There are also gains from ancillary services, such as real estate, hotel accommodation, transportation and the like.

Fiduciary accounts provide a way around the 35 per cent withholding tax already mentioned – they are invested outside Switzerland in the bank's name but at the account holder's risk. Between 1983 and 1984 alone, fiduciary business rose some 24 per cent.[28] This expansion has brought its problems in the form of a veritable army of new financial companies, brokers and investment consultants (collectively known as fiduciaries), not to mention a number of dubious law offices. In an attempt to discipline the somewhat shady end of the market, the canton of Ticino (comprising the towns of Lugano and Chiasso) made registration compulsory for all such firms from the end of 1986.[29]

Despite this heavy commitment to private banking, the Swiss still regard themselves as a much broader financial center (*Finanzplatz Schweiz*), rather than merely as a tax or secrecy haven. For one thing, Switzerland does not charter offshore companies. Swiss-registered companies pay taxes on income, and must have local directors.

The dramatic expansion of Switzerland as an international financial center dates from the 1960s when inflationary policies in the United States led many investors and central banks to move savings and reserves into currencies other than the dollar. With its record of safety, stability, neutrality and low inflation, as well as a freely convertible currency, Switzerland was highly attractive.[30] But the situation has been changing. To the dismay of the Swiss, it is in areas of finance *other than* private banking that Switzerland has steadily lost ground as a world-class financial market to the greater dynamism and innovativeness of

London and New York, as well as to the rapidly evolving centers of the Far East.

Competitive shift

Financial markets have changed dramatically in the past decade and the Swiss have sometimes been slow to keep up. While bankers in London, New York and Tokyo were developing new services, Switzerland continued to rely on its traditional strengths of security and secrecy. For example, the Swiss have had a difficult time figuring out how to court a new type of international investor, pension funds. Although the Swiss never had the most competitive rates, they adroitly catered to wealthy foreigners who wanted safe investments kept away from the local tax man. 'They were happy if you got them a room at the St. Moritz Palace Hotel', commented one banker – an approach that has been rather ineffective with performance-oriented pension fund managers, for example.

With deregulation, new communications technology and round-the-clock trading centered on New York, Tokyo and London, there is an increasing (and certainly premature) tendency for Switzerland to be seen as a discreet backwater, ideally equipped for the wealthy individual, far less so for the professional institutional investor who wants performance first and foremost. Some observers allege that the Swiss are trailing behind both in their ability to invent and adapt new financial instruments and in their willingness to apply the latest trading techniques to make these new transactions work. In futures and options trading, for example, they have lagged, and only in 1988 did Switzerland put into operation a market in traded options and futures (SOFFEX), albeit a highly sophisticated one. At the same time, the long-standing near-monopoly of the major banks on the issuance of Swiss-franc denominated bonds began to erode.[31]

Swiss bankers and financiers also blame the country's declining relative importance on the government's decision to tax a wider range of securities transactions. This has put Switzerland at a disadvantage in competition with other world financial markets. In the international bond market, for example, where the Swiss were dominant just 15 years earlier, there has been a shift of activity to London, where 80 per cent of new international bonds were underwritten during the mid-1980s. Switzerland accounted for only 12 per cent.

Bankers have responded to these challenges by building up operations outside Switzerland. Swiss banks in 1986 had more than $140 billion in overseas assets. UBS, for example, had greatly strengthened its activities in London as the only way to be a major force in the Euromarket. In 1986 it acquired the London brokerage house, Phillips & Drew. It has a seat on the New York Stock Exchange and a Japanese trust banking license. SBC also has a New York seat and has been granted a Japanese securities permit. Crédit Suisse, also a holder of a Japanese trust banking license, now controls First Boston Corporation in New York and Credit Suisse First Boston in London.[32] Most of the major banks have been jockeying as well to break into the West German securities markets.[33] And Swiss portfolio managers have moved some of their business to London as well as the Cayman Islands and other such havens. Even the smaller private banks have realized that they cannot afford to be complacent, and are beginning to diversify their business mix and expand abroad.[34]

A 1987 study estimated that at the end of 1986, the three major banks, UBS, SBC and Crédit Suisse, managed between them portfolio funds in excess of $450 billion. To put that in context, the figures for J. P. Morgan were $62 billion, for Société Generale $19 billion. Geneva's private banks reportedly managed some SFr 100 billion ($71.7 billion) in 1988, the largest shares being accounted for by two banks, Lombard Odier and Pictet & Cie. Annual returns on funds under management averaged 1 per cent, including a standard 0.5 per cent p.a. management fee and a 0.175 per cent custodial fee.[35]

Even so, the Swiss are fully aware that the competition is increasingly fierce and that, to stay ahead on an international scale, they cannot merely rely on tradition. As a result, they are expanding their brokerage facilities and portfolio services into a number of other leading financial centers. They are making greater use of new technologies in portfolio management and trading. They are increasing training programmes – the big three, plus Julius Baer and Vontobel have established a Swiss Banking School in Zurich, and in Geneva the private banks have inaugurated a banking institute. Finally, they are paying more attention to the types of clients they serve to avoid the tarnishing of reputation that can come with a Levine, a Marcos, or a Duvalier.[36]

This new breed of Swiss bankers realizes that future banking success for Switzerland cannot depend on secrecy alone, especially in the light of the unified financial market due to be in place in the EEC by 1992. As one leading banker put it: 'Secrecy attracts attention because it's an emotional issue, but success will depend on things like tax levels for financial services, trading systems, people, electronic systems and clearing systems.'[37]

Ironically, it is the drive to participate fully in world markets that is another major contributory factor weakening Swiss secrecy. A high international profile makes it far more difficult for banks to refuse to cooperate with a foreign government agency, and they are far more vulnerable to outside pressure. This is particularly so as regards the United States, which explains to a great extent the success the SEC has had so far in its attempts to loosen Swiss secrecy in cases involving violation of US securities laws (see Chapter 9). There is a certain amount of bitterness amongst the smaller Swiss banks (whose diversification programmes are far behind those of the big banks) as they perceive their primary asset slowly being eroded as a result of the expansionary plans of the majors.

Even so, private banking and management of financial assets still form the cornerstone of Switzerland's place in the international financial scene. As shown in Chapters 8–10, secrecy has suffered erosion elsewhere as well, and the Swiss bankers' reputation for good sense, caution, discretion and high-quality service is still a valuable asset. Although there have been setbacks of bad publicity, the only one of the major five banks to see its reputation really suffer has been Bank Leu because of its unfortunate involvement with Marcos, Levine and Guinness – all revealed within less than twelve months.[38]

However, the massive inflows of capital have also had some adverse effects on the Swiss economy. The most obvious disadvantage is the periodically severe overvaluation of the franc. Swiss real estate and securities have become very expensive for foreigners, and domestic inflationary pressures have intensified from time to time. The competitiveness of Swiss exports has thus been impaired, only partly offset by the reduced cost of imports. It is sometimes forgotten, for example, that Switzerland imposed severe penalties on foreign account holders in the mid-1970s in order to discourage capital inflows – only the first SFr 50,000 of deposits were eligible to earn interest, and accounts in excess of SFr 100,000 incurred a negative interest of 40 per cent.

The French connection

Following President François Mitterand's election in France in 1981, large amounts of funds began to flow into Geneva's banking community. Estimates of the French share of funds under management by Geneva banks range from 50 to 80 per cent, although some put it much lower. Others suggest that French capital flows into Geneva during the two years after Mitterand's accession exceeded all comparable flows during the seven years of President Valéry Giscard d'Estaing's rule. Overall, French funds in Swiss accounts have been variously estimated at between $3.75 billion and $60 billion.[39]

Whatever the figure, it may have been considerably reduced following an amnesty announced in July 1986 by the newly elected Prime Minister Jacques Chirac. This allowed the repatriation of illegally exported funds on payment of a fine equal to 10 per cent of the amount returned. When the amnesty period ran out in February 1987, it was announced that approximately $2.6 billion had come home.

The French reaction at the time, however, included an enormous beefing-up of manpower on the Swiss border, especially around Geneva, including 800 new customs officers and the assignment of a number of fiscal operatives to Switzerland itself, even though a good deal of the funds transfers are undertaken not in person but rather via commercial transactions.

In 1983, the French fiscal authorities let it be known that they had cracked the computerized account data codes of the Union Bank of Switzerland, and had identified about 5,000 French citizens holding Swiss accounts in violation of French tax and foreign exchange regulations. UBS vehemently denied this, and suggested that the disclosure was a French bluff to elicit admissions of currency smuggling under promise of leniency. In a statement, a UBS deputy director-general emphatically maintained that: 'The lists are false or fabricated by French customs because we do not keep records of account holders by nationality.' The French State Secretary for the Budget replied: 'The French Customs Services has existed for 250 years. It is not in the habit of fabricating false evidence. There are no forgers in the Government . . . The Customs Service has its methods. We have computer experts who know their job.'[40]

The information ostensibly came to the attention of the French authorities in the form of computer print-out, with military cryptographers taking the lead in decoding, yielding the account number, the amount, and the name of the account holder. The French Finance Ministry then ran the names (not identified by nationality) through its computerized income tax files.

However, since tax dodgers may request that any correspondence be held at the Swiss bank, to be picked up personally, it seemed unlikely that the French claim to be able to trace addresses was entirely accurate. Indeed, the official story – as opposed to the press accounts – put the amount of money involved at only $22 million, with 300–400 named account holders ferreted out in part by fiscal agents who physically followed French citizens across the border and, in one case, were arrested and spent two months in a Swiss jail before being released. Even the Greeks got into the act. On the basis of information about the infamous French 'list', the Greek government evidently made overtures to acquire the names of Greek citizens with Swiss accounts.[41]

Other issues

Besides the perennial issue of tax evasion, Swiss financial institutions have also been cited in connection with the export of restricted high-technology products from the United States to the Soviet Union. In 1983, for example, a US court ordered Crédit Suisse to provide information on the financial affairs of an American client accused of illegal exports. Crédit Suisse appealed on the grounds of Swiss secrecy provisions, but the US tax courts denied the appeal, arguing that the alleged crime was neither tax evasion nor a political offense, but rather an outright criminal action involving forged bills of lading and an evasion of US export control legislation.[42]

Although illegal funds (other than tax evasion and flight capital) probably constitute only a miniscule fraction of foreign holdings in Swiss banks, they have become a hot political issue. The Swiss are obviously sensitive to international criticism of their system and its alleged role as an important 'facilitator' of criminal acts committed worldwide. Although Swiss banks certainly cannot be guilty of encouraging or advocating the underlying illegal activities, the available supply of financial secrecy still leaves the country open to charges of aiding and abetting illegal operations through scrupulous protection of all banking transactions, regardless of their nature.

Swiss banks' 'guidance' of political flight capital is, indeed, alleged to be substantial, particularly through Panamanian branches. According to CIA estimates, over 150 wealthy Brazilians were thought to have moved about $14 billion into Swiss accounts during periods of economic difficulty in that country in the early 1980s. The Italian-speaking canton of Ticino is particularly popular with Brazilian and Argentinian businessmen since many of them are of Italian origin and consequently feel comfortable with Ticino's bankers.[43] President Julius Nyerere of Tanzania publicized a proposal from one Swiss bank detailing how he could best shift his financial resources to Switzerland. Overall, it has been estimated that the amount of flight capital in Swiss banks was around SFr 100 billion in 1984.[44]

The defense

Swiss bankers respond to accusations of malpractice by pointing out that really dirty money has no place in Switzerland, since either the client himself or his Swiss lawyer must be known to the bank, and since secrecy is not airtight in cases of investigations of offenses that are defined as being criminal in nature under Swiss law. They point to Austria as offering much greater anonymity (not even a passport being required to open an account). As for tax evasion, Swiss bankers point to excessive taxation in other countries as the primary cause, and also maintain that they do not actively solicit funds that are involved in evading taxes or currency controls. Besides, they argue, there is no obligation for them to collect other people's taxes.

They argue that a large number of conventions for cooperations in legal matters have been concluded between Switzerland and other countries since the Second World War, and that this indicates their desire to eliminate abuses of bank secrecy by criminals. Indeed, Switzerland is granting about 800 foreign requests a year for banking information, mostly under treaties, laws and conventions that did not exist ten years ago.[45] But, as noted, most such cooperation is predicated on the concept of 'bilateral culpability', which means the activity under scrutiny must be a crime in Switzerland itself to fall under the terms of applicable legal assistance conventions. Unfortunately for other countries' authorities, many of the offenses committed by their citizens using Swiss accounts to hide illegally obtained funds are not in fact illegal in Switzerland, including tax evasion and securities laws violations.

But even here things are changing. A law making insider trading a crime came into force in Spring 1988 (see Chapter 10). In October 1987 it cleared the Swiss lower house, the National Council, by a vote of 110 to 3, and was to pass to the upper house, the Council of States, for resolution of certain differences between the two houses. The Council of States wanted to confine the law's application to transactions on the bourse, whereas the National Council wanted to extend it to off-bourse trading as well. The law calls for prison sentences or fines for offenders, and for improved procedures for Swiss judicial assistance in international cases.[46] There is also a plan to define money-laundering and to make it a criminal act punishable by mandatory imprisonment.[47] There is even the possibility that in due course tax evasion will be outlawed. In the words of one Swiss bank chairman: 'Swiss public opinion is moving that way. I think we will have a tax evasion law within ten years.'[48]

On the other hand, the Swiss have no desire to become involved in law enforcement on behalf of the rest of the world, and have taken a strong position that appropriate enforcement activity at home would discourage illegal use of Swiss accounts. They also argue that it is unfair to criticize or condemn Switzerland when other nations permit similar kinds of banking activity, and that increased disclosure in Switzerland would simply encourage the use of other secrecy havens. And while few would defend the rights of plundering dictators, there are many who argue that there is still a vital need for secrecy. 'I have Pakistani clients who could turn round one day and see their government change, or find themselves thrown in jail,' explained one banker. 'Their families would have nothing but their Swiss bank account to rely on. It is more than a banking service I'm providing for these people. It's a life-protecting service.'[49]

All the same, Swiss banking hands are, to some extent, tied. And the concessions that have so far been wrung from them are unlikely to be the last. The concern that the result will be a loss of market share in the secrecy game must be a very real one.

While clients may not feel as comfortable as they once did, they are still not taking their funds away; instead they may just be routing them through other havens to provide extra cover. Reported deposits from Panama and the Caribbean, for example, surged to $25 billion at the end of 1984, from $4 billion in 1978, and there has been a similar trend for deposits from Liechtenstein.[50]

However one looks at it, there can be little doubt that Swiss bankers do still provide a unique service, 'a complete package', for the high net worth individual. And demand for that is unlikely to diminish. A 1987 survey of the Swiss financial sector Arthur Andersen predicted that, while the number of private banks in particular would be likely to fall further (there are currently 24, as compared with more than 200 at the turn of the century and 41 in 1945), for those who survive the future looked prosperous, with an annual growth potential in the asset management field of 10 per cent. Results in 1986 for two of the top private banks would seem to bear this optimism out – Bank Julius Baer increased its gross income by almost 20 per cent; Bank Vontobel by a similar amount ('Commissions have increased tenfold over the past four or five years and the number of portfolios we have under management has increased fivefold').[51]

While there is still a good deal of debate and some serious stonewalling of efforts to obtain cooperation when the laws of other countries are involved, the Swiss are very agile indeed in defending their own interests abroad. For example, Richard Keats was accused in 1982 of dealing in and transporting counterfeit US securities with a face value of over $5.5 million, and later was also accused of placing millions in counterfeit US and foreign bonds with European banks. In Switzerland he was accused of borrowing about $5 million using counterfeit bonds as collateral. When he was finally located in Malaga, Spain, the Swiss were the first to successfully seek his extradition, and also extradited two of his associates from other countries. One European detective noted that it 'was clearly a case of them beating the U.S. to the punch. They are very good about getting things done when their own money is involved.'[52]

The Swiss Banking Commission's 1988 Annual Report is indicative of the Swiss authorities' concern that the country's banking secrecy should only shield legitimate wealth. It specifically stated that, 'the cases of Marcos and Duvalier show just how sensitive it can be for the banks when they accept large assets of foreign leaders.'[53] Indeed, the Commission will require in future that top management rather than lower-ranking employees decide whether to accept business from important foreign officials.

In addition, the report expressed concern about the reasons behind the significant growth of the Swiss banks' offshore investment funds – between end 1986 and 1987, assets under management doubled to more than $2.87 billion, and rose a further 12½ per cent in the first two months of 1988. The Commission was worried that this may reflect an attempt by the banks to sidestep Swiss laws on investment funds.

The report also stated that the Commission would supervise banking practices more closely, paying particular attention to the way in which banks report losses in securities trading and disclose information on debt offerings. It would also cast its supervisory net beyond the banks, to include the operations of all Swiss financial institutions.

Indeed, seasoned observers of Swiss bankers stress their capacity for pragmatism. They suggest that if there is a greater willingness among them to cooperate and compromise in clear-cut cases of wrongdoing, it is because they recognize that it is in their business interests to be so. Quite apart from the wish to compete fully in international financial markets, there is the fact that secrecy remains inviolate for those with nothing to fear from the law. And although honest depositors are not always the wealthiest, they may be the more reliable; they may also object quite strongly to sharing banks with drugs and arms smugglers, fraudsters and cheats, and as 'clean' depositors are still the lifeblood of the business, it may be no bad thing for Swiss institutions to disassociate themselves from the seamier side of the secrecy world.

Notes

1 Cynthia Crossen, 'Look Not Toward the Havens', *Wall Street Journal*, 18 September 1987.
2 Benito Legarda, 'Small Island Economies', *Finance and Development*, June 1984.
3 Permanent Subcommittee on Investigations, Committee on Governmental Affairs, United States Senate, *Crime and Secrecy: The Use of Offshore Banks and Companies* (Washington, DC: US Government Printing Office, 1983), p. 73.
4 'Watch Out Switzerland, Here Comes Tonga', *Institutional Investor*, March 1985, p. 24.
5 *Secrecy in Swiss Banking* (Zurich: Swiss Bankers' Association 1984).
6 Thomas N. Gladwin and Ingo Walter, *Multinationals Under Fire* (New York: John Wiley, 1980), chapter 10.
7 John Tagliabue, 'Swiss Banks: As their International Role Grows, Secrecy Laws Bow to Foreign Pressure', *International Herald Tribune*, 3 June 1986.
8 Ibid.
9 David Lascelles, 'A Hole in the Secret Heart', *Financial Times*, 3 February 1987.
10 Philip Revsin, 'Swiss Accounts Don't Match Exotic Image', *Wall Street Journal*, 21 February 1985.
11 Felix Kessler, 'Neutral Switzerland, Without Enemies, Spending Millions on Fallout Shelters', *Wall Street Journal*, 21 December 1983.
12 'Taking the Secret out of Swiss Banking', *The Economist*, 16 July 1983. See also Maile Hulihan, 'Swiss Vote on Bank Secrecy Curbs After Battle for Hearts and Minds', *Wall Street Journal*, 18 May 1984; John Wicks, 'Swiss Bankers' Code Should Become Law', *Financial Times*, 30 May 1984; and John Wicks, 'Swiss Banks on the Up and Up', *The Banker*, July 1984.
13 George Anders and Margaret Studer, 'Stuck on Tradition, Swiss Banks Discover their Role is Waning as a Financial Center', *Wall Street Journal*, 21 March 1985.
14 Ellen Wallace, 'Swiss Wash Their Laundry', *Euromoney*, April 1987.
15 Jaques Neher, 'Why Secrecy is Crumbling', *International Herald Tribune*, 13 July 1987.
16 'Swiss Bankers Propose Curbs on Secrecy', *Wall Street Journal*, 23 March 1987. See also Margaret Studer, 'Swiss Agency Seeks Tougher Curbs on Bank Secrecy', *Wall Street Journal*, 24 March 1987.
17 'Sensible Lotsen', *Der Spiegel*, No. 20, 1984.
18 'Private Banking: Seek Out Old Fashioned Wealth', *The Economist*, 18 July 1988.
19 Ibid.
20 *Secrecy in Swiss Banking*, op. cit. (n. 5).
21 David Lascelles, op. cit. (n. 9).

22 John Templeman and William Glasgall, 'A Mouse That's Roaring Into Money Management', *Business Week*, 1 February 1988.
23 'Psst . . . I Know This Nice Little Country', *The Economist*, 27 August 1988.
24 Paul Lewis, 'Cracking a Swiss Bank's Code', *New York Times*, 23 September 1983.
25 'Moneymen Feel the Squeeze', Swiss Economy Survey, *The Economist*, 6 September 1986.
26 Margaret Studer, 'Swiss Agency Seeks Tougher Curbs on Bank Secrecy', *Wall Street Journal*, 24 March 1987.
27 'Too Good to be True', *The Economist*, 6 September 1986.
28 John Wicks, 'Dollar Spur for Swiss Bank Assets', *Financial Times*, 26 April 1985.
29 'The Italians' Favourite Swiss Centre', *The Economist*, 6 July 1985.
30 'Moneymen Feel the Squeeze', *op. cit.* (n. 25).
31 Ibid.
32 'Forcing Discreet Money Into the Open', *Euromoney*, November 1986.
33 John Tagliabue, *op. cit.* (n. 7).
34 Genevieve McInnes, 'Swiss Private Banks: Bewilderingly Successful', *Banker International*, August 1987.
35 'Private Banking: Sorting Out the Puzzled Client', *Euromoney*, April 1988.
36 'Switzerland Banking and Finance', *Financial Times*, 14 December 1987.
37 'Will the Old Ways Survive the New Bankers?', *New York Times*, 1 March 1986.
38 Richard Evans, 'Bank Leu – Or Pandora's Box', *Euromoney*, April 1987.
39 'Paris Puts Total on Amnesty', *International Herald Tribune*, 7 February 1987.
40 'Greeks Join the Chorus', *The Economist*, 16 July 1983.
41 *International Herald Tribune*, 13 June 1983.
42 Matthew Winkler, 'Switzerland Beat out US in Extradition of Richard Keats in Bogus Securities Case', *Wall Street Journal*, 29 October 1983.
43 'The Italians' Favourite Swiss Centre', *op. cit.* (n. 29).
44 'Taking the Secret out of Swiss Banking', *op. cit.* (n. 12).
45 Gary Putka, 'Those Famed Swiss Bank Accounts Aren't Quite as Impenetrable as They Used To Be', *Wall Street Journal*, 15 June 1986.
46 'Swiss Closer to Making Insider Trading a Crime', *International Herald Tribune*, 4 October 1987.
47 'Taking Crooks to the Cleaners', *The Economist*, 28 February 1987.
48 David Lascelles, *op. cit.* (n. 9).
49 Gary Putka, *op. cit.* (n. 45).
50 Marcia Berss, 'The Prince That Roared', *Forbes*, 29 April 1985. See also 'The Mouse That Almost Roared', *The Economist*, 21 March 1987.
51 Genevieve McInnes, *op. cit.* (n. 34).
52 As quoted in *International Herald Tribune*, 17 August 1984, p. 1.
53 'Swiss Regulators Say Expansion Abroad of Banks' Investment Funds is Troubling', *Wall Street Journal*, 13 April 1988.

209

8

Global Secrecy Havens

In Chapter 7 we described the pattern of secrecy supply, and illustrated it in terms of one of the principal traditional secrecy centers, Switzerland. In this chapter, we shall discuss some of the other important secret havens. Unlike Switzerland, many of these are non-functional or 'booking' centers.

Caribbean and South Atlantic

Over the years, the Caribbean has become an area abundantly supplied with secrecy havens. The reasons are several. Proximity to the United States is one consideration, supplemented by political risk constrained by vital US interests in the region and the ease of communications with the rest of the world. Geographic location is also important for attracting Latin American flight capital, as is its fortuitous position astride one of the world's major drug routes. And there is the matter of economic development, with most of the Caribbean countries being very small island economies dependent on tourism and primary products, plagued by a lack of options to promote economic growth. Under the circumstances, the financial secrecy business has a great deal to recommend it to planners seeking economic progress. Some examples follow.

Antigua

Antigua has become independent, but is still within the British Commonwealth. It is heavily dependent on tourism, lacks natural resources, and has substantial external debt. No registration requirement is imposed on the establishment of new banks or companies. No assets must be on deposit, and there is no vetting or screening of applicants. An attorney simply presents registration papers and fees, and within a few days the new enterprise has been officially formed.

Antigua has no explicit secrecy provisions, but the government does not know who the beneficial owners of registered companies and banks are because of incomplete or non-existent records. The lawyers involved may know only who forwarded the fees to them, and not on whose behalf they have acted. Moreover, there is no supervision of licensed banks. Antigua has been considering adoption of formal offshore banking legislation with secrecy provisions, and faces a choice of competing with the Cayman Islands for US secrecy business or cooperating with the US authorities. It is felt that, with reasonable US commitment to developing Antigua's banking and company law and general economic development assistance, the country would cooperate in inhibiting criminally tainted funds flows, and in revoking licenses for offshore companies engaged in criminal activities. Antigua may also establish its own central bank through a conversion of the East Caribbean Currency Authority.

Bahamas

The Bahamas lie only 50 miles from the US coast. Tourism contributes about 70 per cent of GNP and there is no significant local market economy. Distribution of income is highly uneven, with high per capita incomes only in Nassau. There is a large underground economy, primarily engaged in narcotics traffic to the United States. Estimates of how much total income now comes from drugs range from 10–20 per cent.[1]

The importance of banking to the Bahamas is primarily defined in terms of the local employment it creates. Between 1,200 and 2,000 Bahamians are engaged in the financial services industry, and the banking sector accounts for 13–15 per cent of GNP. It provides training, as well as the introduction of high-technology data processing and communications facilities.

For about $1,000, any attorney can create a company quickly and easily in the Bahamas. The attorney has no obligation to evaluate the applicant's credentials, character or motives, although reputable lawyers and bankers supposedly will not accept applicants without prior evaluation. The law does not require screening or any reporting of company assets, although the identity of a beneficiary non-resident shareholder has to be disclosed to the authorities. There is no requirement to register trusts. The Bahamas central bank functions well, but does not engage in the supervision or regulation of financial institutions.

Bank secrecy has been covered by criminal law in the Bahamas since 1979, although Bahamian law does provide for the lifting of bank secrecy when an attorney petitions the Supreme Court for a court order to release requested documents. Conditions under which such documents may be released are:

211

- the foreign authority must show that a crime has been committed, proof of which hinges on the requested documents;
- a crime is suspected, proof of which rests on the requested documents; or
- criminal proceedings are already under way abroad.

These conditions pose a dilemma for prosecutors. If enough evidence existed to indict, there would be no need for the requested documents.

The US government has periodically complained about lack of Bahamian cooperation in criminal information requests. The Bahamas response has been that:

- US agencies are ignorant of the means easily available under Bahamian law through which lifting of bank secrecy can be allowed;
- very few US requests for information are made, and, since the requests are so few, there is no evidence of US criminal involvement in the Bahamian system;
- the United States is exporting the responsibility to the Bahamas for its own failures in prevention, detection and prosecution of domestic crime; and
- US banks and firms sometimes vouch for US parties engaged in Bahamian financial business.

The Bahamian government has somewhat changed its policy on foreign tax matters, and now requires that foreigners engaged in the 'tax haven' business obtain local work permits. These are granted sparingly, and the result has been a shift of some banking and other business from the Bahamas to the Cayman Islands. Despite this, the Bahamas has now signed a new treaty with the U.S. to provide for better exchange of information (see Chapter 9).

The Bahamas has long been known for its involvement in the drug trade. In 1984, there was even an internal inquiry into Prime Minister Lynden O. Pindling. It found that although no proof of corruption existed, neither did any satisfactory explanation for the source of much of his wealth. In 1988 his name appeared again when an admitted drug trafficker involved in the Lehder case confessed to paying the Bahamian government $3–5 million in 1980–1, some $400,000 of which allegedly went personally to Pindling. Although Lehder pleaded not guilty to all the charges against him, it appeared that he virtually took over one of the small Bahamian Cays for his operations and that he placed so much cash in Nassau one bank hired extra clerks just to count the bills.

All of this served to tarnish the Bahamas' image as a legitimate financial center. Indeed, some reports indicate that it was struggling to attract new banking business, losing out to rivals such as the Cayman Islands. Some argued that fees are too high, that there was too much red tape and a lack of competent personnel. Others simply indicated that the atmosphere just was not right, 'not the type ... where you like to direct clients'.[2]

The Bahamas has made strong efforts to redress the balance. Since 1985, banks have been required to disclose currency deposits of more than $100,000. The Central Bank has taken its supervisory role more seriously and there has been increased cooperation with the US. It has even been suggested that this anti-drug zeal may have given some liquidity problems. One US Customs Service official estimated that in 1985 $500,000 to $1 million in drug money flowed every week from Bimini, a major smuggling point, to Nassau. After the traffic was stopped, 'Bimini's entire economy dried up.'[3]

The Bahamas remains a leading offshore center. At end-March 1987, commercial banks had total domestic assets of about $1 billion, and their offshore dollar business is known to be many times greater. Banks and trust companies from all over the world are represented, with the largest single group being US institutions, with 97 public licensees, followed by the Swiss with 29 and Canada and the UK with 12 each.

The overall trend is one of continuing growth, and the increase in bank license holders are increasingly active, with the number of non-active holders declining steadily. The Bahamas appears to be taking some business from other centers – Panama's troubles in 1987 and 1988 were part of the reason. In addition, the Bahamas seems to be attracting interest from Hong Kong. In general, newcomers tend to be 'blue chip' institutions, reflecting the Central Bank's policy of favoring well-established institutions.

The type of business done is also expanding. Although Nassau remains an important booking center, this is becoming a less prominent activity. Private banking and trust business, discretionary fund management and mutual fund back-office administration have emerged as main growth areas. Wealthy Latin Americans in particular favor the Bahamas, although private clients come from all over the world.

The absence of tax, exchange controls and regulatory barriers make the Bahamas very appealing, as of course does the financial confidentiality which originates in common law and is reinforced by statute. Certain confidentiality inroads have been made, as discussed in Chapter 10, and the signing with the US of the Mutual Legal Assistance Treaty upset a number of bankers. Even so, it only provides for exchange of information in the case of serious crimes, for example drug trafficking, recognized as such by both governments. The Bahamas remains adamant that 'fishing expeditions' will not be allowed.

The authorities and the Bahamian banking community have heightened their vigilance against unsavory elements. The government expects to play a leading role in global financial markets, but increasingly would prefer this to revolve around legitimate rather than questionable funds. The central bank has tightened its licensing criteria and its supervisory procedures. Since January 1985, a Code of Conduct has been adopted by the Association of International Banks and Trust Companies in the Bahamas and approved by the Central Bank. This sets out standards of conduct and professional ethics governing the relationship between member institutions and their customers.

The stated objectives are to: (1) maintain and enhance the reputation of the Bahamas as an international financial center; (2) prevent the use of banks and trust companies in the Bahamas for criminal purposes; and (3) adhere to the principles of banking confidentiality/secrecy as embodied in Bahamian legislation. Its guidelines include: (1) responsibility to cooperate with the Central Bank, especially in respect of conforming with requirements over the acceptance of large cash deposits; (2) necessity of knowing one's customer; (3) rejection of customers involved in criminal activity; (4) avoidance of acts violating fiscal or foreign exchange laws; (5) maintenance of confidentiality; and (6) disclosure of members' ownership. Penalties for failing to adhere to the Code can include expulsion from the Association.

Bermuda

Bermuda has a very low crime rate and no notable corruption. It also boasts 350 years of political stability. There are no income, capital gains, withholding or estate taxes. The major offshore business is insurance, followed by trust-like personal investment companies. These activities together account for about 40 per cent of GNP. Tourism is also important as an income source, but planning for future economic development focuses more on the expansion of financial activities.

A good relationship with the United States and other countries is recognized as being fundamental to Bermuda's success. Accordingly, Bermuda makes every effort to prevent any use of offshore financial activities by criminal elements. It screens new applicants for offshore business and personal investment companies. The screening is done via referrals of major banks, law firms and insurance companies internationally, supplemented by monetary authority supervision. Like Switzerland, Bermuda has no criminal law governing tax evasion, nor will it violate confidentiality in tax cases.

There are 5,500 offshore trading companies registered in Bermuda, each of which must have local directors who are Bermudans responsible to local authority. Exempt companies must be audited, and directors are held responsible for due diligence in supervision. Management of personal investment companies must also be local, although actual ownership can be foreign.

There is no secrecy law in Bermuda backed by criminal sanction, although a wrongful disclosure statute exists. Confidentiality rests largely on the statutes governing how companies are formed. In either local or exempt companies, nominees may hold shares on behalf of others, and both banks and law firms do in fact hold such shares. Shareholders are obliged to have personal knowledge of beneficial owners, and, in the event of any change in beneficial ownership, the monetary authority must be notified. The monetary authority in turn is obliged, except under court order, not to disclose the names of beneficial owners of record, and it requires all applicants for exempt company status to be recommended by well-known foreign banks and institutions. Small private bank references are not acceptable, since the authority knows that the applicant himself may be the concealed owner of the recommending bank – as can occur with St Vincent, Anguilla or Montserrat banks. The authority also has a computer file of information on all past applicants and on all present owners of exempt companies. Companies in which the applicant has had an interest are on file as well.

Cayman Islands

The Cayman Islands, 475 miles south of Miami, were once the prototypical tax haven. The local economy is stable, and there is an absence of racial tension, poverty and high unemployment. There is little or no taxation of income, profits, gifts, transfers of capital or estates. It is possible to maintain an account in any leading currency and there is no exchange control.[4] The bank secrecy laws appear on the surface to be even more stringent than those in Switzerland – a person can be jailed simply for inquiring about a bank customer's private holdings and financial activities. As a result, the Cayman Islands are generally considered to be the largest money haven in the world, with an estimated $200 billion in deposits.[5] They also rank as one of the most important Eurocurrency booking centers in the world. More than 450 banks and trust companies, some 17,000 companies and over 300 insurance companies are registered there. Banks are required to provide quarterly financial reports, lending guidelines and regular performance reviews. Newly registered institutions must have a quota of local personnel. The Caymans boasted offices of 43 of the 50 largest international banks, and foreign deposits were estimated at somewhere over $220 billion for 1987. The financial sector employs almost 900 people, 75 per cent Cayman citizens.[6]

The Cayman Islands' geographical position and rigid banking secrecy mean that they represent a prime target for bad as well as good money. In 1984, concerned at the ill effects excessive exposure to drug money could have, and under intense pressure from the United States, the Islands enacted a 'Narcotics Drugs Law' allowing the release of information in circumstances where drugs involvement could be shown.

215

Although this was a step away from strict financial secrecy, the Caymans insisted that the commitment to 'full confidentiality for legitimate commercial and tax-planning activities' was in no way reduced.[7] Nevertheless in 1986 a further agreement with the United States was signed, this time guaranteeing cooperation in information-gathering in a whole range of criminal investigations.[8]

While this may be another step toward restricting its secrecy to 'clean' money, it may also reduce the area's popularity considerably in the coming years. On the other hand, the Caymans still have much to offer – the generous tax treatment mentioned above, the fact that they are open for business when Europe is closed, the established financial services they offer, such as fund management and advice on forming corporate entities, the relaxed terms under which new companies may be established (no restriction on residence or nationality of shareholders, no requirement for a register of members or an annual return of shareholders, directors and officers, and the acceptability of a single shareholder).[9] These attractions may at least mitigate the adverse impact of reduced secrecy.

Montserrat

Montserrat is a British colony in the eastern Caribbean. The economy focuses on tourism, customs and excise taxes, property tax, stamp sales, light assembly plants, offshore companies and banking. In recent years there has also been an effort to develop agricultural and industrial areas. In the early 1980s the secrecy business played a relatively prominent role in the island's economic life. In 1981 there were 62 offshore banks, and licensing fees contributed 5 per cent of annual government income. Confidentiality was not guaranteed by stringent laws. Rather, government-sanctioned, purposeful inefficiency and lack of proper record-keeping made total secrecy a fact.

What makes Montserrat of interest is not its erstwhile position as a haven but rather its rapid decline, since it indicates how very rapidly those requiring secrecy will move their assets when they believe their requirements can no longer be met by a particular haven. The number of offshore banks in Montserrat by the end of 1986 had plummeted to 12. The reason? Most bankers attribute the dramatic fall to a new determination by the government to control more effectively the banking sector, and to an agreement between the Finance Minister and the US government that bank secrecy will be waived on a minimal showing of evidence by foreign authorities of wrongdoing – a major change for a place where five years earlier one local official was quoted as saying: 'We are in despair of the law here ever meaning anything.'[10]

Netherlands Antilles

One of the most active Caribbean tax havens is the Netherlands Antilles, since 1954 an autonomous nation within the kingdom of the Netherlands. Its reliance on the financial sector is heavy, and has been made more so since two other major sources of income – an oil refinery and the Western Hemisphere's largest ship-repair dry dock – have fallen on hard times due to worldwide problems in the industries involved. Matters were made worse in January 1986 when Aruba, the second most populous Antilles island, seceded from the other five.[11] In 1988, with unemployment running at 30 per cent, the 2,000 jobs provided by the offshore financial sector in a population of just 200,000 are precious. It produces some 40 per cent of government revenue, 23 per cent of foreign exchange and a quarter of GDP.[12]

The offshore financial sector in the Netherlands Antilles has been built on two foundations – tight local bank secrecy laws and a 1948 tax treaty between the United States and the Netherlands, later extended to the Antilles. Basically, the tax treaty allowed investors who set up Antillean corporations to escape a number of US taxes on a variety of US investments. 'Residents', for example, were exempt from almost all of the 30 per cent US withholding tax on interest income paid to foreigners. As a result, for 40 years the Antilles became one of the most important funnels for foreign investment into the United States. In 1984, some $32 billion in Eurobond investments and a further $11 billion in a variety of other investments, including a significant number of real estate transactions, passed through the Antilles for the US market. But it was not only foreigners who found the islands attractive.[13]

A US borrower could establish a Netherlands Antilles 'paper' corporation, undertake borrowings from foreign lenders, and remit the proceeds to the parent corporation. Interest payments were then made by the US parent to the Antilles captive finance company, essentially free of withholding tax, and subsequently remitted to the ultimate lender – likewise free of all but minimal local taxes and registration fees, which amounted to less than 1 per cent.

From 1974 to 1980, $18 billion in Eurocurrency debt was raised by US corporations in this manner. In 1981 it was $7 billion and in 1982 $14 billion. Of the 30,000 corporations registered with the Curaçao Chamber of Commerce, 25,000 were owned by foreigners in 1983, including such giants as Citicorp, Sears Roebuck and General Motors. The benefits of the reduced interest costs were passed on to the firms' shareholders and to consumers in the form of higher returns and lower prices. Even the US Federal National Mortgage Association proposed a Eurofinancing through the Netherlands Antilles 'window', but this was blocked by former Treasury Secretary Donald Regan in March 1983. In 1981, a total of $1.4 billion was paid by US residents to entities in the Netherlands

Antilles, exceeding by far that paid to any other country. This figure is estimated to have grown dramatically in 1982 and 1983, and probably understates the actual amounts by a wide margin.

However in 1984 the Netherlands Antilles suffered the first setback to this lucrative business. The United States abolished the withholding tax on interest payable to non-residents, thus permitting American companies to raise capital in the Euromarket directly. This of course lessened the incentive for big firms to operate offshore finance subsidiaries, and resulted in a serious decline in this source of income for the Netherlands Antilles. Eurobonds already issued still retained their status, however, and other provisions in the tax treaty – such as protection in real estate transactions – were as relevant as ever.[14] Business continued to boom. Between 1981 and 1986 more than 5,000 offshore companies opened in Curaçao alone, bringing the total number of offshore investment and banking companies incorporated to over 35,000.

In 1987 the United States, concerned about the loopholes open to tax cheats and money launderers, dealt a second blow with the announcement of the total repeal of the tax treaty. The action predictably caused distress and not a little anger in the Antilles. 'I'd characterize it as a national disaster,' commented the Finance Minister, who predicted as much as a 70 per cent fall in government income from the area in the succeeding two years.[15]

But it was from outside the Netherlands Antilles that the greatest reaction came – from outraged US and foreign investors, major US corporations, and the Eurobond markets. By rescinding the treaty, the US Treasury had overnight substantially reduced the intrinsic value of any outstanding bonds issued in the Netherlands Antilles. Prices immediately fell by between 15–20 per cent, wiping millions off investors' holdings. Certain companies began to talk of bond calls, whereby the issuer exercises its privilege to call the bond before its official redemption date at its par value. This would have resulted in yet further losses for investors who had for the most part had to pay well above par on purchase. In July 1986, the Bank of Boston acted, calling in $100 million of 14⅛ per cent 1989 notes.

It was clear that something had to be done. The US Treasury backtracked, announcing only partial termination of the treaty, and upon expiration of the treaty on 1 January 1988, the provisions allowing tax exemption on interest would remain in place.[16]

Although matters no longer looked as black as they had in June 1986, the Netherlands Antilles had certainly lost some of its extraordinary competitive advantage through the repeal of the greater part of the treaty. Even so, the islands still offer a place where money can flow freely and secretly. Import–export agents, film distribution companies, independent oil companies, banks. and others have found doing business in the Netherlands Antilles convenient and congenial, and are likely to continue to do so. Setting up an offshore company is still child's play. Incorporation costs about $1,500, and annual administration fees are just a few thousand dollars. Capital requirements are modest, a minimum of $30,000 of which only 20 per cent needs to be paid in. A range of very helpful financial services exist, including the generation of false invoices.[17] And now locals are looking for ways to capitalize yet further on the stringent bank secrecy laws – ideas such as more liberal ship registration laws and expanded insurance services.

Again, these advantages are attractive to 'dirty' money as well as clean. Until 1984, the Netherlands Antilles had loomed large in US corporate finance on the basis of a legal anomaly; interest of a more unsavory type has grown and prospered in recent years. Ironically, the very aspects that caused the US government to rescind the treaty may well be all that is left to the Netherlands Antilles after its removal. The territory seems to be increasingly used as a conduit for criminal funds, for the laundering of organized crime and drugs money as well as tax evasion. It appears that it still serves as a transfer point rather than a collection point. By the time the money flows through a Netherlands Antilles corporation, the real owners of the funds are so well screened by local Antillean nominees and agents that it is virtually impossible to identify them.

Prominent among the objects of such transactions are foreign-owned land holdings in Florida. Real estate has long been a favorite with secrecy-seeking investors – some estimates indicate that in the early 1980s as much as 20 per cent of all real property in the Miami area was held by companies incorporated in the Antilles.[18] Although the benefits of the tax treaty may have gone, the dense screen provided by a tiering of shell Curaçao corporations, owned through 'bearer shares', is still appealing.

When the US Department of Agriculture wanted to know who owned 1,437 acres purchased in Orange County, Florida, for example, it wrote to the Curaçao International Trust Co., which was managing the company listed as buyer, Debco NV. In reply, the Department was told through a Houston lawyer that Debco NV was a 'wholly owned subsidiary of Pathway Investments NV,' which in turn was described only as 'a corporation organized under the laws of the Netherlands Antilles'.[19]

Whereas the Netherlands Antilles government has accommodated US requests for financial information concerning US citizens, it has been unwilling to yield on disclosures regarding foreigners, making it especially difficult to track criminal financial flows. As one gentleman put it: 'The Antilles? Ideal. Pros. Discreet. In the Antilles you rarely have to pay a bribe and you almost never have to pay a tax.'[20]

219

Channel Islands

The Channel Island havens of Jersey and Guernsey do not fit neatly into the classic image of the offshore center, having a very distinctive character. Jersey, the first sterling offshore banking center, started to develop in the 1960s when the government lifted interest-rate controls. Guernsey followed on some ten years later. Both have built their considerable financial businesses on the basis of the highest standards of conduct and the quality of the services they offer. There are no brass-plate banks; the tax rate stands at a healthy (by haven standards) 20 per cent. But there is complete political stability, major scandals have been avoided and respectability is enhanced by the proximity of the United Kingdom.

In addition, there is relatively little official regulation or control, the authorities being content to outline the type of conduct they expect and to leave the rest to the institutions involved. Indeed, because of the 'legitimate' nature of Channel Islands' business, banks have every interest in guarding their reputation, one of their main assets being their respectability. New clients need good references, if not an introduction, to open an account. Despite this, the Islands have enacted regulations requiring banks to disclose details of accounts where drugs money is thought to be involved, and there is proposed legislation on insider trading.

The factors discussed above, combined with the strength of world markets in the mid-1980s and the significant growth of share-ownership in the United Kingdom, have resulted in massive flows of capital to the Channel Islands – both into those funds and unit trusts marketed by banks based there and into those run by them but marketed by other firms. This in turn has bolstered the already substantial foreign-exchange market. There may be further benefits to come, when the area receives 'designated-territory status' under the UK Financial Services Act, making it possible for Jersey and Guernsey funds to be marketed on the mainland without having to be listed on the London Stock Exchange.

Another major advantage for banks doing business in the Channel Islands is the treatment of loan booking, where there are considerable tax benefits. Both Jersey and Guernsey allow 90 per cent of the profits on loans introduced to Guernsey subsidiaries by parent or associated banks against tax as arrangement fees. That means, with a tax rate of 20 per cent being levied on only 10 per cent of the funds, an effective total charge of just 2 per cent. The result is that many banks use Channel Islands subsidiaries' treasury operations to fund operations in other centers.

The volume of business flooding into the Channel Islands in recent years has however brought its problems. The governments of Jersey and

Guernsey are concerned that unbridled expansion could lead to their economies overheating through overemployment and immigration. At the moment there are no work permit requirements, although residence restrictions hamper banks' abilities to bring in new staff. The situation is likely to be exacerbated, at least in Jersey, when the island's Regulation of Undertakings law is extended to banks, requiring them to gain government permission to take on extra employees.

The combination of heavy demand and staff shortages have forced the banks and authorities to be inventive. One idea, more popular in Guernsey than Jersey, is that of the 'managed bank', whereby a bank would be granted the license to do business on the Islands but would in fact have no physical presence there, its affairs being run on its behalf by an already established bank. 'Any bank which has a large correspondent banking network must see the opportunities,' according to one banker. 'For instance, there is no Scandinavian bank in the Channel Islands, and we have relationships with some which may want to save themselves $750,000 in setting-up costs and get the tax advantages.'[21]

The scheme would be different from a 'brass-plate' operation in three main ways: (1) the newly accepted bank would pay tax directly to the Guernsey authorities rather than simply paying a fee, which is the usual practice for a 'brass-plate'; (2) it would have auditable records in Guernsey, would report to the local authorities, and its records would be inspectable on the island; and (3) its operations would be run by an already established bank.

Gibraltar

Necessity being the mother of invention, Gibraltar was bound to consider offshore banking at some stage. The rock, under three miles long, three-quarters of a mile wide and 1,383 ft high at its peak, is a barren place without agriculture or much industry. Financial services offer one path of economic development. In fact, reports indicate that it has been one of the fastest-growing new offshore banking centers in the world. Moves in this direction began as early as 1967 when the government allowed non-residents to set up tax-exempt companies for offshore business. However, with the dispute over Gibraltar between the United Kingdom and Spain and the consequent Spanish blockade, little progress was made. But with new banking laws to protect depositors in 1983 and the reopening of the border with Spain in 1985, events took a significant turn for the better. With only some $562 million in bank deposits (end 1986) Gibraltar is hardly in the big leagues, but the rate of growth has nevertheless been impressive. Total deposits in 1984 were only around $298 million. By the end of 1987, they were estimated to be as high as $800 million. Meanwhile tax exempt companies were being set up at a rate of around 4,000 a year.

Gibraltar is attractive for a number of reasons. There is zero taxation for non-residents. There are no exchange controls and there is strict banking secrecy. It is in the Continental European time zone, the official language is English, and most professionals are bilingual in Spanish as well. And it has no tax treaty with the United States. It is clear why it has advantages. In an attempt to avoid attracting criminal funds, the government has required banks to conduct genuine banking operations, with an office staffed by at least two managers and support staff. It also insists that it will apply close supervision.[22]

Luxembourg

While Switzerland has gradually been forced to relax its strict stance on financial privacy, Luxembourg has been busy strengthening its bank secrecy laws. In 1981 and again in 1984 its parliament passed new measures that among other things included mandatory jail sentences for anyone making unauthorized disclosures about bank accounts. To gain information on such accounts an order is required from a Luxembourg court. Foreign authorities may only request such an order if the depositor in question has been charged in his home country with an offense that is also a crime in Luxembourg and which also relates to the account under scrutiny.[23] Thus for the first time the long-standing tradition of confidentiality between Luxembourg bankers and their customers has been formally acknowledged. As the Foreign Affairs and Economy Minister put it: 'We discovered that our tight secrecy could be sold all over Europe and all over the world.'[24]

It will be difficult to crack this secrecy. As one US financial regulator put it: 'We could put pressure on Luxembourg banks, but they aren't nearly as exposed as the Swiss.'[25] Luxembourg offers more than secrecy though. It has a long tradition of private banking and its banking and brokerage fees are highly competitive. Its cultural and linguistic pluralism and its political and social stability are also attractive. Its tax system is inviting – international clients are entirely free from any tax on interest, dividends or capital gains and there is no stamp duty.[26] Holding companies may be inexpensively established and maintained, although there are fairly strict legal requirements, concerning for example the assets they may hold, and they too are exempt from tax on dividend and interest income, capital gains and liquidation surplus. There are some 6,000 such companies established in Luxembourg, serving as vehicles for takeovers, mergers, joint ventures, and the investments of wealthy individuals. They are governed by a 1929 law, which was revised in August 1983 to allow mutual funds also to benefit from its terms.

This amalgam of factors has attracted large sums to Luxembourg in recent years. Foreigners' deposits with the 120-odd banks registered in the Grand Duchy jumped almost 40 per cent in 1986 to an estimated $160 billion. This brings Luxembourg into the league of the top tax havens, such as the Cayman Islands and Switzerland.

Although efforts in the private banking field were primarily aimed at creating a new customer base, less affluent than the average Swiss client, some of the super-rich have undoubtedly been enticed into Luxembourg as well. Much of the new business has come from the more modest investors, whom Swiss banks might not consider – 'a second-tier private banking clientele' as the Luxembourg Banking Commissioner described it: 'a huge potential market'.[27]

To cater to such customers, whose means do not permit full-fledged personal investment schemes, the banks have developed a variety of specialist funds, restricted to a certain number of investors. In addition to these, ordinary mutual funds are thriving – at the end of 1984 there were 176 funds incorporated, representing approximately $8.75 billion; a year later the number had risen to 213 funds, with about $14 billion in assets. The figure is expected to go on rising. Luxembourg's strategy of diversifying its financial interests beyond the Eurobond business that was formerly the mainstay of its profitability is paying off. Given the fact that almost 10 per cent of the entire work force was either directly or indirectly employed within the banking sector, and that the share of value-added to gross domestic product by banks and insurance companies is in the region of 15 per cent, it is clear why such success is important to a country with a total area of less than a thousand square miles and a population of 360,000.

Panama

Although it is sometimes grouped with the Caribbean countries in discussions of the suppliers of international financial secrecy, Panama was until recently a rather special case. First, it could be viewed as the only true 'Latin American' secrecy haven. Second, it had since the early 1970s been following an ambitious policy of national development, endeavoring to develop a fully fledged and 'above-board' financial services industry, which would allow it to participate in international financial markets and would provide a springboard of managerial and entrepreneurial development in areas other than banking. The success of this policy must now be in grave doubt, but to understand Panama's past and current position, it is necessary to consider it in the context of these aims.[28]

There are three relevant activity centers in Panama: the banking and business community, its elected government, and its military police, the

National Guard. The financial and business community essentially dictates banking and company legislation. The government seeks to accommodate itself to the business elite and to a growing middle class. Its interests are much the same as those of the banking community, encouraging Panama's role as a financial center. The National Guard must be dealt with whenever foreign authorities seek cooperation in criminal matters. It is said to be 'corrupt', in that offenders such as drugs and arms traffickers can be assured protection from arrest if they have paid an appropriate 'safe conduct' fee. Effective power in the country lies with the head of the National Guard, General Manuel Antonio Noriega. The military has either imposed or deposed the last five presidents.[29]

It has long been accepted that Panama, despite its Parliament and its President, has been ruled in practice by the National Guard since General Omar Torrijos led a coup in 1968. A popular leader of genuine ability, he ruled until his death in an air crash in 1981, achieving a high degree of cohesion within Panamanian society. His successors have been more disappointing, and General Noriega has for some time given cause for concern.

It was not until the 1970s that development of a viable financial industry began. In 1965, there were only 16 'genuine' banks, with total assets of just $250 million. The other 250 were 'brass plates' conducting no real banking operations. The Banking Law of 1970 changed that. This reformed the banking system and established the National Banking Commission, which was to be responsible for its soundness and efficiency. Strict bank licensing procedures were introduced, Panama preferring only to license major international banks already headquartered in responsible foreign countries. It tended to reject applications from banks headquartered in the Caribbean, as well as from major banks' subsidiaries if those subsidiaries were in turn located in the Caribbean. A requirement of $250,000 paid-in capital was imposed. All but two of the 'brass plates' failed. But the major institutions flooded in. For those who could gain entry, the framework was highly attractive, with minimal regulation and stringent secrecy provisions.[30]

Panama had a range of other attractions as well. A special treaty had established the US dollar as legal tender on a par with the Panamanian colon, and indeed the dollar may be viewed as the national currency. There are no exchange controls, nor any form of registration requirements or restrictions on currency shipments into or out of the country. Its location at one of the world's major commercial crossroads and the strategic importance of the Panama Canal also contribute to its viability as a financial center, as do the low taxes on loans and other transactions booked through branches based there.[31] Until 1987, political stability had played a significant role.

Statutes facilitating the establishment of secret registered companies are also relevant. Setting up a Panamanian company is easy and inexpensive. A leading law firm will charge just $800–900 to draw up the necessary papers; some will ask as little as $300. Instructions by telephone or telex are sufficient to get the ball rolling, and a corporation can be 'doing business' anywhere in the world within three days. There are even 'vintage companies' – companies already formed by lawyers and waiting 'on the shelf' to be used. The attorney pays the annual tax of $150 to keep the corporation in good standing until a client turns up who wants a company with a 'history'. As with good wine, one pays for the age.

The actual founder of the company never has to identify himself and there is no income tax payable in Panama as long as transactions are completed outside the country.[32] There is no mechanism for policing offshore activities by such companies. Any inquiries or complaints about an offshore company can be brought to the Ministry of Commerce, but it will only reveal the name of its local agent. There can be no release of information if no crime has been committed in Panama itself. Similarly, once a Panamanian lawyer has set up a shell corporation that can make a cash deposit into a secret account, that account can be accessed by the authorities only through a Panamanian court order showing that a crime has been committed.

By early 1987 Panama had 130 financial institutions, including about 60 commercial banks, of which a dozen were based in the United States. Most of the banks in question maintained full branches. More than a hundred of the institutions were licensed to operate internationally.[33] Bank assets amounted to somewhere between $40 and $50 billion. The financial sector represented around 10 per cent of GNP, and employed over 8,000 people, an important contribution in a country of chronically high unemployment and few other areas of international competitive advantage.[34]

However, despite a serious intention of insuring stable and respectable banking, the Panamanian system had profound flaws that made it an ideal conduit for secret funds flows. The existence of such stringent bank secrecy of course complicates prudential supervision. The central banking authority, for example, was denied any right to audit bank deposits. A bank, once licensed, could engage in extensive laundering or fraud with impunity. The result was that Panama developed into a major center for criminal as well as legitimate funds. In addition to attracting Latin American capital merely seeking safety and offshore tax and exchange-control advantages, the country developed into a key Asia–Europe transshipment point for arms traffic, and played a central role in the Colombia–United States drugs trade.

US customs officials estimate that $500 million of illegally generated drug money passes through its banking system each year. Since the dollar is in effect used as the national currency, old notes are returned to the US Federal Reserve Banks without problem or question. US officials suggest that the very nature of these bills is indicative of the scale of money laundering. In 1982, for example, more than half of the $1 billion returned by one Panamanian bank was in $50 or smaller denominations, raising suspicions that they had been exchanged by money launderers for clean, easier to carry $100 bills.[35] In addition to laundering actual currency Panama also annually feeds billions of dollars electronically into the enormous and almost totally unregulated Eurodollar market, facilitating the flow of drugs profits into legitimate commerce.[36]

The fact that it is Hispanic has helped as well. Latin drugs runners and their launderers can deal with other Latins, whose language and ways of doing business are familiar. This reduces both complexity and inconvenience as well as risk, compared with doing business in the Bahamas or the Cayman Islands.

Examples of Panama's involvement in criminal funds are manifold. Take the case of Ramon Milan-Rodriguez. On 4 May 1983 he was arrested aboard a private Learjet about to take off for Panama, along with $5.4 million in cash. In testimony, it developed that Milan-Rodriguez had run $150 million to Panama over an eight-month period, and that his earnings from this service amounted to over $1 million per year.[37]

Another case of drug money moving to Panama involved Inair Cargo Airlines, a Panamanian-registered carrier making regular runs to Miami. In June 1983, two top airline executives were indicted for conspiracy to ship US currency abroad without declaring it to customs authorities. Particularly interesting in this case was the apparent complicity of the Panamanian National Guard. One $2 million shipment in cartons was evidently guarded by the Panamanian authorities from the time the aircraft landed in Panama City at 4:30 a.m. to the time banks opened at 7:30 a.m. One piece of evidence introduced at the Inair trial was a laminated business card of a member of the National Guard general staff with the following message handwritten on the back: 'The bearer . . . is a personal friend of your superior. Whatever cooperation, I authorize and appreciate.'[38] With such connections, it is little wonder that funds transfers into and out of Panama, even in bags and cartons stuffed with $20 bills, are relatively safe and easy.

Cuba and Nicaragua have used Panamanian companies to circumvent the United States' trade embargoes against them. Both Marcos and Duvalier channeled money through corporations there. Panama was a central point of transfer in the Irangate affair. Exporters regularly sell their goods to their own Panamanian corporations and resell them elsewhere in the name of the Panamanian corporation because in this way profits are untaxed.[39]

The question was whether Panama would degenerate to nothing

more than a major sink for the world's dirty money? The rate of growth in Panamanian offshore deposits (which between 1965 and 1983 ran at a compound rate of over 26 per cent per annum) was reversed in the mid-1980s. This was in part due to the general Latin American economic and debt situation; but it may also have been the result of bad money frightening off good. Certain moves were made. In 1985 the banking commission revoked the license of the First Americas Bank for irregular operations linked to drug dealing, and a code of ethics was drawn up by the bankers' association, allowing the regulatory authorities to investigate any bank exceeding its usual volume of cash flow.[40]

By mid-1987, the problems facing Panama's financial industry were of a much more fundamental nature. Could it survive? The first signs of the upheavals to come were perhaps when, in mid-1986, General Noriega was accused of deep personal involvement in drugs running and money laundering and later indicted by a US court in Miami. He denied vehemently any connection, pointing out that bank transactions and regulation were outside the scope of the military and citing his close work with the US Drug Enforcement Administration as proof of his good faith.[41] Perhaps in an attempt to put action to his words, he persuaded the country's national assembly to pass legislation in early 1987 requiring Panama's banks to provide information about the financial dealings of suspected narcotics kingpins and permitting previously sacrosanct numbered bank accounts to be frozen. The new law also accelerated the extradition of foreigners suspected of drug offenses.[42]

In May 1987, as part of a US campaign against the laundering of drug money, the Panamanian government froze some 54 accounts at 18 banks, involving around $10 million. The manner in which this was done was regarded by bankers and lawyers as arbitrary, and understandably was not good for confidence in the Panamanian financial sector.[43]

Worse was to come. In June 1987, Colonel Roberto Diaz Herrera accused General Noriega of corruption, ballot-rigging and political assassination.[44] On June 26, the US Senate passed a resolution calling on Noriega to step aside pending an independent investigation into the charges against him. He refused. The resultant strikes, riots, repression, US economic sanctions and widespread unrest have done nothing to calm financial nerves.[45] In an effort to give the appearance that he still enjoyed popular support, Noriega organized rallies and wrote off certain debts – all to the further alarm of the financial community who knew that these debts were being covered out of government overdrafts. Panama in 1988 faced a $350 million budget deficit and fell behind on payments of both principal and interest owed to foreign governments.

Accusations against Noriega intensified in 1987 and 1988 and included drugs and arms trafficking, the murder of a prominent opponent, rigging the 1984 elections and forcing out a series of civilian presidents who failed to meet with his approval. He was allegedly recruited by the CIA in 1966 and is thought to have played a role in the Iran-Contra affair. It is suspected that he conspired with Oliver North to dispatch, then intercept, a shipment of East German arms to El Salvador's leftist guerrillas with the aim of blaming Nicaragua for supplying the weapons and thus adding fuel to charges that the Sandinistas were engaged in exporting revolution.[46] He was also believed to have supplied Cuba with US intelligence and high-technology goods. 'He is a businessman. Contras, Sandinistas, Cubans, the CIA – he deals with them all to make money.'[47]

It was widely accepted that the Noriega empire incorporated the Panama Defense Forces. According to the Senate Foreign Relations Subcommittee on Terrorism, Narcotics and International Affairs, the General demanded a cut of almost all tainted funds deposited in Panama's banks. Drug traffickers and money launderers who refused to pay were liable to have their shipments hijacked. This would certainly correspond to the testimony of Ramon Milan-Rodriguez, cited earlier, who claimed to have paid Noriega some $10 million a month as protection money for his laundering activities.[48]

Matters came to a head in February 1988, when in two separate cases in Florida, Noriega was indicted for drug and laundering offences. In Tampa, he was accused of conspiring to import and distribute more than 1 million pounds of marijuana into the US. The chief witness in the case testified that he had personally delivered at least $900,000 in bribes to Noriega in 1983 and 1984, in return for a diplomatic passport, a multimillion dollar letter of credit, and safe passage for thousands of pounds of hashish. In Miami, the General was charged with accepting $4.6 million to allow Colombian shipments of over 4,000 pounds of cocaine to pass through Panama for the US. He allegedly also permitted the Colombians to establish a cocaine-processing plant on Panamanian soil, and temporarily to relocate their headquarters there after the murder of the Colombian Justice Minister in 1985.[49] A guilty verdict in both cases would mean that Noriega would be arrested if he entered the US or any other country with an extradition treaty with the US.

These developments naturally took their toll on Panama's stability. President Eric Arturo Delvalle promptly sacked the General as commander of the National Guard, only to find that Noriega could not be so easily removed and that instead it was Delvalle who was packing his bags. The US position was that the president's dismissal had been unconstitutional, and agreed to his request to freeze Panamanian assets in the US amounting to some $50 million. The US also stopped payment due under the Panama Canal treaties. By March 1988, the Panamanian Treasury had total cash resources around $40 million although its public payroll alone is $65 million a month. There followed months of hard times in Panama, even as Noriega clung to power, causing the US to give up its pressure tactics in the summer of 1988.

The result has been a general stampede for the exit by those with funds deposited in the country. It is estimated that between June and August 1987, some $3–5 billion, or 10 per cent of total bank deposits, fled the area, and that up to $15 billion had fled the country by mid-1988.[50] As one diplomat in Panama put it, 'There's nothing as nervous as a million dirty dollars.'[51]

All of this was disastrous for an economy that remains two-thirds service based and depends on the free transit of ships through the canal, goods through its $4.4 billion free trade zone and money through its 125 banks. It seemed highly unlikely that Panama could survive as a leading international financial center as depositors rushed to withdraw cash and the Panama National Bank was in no state to bail out the institutions affected. Most importantly, confidence in the country as a financial center has been shaken, perhaps terminally.

During 1987 and 1988 bank deposits in Panama dropped from $37 billion to less than $15 billion. Several foreign banks including Bankers Trust Company of New York, Republic National Bank of New York and First National Bank of Chicago have closed their Panamanian operations and more were expected to follow suit.

With the GNP of Panama expected to plunge 10 to 15 per cent in 1988, the government unable to meet its payroll commitments, and unemployment running at 30 per cent and growing, the poor were increasingly leaving Panama City for the countryside while middle-class professionals were emigrating in increasing numbers.

Other havens

As indicated in Table 7.1, there are a number of other secrecy havens. The New Hebrides is a tax haven in the South Pacific. It has attracted investors from Asia, Australia and the West Coast of the United States. The most popular form of corporation in the New Hebrides is the 'exempt company', which conducts all business outside the islands and is protected by strict secrecy laws.

Austria

Austria has a tradition of bank secrecy dating back to the Austro-Hungarian Empire. This tradition was reinforced by a 1979 law codifying bank secrecy. It allows a depositor to open an account without revealing his or her name or true identity, and the account remains anonymous as long as the depositor wishes – a form of total privacy unavailable even in Switzerland.

Given this level of secrecy and discretion one would expect the money launderers and drug traffickers to be rushing in. But Austria has one or two drawbacks. Most of the big banks are in part state-owned, making them understandably unattractive to the international criminal. In addition the country's geographical position in the shadow of the Soviet Union perhaps makes some clients nervous. And the Austrian schilling lacks the international profile of the Swiss franc.

Hong Kong

In Hong Kong bank secrecy laws are very strict, with the result that the colony has a reputation as one of the world's important 'laundries'. Generally speaking the funds laundered do not relate to the territory's own criminals (who tend to use more traditional underground systems, such as gold shop networks), but to international crime syndicates. Although Hong Kong has a range of special units, including the police Commercial Crime Bureau, the Independent Commission Against Corruption and the Special Commercial Crime Unit of the Territory's Legal Department, these tend to be underfunded and are also struggling well with widespread lack of political will, not to mention distinct unhelpfulness on the part of the banks. At a 1987 workshop on economic crime, not one of the banks contributed to the seminars. There is also the complicating factor of the territory's return to Chinese rule in 1997 – it is thought, for example, that any attempt to monitor capital flows now would simply be viewed as the precursor to the exchange control likely to be imposed then. So for the moment at least it looks as though Hong Kong's attractions to the secrecy seeker will remain undiminished.[52]

British Virgin Islands

The British Virgin Islands are popular as well. Exempt companies can be formed to engage in any activity that is not illegal in the BVI. There are no capital gains, turnover or net worth taxes and no estate duties. Unlike a number of its Caribbean cousins, the BVI has refused for the time being to agree to new provisions to facilitate US information-gathering.[53]

Lebanon

Even in Beirut, the financial secrecy business is thriving. In the decade of strife up to 1986 in Lebanon, only 2 out of 92 banks went out of business. The bank-secrecy laws – tougher than those in Switzerland – make Beirut's financial institutions highly attractive for those wanting to move large sums of money around with no questions asked. It seems that this and its geographical position are increasingly making Beirut into a major center for the arms trade. Arms deals have even been said to account for sudden mysterious rises in value of the Lebanese pound.[54]

United States

In countries such as France, West Germany, the United Kingdom and the United States, banks are bound either by law or by a code of discretion to maintain secrecy.

Deak & Co.

Among US financial institutions, the supply of international secrecy services has perhaps been most closely associated with Deak & Co. and its affiliates. Besides accusations of laundering drug money, including $7.6 million deposited by middle-aged and older women working as couriers, '. . . the company has long provided the anonymous and convuluted transactions prized by people trying to shield their money from coups, tax collectors, and police departments.'[55] This included the attraction of large mail deposits from Latin America, especially Argentina. It also included running funds for Lockheed to Asia to use in bribing officials during 1969–75 to influence aircraft procurement. 'In 15 deliveries, Deak & Co. moved $8.3 million to Hong Kong, where a Spanish priest representing Lockheed took the cash and carried it to Japan in a flight bag or in cardboard boxes labeled "oranges".'[56] According to a Deak spokesman, 'Lockheed Corporation came in and asked us to make a payment. We made a payment. The fact that the money was used later for bribes is Lockheed's shame, not ours.'[57] And in 1978 Deak & Co. was accused of taking a deposit of $11 million by two Philippine businessmen without filing the required federal reports. All this notoriety attracted so much attention that a substantial number of secrecy-seeking clients seem to have pulled out, leading to a liquidity crisis that added to already existing business problems and caused Deak & Co. to file for bankruptcy late in 1984.

Deak & Co. estimated its debts at about $60 million. The company announced that it would repay depositors by selling off a number of its healthier subsidiaries. However, beginning in December 1984, hundreds of creditors lined up, and it appeared not only that debts exceeded $60 million, but that the proceeds from the sale of assets might not cover them. Two groups of large depositors emerged with substantial claims: the Committee of Unsecured Creditors in the United States and the Hong Kong Creditors' Committee in Hong Kong.

At one time, Hong Kong creditors were apparently under the impression that their money was deposited locally, or maybe across the Pearl River estuary in the unregulated banking center of Macao. The only thing clear was that $26 million in depositor funds were missing. Funds transferred by Hong Kong to the Deak office in Macao apparently never reach their destination. The Hong Kong creditors also discovered that neither Deak-Perera Far East in Hong Kong nor Deak & Co. Macao Ltd

231

were licensed to accept deposits. The Macao office told creditors it had no records of the deposits from Hong Kong. With no proof that they were depositors, Hong Kong creditors were fighting to be recognized. A further complication was that Deak's US operations regularly borrowed from the Hong Kong subsidiary whenever New York ran short of cash. The amount thus borrowed was pegged at $15 million.[58]

Taken together, the problems motivated Deak's Hong Kong management to close the office doors. Under pressure from local creditors, the Hong Kong banking authorities intervened by assigning a provisional liquidator to find whatever assets remained and sell those that might lose value over time. The action came too late, however, as Deak insiders estimated that only $9 million of the creditors' original $26 million in cash remained in Hong Kong. Finally, in January 1985, Lark International Ltd, a Hong Kong conglomerate, purchased Deak-Perera Far East's operations for $385,000, which will go to Hong Kong creditors. Confusion still remained about which assets belonged to which of Deak's worldwide affiliates.

The bearer securities problem

In order to keep track of tax reporting on interest income, the US government ended the availability of domestic bearer bonds (previously issued mainly by municipal governments) on 1 July 1983. Old bearer bonds immediately increased in price slightly to reflect the increased value of their confidentiality, even though they traditionally sold a fraction below registered bonds of the same quality because of the virtual impossibility of tracing them if stolen and the resulting differential in warehousing risk.

Almost all municipal bonds issued in the United States before 1983 were bearer bonds, a feature which made them desirable instruments for investors wishing to evade taxes. Since that time, all new issues have been in registered form, with ownership recorded on central computers. Outstanding municipal bearer bonds, which amount to $270 billion, or more than one third of the total US municipal bond market in 1988, have continued to trade and have commanded a market premium of about $25 for each $1,000 face amount – effectively representing the value of the secrecy component. Beginning in September 1988, however, whenever an outstanding trade in a municipal bearer bond is settled, the national clearing house that handles most municipal bonds trades will have to convert it into bearer form. Over a two-year period, those bonds stored at the clearing house will likewise be converted into registered form. The view was that investors who value the bearer feature would withdraw their bonds from the clearing house and that the premium for the bearer bonds would increase as the supply decreased. The outstanding bearer bonds will continue to trade – outside the clearing house.[59]

Table 8.1 *Withholding tax on bond interest*

Country	Interest payable to	Eurobonds	Other corporate	Public sector
United	Residents[1]	0 or 20%	0 or 20%	0 or 20%
States	Non-residents[2]	0 or 30%	0 or 30%	0 or 30%
Britain	Residents	0[3]	30%	30%
	Non-residents	0[3]	30%	0 or 30%[4]
West	Residents	0	0	0
Germany	Non-residents[5]	25%	0 or 25%	25%
France	Residents[6]	0 or 10–12%	0 or 10–12%	0 or 10–12%
	Non-residents[5]	25%	25 or 45–50%[7]	25%
Switzerland	Residents	0 or 35%	0 or 35%	0 or 35%
	Non-residents[8]	35%	35%	35%
Holland	Residents	0	0	0
	Non-residents	0	0	0
Belgium	Residents[9]	0 or 25%	0 or 25%	0 or 25%
	Non-residents[9]	0 or 25%	0 or 25%	0 or 25%
Japan	Residents	0	0	0
	Non-residents	20%	20%	20%

Notes:
1. back-up witholding tax until taxpayer identication
2. no tax on 'portfolio' interest
3. with certain restrictions
4. no tax on interest on designated issues
5. exemptions announced/being considered
6. possible tax of 10–12%, except on government bonds and bonds issued by French companies abroad
7. tax on negotiable instruments 25%, non-negotiable 45%–50%
8. no tax on interest on bonds issued by non-Swiss borrowers
9. exemption for interest paid to certain companies and if funds are not used in a Belgian business

Source: The Economist, 27 October 1984, p. 81, from data compiled by Price Waterhouse.

In 1984, the United States repealed a 30 per cent withholding tax on interest paid to foreign purchasers of domestic bonds. Withholding has traditionally made such bonds less attractive than those issued in jurisdictions that have no such provisions (such as the Netherlands Antilles) or in the Eurobond market, and in jurisdictions that rebate most or all of the tax (such as Switzerland). Repeal was designed to put the US capital market on a par with these foreign and offshore financial centers and reposition that market more favorably, while at the same time giving US private and public sector borrowers better access to foreign capital.

One sticky point emerged, however, on the matter of secrecy. Whereas bonds in the United States can be issued only in registered form (with interest payable only to the registered owner), the bearer bonds that are common abroad (interest payable to anyone presenting a valid coupon) are obviously more attractive to investors intent on secrecy for tax evasion and other reasons.

Bearer bonds have long been attractive to those on the run from taxes or adverse political developments. According to Hans-Joerg Rudloff of Credit Suisse First Boston Ltd (a leading underwriter of Eurobonds): 'We in Europe have been through civil wars, revolutions, world wars and the confiscatory policies of socialist and communist governments. Whoever saves and has capital wants to protect himself from these events.'[60]

Table 8.1 indicates the rules applying to withholding of tax on bond interest in a number of major issuing countries, for both residents and non-residents. Interest withholding repeal coupled to bearer securities could make the United States the largest and most attractive tax haven of all for non-residents, with the potential of greatly increasing the $86 billion of foreign capital inflows recorded in 1983. One motive (more or less unspoken) was to gain still greater access to foreign savings to finance a large US budget deficit and help keep the lid on domestic interest rates.

Naturally, there were howls of protest from foreign governments, including some whose markets have traditionally been used as tax and secrecy havens. The most telling objections to the prospect of bearer securities emerged at home, however, with the possibility that such securities could be used by US residents (for example, through purchases by third parties) for purposes of tax evasion and money laundering. Shortly after withholding repeal, the New York firm of Salomon Brothers announced a repackaging of $1.7 billion in US Treasury securities in the form of Certificates of Accrual on Treasury Securities (CATS), fully backed by the securities themselves held in trust and sold at discount to investors.

The Treasury was caught in a bind. Issuing bearer bonds would clearly foster tax evasion by residents of the United States and was unanimously deemed unacceptable by a non-binding Senate resolution and threatened future legislation. Yet issuing registered bonds would make them unappealing to foreign investors. So a compromise solution was devised that pleased no one. The 'special registered securities' require buyers to certify that they are not US citizens, and the investment house must provide recertification each time interest is paid, yet without revealing the identity of the bondholder to the Treasury. This created a potential tax liability for securities dealers in the case of erroneous certification – prompting them to ask investors for more information than actually needed and potentially alienating them – as well as producing a large amount of paperwork. Swiss banks in particular fielded strong objections on both grounds, as well as the likelihood that the Treasury's requirements would conflict with Swiss secrecy laws. Resale of such securities could be made more difficult, and in particular resale in the US domestic bond market automatically precludes their further resale offshore.[61]

An interesting addendum to the whole affair was that less than a year after the US move the Japanese retaliated. They had maintained a 20 per cent withholding tax for non-residents on Euro-Yen bonds issued by Japanese companies. But that was repealed and now such bonds are tax free to foreign investors.

Summary

The motivation underlying the supply of financial secrecy in the international environment is clear – economic gain. Whether it involves individual vendors, lawyers, accountants and other intermediaries, or entire countries, secrecy-related financial services can be provided at a substantial 'mark-up' over their actual cost. The quality of those services is rather diverse, as we have seen. It depends on the professional competence, honesty and integrity of the vendor, as well as the legal safeguards and economic/political risks associated with his country.

Chapter 7 clearly indicated the degree of diversity that exists in the pattern of demand for financial secrecy. The same degree of diversity exists in the pattern of supply. Risk-averse tax evaders will prefer some secrecy havens over others. Crooks will be similarly selective. Geographic location, language and related factors enter the picture as well.

Where there are gains there will be competition, and this is no different in the secrecy game. Individual vendors compete, and so do their governments. Secrecy attributes are vigorously protected, since their erosion will quickly drive money out. New and innovative secrecy attributes are eagerly sought after, although in most cases they cannot be created overnight and marketing them can pose a difficult problem. A competitive hierarchy clearly exists, with very significant gains going to the pre-eminent, established secrecy centers, notably Switzerland, and rather limited benefits accruing at the more highly competitive 'booking' end of the market.

Notes

1 'Her Majesty's Drug and Bank Capital', *The Economist*, 12 October 1985.
2 'How Drugs Turned the Tide Against Bahamas' Banks', *Business Week*, 23 May 1988.
3 Ibid.
4 Ian Lyon, 'Paradise Under Pressure', *Investment International*, June 1987.
5 Ibid.
6 Thomas C. Jefferson and Vassel G. Johnson, 'Cayman Commits Itself to Financial Confidentiality', *Taxes International*, February 1985.
7 Ibid.
8 Andy Pasztor and Sonia Nazario, 'Cayman Islands Grant U.S. Access to Offshore Bank Data', *Wall Street Journal*, 3 July 1986.

9   Ian Lyon, 'Why Choose Cayman?', *Investment International*, June 1987.
10 Allan Dodds Frank, 'New Hub for an Old Web', *Forbes*, 7 April 1986.
11 Charles F. McCoy, 'Netherlands Antilles Minus a Tax Treaty is Tax-Paradise Lost', *Wall Street Journal*, 31 July 1987.
12 R. Eliot Rosen, 'Treasury's Blunder in Paradise', *New York Times*, 4 October 1987.
13 'The Antilles Heel', *Wall Street Journal*, 15 July 1987.
14 Charles F. McCoy, 'Netherlands Antilles Minus a Tax Treaty is Tax-Paradise Lost', *Wall Street Journal*, 31 July 1987.
15 'The Antilles Heel', *op. cit.* (n. 13).
16 R. Eliot Rosen, *op. cit.* (n. 12).
17 Allan Dodds Frank, *op. cit.* (n. 10).
18 Ibid.
19 Edward Cody, 'US Seeks to Reduce Loss of Revenues in Fiscal Fuzz of Caribbean Tax Havens', *Washington Post*, 15 June 1983. See also Alan Murray, 'We find it Very Hard to Believe that J. P. Morgan Began this Way', *Wall Street Journal*, 4 April 1985.
20 Charles F. McCoy, *op. cit.* (n. 11).
21 Jason Nisse, 'Channel Islands – Too Much of a Good Thing?', *The Banker*, August 1987.
22 Nicholas Bray, 'Rock Solid?', *Wall Street Journal*, 24 March 1987.
23 Edwin A. Finn, Jr and Tatiana Pouchine, 'Luxembourg: Colour it Green', *Forbes*, 28 April 1987.
24 'Luxembourg Makes Private Clients Feel Welcome', *International Herald Tribune*, 24 February 1986.
25 'Banking and Finance in Luxembourg', *International Herald Tribune*, 2 July 1986.
26 Ibid.
27 Richard Evans, 'Forcing Discreet Money Into the Open', *Euromoney*, November 1986. See also Richard A. Gordon, *Tax Havens and their Use by US Taxpayers – An Overview* (The Gordon Report) (Washington, DC: Internal Revenue Service, 12 January 1981), p. 123.
28 Donald Lessard and Adrian Tschoegl, 'Panama's International Banking Center: Where Does It Stand and What Can be Done to Insure Its Continued Viability and Increase Its Contributions to the Panamanian Economy?', *International Business and Banking Discussion Paper Series*, University of Miami, January 1985.
29 James LeMoyne, 'Panama Military Leader Denies Allegations of Crime Activities', *International Herald Tribune*, 19 June 1986.
30 Donald Lessard and Adrian Tschoegl, *op. cit.* (n. 28).
31 Larry Rohter, 'Bank Uncertainty in Panama', *New York Times*, 10 August 1987.
32 Joseph B. Treatser, 'Panama Offers a Haven for Shadowy Concerns', *New York Times*, 21 December 1986.
33 Larry Rohter, 'Bank Uncertainty in Panama', *New York Times*, 10 August 1987.
34 Allan Dodds Frank, 'See No Evil', *Forbes*, 6 October 1986. See also Julia Preston, 'In Panama, Turmoil Disturbs Peaceful Haven for International Bankers', *International Herald Tribune*, 11 July 1987; and Peter Ford, 'Panama's Bankers Weather Civil Unrest', *Financial Times*, 21 July 1987.
35 Richard Evans, *op. cit.* (n. 27).
36 Allan Dodds Frank, *op. cit.* (n. 34).
37 Stanley Penn, 'Top Spot to Deposit Illegal Narcotics Profits', *Wall Street Journal*, 16 October 1983.
38 Ibid.
39 Joseph B. Treatser, *op. cit.* (n. 32).
40 Richard Evans, *op. cit.* (n. 27).
41 David Warsh, 'The Money Launderers Stay a Step Ahead', *Boston Globe*, 15 June 1986.
42 John Moody, 'Dirty Dollars', *Time*, 19 January 1987.
43 Larry Rohter, *op. cit.* (n. 33).
44 John Borell, 'Bankers With a Bad Case of Nerves', *Time*, 31 August 1987.
45 Julia Preston, 'In Panama, Turmoil Disturbs Peaceful Haven for International Bankers', *International Herald Tribune*, 11 July 1987.
46 David Gardner, 'General Manuel Antonio Noriega, Master Manipulator in a World of Intrigue', *Financial Times*, 18 March 1988.
47 Laurence Zuckerman, 'Wanted: Noriega,' *Time*, 15 February 1988.

48 Robert E. Taylor, 'Ex-Smuggler Tells of Huge Drug Profits Laundered, Placed at Major US Banks', *Wall Street Journal*, 12 February 1988.
49 Ed Magnuson, 'Tears of Rage', *Time*, 14 March 1988.
50 Peter Ford, 'Panama's Bankers Weather Civil Unrest', *Financial Times*, 21 July 1987.
51 John Moody, *op. cit.* (n. 42).
52 John Mulcahy, 'The Chinese Laundry', *Far Eastern Economic Review*, 20 August 1987.
53 Ian Lyon, *op. cit.* (n. 4).
54 'The Surprising Boom for Beirut Banks', *Newsweek*, 26 August 1986.
55 'How Deak & Co. Got Caught in its Own Tangled Web', *Business Week*, 24 December 1984.
56 'Collapse of Deak & Company', *New York Times*, 10 December 1984.
57 Ibid., p. D4.
58 Sarah Bartlett and Dorinda Elliott, 'The Mess at Deak & Co. is Worse than Anyone Thought', *Business Week*, 11 February 1985, p. 20.
59 Alexandra Peers, 'Municipal Securities Ends Bearer Bonds' Anonymity', *Asian Wall Street Journal*, 23 August 1988.
60 'Braking in the Fast Lane', *Newsweek*, 27 August 1984.
61 'Why the Treasury's Plan to Sell Debt Overseas May Not Fly', *Business Week*, 22 October 1984. p. 129. See also Matthew Winkler, 'U.S. Change in Rule on Withholding is Reshaping Eurodollar Bond Market', *Wall Street Journal*, 20 June 1985, and Bob Hagerty, 'Japanese Snap up the Bulk of Special Treasury Issue', *International Herald Tribune*, 3 June 1985.

9

Combating International Financial Secrecy: Unilateral Initiatives

Given the discussion of the demand for financial secrecy presented in Chapters 3–8, it is little wonder that governments around the world have put a high priority on finding ways to control secret money. In doing so, they often seem to confuse cause and effect, disease and symptom.

Secret money itself is not the root cause of anything. But it makes things possible – it *facilitates*. Governments' inability or unwillingness to do very much about the underlying causes of financial secrecy perforce drives policymakers to attempt to deal with the symptoms. Yet in some cases this may be the only viable option. Funds spent combating money laundering may produce far better results than an equivalent expenditure on the direct enforcement of drugs laws, for example.

Like the market for secret money itself, policies to control it can be attempted on both the supply and demand side. With respect to the supply of international financial secrecy, it may be possible to convince foreign governments to facilitate disclosure, or to crack down on secrecy vendors within their borders – or at least to encourage them to exercise self-discipline. Or it may be possible to reach bilateral accords, even multilateral ones, that would contain substantial disclosures or investigative provisions. All such efforts require the exercise of power (bargaining leverage, intergovernmental arm-twisting) or cooperation – more likely the former. Regarding demand, it may be possible to crack down on secret financial flows by increasing penalties, reporting requirements and enforcement efforts, and by raising the probability of getting caught and the pain associated with punishment. But, like water, secret money will always find a way around attempts to control it as long as the underlying incentives are there. It can be temporarily dammed-up, diverted and made more costly, but it will invariably

238

resurface. In this chapter we shall outline some of the dimensions of controlling secret money, and evaluate their prospects for success.

Self-control

It would, of course, be nice to think that financial institutions and other intermediaries in the secrecy business will adhere strictly to the law, and even exercise a certain amount of discretion that goes beyond the law. To a considerable extent, they do. It is not good for business for financial institutions to be named in newspaper exposés of narcotics trafficking, child pornography or egregious political corruption. For most of the world's major financial institutions, abusive financial secrecy clearly constitutes a tiny fraction of their overall activities, and the possibility of contamination of legitimate business is anathema to senior management. Such institutions would be expected to stay well clear of any dealings that might be tainted – or at the very least have one or more intermediaries provide the necessary 'insulation'.

The almost panic reactions of leading firms on Wall Street to the revelations of malpractice by insider traders such as Levine and Boesky were indicative of how highly prized 'a good name' can be. Throughout the latter part of 1986 and beginning of 1987, firms were involved in a spate of security procedure reviews; there were internal investigations, investigations invited from external experts, memoranda to employees.[1] Offices were debugged, sophisticated locks installed, electronic rather than paper lists required for confidential items, even lie detectors and drug tests for recruits. The head of Drexel Burnham Lambert told his staff: 'Because the integrity and the perceived integrity of our markets and our firm is the jugular vein of our business, we have never and must never tolerate any violations of the law or of the firm's and industry's rules.'[2]

In any case, there has to be some perceived benefit for the institution involved. The case of insider trading is fairly clear-cut in this respect – there is a reputation and business to be lost and nothing much to be gained. But the case of capital flight, for example, is more difficult. Holding deposits for a few wealthy foreign clients is arguably far less offensive to a financial institution than having an insider trader on the staff, and it is certainly more profitable. So the vested interest element of self-control evaporates, reducing its likelihood for success as it does so. This may be lamentable, but as one banker has put it, 'there is no moral issue; if we don't do it, the Swiss will.'[3]

However, self-control is easier said than done, particularly in a very competitive financial environment and within often decentralized institutions. It requires a viable system of highly centralized management information and control of domestic and international branches and affiliates, as well as a consistent and unambiguous supervisory environment on the part of the regulatory authorities. These conditions are not always met.

For example, we know from Chapter 2 that the creation of trusts, other than direct transfers, is used to place funds offshore, primarily for tax avoidance or evasion. One major US international bank, when accepting trust accounts for administration in a higher-yield Euro-branch, stipulates that its clients consent in advance to disclosure, and the bank reserves the right to provide information to authorities as it deems necessary. This waiver supersedes any client rights under local secrecy laws abroad. For deposits held onshore, there is no need for contractual waivers. In the United States, federal authorities may approach a bank for access to information under the Right to Financial Privacy Statutes.

The majority of banks in tax havens are subject to control by their parent banks. These in turn are supervised by their own central banks and other regulatory authorities. Not surprisingly, one finds great variation among haven banks as well as bank headquarters in rules regarding secrecy and acceptance of currency deposits of dubious origin. There are also policy variations among offshore branches of the same bank. As Chapter 8 noted, in the Caymans or Panama the majority of banks, whether domestic or foreign-owned, are said to accept suitcase currency.

Central banks or other regulatory controls are probably most strict among banks headquartered in the major trading nations. However, some banks are suspected not only of being negligent with regard to their offshore branches' policies, but also of tolerating greater laxity in standards on the part of local managers with respect to their dealings with suspect clients. Expatriate managers' direct involvement in criminal activities, as well as questionable relations with local officials, do not seem to be uncommon. Besides the obvious incentive to become involved in criminal activities, local managers could find that they are actually punished for honesty. There have been instances where parent banks removed competent offshore managers for their refusal to participate in highly questionable financial activities.

According to a US Senate staff study, Africa, Central America and the Caribbean were the areas most vulnerable to bank involvement in politically corrupt or direct criminal matters and where suitable controls might not be exercised by headquarters.[4] Of the three regions, the Caribbean (including Panama) is said to be the most vulnerable of all. Conceptually, external control of foreign branches should probably come from home-country central banks. The supervision required, however, is not an audit of books but an audit of conduct.

Besides internal control and audit problems – and a heterogeneous external regulatory environment – there is also the problem of diverse views on the legal and moral status of secret money. The US or British tax evader who puts his money in Switzerland is welcome there. As long as he has not committed an act of fraud, he has broken no Swiss law. The Mexican businessman concerned with economic stability at home is welcome to place his assets in the United States, even though he might be considered a traitor back home. In the secrecy game, the gray areas are enormous, which makes it very difficult or impossible to define the 'correct' action on the part of the financial intermediaries, particularly those physically present in a number of different countries.

There is also the omnipresence of 'see no evil' operators who may be on the fringes in terms of overall financial significance but who may also carry disproportionate weight as intermediaries and middlemen in questionable transactions. The apparent voluntary cooperation of some of these banks in money laundering has been impressive. According to one US investigator posing as a courier: 'The banks were delighted to deal with me when I was "dirty". Bank guards were always willing to carry crates of money into a back room with the counting machines. Cash reporting requirements never hindered the banks, since they could afford to pay the fines if caught.'[5]

According to the testimony of a pilot before the President's Commission on Organized Crime:

When depositing money at Miami banks ... the clerks obligingly broke his large deposits into several smaller ones so he could avoid Federal [report] regulations ... When the volume of cash increased, [he] banked in the Bahamas. He recalled flying to a Bahamian bank carrying a large plastic trash bag full of bills. At the bank he sat talking with a bank official, the garbage bag of bills between his feet, and bargained over the banking fee. The banker finally charged a 1 percent 'counting fee' to accept the deposit. Eventually he had to buy an expensive money-counting machine.[6]

Diversity and inconsistency in the legal and behavioral picture, coupled to competitive, regulatory and control difficulties (both internal and external) limit governments' reliance on financial institutions themselves as levers in any crackdown on illegal activities giving rise to secret money flows. Rather, the majority of efforts have tended to run the other way – measures to deal directly with the flows themselves, which in turn impact on the institutions involved.

National government initiatives

There are a number of things governments can do within their own borders to try to affect, directly or indirectly, the secret money business.

Even without international flows, such action will never been entirely effective. For example, someone who wants a payment by check converted to cash can get it done (for a fee) through a check-cashing service, which assumes the risk of non-payment, or by cashing it at his bank and waiting until it clears or having a 'hold' put on sufficient funds maintained in an account to cover the principal amount. Alternatively, in the United States 'money orders' can be purchased in blank form from a number of vendors, which can then be used to make payments without significant identification of the payer. Still, things can be made more difficult and more expensive for the secrecy seeker, by countries acting on their own.

The US Bank Secrecy Act

One example is the US Bank Secrecy Act – the popular name for the Currency & Foreign Transactions Reporting Act of 1970. Under this legislation, the federal government has the authority to monitor large cash transactions and the export and import of large amounts of currency by means of reporting requirements imposed on banks and individuals. Although these requirements were intended to disrupt the laundering of cash for criminal purposes, effective enforcement was recognized as being difficult. A criminal already breaking the law would obviously care far less than law-abiding citizens about compliance with reporting requirements. However, a significant purpose of requiring the filing of these so-called CTR reports was to provide the Department of Justice with a means to obtain court convictions in criminal cases. This is because it is much easier to establish a criminal violation when a report is not filed than to prove the person's criminal activities. The penalty for failure to file a CTR report is either a year in prison or a fine of $10,000, or both. If failure to report is linked to other criminal activities, a much stiffer penalty is imposed – five years in jail or $500,000 in fines, or both.

With respect to financial institutions, the Bank Secrecy Act mandates that all depositors of over $10,000 in cash must be identified by name and source of funds, except for volume depositors like retail outlets. These may be exempted, although exempt lists must also be reported to the government. The same is true of telex transfers in excess of $10,000.

The Act imposes on the Secretary of the Treasury the responsibility for assuring compliance. The Secretary may then delegate responsibility to various bank regulatory agencies – the Comptroller of the Currency and the Federal Reserve Board.

Both the Comptroller and the Federal Reserve accorded low priority to the transaction reporting requirement in their respective bank examinations. To them, the bank's examination process is defined conventionally, focusing principally on the determination of the institution's financial condition and whether it is operating in a safe and sound manner. Neither seems ready to expand its role to cover closer offshore supervision, nor are they prepared to deal with criminal activities offshore that may be related to US banking activities. Both agencies have also noted a legal impediment: the Right to Financial Privacy Act of 1978. This legislation significantly restricted government agencies from transferring financial records or information of bank customers to other agencies or departments.

Within the Treasury Department, the Drug Enforcement Administration (DEA) is subordinate to the FBI and is on the front line with respect to investigations of the flow of money through offshore accounts. The prevalence of narcotics cases, however, is not proof that drugs money constitutes the largest element of crime-related offshore financial activities. It may simply reflect the intensity of the enforcement effort because of the moral, social and political concerns associated with narcotics. Also within the Treasury, the US Customs Service was given expanded search authority under the Bank Secrecy Act, with respect to both departing and incoming travelers. However, a 1981 survey found that few departing passengers bothered to fill out the CTR forms – one or two per week at JFK International Airport in New York and two or three per month at Chicago's O'Hare – although a far larger number of incoming passengers filled them out, apparently because the CTR requirement is listed on the mandatory customs forms while no forms are required to be filled out by passengers leaving the country.

An analysis of 1981 CTR forms relating to Panama showed $139 million of cash deposits, $6.5 million of withdrawals, and $9.7 million in other transactions, for a total of $155.2 million, with 86 per cent of those funds identified as being related to drug laundering operations.

> In fact, the great percentage . . . is money from the streets of US cities which was deposited into accounts of alleged currency exchanges using Panamanian addresses. The exchanges have been found to be owned and operated by Colombians who are in the business of laundering drug proceeds for other Colombian drug traffickers.[7]

Such information, of course, reflects only a tiny fraction of the actual funds flows, the vast majority of which never get anywhere near compliance with the government's CTR reporting requirements. In one experiment, the Federal Reserve Bank of New York marked large numbers of $100 bills, which were then put into circulation locally. Within a fairly short period of time, a sizeable proportion of them turned up in Miami, having been caught up in the wash of currency to South Florida ultimately destined for domestic and offshore money laundering.

Operation Greenback

In June 1980 Operation Greenback was set up in Miami in an attempt to break the back of money laundries there. It was a joint effort of the Treasury and Justice Departments, involving use of the reporting requirements established under the Bank Secrecy Act:

> IRS and Customs in Operation Greenback used a sort of a rock and a hard place approach in order to get at these people. They basically go in and say: Mr. Hughes, excuse me, but where did you get that £1 million that you put in the bank last week? And if you had already been presented with an IRS and a Customs agent there wasn't too much you could say about it. You either had to say that money was generated inside the United States, and you knew darn well your tax year was going to be closed out, or you would have to tell me, for instance, that you brought the money from Colombia or Panama or elsewhere, and there was no form to back it up ... We had a large number of individuals cooperate with us because they could not explain where they got their cash. It was a very good technique that we used between us.[8]

Early successes were perhaps not as great as such enthusiasm would suggest. But the operation was nevertheless considered sufficiently worthwhile to serve as a model for the establishment in February 1983 of the Organized Crime Drug Enforcement Task Forces (OCDE),[9] a network of multi-agency narcotics/financial task forces spread throughout the country. Operation Greenback itself became part of the Miami OCDE force in October 1984, by which time its efforts had resulted in indictments against 215 individuals from 82 organizations, seizure of $38.8 million of suspect currency, $14.6 million in property, and total fines and taxes in excess of $120 million.[10]

Between February 1983 and April 1985 the OCDEs produced 1,300 indictments, 460 convictions, $81.8 million in money seized and $34.3 million in property. They are believed to have destroyed 18 major laundering enterprises, which laundered a documented total of $2.8 billion.[11]

In early 1984, a further plan was set up under the auspices of Operation Greenback, again with a wider field of play than Florida.[12] Known as Operation Tracer, it was the largest operation of its kind in US history, involving raids on dozens of Puerto Rican banks and seizure of more than $100 million of allegedly drug-related money.[13] It culminated in June 1985 with the arrest in Puerto Rico of 17 people involved in major laundering schemes. Some of the individuals were high-ranking bank officials, one even a prominent savings and loan institution president. The Bank Secrecy Act made it possible for the government to charge the

17 with failure properly to report large cash transactions as well as with conspiracy.[14]

Still, a decade and a half after its passage, the US Bank Secrecy Act and its administration had failed in two important aspects. First, the Act did not slow down or stop movements of illegally obtained currency from the United States. Second, while some successful prosecutions did provide an inkling of the 'big money' involved in these movements, the Act failed to yield sufficient data about onshore and offshore money laundering. Insufficient data, in turn, hindered the formulation of policy and the development of appropriate legislative, administrative and diplomatic remedies.

For their part, bankers continued to argue that it is not appropriate for them to police financial transactions. Even failure to meet government reporting requirements is laid to the action of individual bank employees, rather than the systematic practice of the banks themselves. Yet according to Rudolph W. Giuliani, US Attorney in Manhattan:

> The law placed the responsibility on banks to obtain and report concerning domestic and foreign transactions. And similarly, irrespective of legal ramifications, any bank that allows itself to be used as a conduit for drug money is in danger of severely damaging its image and its reputation for prudence and integrity. At the same time, it is exposing its employees, who have to deal with many sensitive situations, to being tempted to involve themselves in crime.[15]

The Bank of Boston case

In early 1985 it was revealed that, in direct violation of its reporting obligations under the Bank Secrecy Act, the Bank of Boston had failed to report to the government 1,163 currency transactions amounting to $1.22 billion, mainly with Swiss correspondent banks. In February the bank pleaded guilty to a felony charge of 'knowingly and willfully' failing to report, and was fined $500,000, at that time the largest penalty ever imposed on a financial institution for violations of the reporting requirements.[16]

Equally embarrassing was the fact that the bank had also undertaken a string of cash dealings with the Angiulo family, reputedly the leading organized crime group in Massachusetts. The Angiulos and associates had been allowed to deposit shopping bags of cash and buy cashier's checks without filing any CTR reports. Two companies headed by the family were placed on the bank's list of those customers exempt from reporting.[17] It was stated that there was no collusion between bank officers and the Angiulos.[18]

William Brown, chairman of Bank of Boston Corp., claimed that the bank had failed to report both the domestic and international currency transactions as required because its officers were not familiar with the law. However, Treasury officials pointed to the Bank's repeated violations even after having been notified, and wondered how a large bank could have been totally oblivious to the widely publicized regulation. Several weeks later, the bank revealed an additional $110 million in unreported cash transactions, mostly with Canada and Haiti.[19]

In March 1985, to the Reagan administration's embarrassment, Comptroller of the Currency C. Todd Conover told a Senate committee that his agency had made the same mistake as the Bank of Boston officers. The Comptroller's bank examiners missed the irregularities during a special investigation conducted at the Bank of Boston in 1982. The Treasury expressed fears that the Comptroller's admission could provide ammunition for banks seeking immunity from prosecution if they disclosed that they, too, had failed to report currency transactions as required under the Bank Secrecy Act. Almost immediately, several banks did in fact seek immunity.[20]

As far as government officials were initially able to determine, the Bank of Boston violations were mainly due to 'systems failure'. That is, most of the employees involved failed to comply with the CTR reporting requirement out of ignorance, and their failure was not picked up by bank officers up the line. Nevertheless, suspicions had been aroused that at least some were actively involved in money laundering – suspicions reinforced by instances in the past of bank managements' non-reporting in return for kickbacks from criminals and their associates. The Garfield Bank and the Pan American International Bank serve as examples. Garfield was hit with $2.3 million in fines, penalties, back taxes, and interest. Pan American fines were smaller, but its former vice-chairman was sentenced to prison. As long ago as 1977, Chemical Bank in New York fired 24 employees for cooperating in money-laundering schemes and paid more than $200,000 in fines. In 1983, Republic National Bank admitted it had not reported $165,000 in cash business from cocaine dealers and paid a $15,000 fine. The Rockland Trust Co., a small bank in Plymouth, Massachusetts, and officers of the Ansonian Credit Union in Boston, were indicted in 1984 for failing to file currency reports. Overall, by early 1985, 21 banks had been penalized for failing to report currency transactions of more than $10,000.[21] But it was with the Bank of Boston case that the true extent of violations fully began to be grasped.

The Justice Department investigation of the Angiulo family in Boston also uncovered connections with the brokerage firms of E. F. Hutton and Cowen & Co., as well as the Provident Institution for Savings. The Angiulos bought $520,000 in cashier's checks from the Provident and the Bank of Boston, payable to Cowen. Cowen claimed that one of its retail managers inherited the Angiulo accounts from a colleague at E. F. Hutton and brought them with him when he transferred to the firm in

1980. In March 1986, the Provident was fined $100,000 for its failures to report large transactions totalling almost $1 million, including those of the Angiulos.[22]

Other banks began confessing. In July 1985, a Treasury official was quoted as saying: 'After the Bank of Boston fines about 40 banks have come forward to report violations to us.'[23] By August, some 60 banks were under Treasury scrutiny.[24] Already in March, four major New York banks were in the spotlight. Chemical Bank admitted 857 unreported cash transactions worth $25.9 million since 1980, most reportedly with US foreign exchange brokers. Irving Trust Company listed 1,659 transactions with 38 foreign banks worth $292 million, while Manufacturers Hanover Trust Company listed $140 million covering 1,400 international currency transactions – both banks cited 'oversights' and 'systems failure'. Chase Manhattan did not make its disclosure public, but the figures were thought to be close to those of Manufacturers Hanover Trust.[25] The total fines imposed on the four were $1.2 million.[26] These were based on the number of unreported transactions in each case. Before 1984 the maximum penalty per transaction had originally been $1,000, but this had been increased to $10,000. However, reductions were made for the New York banks because of their cooperation with the Treasury. The fines were criticized in Congress as merely a 'pittance'.

In the Fall of 1985, two more Boston banks came forward. The Bank of New England, the region's second largest bank, admitted to two sets of unreported cash transactions, and the area's third largest bank, the Shawmut Bank of Boston, confessed to over $190 million in transactions with foreign banks and improperly exempting 27 customers. The Bank of New England was in the end found guilty of 31 failures to report cash withdrawals by a convicted gambler in 1983 and 1984. It was fined $1.2 million which it appealed, noting that its violations were due to 'organizational indifference' not criminal intent, and therefore it should not be held liable. But the original judgement was upheld by the Supreme Court in November 1987.[27]

Meanwhile, investigations into Crocker National Bank had been proceeding, resulting at the end of August 1987 in a massive $2.25 million fine, for failing to report 7,877 cash transactions totalling $3.98 billion. Crocker's case differed from the others because it had not voluntarily disclosed its currency violations. These were discovered by the Comptroller of the Currency, and only then did the bank cooperate with the Treasury. Of the $3.98 billion in question, some $3.43 billion involved six Hong Kong banks that had shipped large amounts of US currency to Crocker's main San Francisco office. Crocker branches near the US–Mexican border, however, also did some brisk illicit business.[28] The Treasury stated that they had, through Crocker's violations, been 'deprived of potentially important law-enforcement leads that could have been useful in drug, tax and laundering investigations'. Crocker was 'outraged' at the innuendo that it had been knowingly involved with criminal funds, but the Treasury's suggestion that somebody ought to have at least been suspicious hardly seems unreasonable.[29]

The E. F. Hutton case

Banks have not been the only financial institutions implicated in US money laundering related to organized crime and narcotics trafficking. The brokerage firm of E. F. Hutton accepted more than $13 million in cash during a five-month period in 1982, most of it delivered by Franco Della Torre, one of 38 people indicted in the $1.65 billion 'Pizza Connection' heroin case (see Chapter 3). The money eventually was placed in accounts opened at Hutton's office in Lugano, Switzerland, registered in the names of Traex, Acacias Development Corp. and P.G.K. Holding, and controlled by Della Torre associates. In Switzerland, the money was handled by men who acted as professional money launderers for Giuseppe Bono, an alleged Mafia boss arrested in the Milan area in 1983. Much of the money ended up invested in northern Italy. Interestingly, and a sign perhaps of Swiss determination not to be shown to tolerate 'serious' crime, the four Swiss who allegedly acted as consultants for recycling the money were tried in Lugano in 1985.[30]

Hutton was not charged with any violations of law because it had in fact complied with the Bank Secrecy Act by filing CTR reports for all of the cash transactions exceeding $10,000. However, the FBI and the US Customs Service remained perturbed by indications that Hutton's actions supported and protected the alleged money launderers. For example, the company arranged personal security for Della Torre from his hotel to the financial institutions in which the money was deposited. In addition, the amount of the deposits should have caused alarm, as they did at Merrill Lynch, where Della Torre had earlier made questionable cash deposits of $4.9 million and which had declined to accept further funds and closed the account. Della Torre then went to Hutton.

Further confusion about Hutton's role emerged in October 1982, when the firm was served with a federal grand jury subpoena to provide information regarding Della Torre and the Swiss accounts. Hutton officials promptly notified a Della Torre associate in Switzerland of the subpoena, despite specific requests by the government that no such disclosure be made. The firm's attorneys requested immunity for Hutton officials. Since no charges had been filed, the government's question naturally was 'immunity from what?'

Hutton's actions remained under intensive review. Indeed, the head of the firm's futures division, Arnold Phelan, was placed on leave of absence while his role in the various transactions contributing to the laundering operation was being considered. What the firm did, according to one Treasury agent, was 'right on the knife-edge [between legal and illicit conduct] and, depending on the intention, could amount to an obstruction of justice.'[31]

In 1988, Hutton pleaded guilty to federal money laundering charges for offenses that took place between 1982 and 1984 at its Providence, RI office. It paid over $1 million in fines. The company also faced criminal charges in the US District Court relating to alleged failure to report at least $532,000 in currency transactions, some of them with organized crime figures. A felony conviction could result in the company being forced to suspend investment services, although the successor firm, Shearson Lehman Hutton, hoped for waivers of such a penalty by the SEC.[32]

Laundering and CTRs figured prominently in the case of another well known securities firm, Shearson Lehman, at that time the United States' third largest brokerage house. In a case that was expected to break new legal ground, the company was indicted on 26 June 1986, together with its former Philadelphia sales manager, Herbert L. Cantley, on two counts of conspiracy, 36 counts of failure to report currency transactions, and three counts of concealment of material facts. In addition, Cantley and six other Philadelphia men were charged with conspiracy and operating an illegal sports gambling enterprise.

These charges, amounting to the overall accusation that Shearson Lehman had laundered some $1.2 million, were tantamount to the government's saying that it viewed the company as criminally liable for the actions of one of its employees, regardless of whether it was aware of them or not. As the senior legislative counsel for the American Bankers Association expressed it: 'The big question is when do you attribute an individual's knowledge to a corporation?'. It has been suggested that in fact Shearson chose to ignore Cantley's criminal activities out of eagerness for commissions. And some think that the company's indictment was a deliberate attempt on the part of the government authorities to 'persuade' financial institutions into a more active role in the fight against organized crime.[33]

The Paine Webber securities firm also attracted embarrassing attention in January 1987, when a former vice-president of the firm, Gary D. Eder, was indicted on charges that he had helped clients move more than $700,000 in cash into their accounts in a way that avoided reporting the transactions to the IRS. Between August 1981 and July 1983, Eder allegedly received cash in excess of $10,000 on several occasions, but deposited the funds into his clients' accounts in amounts of just under $10,000 in several different days. There is no indication that laundering was involved, and the scheme simply seems to have been tax-oriented.[34]

In the first case involving a criminal indictment of a financial institution involved in drug laundering, the US Federal Government, in early

October 1988, charged that Bank of Credit & Commerce International (BCCI) and nine of its officers were involved in laundering more than $32 million in drug money.

Federal prosecutors alleged that bank officers of the Tampa, New York and Houston branches of BCCI – a large and rapidly growing, Luxembourg-based international bank that was started in the early 1970s and now owned primarily by Middle East interests through a Cayman Island holding company – took funds they knew to be from US cocaine sales, invested them in certificates of deposit issued by BCCI branches in France, Britain, Luxembourg, the Bahamas, Panama and South America, and made to drug dealers loans to be repaid later with proceeds from the maturing certificates of deposit.

The loan proceeds were eventually wired back to the BCCI branch in Florida. On the return trip and thereafter, the funds involved would not have been subject to the $10,000 currency transaction reporting requirement, they could be transferred to members of the so-called Medellin drug cartel in Colombia without detection through Uruguay.

Because at each stage in the chain bank fees and interest spreads would be deducted, the circuitous routing of funds – highly profitable for BCCI – would have been quite costly to the beneficiaries of the laundry operation. Presumably, it was designed with the sole purpose of confusing law enforcement agencies. BCCI had previously come under suspicion of drug money laundering as one of the bankers to General Manuel Noriega, the Panamanian leader indicted in the US on drug charges but never brought to trial.

In a two-year investigation involving British and French government cooperation, US federal investigators posed as professional money launderers and approached BCCI with a number of transactions. Although initially the undercover investigators proposed methods for laundering the funds, they alleged that BCCI officers themselves suggested innovations. In the coordinated October 1988 arrests in financial centers in Europe and the United States, 80 people were rounded up. On conviction the major defendants could face up to life imprisonment and fines totalling more than $5 million. BCCI itself could face maximum fines of more than $45 million.[35]

New initiatives

As a result of the Bank of Boston revelations, US banks appear to be increasing internal controls to guard against money laundering, including greater emphasis on training programs, revised policies, and improved computer software. Training programs teach tellers to identify launderers. New policies make cashier's checks available to regular customers only. Data processing software has become available that produces daily lists of accounts with cash transactions of more than $10,000.

The US Treasury carried forward its offensive against money laundering, beginning in July 1984, with a broad set of proposals that would require banks to supplement the already mandated disclosure of international currency movements in excess of $5,000 with:

- all credit card charges received or shipped by financial institutions, including date, amount of charge, and submitting merchant;
- all travelers check transactions, overseas checks and drafts, including the names of payee and payer, names of enforcers, date and amount; and
- all transfers of securities, certificates of deposit, commercial paper and wire funds transfers.

Two years later, in August 1986, it continued in the same vein with further suggestions for modification in reporting and recording cash transactions. Banks were to:

- record all cash purchases of cashier's checks, money orders or travelers' checks of more than $3,000;
- report such purchases if they totalled more than $10,000 in a single day;
- report any type of multiple cash transactions by one customer totalling more than $10,000 in a single day.

In addition, it would no longer be satisfactory merely to keep a list of 'exempt' customers (i.e. high-volume cash customers, such as retailers); statements signed by those customers and explaining why they were exempt were to be provided.[36]

The various reporting and record-keeping requirements had in addition been extended to cover a greater variety of institutions. As well as banks and other financial organizations, such as brokerage houses, as well as gambling casinos had, from 7 May 1985, been brought into the CTR net.

Meanwhile the President's Commission on Organized Crime had come to the conclusion that banks, brokers and casinos were undeniably, whether wittingly or not, involved in the laundering of criminal funds. The Commission had been established by President Reagan on 28 July 1983 with a mandate to investigate the scope of organized crime in the United States. Its final report was to be submitted by 1 March 1986, but it issued also a number of interim reports. One of these, 'The Cash Connection', released in 1984, considered in depth the aspect of money laundering and the involvement of the financial institutions. It suggested that of the $5–15 billion from the narcotics trade alone in 1984, some two-thirds passed through US financial institutions.

These findings, compounded by the subsequent discoveries of violations of Bank Secrecy Act reporting requirements, gave rise to grave concern on the part of the authorities. Research was making it clear that the laundering of funds was indispensable for the success and profitability of large-scale organized criminal activity. Equally clear was the fact that attacking the funds themselves was an efficacious way of attacking the underlying crime. If the money could be traced, it would often lead to the figures at the top; if it could be seized, it would serve as devastating evidence at a criminal trial; if it could be forfeited to the authorities, it deprived a criminal enterprise of its lifeblood. Unfortunately, it was equally obvious that professionals and institutions who should have been above reproach were by no means impervious to the corrupting influence of the vast funds involved. 'We are particularly concerned', noted the Senate Permanent Subcommittee on Investigations, 'about the impact such activities may have on both the integrity and safety and soundness of the nation's financial institutions.'[37]

It became clear that, quite apart from stricter surveillance of reporting and increased penalties for non-compliance, other moves had to be taken. Discouraged and disturbed as well by what it saw as irresponsible lack of interest on the part of financial institutions, the Reagan administration began seriously to consider new legislation to combat laundering. Attorney General Edwin Meese stressed the need for more effective weapons in the fight, likening money launderers to the 'fences' used by burglars.[38]

Under existing laws money laundering, as we have seen, could only be prosecuted either as a violation of the reporting requirements of the Bank Secrecy Act or as a conspiracy to defraud the government by obstructing the filing of accurate reports.[39] This made successful prosecution extremely difficult. It was felt that the only truly viable solution was to make the act of laundering itself a felony, thus opening the way as well to prosecution of anyone who aided or abetted the action.[40] The Senate Permanent Subcommittee on Investigations recommended that: 'The enactment of a statute which directly addresses the problem of money laundering would be a significant addition to the federal arsenal and would greatly assist law enforcement's ongoing fight against criminal activity in this country.'[41] It also reported that: 'The courts are jammed up in South Florida. One of the interests we have ... in the money laundering bill ... is that [it places] greater emphasis on the crime itself. We have some difficulty convincing not the courts, not the juries, but the judges, really, of the fact that people who handle the cash are just as guilty as people who handle the powder.'[42]

During the course of 1985 five separate bills were in fact considered. There were certain (in some cases quite major) differences between them. We confine ourselves here to a summary of the essential points that evolved.

First, as discussed above, the act of classic money laundering, that is helping to disguise criminal proceeds, was to be made illegal. Penalties suggested included imprisonment for from five to 20 years and fines of from $250,000 to five times the monetary value of the instruments involved.[43]

Second, the definition of money laundering was to be extended. It was now to apply to anyone who 'knowingly engaged or attempted to engage in a monetary transaction (of more than $10,000) in criminally derived property.'[44] It would thus be a crime, for example, for a car dealer or a real estate agent, let alone a banker, to accept cash if the government could show that in doing so he or she was 'recklessly disregarding' the unlawful source of the funds.[45] It was considered necessary to extend the definition in this way in order to 'catch' those who were 'willfully blind' to the source of the funds with which they were dealing and who were thus both facilitating the act of money laundering and benefiting from it.

Third, the Treasury should have direct access to bank records if it is required for its investigations. It would be granted direct summons authority for both financial institution witnesses and documents.[46]

Fourth, combined with this there was to be generally easier access to financial records for any government agency investigating laundering offenses. In 1978, the Right to Financial Privacy Act had set down strict criteria for such access. While bankers were expected to inform law officers of suspicious activities by their customers, the authorities were required to obtain a warrant or a subpoena entitling them to view the individual's records before they could proceed. In addition, the individual was to be informed of the investigation unless the court specifically relieved the authorities of the obligation to do so. There were also restrictions on transferring information between government agencies.[47] All of this was to be amended. Agents would no longer need a judge's permission; bank employees would be exempt from the requirement to inform an individual of an investigation;[48] transfers between agencies would be permissible and on top of it all there would be a provision forbidding states from restricting authorities' access to bank records.

'The object', the Senate Permanent Subcommittee noted, 'is simply to enable – not to compel – financial institutions to notify law enforcement authorities of possible illegal activity without incurring civil liability under the Right to Financial Privacy Act'[49] and to ensure that 'state financial privacy laws that are more restrictive than the Right to Financial Privacy Act do not create an impediment to the effective investigation of Federal crimes.'[50]

Fifth, seizure and forfeiture of money laundering funds was to be introduced. Hitherto the government had only been able to seize proceeds from narcotics transactions if it had proved that the defendant was guilty of the underlying narcotics offense or at least knew that the funds derived directly from a specific drug transaction. It could thus be difficult to seize 'dirty money' from a launderer who could not be proved to have definite knowledge of the exact origin of the funds in question. The Senate Permanent Subcommittee argued that: 'A specific forfeiture provision for the funds involved in money laundering ... is a somewhat more direct way of focussing the attention of the court on the specific reprehensible conduct, money laundering, that justifies forfeiting the money and thus separating the criminal from the fruits of his crime than is proceeding under the drug forfeiture statutes.'[51]

It is not difficult to imagine the outcry these sweeping proposals caused. They were condemned as overkill by bankers, and even raised possible constitutional questions. A spokesman for the American Bankers Association was quoted as saying that 'the Fourth Amendment to the United States Constitution prohibits not only illegal search and seizure but also protects individuals from unreasonable invasion of legitimate privacy interests at the hands of the government ... This law would virtually repeal all the protections established by Congress in 1978 when it approved the Financial Privacy Act'. 'Financial institutions', he continued, 'are in a poor position to complain that the Feds want to do too much, when they themselves have done so little. I think that's the tragedy of all this.'[52] Concern was also expressed by the American Bar Association and the American Civil Liberties Union (ACLU), who were gravely disturbed by what they saw as an onslaught on citizens' rights.[53]

For the most part, these groups accepted the need for some sort of offensive against money laundering; their worries were about how this would be done in the legislation proposed. Three main issues of concern emerged.

First, the extension of the definition of money launderer to include one who acted with reckless disregard of the source of funds he touched was particularly controversial. It was suggested that the definition was just too broad – as drafted it could apply to any number of innocent people going about their daily business,[54] and in particular it would put a quite intolerable burden on the ordinary bank teller, who would be expected to tell when an apparently normal transaction was shady. 'Entire classes of people who are not involved in illegal activity under [these] money laundering definitions ... could subject themselves to prosecution.'[55] 'I think the administration bill is far too reaching and is subject to too much abuse when you put what is essentially a negligence standard into the criminal law.'[56] 'These bills turn the emphasis from the criminal activity of the drug dealer to the bank teller – to the average law abiding man and woman.'[57]

As we saw earlier the question of 'reckless disregard' was also a very relevant issue to lawyers acting on behalf of criminals and receiving fees from them. Because of the special relationship of a lawyer and his client, a defense attorney would quite probably be aware of the source of the funds that went to pay his fees. Would it really be just for that to lay him open to prosecution as a money launderer? As one law professor put it: 'The bill is ominous. It gives the government tremendous coercive power over defense lawyers.'[58]

Second, the role of the attorney and the whole question of a man's right to counsel under the Sixth Amendment was at the center of the second major objection to the proposals. It was pointed out that seizure and forfeiture of proceeds before trial was tantamount to removing the presumption of innocence on which the US legal system functions. In addition, the confiscation of the defendant's assets (before any findings of fact) left him without the resources to pay for an attorney. The US administration's argument was that in that case the defendant would be represented by a court-appointed counsel, like any other accused without financial backing; why should ill-gotten gains allow the alleged drug-dealer or launderer his choice of representative when more ordinary alleged criminals had to be content with what they were given?[59]

The third major concern was over the implications of the legislation for financial privacy. It clearly attacked the heart of the protections afforded by the Financial Privacy Act. And according to the American Bankers Association and ACLU it did so unnecessarily. They pointed out that provisions already existed whereby in certain circumstances banks could inform the government that they held information that might be relevant to a possible violation of the law; notification to a customer of investigations underway could be delayed and records could be passed between government agencies.[60] Such provisions were not as sweeping as those suggested, but they were sufficient.

Discussion and redrafting continued throughout 1985. The Hearings before the Subcommittee on Crime on the subject provide a fascinating picture of the issues under debate. In July 1986 the Comprehensive Money Laundering Prevention Act was passed by the House of Representatives Banking Committee, and the Money Laundering Control Act was passed by the House Judiciary Committee.[61] In October 1986, the Anti-Drug Abuse Act was signed into law.[62] It contained all the major provisions outlined above, and penalties for the crime of money laundering were set at a maximum of 10 years imprisonment with fines of up to $250,000.

Another US unilateral initiative would involve establishing an ad hoc federal commission whose functions would include accumulation and dissemination of information, coordination of inter-agency and inter-governmental activities, and provision of personnel and support to countries seeking to improve their bank supervision and control arrangements, and to provide a financial investigative service. The United States has had very little in the way of a truly coordinated approach to these problems, although there is a general consensus among government agencies that cooperation is needed to improve investigation of offshore criminal activities. As yet, however, there are no guidelines as to possible procedures, nor is there an accessible inventory of work done by the various government agencies. In the State Department, for example, attention to Caribbean matters has always been of low priority. The Internal Revenue Service did publish the Gordon Report on tax havens in 1981,[63] while the Customs Service was among the first to recognize the role of banks in laundering narcotics money. However, there has clearly been inadequate use of the Currency Transaction Reports and the Currency and Monetary Instrument Reports for control purposes.

The US courts have also contributed to the attempted diminution of money laundering. In the 1983 trial of money launderer Eduardo Orozco Prada, discussed in Chapter 6, two new legal precedents were established.

First, the prosecution convinced the jury that Orozco was himself a 'financial institution', and was therefore required to file Currency Transaction Reports. This means that if a launderer is discovered to have bought 20 cashier's checks of $5,000 with an original $100,000, he could be held in violation of the Bank Secrecy Act for not having filed reports for the whole amount, with penalties set accordingly.

Second, the prosecution secured the conviction of Orozco as a co-conspirator who was 'aiding and abetting' drug traffickers, even though Orozco had a policy of never dealing directly with anyone who had a drug conviction. Previously, money launderers could work with impunity as long as they kept their operations separate from their drug-dealing counterparts. And in 1986 the Court of Appeals upheld attachment by US marshals of more than $3 million of a Panamanian bank's alleged drug money, on deposit in the United States, via a Colombian bank's accounts at Irving Trust, Chemical Bank, Marine Midland, First Chicago and Philadelphia National Bank. A US Customs Special Agent explained the relevance of this decision: 'Now the government can pursue alleged drug proceeds as they are moved to a second or a third bank in any form, including credit balances or cash. If we can track the money, we can seize it.'[64]

The various points at issue in these decisions have now been incorporated into the Anti-Drug Abuse Act. But it is interesting to note that the courts had been moving in that direction anyway. Interesting, too, is the fact that the increased power to seize illicit funds has resulted in a windfall for bodies such as the Drug Enforcement Administration. In 1986 it made an operating profit of $30 million, and it has hundreds of millions of dollars in assets ranging from aircraft to a golf course.[65]

It remains to be seen what effect this range of initiatives will have. They have certainly made smurfing far more difficult, for example. But as one Washington attorney has put it: 'One thing I can tell you, the biggest traffickers aren't smurfing. The easiest way to deal with drug money is to lug the currency out of the country.' Other investigators and bankers familiar with clandestine currency movements tend to agree. It is still very difficult for the US Customs Service to detect physical cash on its way out of the country; once the funds are in a banking-secrecy country, the return of it 'legally' is relatively simple. The most common method is the issuance of loans from third-party banks that use the original 'dirty' deposits as collateral.[66] Laundering itself is now a crime in the United States, and so prosecution of those suspected is at least more straightforward and as such has more chance of success. In addition, as places such as Switzerland, the Caymans and the Bahamas become more cooperative, laundering will prove more tricky. Nevertheless, there remains a long road ahead.

Money laundering has, of course, not been the only field of attack for the US administration. It has been engaged in a general war against white-collar crime. This involves the major problem of insider trading (see Chapter 10), as well as bank fraud, defense procurement and tax evasion.

Several laws have been passed in the United States over the past 20 years to counter white collar crime, besides the 1970 Bank Secrecy Act. In the same year the Racketeer Influenced and Corrupt Organizations Act (RICO) was passed. This was aimed at offenders displaying 'a pattern of racketeering activity', i.e. organized criminals. In 1977 the Foreign Corrupt Practices Act forbade companies to use bribes, even for foreigners used to considering them as a part of their pay. In 1984 the Comprehensive Crime Control Act came into being, aimed in part at preventing bank fraud. The need for such legislation was perhaps highlighted by the findings in 1983 of the House Committee on Government Operations. It found in a study of 105 bank and savings and loan failures that criminal activity by insiders figured in more than half the bank failures and one quarter of the failures of savings and loan institutions. It was under the Act's powers that the Department of Justice enjoined E. F. Hutton from future use of the cash-management procedures that had made its 'check-kiting' operation possible.[67] The Act has also extended the government's ability to pursue the assets of hardcore criminals. It has made possible, for example, the seeking of restraining orders from the courts, prohibiting defendants from transferring property pending the outcome of their trials.[68] In addition it expanded bank bribery provisions to cover situations where corrupt bank officials are 'paid off' to launder funds.[69]

In the fight against the sort of malpractice seen in the GE defense procurement fraud case (see Chapter 5), the Defense Procurement

Fraud Unit has played a major role. This is a joint effort of the Departments of Justice and Defense. Its responsibilities include analyzing the evidence in potential fraud cases, prosecuting some, referring others to the US Attorneys or to the Fraud section in Washington and monitoring the progress of cases.[70]

Tax evasion has, of course, been another major area of concern. It has been suggested that the loss of tax morality in the United States has, in part at least, been due to the perceived unfairness of the tax system, and that an element of curative action should perhaps therefore involve changes in the framework which encourages tax cheating. This is by no means straightforward or foolproof, but initiatives along such lines are certainly worth consideration. As we have seen, a decision to act illegally in this respect is likely to have been made in the light of risk–reward assessments. If the reward for avoiding taxes is diminished (because tax rates are lower) the risk of punishment is commensurately less worth taking. If this is combined with more effective detection methods and stiffer penalties for those cheating (i.e. the risk is increased) the whole exercise becomes even less attractive. It is this several-pronged attack that has been adopted in recent years.

In 1981 the Economic Recovery Tax Act reduced high-bracket rates; the following year, the IRS reported that three of the four taxpayer classes with increased voluntary compliance levels were the high income classes, the very ones with the largest rate reductions. Under the Tax Reform Act of 1986, the top tax rate fell to 34 per cent and in 1988 to 28 per cent.[71] This, along with elimination of loopholes widely considered unfair, may well reduce further the incentive for concealing income.[72]

Beyond this, there is of course the deep and growing concern in the US that the vast flow of drugs into the country continues unabated. New methods of combating the problem are continually sought. As we have discussed, one of the most powerful of these is to attack the flow of profits rather than the goods themselves – easier said than done due to the ingenuity of the people involved, the high stakes for which they are playing and the complexity of today's financial markets. As a spokesman at a White House conference said, 'Money laundering is an art form limited only by imagination.'[73]

The Government continues with undercover investigations along the lines of Operation Greenback and Operation Tracer. The latest, and the largest, Operation Pisces and Operation Cashweb/Expressway, drew to a close in 1987. It had spanned three years, during which time it documented cases in which Panamanian banks laundered some $275 million for Colombian cocaine rings. The money began in cash form and was deposited in banks in major US cities. It was then normally wired to Panamanian bank accounts designated by the traffickers. Some was sent on to Colombia, often to currency-exchange houses. Between 30 and 40 of Panama's 120 banks were involved. Some $60 million was seized and almost all the 200 defendants have pleaded guilty.[74]

Research has been carried out into what happens to US currency, especially $100 bills, in the hope that this will provide information useful to investigators. US treasury data show that the percentage of $100 bills in circulation has increased steadily during the 1980s, to the level that almost half the total currency in circulation was made up of hundreds as of 1988. Apparently half the $5 billion in hundreds printed every year have been shipped abroad. There is no normal economic explanation for this appetite for large bills, especially as most sizeable, legitimate transactions involve checks or noncash instruments. But the $100 bill is attractive to the launderer trying to get the thousands of small denomination bills collected 'on the street' into manageable form.

Another effort, this time to put pressure on other countries to provide assistance, has been to draw up a list of nations certified as cooperating with the US in reducing the production or transport of drugs. If a nation is 'decertified' it loses half its US economic aid and faces American opposition to requests for loans from international lending agencies. The only decertified nations in recent years have been Iran, Afghanistan and Syria, although in 1988 Panama was added to the list. The efficacy of this method is open to question given the fact that such countries as the Bahamas, Colombia and Mexico retain certified status. In justification, former Attorney General Edwin Meese was quoted as saying, 'We have to recognize that in some countries the government is fully cooperative. They are less than fully successful because of intimidation, bribery and corruption.'[75]

In 1987, the US DEA seized $500 million in assets of drug traffickers, a sum equal to the department's annual budget. Antidrug agencies at all levels combined to intercept 356 kg of heroin and 35,970 kg of cocaine, as compared with 1981 figures of 209 kg and 1,872 kg respectively.

Still, there is a sense of despondency in many areas. The US Attorney for New York, Rudolph Giuliani, was concerned that the State Department is disinterested and complacent. 'They don't want to deal with it. Yet it is just as important as our relations with the Soviet Union or the Middle East.' And in response to former President Ronald Reagan's optimism that the corner is being turned in the anti-drug crusade, one federal agent's comment was quite simply, 'Yeah, we turned the corner – and there was an army coming.'[76]

The long arm of the tax man

Much of the money that is concealed from the tax authorities, of course, goes offshore to secrecy havens. There is no legal way of keeping such offshore deposits from the IRS. Since 1976, US taxpayers have been required to report any foreign account, originally of more than $5,000, now more than $10,000, on their tax form. The country, though not the bank, where the deposit is held, must be stated.[77] In 1983, some 151,000 taxpayers reported such accounts, but at least that many again should have done so and failed to report.

There is a similar problem of non-reporting with US citizens residing abroad. To avoid US taxes, an American must sacrifice his citizenship – simply living overseas is not enough. Taxes are due just the same. The result is that many Americans living outside the United States fail to file tax returns. The IRS calculates that this applies to some 61 per cent of those subject to US tax, amounting to an annual loss to the Treasury of $620 million to $2.1 billion.[78]

Combined with the attempt to render the domestic tax legislation less onerous, recent reforms have also sought to tighten up on the few remaining legal loopholes making offshore havens attractive. Until 1962, it had been possible for US taxpayers to defer payment of income tax by diverting profits to foreign subsidiaries, using techniques such as payment of excessive insurance premiums. The 1962 Act stopped that, but nevertheless left a major loophole – it only applied if the foreign entity was 50 per cent or more owned by US taxpayers. It was thus still possible for an American to join a foreign citizen in setting up a company in a country such as the Caymans and, provided he owned less than half of the company, his earnings would remain exempt from both Cayman and US taxes as long as the earnings accrued offshore. When the American eventually sold his shares, the profits would be charged to the relatively low capital gains tax rate rather than the higher income tax rate.[79]

No longer. Provisions in the 1986 Tax Act deal once and for all with such 'passive foreign investment companies'. Now tax is due at the normal rate, and a penalty of non-deductible interest will be imposed on the deferral.[80]

This provision has caused some concern as well, however, for legitimate business. It was previously the practice that earnings from offshore subsidiaries were divided between 'good' and 'tainted'. In the case of the former, no US tax was due until the subsidiary transmitted dividends to the parent; in the latter case, taxes had to be paid immediately. Under the 1986 reforms, the tainted category was greatly extended, since the penalty will apply if either 50 per cent of a fund's assets or 75 per cent of its income is 'passive', i.e. not earned from actively engaging in trade or business.[81] This could well cover a large number of US companies' foreign subsidiaries – particularly in the high-tech field, the assets test may be easy to fail. And once a subsidiary is denoted as a passive holding company the classification is irrevocable. US multinationals have vociferously expressed their distress at this treatment, arguing that they need the deferral of tax on foreign profits to compete internationally. But at the time of going to press the provisions stand unchanged.[82]

Despite the various moves, the problem of detection remains. In fiscal 1985 the IRS recommended only 213 cases of offshore tax shelter abuse for prosecution. Only 10 led to convictions and 39 to guilty pleas. One of the major problems facing the IRS in dealing with overseas havens is its auditors' lack of experience in handling cases involving unreachable foreign documents. However, since the federal war on money laundering began in earnest in 1980 with Operation Greenback, the IRS has gradually begun to benefit from the cracks developing in certain havens' secrecy and has begun to develop its own body of expertise. 'We're not in for any surprises anymore,' explained one IRS criminal investigator.[83]

The IRS makes use of the 'intelligence community' far more, cooperates with other federal agencies, and has learned some useful tactics for getting the information it wants. In the Ghidoni case, for example, it asked a US court to order Mr Ghidoni (a Tallahassee businessman who had allegedly diverted more than $1.3 million of his profits to an offshore account) to sign a statement allowing his Cayman Islands bank to release the records – the Fifth Amendment right against self-incrimination does not apply to bank records.[84]

In 1984 and 1985 the IRS formalized its pursuit of evaders in Operation Dome (Domestic–Offshore Monetary Exchange). In addition, certain legislation has proved helpful. For example, under the 1986 tax reforms, anyone claiming exemptions for a dependent aged more than five years must now provide his social security number, which makes it far easier to track down phoney claimants, and there are new penalties for wrong social security numbers on bank accounts.[85]

The computer power of the IRS has also been vastly increased. It is thought that IRS computers in 1987 were capable of matching against individual taxpayers' returns virtually all of the 664 million wage, interest, dividend, capital gain, home sale and state income tax reports that were filed by payers. Manpower is on the increase too. In the years 1987–9 the IRS was scheduled to hire 2,500 new auditors, an increase in auditing staff of some 26 per cent.[86]

Patterns of national action

It is not only the United States, of course, that has made unilateral efforts to come to grips with the underlying causes of secret money flows, and with the flows themselves – even countries that are among the beneficiaries have taken action.

In 1984, after the assassination of the Colombian Justice Minister, Rodrigo Lara Bonilla, the government declared a state of siege and began its first serious crackdown on the drugs trade, with potentially far-reaching consequences for the national economy. Colombia is the largest narcotics supplier to the United States after Mexico, providing some 75 per cent of cocaine consumption. Drugs are estimated to exceed both coffee and cut flowers in export value and are Colombia's largest earner of foreign exchange. The effects of the crackdown were felt immediately in the black market exchange rate, where the dollar quickly appreciated in response to the projected decline of currency inflows attributable to drugs export cuts.

Other Latin American countries, also eager to reduce their economic dependency on narcotics, have made attempts to fight the secret drugs flows at source. In Bolivia, for example, some 350 members of the Leopards, a special unit of the Bolivian national police, were sent into the Chapare region, where coca is a major cash crop. With the help of US troops, they succeeded in late summer 1986 in closing around 100 drug processing plants in the area. Peru, Ecuador, and to a lesser extent, Brazil have also sought US help to begin the fight.[87] In Mexico, as well, drugs have been seized, ceremonial public drug-burnings carried out, and, according to some sources, as many as 27 per cent of the country's army had been put to work on anti-drug efforts, notably the eradication of poppy and marijuana fields.

The success of all this is, of course, highly uncertain – with corruption weakening effectiveness.[88] There is also undoubtedly a certain resentment in some quarters that the US administration is so vociferous about the need for anti-drug action. It is pointed out, and not only by Latin Americans, that much of the demand for narcotics stems after all from the United States. Rather than criticize producers, traffickers and launderers, it would perhaps do well to address the underlying problems of its own society that lead to such widespread abuse.[89]

For the United Kingdom the main drugs threat comes not from Latin America but from Asia, with a significant proportion of imports passing through India. In 1986, 70 per cent of Pakistani and Afghan heroin arriving in the United Kingdom was trafficked through India (up from 49 per cent in 1985 and 23 per cent in 1983). There are now also fears that India itself, already the world's largest legal producer of opium, is becoming an illicit heroin producer. The United Kingdom government has made several requests to be allowed to base British customs officials on Indian soil in an attempt to stem the flow, but the Indians have been consistently uncooperative.

In an effort to attack the problem from another side, by getting at the proceeds, amendments were made to the Drug Trafficking Offences Bill. Since 1924 and the Tournier case precedent,[90] British banks had been bound to a legal duty of confidentiality, with the result that bank officials had felt unable to inform the police authorities of suspicious behavior for fear of being sued by their customers for breach of confidence. The new amendment, while not making it a statutory obligation for banks to pass on their suspicions of drugs dealing, now provides them with complete legal immunity should they choose to do so.[91]

The United Kingdom has also introduced the Forfeiture Act, which has expanded the range of offenses under which assets may be seized by the authorities – another move to attack the lifeblood of criminals by seizing the funds that finance their nefarious operations.[92]

In Italy, a 1982 law allows the tax police to inspect the bank accounts and other financial holdings of anyone suspected of having Mafia links. In effect, the suspect is guilty until proven innocent.[93]

Other efforts to control laundering include a Council of Europe 1985 meeting on 'financial assets of criminal organizations', a United Kingdom parliamentary proposal to expand government wiretapping authority to include currency transactions, and Interpol's design of model banking legislation for the Caribbean. In fact, the Bahamas have, since January 1985, had their own specific code of banking conduct. And, as noted in Chapter 7, there are even ponderous moves in Switzerland to outlaw laundering.

No cash transactions reporting rule such as exists in the United States has been applied in Canada, even though three of the five major Canadian banks (Bank of Nova Scotia, Canadian Imperial Bank of Commerce, and Royal Bank of Canada) have extensive branch networks in the Caribbean. However, the Bank of Nova Scotia case (discussed in the following section) and the Bank of Boston revelations in the United States increased pressure in Canada for some sort of initiative to address the money-laundering issue. In March 1985, the Inspector-General of Banks in Ottawa asked financial institutions to strengthen know-your-client-rules and to alert their branches both in the Caribbean and on the US border against cash purchase of large-denomination drafts, major swings in daily cash balances, and conversions of large amounts of US dollars into other currencies.[94]

Banking authorities in other major financial centers such as London, Hong Kong and Frankfurt do not monitor large cash transactions. And many international bank managers appear to want things to stay that way. 'Top management is less worried about snuffing out unsavory depositors and more worried about preserving Frankfurt's role as an international financial center,' commented an officer at a major West German bank.[95] Political factors also complicate international regulatory efforts abroad. The head of the City of London's fraud squad reportedly must go through slow diplomatic channels every time his inquiries lead to continental Europe. It is not unusual for the wait to be more than a year.

In a battle against under-invoicing of international trade transactions, the Indonesian government appointed on 1 May 1985 Société Générale de Surveillance (SGS), a private Geneva-based firm, to inspect and certify imports in their country of origin and exports at their port of destination. An Indonesian buyer making payment by letter of credit would be required to inform SGS of the deal at its Indonesian coordinating office in the country of the seller. SGS then physically inspects the goods to ensure that they are in line with specifications, are correctly classified, and conform to the invoice terms. SGS also makes a 'price comparison' to ensure that the price agreed between buyer and seller is, within reasonable limits, in line with the export price prevailing at the time of the deal. Finally, if SGS is satisfied it issues a 'clean bill of findings', known as an LKP in Indonesia, which along with a bill of lading is used by the seller's bank to receive payment. The importer's bank then uses the LKP to collect the taxes and duties, and eventually the importer uses the bank receipt to collect his goods at port without any customs intervention.

If SGS finds any discrepancy in price, classification, etc., the local importer has to pay duty on the full value assessed by SGS and higher duties where goods are misclassified to incur lower tariffs. The seller, of course, receives payment according to the original agreement. This 'comprehensive import supervision scheme' of SGS was expected to check the high volume of smuggling, misclassification and mispricing of goods, particularly in Singapore–Indonesia trade. Such schemes had already been applied in a variety of other countries, including Mexico, Zaire, Angola and Nigeria; and in April 1986 Ecuador joined the list.

In Burma in 1985, as an initiative against black marketeers, the authorities reissued part of the country's currency, the kyat. Working on the basis that traders would be holding a lot of cash, the government stipulated that six weeks would be given to turn in high denomination notes. The first 5,000 kyat (about $575) would be immediately exchanged for the new currency. Half of the remainder could also be exchanged, but the other half would be confiscated unless the holder could prove it was acquired legally. If not, he would face up to five years imprisonment into the bargain. Vietnam carried out a similar scheme in 1984.[96]

A final example comes from Hong Kong. Irked by a spate of abusive equipment-leasing tax shelter schemes, officials proposed new, wide-ranging legislation to help tax collection. The tax authorities would be entitled to take steps against any firm or person if they were 'of the opinion' that a purpose of any transaction is to avoid taxes. And if there is a guilty finding, the penalties at the disposal of the tax authorities are (1) to void the transaction, (2) to force completion of the deal but without the tax benefit, or (3) take measures necessary to void the transaction.[97]

Notes

1 James Sterngold, 'Wall Street, Hit by Insider Cases, Reviews Security', *International Herald Tribune*, 6 September 1986.
2 James Sterngold, 'Security-Conscious Wall Street', *New York Times*, 14 July 1986.

3   Karin Lissakers, 'Money in Flight: Bankers Drive the Getaway Cars', *International Herald Tribune*, 6 March 1986.
4   Permanent Subcommittee on Investigations, Committee on Governmental Affairs, United States Senate, *Crime and Secrecy: The Use of Offshore Banks and Companies* (Washington, DC: US Government Printing Office, 1983).
5   Penny Lernoux, 'The Seamy Side of Florida Banking', *New York Times*, 5 February 1985.
6   'Drug Smugglers Say Hard Part is What to do with Money', *New York Times*, 29 November 1984.
7   Richard A. Gordon, *Tax Havens and Their Use by United States Taxpayers* (Washington, DC: Internal Revenue Service, 1981), p. 82.
8   Permanent Subcommittee on Investigations, *op. cit.* (n. 4), pp. 4–5.
9   Ibid., p. 300.
10 Ibid., pp. 308–9.
11 Ibid., pp. 4–5.
12 'Laundering Schemes Traced to Puerto Rico', *New York Times*, 9 June 1985.
13 Richard Evans, 'Forcing Discreet Money Into the Open', *Euromoney*, November 1986.
14 Richard A. Gordon, *op. cit.* (n. 7), p. 82.
15 Penny Lernoux, *op. cit.* (n. 5).
16 Bob Davis, 'Bank of Boston Unit's Fine Criticized as Inadequate by House Banking Panel', *Wall Street Journal*, 4 April 1985.
17 Bob Davis, 'Bank of Boston Report Criticizes Firm Chief Over Cash-Reporting Violations', *Wall Street Journal*, 5 April 1985.
18 James Sterngold, 'Bank of Boston Details Its Failures', *New York Times*, 25 July 1985.
19 Fox Butterfield, 'Bank of Boston Reiterates Denial on Employees', *New York Times*, 28 February 1985; Fox Butterfield, 'Boston Bank Calls Misuse of Cash Unwitting', *New York Times*, 22 February 1985, p. 1; Bob Davis, 'Bank of Boston Currency Moves Foundation in Probe', *Wall Street Journal*, 10 February 1985; Alex Beam, 'Bank of Boston: A Public Relations Nightmare', *Business Week*, 4 March 1985, p. 38; Nathaniel C. Nash, 'Bank of Boston Officer Says He Erred on Rule', *New York Times*, 13 March 1985; Bob Davis, 'US Says Bank of Boston Unit was Told It Broke Law 2 Years Before Compliance', *Wall Street Journal*, 28 February 1985, p. 16; Fox Butterfield, 'US Says Boston Bank Know of Rule on Cash', *New York Times*, 27 February 1985, p. 1; Fox Butterfield, 'US Jury Reported Investigating 2 Ex-Employees of Boston Bank', *New York Times*, 25 February 1985, p. 1; 'Bank of Boston', *The Economist*, 23 February 1985, p. 87.
20 Fox Butterfield, 'Boston Bank Cites "Systems Failure"', *New York Times*, 12 February 1985; Fox Butterfield, 'Statement by Boston Bank Due', *New York Times*, 10 February 1985 p. 1; 'US Clarifies Letter on Bank', *New York Times*, 2 March 1985; 'When Banks Launder Dirty Money', *New York Times*, 16 February 1985.
21 James Rowe, 'Bank Regulators Track Paper Trails in Search of Laundered Transactions', *Washington Post*, 3 March 1985; Nathaniel C. Nash, '41 Banks Studied on Cash Rules', *New York Times*, 5 March 1985.
22 'Boston Bank Pays Big Fine', *New York Times*, 2 February 1986. See also Lois Therrien, Blanca Riemer and Daniel Moskowitz, 'An All-Out Attack on Banks That Launder Money', *Business Week*, 25 February 1985, p. 30.
23 Nathaniel C. Nash, '4 New York Banks Face Fines by US in Cash Violations', *New York Times*, 18 June 1985.
24 Monica Langley and Paul Cox, 'Treasury Fines Crocker Unit $2,250,000 for Failing to Report Cash Transactions', *Wall Street Journal*, 28 August 1985.
25 Nathaniel C. Nash, *op. cit.* (n. 23).
26 Monica Langley, 'Currency Laws Found Violated by 2 Big Banks', *Wall Street Journal*, 26 July 1985.
27 Stephen Wermiel, 'Top Court Lets Boston Bank's Penalty Stand', *Wall Street Journal*, 10 November 1987.
28 Monica Langley and Paul Cox, *op. cit.* (n. 24).
29 Monica Langley and G. Christian Hill, 'Crocker and Treasury Clash Sharply in Wake of Fine for Reporting Violations', *Wall Street Journal*, 29 August 1985. Also see Robert M. Garsson, 'Professor Raps Banks' Attitude on Secrecy Act', *American Banker*, 5 December

1985; and Jan Wong, 'U.S. Attorney Expects to Indict Banks in Boston for Currency-Law Violations', *Wall Street Journal*, 29 August 1985.

30   'The Italians' Favourite Swiss Centre', *The Economist*, 6 July 1985; and 'Hutton Official on Leave in Laundering Case', *New York Times*, 15 July 1987. See also Alex Beam, 'Two Brokerages Get Tangled in the Money Laundering Net', *Business Week*, 11 March 1985, p. 37. Blanca Riemer and Lois Therrien, 'Money Laundering: The Defense Gets a Star Witness', *Business Week*, 28 March 1985, p. 27; James Sterngold, 'Boston Bank Cites More Violations', *New York Times*, 29 March 1985; 'More Banks Say They Didn't Report Transfers Totalling Millions of Dollars', *Wall Street Journal*, 28 March 1985; Robert A. Bennett, 'Two Banks Broke US Cash Rules', *New York Times*, 28 March 1985; Daniel Hertzberg, 'Chemical Bank Says It Failed to Report \$25.9 Million in Cash Moves Since 1980', *Wall Street Journal*, 27 March 1985; Fox Butterfield, 'A Second Bank in Boston Says It Didn't Report Big Cash Transfers', *New York Times*, 9 March 1985; David Wessel and Monical Langley, 'Boston Banks Didn't Report Cash Transfers', *Wall Street Journal*, 11 March 1985.

31   Roger Cohen, 'Laundry Service: How the Mob is Using Financial Institutions to Disguise Its Gains', *Wall Street Journal*, 12 March 1985, p. 1. In May 1985, E. F. Hutton pleaded guilty to criminal fraud charges involving a massive scheme to overdraw checking accounts with US banks, involving 200 counts of felony. See 'E. F. Hutton: It's Not Over Yet', *Newsweek*, 20 May 1985, and Nathaniel C. Nash, 'E. F. Hutton Guilty in Bank Fraud; Penalties Could Top \$10 Million', *New York Times*, 3 May 1985.

32   'E. F. Hutton pleads guilty in money-laundering case', *International Herald Tribune*, 18 May 1988.

33   Lindsey Gruson, 'The Shearson Case Opens New Ground', *New York Times*, 14 July 1986.

34   Kenneth N. Gilpin, 'Ex-Broker Indicted in Cash Scheme', *New York Times*, 14 March 1987.

35   See Jeffrey Schmaltz, 'Bank Is Charged by US with Money-laundering', *New York Times*, 12 October, 1988; Richard Donkin, 'Luxembourg-based Bank Indicted on Drug Money Charge', *Financial Times*, 12 October, 1988; Robert Graham, 'Dirty Money in Clean Hands', *Financial Times*, 12 October 1988; Andy Pasztor, 'BCCI, 2 Units, 9 Bank Officials Charged with Conspiring to Launder \$32 Million', *Wall Street Journal*, 12 October, 1988; and Peter Truell, 'Luxembourg-based but Global, BCCI Is One of the Fastest-Growing Banks', *Wall Street Journal*, 12 October, 1988.

36   'Stricter Reporting of Cash Dealings at Banks Proposed', *Wall Street Journal*, 20 August 1986.

37   Permanent Subcommittee on Investigations, *op. cit.* (n. 4), p. 415.

38   David Burnham, 'Money-Laundering Bill Seen as Privacy Threat', *New York Times*, 23 June 1985.

39   Permanent Subcommittee on Investigations, *op. cit.* (n. 4), p. 416.

40   Patrick Cox, 'More Laws Won't Hamper Drug-Money Launderers', *Wall Street Journal*, 14 December 1987.

41   Permanent Subcommittee on Investigations, *op. cit.* (n. 4), p. 94.

42   Ibid., p. 299.

43   Ibid., p. 41.

44   Patrick Cox, *op. cit.* (n. 40).

45   Michael Allen, 'Defense Lawyers Fear Becoming Targets Under Sweeping Money-Laundering Law', *Wall Street Journal*, 2 December 1986. See also Paula Dwyer, 'Big Brother Wants to See Your Bankbook', *Business Week*, 16 September 1985.

46   Permanent Subcommittee on Investigations, *op. cit.* (n. 4), p. 238.

47   David Burnham, *op. cit.* (n. 38).

48   Paula Dwyer, *op. cit.* (n. 45).

49   Permanent Subcommittee on Investigations, *op. cit.* (n. 4), p. 275.

50   Ibid., p. 277.

51   Ibid., pp. 294–5.

52   Ibid., p. 287.

53   David Burnham, *op. cit.* (n. 38). See also Patrick Cox, *op. cit.* (n. 40).

54   Permanent Subcommittee on Investigations, *op. cit.* (n. 4), p. 444.

55 Ibid., p. 445.
56 Ibid., p. 123.
57 Ibid., p. 111.
58 David Burnham, *op. cit.* (n. 38).
59 Permanent Subcommittee on Investigations, *op. cit.* (n. 4), pp. 369–72, 482–7. See also David Burnham, 'Treasury Wants More Foreign Data from Banks', *New York Times*, 3 July 1984. See also David Burnham, *op. cit.* (n. 38).
60 Permanent Subcommittee on Investigations, *op. cit.* (n. 4), pp. 386, 523–5.
61 Richard Evans, *op. cit.* (n. 13).
62 David Burnham, *op. cit.* (n. 38).
63 Richard A. Gordon, *op. cit.* (n. 7).
64 Allan Dodds Frank, 'See No Evil', *Forbes*, 6 October 1986.
65 John Mulcahy, 'The Chinese Laundry', *Far Eastern Economic Review*, 20 August 1987.
66 Patrick Cox, *op. cit.* (n. 40).
67 Carol J. Loomis, 'Limited War on White Collar Crime', *Fortune*, 22 July 1985.
68 Michael Allen, *op. cit.* (n. 45).
69 Permanent Subcommittee on Investigations, *op. cit.* (n. 4), p. 31.
70 Carol J. Loomis, *op. cit.* (n. 67).
71 Cynthia Crossen, 'Look Not Toward the Havens', *Wall Street Journal*, 18 September 1987.
72 Charles N. Stabler, 'Underground Economy May Start Shrinking', *Wall Street Journal*, 25 August 1986.
73 Jeff Gerth, 'Vast Flow of Cash Threatens Currency, Banks and Economies', *New York Times*, 11 April 1988.
74 Ibid.
75 Ed Magnuson, 'Tears of Rage,' *Time*, 14 March 1988.
76 Ibid.
77 Suzanne Woolley 'Opening a Swiss Bank Account is No Big Secret', *Business Week*, 4 April 1985.
78 Cynthia Crossen, *op. cit.* (n. 71).
79 Ibid.
80 Ibid. See also Laura Saunders, 'Innocent Victims', *Forbes*, 5 October 1987.
81 Cynthia Crossen, *op. cit.* (n. 71).
82 Ibid.
83 Thomas E. Ricks, 'Tax Evaders Find Foreign Banks Aren't Havens of Secrecy Anymore', *Wall Street Journal*, 14 August 1985.
84 Ibid.
85 Adam Snitzer, 'Stash Accounting', *Forbes*, 6 April 1987. See also Sara Bartlett, G. David Wallace, Carla Anne Robbins, Lois Therrien, Ronald Grover, Blanca Riemer and John Rossant, 'Money Laundering', *Business Week*, 18 March 1985, p. 74.
86 Ibid.
87 Jeffrey Ryser and Bill Javetsky, 'Can South America's Addict Economies Ever Break Free?', *Business Week*, 22 September 1986.
88 William Branigin, 'Mexican Antidrug Campaign Failing to Stem Flow Into US', *Washington Post*, 4 August 1987. See also Anne B. Fisher, 'Money Laundering', *Fortune*, 1 April 1985, p. 34.
89 Ian Lyon, 'Paradise Under Pressure', *Investment International*, June 1987.
90 Christopher Stoakes, 'The People vs Confidentiality', *Euromoney*, August 1986.
91 Sarah Helm and Simon Freeman, 'Banks to be Protected Over Drugs Cash Tip-Off', *Sunday Times*, 4 May 1986.
92 John Mulcahy, *op. cit.* (n. 65).
93 Roger Cohen, *op. cit.* (n. 31), p. 1.
94 'Limit Bank Secrecy', *The Economist*, 5 April 1986.
95 Keith Grant, 'Latin American Nations See Progress in Slowing Capital Flight', *International Herald Tribune*, 29 April 1986.
96 'A Loss of Liquidity in Rangoon', *The Economist*, 16 November 1985. See also Chris Sherwell, 'Indonesia Cleans Up Its Ports and Customs', *Financial Times*, 12 June 1985.
97 Laura Saunders, 'And Then There is Hong Kong', *Forbes*, 23 September 1985.

10

Combating International Financial Secrecy: Patterns of Cooperation and External Pressure

Given the apparent limits on the effectiveness of unilateral attempts to deal with flows of secret money, much effort has been devoted to securing cooperation from countries around the world that serve as secrecy havens. Occasionally this leads to intergovernmental friction – with the financial institutions caught in the middle.

Mutual assistance

Historically, probably the most common form of cooperation is bilateral tax treaties. However, the US House Ways and Means Committee has found that some tax treaties, while having as their objective the elimination of double taxation, are often abused by third-country residents to avoid paying either US or third-country taxes. This kind of abuse is commonly known as 'treaty shopping'. Two treaties that have been extensively used by 'treaty shoppers' are those between the United States and the Netherlands Antilles, and between the United States and the British Virgin Islands. The United States elected to cancel the latter at the end of 1982 and, as we discussed earlier, the former was repealed (apart from the interest provisions) with effect from January 1988.

Certainly the most visible efforts at cooperation have taken place between the United States and Switzerland. Despite tenacious efforts by Swiss officials and banks to uphold rigid disclosure limits, some compromises have been reached. Limited mutual assistance treaties are the primary vehicles, and the Swiss government has been cooperative in devising methods of assistance.

The bilateral assistance efforts between the United States and Switzerland began in 1951 with the ratification of the Swiss–American Tax Convention. In 1973, the Swiss–American Treaty on Mutual Assistance on Criminal Matters was ratified. This treaty broke new ground in that the Swiss agreed to pierce the veil of bank secrecy in criminal cases that do not involve crimes in Switzerland – for example, the activities of US organized crime. This waiver of the principle of mutual penal liability was an important breakthrough for the US authorities, and eliminated some of the protection previously afforded US organized crime figures by Switzerland. The treaty came into force in 1977.

Despite some difficulties in coming to agreement, the treaty has been successfully used in over 200 cases of criminal prosecution brought in the United States. In 1983, a law on International Mutual Assistance on Criminal Matters extended the bilateral treaty's provisions to all other countries. The line between tax evasion and tax fraud is a problem that remains to be clearly defined.

Although Switzerland only registers Swiss companies, the law does allow the beneficial owner to be hidden behind offshore companies. As noted in Chapter 4, Swiss attorneys can routinely purchase companies in Liechtenstein, Panama, the Cayman Islands or elsewhere without leaving their offices. The 'layering' of secrecy is achieved through complex arrangements involving nominee companies and accounts, and this complicates any attempts to achieve disclosure through cooperation.

According to one account, Markus Lusser, president of the Swiss National Bank, supports further legislation against the use of Switzerland for illicit transactions via additional limits on financial secrecy.

> I am very much in favor of greater due diligence by the banks; their attitude has been too lenient. It isn't enough for the banks to know the person opening an account. They must also try to find out if there is a beneficial owner. The banks should always have doubts about whose money is actually being deposited. Some of the worst abuses are by Swiss lawyers, who themselves open numbered accounts on behalf of unnamed foreign clients. The lawyers act more like international portfolio managers than responsible attorneys. We need new legislation by the Swiss government to prevent money laundering.[1]

Moreover, contrary to the official views of the Swiss government, some Swiss bankers insist that it is silly to forgo the potential profits involved since the funds will simply go somewhere else instead. Consequently, there has long been tension between the business community and the authorities when it comes to deciding what banking information is to be provided to foreign authorities. The bankers continue to maintain that they should certainly not be pressured to police tax evasion and violations of exchange controls in other countries. This, they argue, is the responsibility of national authorities that often change the rules and, in any case, are responsible for punitive taxation that gives rise to evasion in the first place. According to one source:

If the U.S. can provide us with information about criminal funds sources and the Swiss lawyers or banks they use, then we can act. Unless the U.S. tells us, how can we know? Is it not easier to learn in the U.S. who the criminals are and how they export funds, than to come here after the black has been dyed white? If the U.S. genuinely wishes us to take action against their criminals, then transmit to our Minister of Justice the list of names and their companies. We will act. It is that simple.[2]

Nevertheless, Swiss banks have taken some cooperative steps to curb abuses of financial secrecy. The *Vereinbarung* discussed in Chapter 4, and its application, is one example. One Swiss bank, Union Bank of Switzerland, reportedly requires that any account opened by someone recognized as a politician from another country must be notified to senior management. It is said that such accounts have indeed been refused on occasion. Despite the resounding defeat of the 1984 bank secrecy referendum by the Swiss voters, revision of the Swiss banking law has proceeded apace and there were a number of indications that it would contain tougher provisions on the abuse of secrecy, enforcement, and the closing of loopholes in the law.

In November 1987, the Swiss Justice Minister and the US Attorney General signed a new memorandum setting out revised guidelines for mutual legal assistance. The principle of 'double criminality' continues to apply.

In June 1988, the Swiss Supreme Court voted 8 to 1 to force those subject to criminal investigations to authorize Swiss banks to disclose account records in overseas locations such as the Cayman Islands and Bermuda – cases where the customer's consent is necessary in order for banks to comply with subpoenas.[3]

Given the stringent code of secrecy still enshrined in Swiss law and the fact that tax evasion is still not a crime, this means that the Swiss banks retain a significant competitive advantage on this front. The Swiss have, by patient negotiation, persuaded the Americans to see the inadvisability of their extraterritorial approaches. For those enjoying the joke that Swiss secrecy is as full of holes as Emmental cheese, it would be worth remembering the Swiss view on Emmental imitators, 'Anyone can make the holes, but only the Swiss can make the cheese.'[4]

Nevertheless, concessions have been made. While the Americans have agreed to work through established channels and to avoid 'unilateral compulsory measures,' applying instead 'moderation and constraint', the Swiss have agreed to speed up procedures. The tactic of appealing on the ground of violation of vital Swiss interests has been restricted to Swiss citizens or permanent residents and owners of Swiss companies. Moreover, appeals must henceforth be lodged within ten days of judgement.

Meantime the Pope, on a 1984 visit to Switzerland, cautioned its citizens to insure that its banking system not be used to promote war and injustice throughout the world. 'As a democratically constituted society you must watch vigilantly over all that goes on in this powerful world of money ... The world of finance, too, is a world of human beings – our world, subject to the consciences of all of us. Ethical principles apply to it, too.'[5]

Similar sentiments have been couched in less gentle terms. A former Swiss missionary in Peru was quoted as saying: 'Our banks belong to a system which injures a great mass of humanity. In accepting flight capital they are stamping and kicking the fundamental basis of every Christian ethic of love and justice.' And one Brazilian archbishop went as far as to ask: 'Are you aware that the tears, sweat and blood of the masses of the underdeveloped countries are tied to this money?'[6]

As noted in Chapter 5, in 1984 the Cayman Islands passed the so-called Narcotics Drug Law.[7] This disclosure pact with the United States was negotiated with the help of the British authorities, who handle external affairs for the islands.[8]

Under the agreement, the Cayman Islands government will release financial information regarding drugs cases within about two weeks of receiving a request from the US authorities, making a major potential dent in the estimated $20–30 billion in illicit funds laundered annually through the Caribbean countries. The request must be certified to be drugs-related and necessary for the prosecution of the case, and the records are to be accompanied by an affidavit attesting to their authenticity. The agreement was considered a possible model for comparable arrangements with other countries in the region.[9] Nevertheless, it was negotiated without the fanfare that might ruin the Caymans' image as a secrecy haven.[10]

However, the pact that followed two years later may prove more detrimental. In July 1986 the Caymans signed a treaty giving US law-enforcement officials access to bank records in most types of criminal investigations, ranging from mail fraud through corrupt activities by US contractors to insider trading cases. Even alleged tax evasion is within its scope, provided US prosecutors suspect that the disputed income derives from illegal activities. It was hoped that the agreement would serve as a basis for other mutual legal assistance treaties with offshore centers, and agreements with Bermuda and the Bahamas are indeed also now in place. The British Virgin Islands, on the other hand, remain unhelpful – even though their refusal to cooperate has cost them a new tax treaty with the United States.[11]

Reactions in the Caymans have been mixed. Some were surprised at the breadth of the pact. 'It covers virtually everything except tax fraud,' said one bewildered banker.[12] But others believe it is a necessary part of the Islands' attempt to clean up their image, to develop tourism and growth in legitimate financial business in the banking and insurance industries. 'This agreement may frighten some people away,' predicts the president of the Cayman Islands Bankers Association, 'but probably those are the people we want to frighten away.'[13]

In response to an increase in drugs smuggling from the Caribbean and South America through the Turks and Caicos Islands, the US Drug Enforcement Administration in 1983 asked the Islands' government to help reduce the flow. The British protectorate agreed, and indeed invited Federal agents to the Islands to assist in the effort. It was suspected that Colombian drugs smugglers were flying large amounts of cocaine to the Islands, where the cargoes were broken up for delivery to South Florida by fast, small boats island-hopping through the Bahamas.[14]

An ironic twist to the cooperation between the two governments was that undercover operations led to the arrest of three high-ranking Turks and Caicos Island officials. On 5 March 1985, the highest elected official, Chief Minister Norman Saunders, the Minister of Commerce and Development Stafford Missick, Legislator Aulden Smith, and business-man André Fournier, were arrested in Miami and charged with plotting to use the Islands as a base to smuggle narcotics into the United States. A British Embassy spokesperson said that the officials did not have diplomatic immunity because they were in the United States on 'private business'. They were subsequently convicted and sentenced to jail for accepting bribes to allow use of the islands as a transit point for cocaine to the US.[15]

In September 1986, an interim agreement was signed with the Turks and Caicos allowing US prosecutors access to previously secret bank records in a limited number of major narcotics investigations. Nego-tiations continued with a view to producing in due course a comprehen-sive legal assistance treaty.[16]

One of the most recalcitrant of the secrecy havens has been Panama. According to one US Justice Department official: 'You just don't get records out of Panama. They probably have the tightest secrecy laws. I know of no subpoenas that have been successful.'[17] The United States has consistently placed pressure on the government to be more responsive, and in early 1987, perhaps due to concern at his image in the United States, General Noriega encouraged the national assembly to assist. A new law was passed requiring banks to divulge details of the financial dealings of drugs barons, permitting the freezing of numbered accounts and even allowing for the extradition of foreigners suspected of drugs offenses. Nevertheless, given the nature of Panama's political situation and the possibly questionable honesty of the General, the Administration could be forgiven for being wary. Says one Washington official: 'We'll be looking very carefully at how the new law is enforced.'[18]

The United States has made progress on other fronts, however. As well as the treaties with Switzerland, the Caymans, Bermuda, the Bahamas and the Turks and Caicos, it has also signed agreements since 1977 for cooperation with the Netherlands, Turkey, Canada and Thailand.[19] However, given the potential economic costs of proceeding against financial secrecy in a cooperative manner at the request of another government, it is little wonder that most international efforts to attack secret money have involved a good deal of diplomatic and economic pressure, as well as outright arm-twisting.[20]

Pressure tactics

Take the case of a US grand jury's investigation of a criminal fraud in the early 1980s. Relevant bank records were subpoenaed from the Bahamas branch of the Bank of Nova Scotia, headquartered in Toronto via a US branch of the bank. This method of serving a subpoena on a foreign bank was established in the *Quigg* case in 1981. Here the document was addressed to the Canadian bank in general, though delivered to its New York branch. This was held to be effective on the head office, which was doing business in the United States through its New York branch. The head office was then deemed to be in a position to order its branch in the offshore haven (in this case the Bahamas) to release the relevant documents – and if it refused to do so could be punished through its US branch for failing to comply.[21]

In the *Nova Scotia* case the bank, citing the Bahamas Bank and Trust Companies Regulation Act, which prohibits the release of documents to foreign authorities without official authorization, refused to comply. At this point the US judge followed the 'balancing test' criterion, established in 1968 in the *Loveland* case, to decide, in simple terms, whose laws should predominate. In *Loveland*, the head office of Citibank in New York had been served with a subpoena requiring the production of records from its West German branch. It argued that compliance would put it in breach of West German civil (though not criminal) law, which could expose it to a claim for damages from the client. In considering whether US or West German law should prevail, the court tried to weigh an amalgam of factors – the vital national interests of the two countries, the hardship that inconsistent enforcement would impose on the bank caught in the middle, etc. The court concluded that for the United States the violations under investigation were of a criminal nature, whereas breach of bank secrecy was only a civil offense in West Germany, and that US interests should therefore dominate.

However, in the case of the Bank of Nova Scotia, it was a criminal offense in the Bahamas for the bank to produce documents. All the same, the ruling went in favor of the US investigation again. A federal judge in Florida thereupon fined the bank $500 per day on a contempt of court citation in late 1981, fines that were affirmed by a federal appeals court in 1983 and let stand by the Supreme Court itself. Subsequently, the judge increased the fine to $25,000 per day, whereupon the bank turned over the requested documents.

The Bahamian government undertook a criminal investigation of the Bank of Nova Scotia's violation of local disclosure laws, threatening a fine of $15,000 and two years' imprisonment for those involved. It also sent strong letters to President Reagan and Vice-President Bush, protesting US legal extraterritoriality and further straining diplomatic relations over the matter of financial disclosure. The US government, meanwhile, announced its intention to continue to press for disclosure in whatever ways seem appropriate in criminal cases where the countries concerned fail to reach a reasonable accommodation between bank secrecy and the requirements of bona fide, reasonable law enforcement interests.[22]

An almost identical sequence of events involved the Bank of Nova Scotia in connection with marijuana smuggling into Florida and channeling of the proceeds to Cayman Islands accounts, as well as a number of cases of tax evasion. Again the United States subpoenaed the bank to reveal information on 4 March 1983, and again the bank's US subsidiary was fined $25,000 per day beginning 20 October 1983, when it failed to do so – even though it had explained that under Caymans law it could release the documents if the United States would prepare an affidavit for the Caymans Grand Court giving details of why the interests of justice would be served if the information were passed over (which the United States had refused to do).

The bank appealed the fine – supported by four parties, the Canadian Bankers Association, and the governments of Canada, the Cayman Islands and the United Kingdom. But to no avail. The Caymans issued an injunction forbidding the bank from giving up the documents, although under severe pressure from the bank itself and from the United States it later relented and eventually accepted the broad degree of disclosure mentioned earlier. The Bank of Nova Scotia was caught in the middle, with exceedingly high stakes as the largest Canadian bank operating in both the United States and the Caribbean. It continued to appeal the US ruling while the Canadian, Cayman and British governments protested bitterly over the extra-territorial application of US law. But in the end, some 30–40 subpoenas later and with a fine amounting to $1.8 million, the Bank of Nova Scotia had been forced to surrender everything the United States wanted. It made a final appeal over the level of its fine. This was refused on 7 January 1985.

There are several disturbing aspects of the Bank of Nova Scotia affair. Some commentators have suggested that the aggressive course of action followed by the United States was unnecessary and perhaps deliberately heavy-handed to establish precedents for future document-gathering. Although the case began before the 1984 Cayman Islands Narcotic Drugs Law, there was apparently in existence at the time a secret exchange-of-letters between the United States and the Caymans setting out an agreed procedure for securing bank records and other information pertinent to US criminal investigations. Evidence seems to indicate that the United States made no attempt to use this procedure, even though the authorities may have at one stage given the impression that they would do so, given the fact that the international rules of comity in any case required them to act first on a cooperative rather than an antagonistic basis. It has also been suggested that when the bank, the Caymans and the United Kingdom governments attempted to raise the issue they were prevented by a technicality from producing their evidence.

It has been pointed out as well that in other cases the United States has resorted to strong-arm tactics before exhausting more friendly approaches. In a 1984 tax evasion action against Gucci Shops, Inc., a US court ordered the Chase Manhattan Bank to turn over Hong Kong financial records. The bank was held in contempt and threatened with a fine of $15,000 per day, even though a Hong Kong court ruled that the records in question would remain blocked. Chase was caught in the middle and appealed. Only after this had been refused did the US Attorney issue letters-rogatory to Hong Kong, thus seeking the documents on a cooperative government-to-government basis, a course of action that had been available all along.

Similarly, in the Marc Rich & Co. case the US Justice Department refused to request documents from the Swiss under the International Mutual Assistance on Criminal Matters Agreement available to it until the fine of $50,000 per day imposed on the company had been confirmed under appeal.

Of the $1.8 million fine imposed on the Bank of Nova Scotia, $1.3 million related to four carbon copies that had been originally overlooked by the bank and were consequently delivered late. They provided no material information that had not appeared in documents already surrendered, and it was a bank official, not the prosecution, who discovered their omission and rectified it. Yet, even under appeal in the US Supreme Court, the $1.3 million was considered reasonable and allowed to stand.[23]

It could be said that the emerging US view has thus been that the information requirements of domestic legal proceedings take precedence over the financial secrecy statutes of other countries, including compliance with a subpoena served on US soil – all to the intense displeasure of governments such as those of the United Kingdom, Canada, Switzerland and the Cayman Islands. In the process the United States has been widely accused of extending the application of its laws well beyond its national boundaries in the effort to crack financial secrecy used for criminal purposes.[24] According to one analysis of foreign reactions to this US extraterritorial reach:

> It is critically noted that Americans resort to legislation for all manner of purposes, overusing statutes, lawyers and litigation, not realizing that the problem is not one of legislation but of what people's morals really are as expressed in their deeds. The U.S. optimism about the morally educative function of further law is dismissed. Consequently, the American tendency to seek to expand its legislative approach worldwide is resented and resisted.
>
> The U.S. has the tendency to seek to legalize [legislate for] the whole world. One *must* not assist the U.S. in this wrongful activity. While all nations must assist one another in preventing the use by criminals of havens, and everyone must agree to interfere in crime itself, other nations cannot accept underlying U.S. views, values and exported problems.[25]

There has been concern over this tendency in the United States itself. The rescinding of the Netherlands Antilles tax treaty, for instance, was seen by some as just another example of a growing trend. As the *Wall Street Journal* put it: 'The Netherlands Antilles tax-treaty fiasco, [is] a perfect example of foreign-affairs confusion caused by the recent executive-branch campaign to extend America's tax and regulatory reach beyond U.S. shores ... the Treasury was playing macho about its efforts to make other jurisdictions play by U.S. rules on information sharing.' It continued: 'We have the sense that the various departments of the government – Treasury, the Securities and Exchange Commission, the State and Justice departments – have had all sorts of aides racing around the world trying to impose regimes under which the U.S. can monitor and control capital moving into and out of the country.'[26]

Nevertheless, a number of proposals have been made in the United States to try to come to grips more effectively with the problem of secrecy havens abroad in the absence of the desired degree of cooperation from foreign governments. This includes increasing further the responsibility of bank officials to report unusual account activity, notifying US banks of foreign banks against which fraud complaints are pending, prohibiting foreign banks that fail to provide information in criminal cases from doing business in the United States, and requiring a new visa of US residents for each visit to a foreign secrecy center.[27]

The Gordon Report to the Internal Revenue Service came up with a series of rather draconian measures against countries declared to be 'non cooperating offshore havens'.[28] These would prohibit US airlines from serving such countries, bar US banks from doing business there, apply a 59 per cent withholding tax on any dividends and interest due to residents of these countries, and tax all loans from their institutions to domestic residents as ordinary income. Other measures would include denial of landing rights to airlines from non-cooperating countries, eliminating customs pre-clearance arrangements, requiring special visas for travel to such countries, denying voting rights on stocks held there, denying purchasing rights to US assets, denying tax deductions for business travel to a haven and associated expenses, denying banks with operations there the right to do business in the United States, and blocking the accounts of non-cooperating banks in criminal cases involving havens.

One hope for the United States to penetrate banking and commercial secrecy in the Caribbean has been the Reagan administration's Caribbean Basin Initiative (CBI). The administration proposed that Caribbean countries that participate in the investment tax incentives incorporated in the plan be required to cooperate fully in US tax investigations involving US citizens. Under this proposal, US citizens who invest in any of the 30 eligible countries would be entitled to an investment tax credit only if the country enter into a bilateral executive tax agreement with the United States. Furthermore,

[the CBI agreement] shall provide for the exchange of such information as may be necessary and appropriate to carry out and enforce the tax laws of the U.S. and the beneficiary country, including information which might otherwise be subject to non-disclosure provisions of the local law of the beneficiary country such as provisions respecting bank secrecy and bearer shares.

The Ways and Means Committee of the US House of Representatives, in recognizing that the economies of countries such as Bermuda and the Bahamas are highly dependent upon US tourist dollars, likewise took a carrot-and-stick approach to bring pressure to bear. Instead of the proposed investment tax credit, the Committee substituted an *indirect* incentive to Caribbean tourist countries – tax deductions for US citizens attending conventions, seminars and similar meetings in any of the Caribbean countries and Bermuda. Tied to the offer of favorable treatment was the requirement that, before any tax-deductible convention opens, the host country must have in force an agreement with the United States to exchange tax information. At the time of writing, Jamaica is the only Caribbean country where the convention deduction applies. In return for the deduction, Jamaica made substantial concessions in anti-treaty shopping provisions, and promised to negotiate a mutual assistance treaty concerning criminal matters in general.

As is true of most other countries, the British view of the regulatory implications of international financial secrecy is far more relaxed than the official US position. While the authorities generally acknowledge that the regulatory/supervisory situation in some countries is corrupt, inefficient and inept, and that others see it in their own interest to supply secrecy services, they consider that the fundamental problems lie in the home countries themselves. These include dysfunctional tax systems, inadequate domestic law enforcement, confusion and conflict among the responsible agencies, and similar factors that either create incentives to take advantage of international financial secrecy or minimize the disincentives.[29]

Combating insider trading

Certainly in no area of the secrecy business has the effort to use inter-governmental cooperation and pressure to enhance the degree of disclosure been pursued more consistently and vigorously than against insider trading – identified in Chapter 3 as perhaps the principal source of secrecy demand emanating from illegal activities in the securities markets.

Historically, when foreign entities have been involved in questionable securities transactions under review by the Securities and Exchange Commission in the United States, comity (mutual respect for the laws of foreign countries) was weighed heavily by judges in deciding on the enforcement of subpoenas. Under well-established principles of international law, a US court has no authority to enforce domestically issued subpoenas against a foreign national in his own country. Thus, even after the allocation of staff time and expense in compliance actions of this type, the SEC could still face defeat, since efforts to pry open foreign bank secrecy usually prove fruitless. This has clearly defined the limits of the SEC's enforcement power in insider trading cases involving foreign financial institutions and foreign nationals.

Foreign financial secrecy laws and blocking statutes were thus alleged to contribute a lack of symmetry to the rights and obligations of participants in US financial markets. These markets are among the most important in the world, and attract borrowers and lenders globally within the growing interlinkage of financial centers.

The dollar and the integrity of our capital markets stand at the center of the world economic order. Stock and bond purchases in the United States by foreign persons or institutions have more than doubled in four years, to $53 billion in 1982. Our markets are also a source of

278

capital for foreigners. About 250 foreign issuers and 25 foreign governments have securities registered with the SEC.[30]

In 1985 the stock market value of all publicly traded American companies accounted for 48 per cent of the world market, as compared with 22.5 per cent for Japan and 8.1 per cent for the United Kingdom.[31]

Yet, while all players assumed they had the right to gain access to these markets, not all acknowledged an obligation to comply with regulations designed to prevent their abuse.

Foreign individuals and entities were thus considered to have the best of two worlds – the participation in US capital markets and the cloak of foreign financial secrecy – which in effect enabled foreigners to engage in securities transactions illegal under US laws and yet avoid US sanctions. A double standard was alleged to prevail – a strict standard of conduct for persons effecting transactions domestically and a lesser enforcement standard for foreigners or for persons or entities employing a foreign intermediary:

Clearly, participants who place orders for financial assets through a secrecy jurisdiction may be able to escape their obligations under U.S. financial regulations. Similarly, players who maintain records in jurisdictions that apply blocking laws can do likewise by seeking to have their disclosure to U.S. authorities prevented.[32]

One problem with the development of truly global, 24-hour securities trading is that investments by foreign institutions in US securities would doubtless increase, including those from countries with secrecy laws. Already US securities firms have reportedly felt leery about trading with Swiss and some other foreign banks because they cannot be sure the banks' customers are not trading on inside information.[33] In addition, round-the-clock trading may well give rise to problems in clearing and settling stock trades. US securities trade for settlement in five days, Japanese in four. In the United Kingdom, certain stocks are for settlement next day, and others are on an account basis with settlement anywhere between a week and four weeks later. As for Italy, the whole business is entirely uncertain. These discrepancies create enormous risks for brokers, as well as significant possibilities for abuses.[34]

Even in countries which are not secrecy havens, insider trading has tended to be less of an issue than in the United States. Requirements both for companies and investors in the other major world markets are on the whole less stringent than in the United States. This is one more complicating factor for the SEC since it raises the question of whether its tight regulation could in fact drive business overseas. There is a body of opinion which is seriously concerned that excessive securities' laws will hamper US investors and brokerage firms from competing on an equal footing with their counterparts in other countries. As a vice-president of Lehman Brothers International Securities in London expressed it at the time: 'The SEC cannot afford to keep up its strong arm, policeman-of-the-world image. The markets here are getting too efficient and will continue to draw business away if they insist on unreasonable requirements.'[35]

Quite apart from these difficulties, the SEC has been woefully understaffed. Between 1976 and 1985 the volume of securities traded was estimated to have risen by 800 per cent; in the same period the SEC's enforcement staff dropped by 5 per cent. Even so, it remains determined to stamp out insider trading. Between May 1982 and May 1986 the SEC filed some 77 suits more than it had started in the preceding 32 years.[36] Since 1984 it has been aided by the availability of the threefold penalty, whereby it may recover three times the profits or losses made or avoided through malpractice.[37] It now has a massive computer back-up reputedly providing details from golf club membership to school background on those working in the industry, and undercover agents have even been sent to Wall Street cocktail parties in quest of illicit exchanges of information.[38]

The tone for this level of commitment to a fair market for all was set as long ago as 1981, when Judge Milton Pollack stated during a case involving the St Joe Minerals Corporation (see below): 'It would be a travesty of Justice to permit a foreign company to invade American markets, violate American laws, if they were indeed violated, withdraw profits and resist accountability for itself and its principals for the illegality by claiming their anonymity under foreign law.' The US Supreme Court later upheld the view that persons who purposefully avail themselves of the privilege of conducting activities in US securities markets should be subject to the full enforcement and protection of its laws.

In an attempt to restore symmetry to the rights and obligations of participants in US financial markets the SEC initiated a plan to negotiate individual disclosure agreements with each of the 25-odd countries that have secrecy or blocking laws. Some progress has been made, but it is a slow and laborious task.

In the meantime, the SEC has pursued a variety of other routes to achieve its goal, often using individual cases to try to crack foreign bank secrecy used to shield individuals violating American securities laws. On occasions, tactics akin to those discussed in the previous section have been employed. In the case of Dennis Levine, for example, a representative of Bank Leu was quoted as saying: 'We cooperated to protect our interests, because we didn't want to get served with a subpoena at our branch in New York.'[39]

Two landmarks in the SEC pursuit of foreign miscreants were the St Joe Minerals Corporation and the Santa Fe International Corporation cases.

St Joe Minerals Corporation

In the St Joe Minerals Corporation case it was again the threat of the fine sanction that finally produced the records required. The SEC had charged that an Italian investor used privileged merger information to purchase stock and options in St Joe through the Banca della Svizzera Italiana (BSI) in Lugano. The privileged information involved the likelihood of a takeover by Seagram Corporation.[40] The SEC filed an injunction and served a subpoena on BSI's US subsidiary in order to obtain documents of the transactions in question. When the documents were not forthcoming, a US judge threatened a fine of $50,000 a day for each day of non-compliance, plus a ban on trading in the US markets. The bank, however, managed to obtain a waiver of Swiss bank secrecy laws from its customer and finally produced the identity of the individual in question.[41]

St Joe was also highly relevant for another reason, since it was over this issue that bilateral efforts between the United States and Switzerland to curb insider trading could be said really to have begun. Swiss officials resented the pressure imposed on its banks by US authorities, but agreed to draft temporary measures to combat insider trading until appropriate legislation could be passed. Independently, the Swiss commercial banks indicated their willingness to cooperate with SEC officials by requiring their foreign customers to sign waiver forms permitting disclosure of information identifying clients when evidence is presented by enforcement authorities showing a possible violation of US securities laws.

After five months of debate and negotiation, an agreement was reached between the Swiss authorities and the SEC establishing a procedure permitting the SEC to make a formal request for customer information from Swiss authorities. This Memorandum of Understanding and Private Agreement, as it was called, formed the basis of the eleven-article Convention 16 drafted by the Swiss Bankers' Association.[42] In this the institutions committed themselves to provide information requested by the SEC to a three-member Commission appointed by the Association.

The Commission's members were not to hold executive posts in any banking establishment. The Commission was given authority to refuse SEC requests for information if it felt that the evidence of illicit conduct was insufficient. Complaints immediately arose from customers of Swiss financial institutions, reflecting the fear of possible disclosure to US tax authorities. Perhaps as a *quid pro quo*, Swiss bank officials required a rather strong showing of proof before information could be released.

Santa Fe International Corporation

The Santa Fe International Corporation case evolved along rather different lines to the St Joe case. It took four years of painstaking

281

detective work by the SEC to complete, work that eventually established a network of investors spreading from the Middle East to France, Switzerland and the United Kingdom.[43]

In Autumn 1981, the SEC found evidence of substantial purchases of stock and call options in Santa Fe International just before its takeover by Kuwaiti Petroleum Corporation, apparently undertaken by individuals acting through Swiss intermediaries. Insider trading seemed clearly to be involved. Santa Fe's stock price more than doubled just days before the offer was made public and a call option, standing at less than 60 cents on 23 September, was at $15.875 by 6 October, just after the bid was announced.[44] Indeed, it was later established that investors in the options had on average taken home profits of 1,300 per cent.[45] Swiss secrecy, of course, barred disclosure of the purchasers' identity.

At first the SEC was working in the dark, but within a month it had the first name – Faisal al Massauod al Fuhaid, a Kuwaiti businessman with close ties to Kuwaiti government officials – who had opened an account with Merrill Lynch's Kuwait office on 22 September simply to acquire a large number of Santa Fe options.[46] The SEC sued Fuhaid and 'certain unknown purchasers' immediately, and the chase was on. At the SEC's request, a US federal judge froze the profits determined by the courts to have been illegally channeled through Swiss accounts. The SEC traced the proceeds to a bank account in the New York offices of Banca della Svizzera Italiana and persuaded a federal judge to freeze $2 million of the bank's assets pending the outcome of the subsequent negotiations.

The SEC appealed to the Swiss under the 1977 Treaty on mutual assistance in criminal matters, and investigations took an encouraging turn when the lower court, the Office for Police Matters, upheld the request. However, the ruling was predictably immediately appealed and reversed by the Swiss Federal Tribunal in January 1983.[47]

Meanwhile there had been an unexpected breakthrough. Darius Keaton, a non-executive director at Santa Fe, came forward and under an arrangement whereby he neither admitted nor denied charges (a technicality to prevent future civil charges), settled with the SEC, surrendering profits of around $275,000. But he still faced criminal charges, and in March 1987 pleaded guilty on the two felony counts of trading on advance knowledge and passing on information.[48]

It became apparent that Keaton had tipped off a number of overseas businessmen, including one Costandi Nasser, a Jordanian-born Lebanese executive who also had ties with Fuhaid.[49] The pieces of the puzzle were beginning to fit together.

In May 1984, after almost three years of US pressure, the Swiss Federal Tribunal in Lausanne reversed its earlier decision and ordered Crédit Suisse, Swiss Bank Corporation, Lombard Odier and the Swiss branches of Chase Manhattan and Citibank to turn over to the SEC certain account information and order tickets regarding the Santa Fe

International insider trading case. Whereas the SEC's original complaint to the Swiss court had been thrown out because it had failed to prove that the alleged securities law violations represented a crime in Switzerland, a second SEC attempt successfully linked information by the Kuwaiti tipster to the illegal transactions in a way that constituted a violation of Article 162 of the Swiss penal code (disclosure of business secrets to third parties).

In February 1985, the Swiss Federal Council approved release of the information and the documents were sent.[50] The Swiss Justice Ministry said the government had rejected a plea by unnamed individuals who had asked that assistance not be granted. The information provided was enough to lead to a series of out-of-court settlements,[51] the last of which involved seven individuals, including the Interior Minister of Qatar and the surrendering of profits totalling $7.8 million.[52] A special claims fund was set up with the money to reimburse investors who lost money in Santa Fe trading in 1981.[53]

Both the SEC and the Swiss banks claimed victory. The SEC argued that cooperation had won over confrontation. According to a Justice Department official, the case '. . . will signal to those who would trade on the basis of inside information that Swiss bank secrecy is no longer available as a shield from SEC investigations.'[54] The banks argued that the duration and cost of the legal proceedings would effectively discourage any further US incursions into Swiss bank secrecy in pursuit of securities law violations except under the most egregious of circumstances. Looming in the background, however, were continued rumblings in the US Congress to curtail severely Swiss banks' access to US securities markets unless effective cooperation continues.

IU International Corporation and Ellis AG

Two other cases relevant to the SEC's various attempts to extract information on insider trading from Switzerland are those of IU International Corporation and Ellis AG. In the former, allegations were made that John Seabrook, former chairman of IU, had raided the company's treasury and deposited the proceeds in Swiss accounts. Switzerland's highest court ruled that the SEC was entitled to information regarding Seabrook's account in the pursuit of its investigation of fraud charges.

The full ramifications of the Ellis AG case remain to be established. In general terms, the SEC has alleged that between October 1981 and mid-1984 this Zurich-based stockbroker put through deals in more than 60 US companies for principals thought to have been acting on takeover tips. It is suspected that dozens of clients were involved and illicitly gained profits might be in excess of $100 million.[55] It seems that a number of the defendants obtained advance information on pending deals, possibly from materials at a major New York law firm, and used it as a basis for illegal trades through Ellis – coupled to a tax evasion scheme designed to protect the gains.

The SEC made strenuous representations to the Swiss authorities for records. Its first request, as with Santa Fe under the Mutual Assistance treaty, was rejected as the charge was for insider trading, not at that time a crime in Switzerland.[56] Convention 16 did not help either, since it only covers banks, not brokerage firms. Ellis' principals, Claude and George Dreifuss, said they would like to help, but that Swiss law made it impossible.[57] It seems material in this context that, in 1984, in another case involving insider trading in Marathon Oil call options in 1981, it was shown that the Dreifuss brothers had each accepted $10,000 from two of the defendants to place the orders.[58]

However, a second request was made by the SEC, based this time on an illegality in Switzerland, the passing of company secrets to third parties. The request was this time granted and upheld on appeal in October 1985 by the Swiss Federal Court.[59]

One of the startling aspects emerging from the evidence is the possibility of circumstantial connections between the Levine case and the Ellis dealings. Three significant coincidences have been noted: (1) Trading by Levine often paralleled that by Ellis investors. Of the 18 issues named in SEC Ellis court papers, Levine took positions in seven. Sources say that such parallels are even more striking in the more than 40 at that point undisclosed Ellis stock trades. (2) Bank Leu, the bank involved in the Levine case, has had business ties with Ellis. Until late 1984 Ellis was owned by an affiliate of A. Sarasin & Cie, a Basel bank, with a senior partner on the board of Zurich-based Bank Leu. (3) In all seven Levine–Ellis linkages were found where the law firm Wachtell, Lipton, Rosen and Katz represented the raider or initiator.[60]

A study by the General Accounting Office reveals how significant the 'foreign question' is. In 1986 and 1987, a total of 609 possible insider trading offenses were placed for investigation with the SEC by US exchanges. Of these, 226 involved 'suspicious trades executed through foreign institutions.' In one case (thought to be that of the hostile tender by Limited Inc. in 1984 for Carter Hawley Hale Stores Inc., where foreign entities are calculated to have made some $1.7 million in profits), approximately 30 firms in 10 countries traded 265,900 shares of the target company in the six days prior to the bid.

The report suggested three possible strategies for the SEC in order to strengthen its attack against illicit dealing emanating abroad: (1) The SEC should analyze trends in suspicious overseas trading to provide a data base that might be used as a negotiating tool with foreign governments and institutions, (2) it should require US brokerage firms processing orders from foreign institutions to break out the order into individual transactions rather than handle it in bulk through an 'omnibus' account as is the existing practice, (3) information obtained by the SEC from foreign governments should be exempted from the Freedom of Information Act requirements. The latter is important because foreign regulators are reluctant to pass details to the SEC as confidentiality cannot be guaranteed since, under the Freedom of Information Act, the SEC can be required to release its files once an investigation is closed.[61]

Waiver by conduct

One of the more confrontational of the SEC's efforts was the 'waiver by conduct' proposal suggested in 1984 by John Fedders, former chief of the SEC's Enforcement Division, in the light of indications that almost all of an estimated $79.8 billion in foreign purchases of stocks and bonds on US exchanges in 1983 originated in countries that have either secrecy or blocking statutes. Under the proposal, US securities trading tickets and confirmations would be considered to imply consent on the part of traders to waive any and all secrecy rights. Quite apart from the impractical nature of the idea, it raised yet again the issue of US extraterritorial application of law. The Swiss, as the largest foreign purchasers of US equities, were unimpressed.

According to one perceptive analysis of Swiss views,

> . . . we have seen that there is reticence to serve the U.S. as an outpost for its 'detour' approach to criminal prosecution. Any demands for further reductions in bank secrecy strike at the heart both of commercial interests, where secrecy is seen as essential for business success and for Swiss bank primacy in commerce, and of Swiss sentiments that individual privacy must take precedence over the interests of the state.
>
> If one respects freedom, as protected by financial privacy, one does not wish to know, nor encourage others to be able to know, about how people earn or handle their money. This is a Swiss view. The Americans have no respect for freedom or for privacy. They encourage government interference in citizens' lives. The price of the Swiss view is that we will not know about criminality. The price of the American view is that the citizen is neither private nor free, for his own government is his enemy.[62]

The idea was later dropped.[63]

Despite the conspicuous failure of the waiver by conduct proposal, success has been achieved on other fronts. Swiss cooperation has gradually increased. Quite apart from Convention 16, there is the real insider trading law taking effect in 1988. It has been pointed out that the Convention was designed to remain in force only until such a law was enacted.[64] Even so, the new law will surely make far easier requests made under the 1977 treaty for Mutual Assistance on Criminal Matters.

The Swiss Minister of Justice and US Attorney General were in any case scheduled to sign a new memorandum of understanding on procedures for cooperation between the two countries in criminal investigations. In addition, it was anticipated that diplomatic notes will be exchanged by the Justice Minister and a State Department official to allow the SEC greater access to evidence for civil insider trading cases.[65]

In other areas, the SEC has established a policy of insisting on bilateral accords before it authorizes new electronic international trading links. Partly as a result of this approach, the Committee reached in 1985 informal agreements with the Quebec and Ontario securities regulators to cooperate in information sharing.[66] The first formal agency to agency arrangement came in May 1986, when the SEC and its Japanese counterpart agreed to exchange surveillance and investigative information in cases involving securities law violations.[67] Four months later a similar agreement was announced between the SEC and the United Kingdom. British and US securities and commodity regulators had previously cooperated on a case-by-case basis, but an organized framework will make exchange of information far easier and more certain. The agreement may in due course be replaced by a more comprehensive treaty for joint combating of international securities frauds.[68]

In January 1987, France signed mutual aid agreements with the SEC allowing regulators to share data on trading.[69] The Netherlands and Italy also have information-sharing treaties with the United States that theoretically could help bilateral investigations into insider trading.[70]

The SEC views these agreements, particularly those with major markets such as Japan and the United Kingdom, as very important breakthroughs. There is a belief that, if there is a free exchange of information between the countries where the main markets are located, it should facilitate the detection of malfeasance from other smaller financial centers.[71] In this search for a common ground, which could also serve to safeguard the attractiveness of the US markets vis-à-vis their competitors, the SEC has sought comment on the possible development of a common prospectus for public debt and stock offerings in the United States, Canada and the United Kingdom, a step which could, if successful, be extended to other EEC countries and beyond. It has also proposed an agreement under which governments would recognize the filings of foreign companies, provided they meet the disclosure requirements of their own countries. Still, as one SEC expert put it: 'If you let a foreign company offer securities with considerable less disclosure, you will have American companies coming to you asking why they can't follow the same rule.'[72]

Combating insider trading in Europe, Asia and Latin America

As noted earlier, countries other than the United States tend to have had a more relaxed view of insider trading. It is difficult to know why exactly this should have been the case, although it is not unreasonable to believe that the generally higher level of public participation in markets in the United States may be a contributory factor. Only one in forty people in France, for example, owns shares, whereas in the United States the figure is closer to one in five.[73]

Whatever the reasons, the attitudes are certainly somewhat different in other countries than in the United States. In Japan, despite the existence for almost forty years of US-style securities laws, insider trading is considered to be rife and prosecutions are rare (only five in four decades). In the United Kingdom and France insider trading is now illegal but these countries are the exception rather than the rule. Elsewhere in Europe it is a rather different story.

In West Germany the stock market relies on voluntary guidelines used by listed companies and banks as a code of honor.[74] But these do not bind lawyers, accountants or journalists, who regularly know earnings results, for example, several days before they are made public.[75] In Italy, the Netherlands and Belgium insider trading is not a crime at all.[76] In Austria, the bank secrecy provisions of the Banking Act make it a criminal offense for an employee to use information made available to the bank for his or another's advantage – but that is far too narrow to amount to any real ban on insider trading.

In Luxembourg, Article 311 of the penal code makes it an offense to manipulate fraudulently the price of public notes, but most lawyers agree that this would not apply to insider dealing. Looking further afield, while insider trading is discouraged in Hong Kong it is not a criminal offense; in Venezuela and Brazil, no law forbids insider trading, although the exchange authorities do have regulations against it. In India, the only restriction is the general legal principle that no officer of a company may use information obtained while working for that company for personal advantage and to the detriment of the share-holders. In South Africa and Malaysia, where insider trading is prohibited, it is to no avail whatsoever in that the manpower and administrative capabilities to police and prosecute it are totally insufficient.[77]

However, there are signs that such attitudes may be changing in a number of countries. This may in part be the result of US pressure. But other factors are at play as well. As the United States worries that it may lose market share through excessive regulation, other major markets are concerned that too much malpractice in their securities markets gives them a bad name, and will drive investors elsewhere. As one banker noted: 'To attract international capital is the litmus test of success. People are afraid to play in markets where they don't know the rules. A market has to be perceived as fair and honest, or else it won't attract foreign capital.'[78]

Recent egregious examples of insider trading, in other markets as well as on Wall Street, have brought the whole issue into sharper focus. The

Guinness scandal in the United Kingdom, for example, had the opposition Labour Party calling for imposition of SEC-style regulation and, in response, the government strengthened rules on disclosure during merger battles.[79] The growth in private share ownership occurring throughout Europe may also have an effect. If markets are perceived by the individual investor to be unfair, voting pressure for regulation may well increase.[80]

In the United Kingdom major changes in the way the Stock Exchange functions have also contributed to concern. On 27 October 1986 – Big Bang – minimum commissions in the London market were abolished. With this move, the old system of 'single-capacity', according to which broker and market-maker functions were strictly divided between separate firms, also disappeared. In addition, restrictions preventing banks from engaging in securities transactions were lifted.

In this new world, where brokers, market-makers and bankers are under one roof, the temptations and possibilities for insider dealing are sharply increased.[81] Added to this is the fact that London, like New York, has experienced a significant upsurge in takeover business. In view of London Stock Exchange estimates that 80 per cent of suspected insider trading deals occur immediately before or during a takeover bid,[82] it is easy to appreciate the concern. Finally, there is concern that the increasing tendency to raise cash not from existing shareholders through the traditional rights issue, but from the public markets, increases the opportunity for leaks of sensitive information.[83]

Before 1980, the Stock Exchange itself 'policed' the activities of its members and investors. However, under the Companies Act of 1980 insider trading actually became a criminal offense. The law was updated, though not materially changed, in 1985 in the Company Securities (Insider Dealing) Act. The penalty on conviction is a prison term of up to two years and an unlimited fine, both determined by the judge.[84] There have been proposals to increase the prison term to seven years. Under this system the London Stock Exchange still carries out preliminary investigations, but if it considers that the evidence is sufficient it hands the matter over to the Department of Trade and Industry which may initiate a prosecution. The record of success by the mid-1980s was not impressive. Out of the 284 full-scale investigations carried out by the Stock Exchange between 1980 and early 1986, only 93 had been referred to the DTI. Of these 93 only five resulted in prosecution, out of which came three convictions.

To some extent, the United Kingdom authorities faced similar obstacles as did their US counterparts. Out of the 284, 50 were apparently frustrated because of the use of offshore companies based in areas such as the Caribbean or Liberia.[85] But in addition to this there were flaws in the legislation preventing full investigation. For instance, while the government could compel suspects to show their records, it could not compel them to respond orally to questions.[86]

In 1986 the Financial Services Act was passed, in which the new regulatory structure of the City of London was set out. Under this Act the right to silence is lost to a defendant, who can be charged with contempt of court for refusing to answer questions. Other reforms facilitating the investigators' task are included and a new watchdog agency, the Securities and Investments Board, has been established.

There appears to be a new determination to punish insider trading in the United Kingdom, as the treatment of Geoffrey Collier, a Morgan Grenfell banker charged with insider trading indicates. In order to aid investigations into his case, the government supposedly hastened the implementation of the insider provisions in the new law.[87] The United Kingdom is also beginning to participate in international mutual assistance agreements. It now has one, as we discussed above, with the United States and is currently negotiating a similar pact with Japan.[88]

As noted in Chapter 7, Switzerland promulgated an insider trading law in 1988. The Swiss Investors' Protection Association fiercely opposed the law, and indeed attempted to force a referendum on the issue. The attempt failed, however, and the law came into effect on 1 July 1988. Insider trading is now a criminal offense punishable by a prison sentence of up to three years or by a fine. The law applies only to those connected with a specific company or deal, or those receiving direct inside information. Acting on a tip overheard by chance, for example, is not illegal.

There has been some concern that, due to the law's structure and triggering mechanism, normally legitimate actions will also fall into its net. There is, for instance, no threshold set at which a bidding corporation must disclose its shareholding interest – in the US it is 5 per cent, in France 20 per cent. As a result, it is argued, it may be that an announcement strictly would have to be made on the purchase of the first share if the move were liable to have a significant effect on the stock price. That is, any purchase of a sizeable equity interest of a company might conceivably be construed as legal only after publication of the purchase. The Swiss Ministry of Justice has stated that in practice the law will not be applied in such a manner, but it is a weakness in its drafting.

In their actions on insider trading, the Swiss have to a certain extent given in to US pressure. Critics of the law have dubbed it the *Lex Americana*. Even so it may represent, like the November 1987 Memorandum, an acceptance by the authorities that ultimately insider trading does in fact erode investor confidence, thus damaging the market.[89]

Elsewhere in Europe too new steps are being tried or at least considered. France, like the United Kingdom, already views insider trading as a crime, punishable with up to two years' imprisonment and an $800,000 fine, and has been involved in discussions over information-sharing with Japan and the United Kingdom.[90] The Netherlands has introduced an insider trading code and legislation to make it a crime. Norway also has such a code and Belgium has had the issue under review.[91]

Even in West Germany, changes can be detected. Although they have been short on monitoring resources, the authorities caught their first insider trader in August 1986. In October 1985 the stock of the diversified electrical concern AEG had risen almost 30 per cent in the ten days before Daimler Benz announced its takeover bid for the company. It transpired that Klaus Kuhn, AEG's former chairman, had bought 700 shares in September 1985 when acquisition talks were going on, and had allegedly profited by $7,800 by selling the shares after the Daimler bid in October. As a penalty he repaid the profit to AEG.[92]

West German market officials have also begun to meet periodically regulators from the United States, Japan, the United Kingdom and France and from that process formal and informal agreements are gradually emerging.[93]

In line with its plans for greater financial integration in Europe by the early 1990s, the EEC Commission has prepared a draft directive on insider trading designed to standardize treatment throughout the 12 member states. It is proposed to make insider trading illegal everywhere and to include in the legislation a precise definition of those considered to be engaged in insider trading.[94]

Outside Europe, Hong Kong and Canada are worthy of note. In the former, discussions have proceeded on the possibility of making insider trading a criminal offense. In Canada, the Province of Ontario, which regulates Canada's key Toronto stock market, has widened its definition of insiders and raised penalties for offenders.[95]

Worried that international investors would lose confidence in the Tokyo Stock Exchange, the Japanese government announced new regulations to outlaw the traditional Japanese financial practice of insider trading in 1988. In a country where equal access to information has never been the norm and seldom a goal, no one has ever been sent to prison for insider trading. The use and leakage of market-sensitive information by those privy to it has been seen as an appropriate way of increasing corporate profitability, maintaining friendships, returning political favors, and cementing relationships between broker and investor.

In October 1986, just before Recruit Cosmos Company went public, it sold unlisted shares to 80 politicians and journalists, including aides to Prime Minister Noboru Takeshita, who reaped the subsequent rewards – largely for the benefit of the ruling Liberal Democratic Party – as a result of the stock's quadrupling in value. Although the case has been investigated and subsequently widely criticized, no law was apparently broken – although it did lead to the resignation of Foreign Minister Miyazawa in 1988.

Nor, it seems, were laws violated when the Hanshin Sogo Bank, acting on warnings from its client, Tateho Chemical Industries, sold millions of Tateho shares hours before the company announced that it had lost more than $210 million in the bond futures market. No charges were filed against those involved. 'We could only prove that the bank had a vague sense of crisis,' said one investigator. With the 1988 legislation, the vagueness is being clarified, at least statutorily.

Henceforth, directors of publicly quoted corporations will be obliged to disclose dealings in their own company's stock. Companies will be required to issue statements when potentially sensitive decisions are made. Companies will also be urged to report earnings quarterly, rather than semi-annually. And the government will have wide powers to investigate companies and individuals suspected of infringement.

Market leader Nomura Securities has repeatedly altered the environment where a company's portfolio manager was often its corporate finance advisor as well, by erecting 'Chinese Walls' – Wall Street jargon for ostensibly impenetrable barriers to information flow between different units of a single securities firm – in its organization. Violators who pass along sensitive information are to be dismissed.

Given the long-standing traditions of elitism in the securities business in Japan, it is nevertheless debatable whether the apparently sincere attempts to rein in insider trading abuses will be fully effective.[96]

Multilateral approaches

Multilateral initiatives and general behavioral codes have also been suggested to combat secret money. One such initiative would involve the International Monetary Fund. It is felt that, given the reputation of the IMF, any pronouncement of its interest in ethical conduct could carry some weight in the international banking community. Education of banking personnel, expansion of technical competence of local governments to engage in effective supervision and creation of independent teams to run central bank authorities in problem countries are some long-range suggestions. In any country where the Fund is providing standby facilities, the possibility exists for the IMF to require the central bank to extend its supervision of commercial banks and to intensify deposit diligence.

The argument is that criminals will cause a country already in difficulty to suffer further losses through fraud and other crimes. The effects are often underestimated, and may include serious problems such as distortions in the supply of labor, volatility in equity and commodity markets, and misallocation of resources where illegally funded front businesses are able to monopolize industries because of cheap funding.[97] So the IMF could have a legitimate role to play consistent with its broader mandate.

Other methods to create disincentives to secret money flows include a coordinated increase in regulation through central banks in home countries and a rigid imposition of a carefully policed 'due diligence' requirement that would seek to ban criminal monies from the banking system. This would involve an expanded communication network allowing access to certain central files and to the credit, police and banking authorities of any nation for the purpose of inquiry. A disciplined, ethical Bar would be responsible for policing nominees' diligence in screening the clients they represent. It would also be necessary to have a cadre of investigators capable of examining the business aspects of crime. The investigators would be sworn to observe local secrecy laws during the presence 'on assignment' to any national jurisdiction. Flight capital or funds escaping taxes or exchange controls would not be included in the diligence check, although the lack of international consensus on tax policy could make it difficult to enforce effectively any such diligence requirements.

In April 1988, it was announced that international banking supervisors were jointly drawing up a code of conduct (similar to that developed from the Swiss Gentlemen's Agreement) to be followed by banks of all the major banking nations. The aim of this multilateral effort would be to end bank involvement with money arising from fraud, tax evasion and other criminal acts.

The two principal undertakings would probably consist of the requirement to ascertain the true identity of a client and the prevention of the abuse of banking secrecy to conceal the criminal source of funds. The goal is particularly to end the 'no questions asked' practices adopted by certain banks.

It seemed unlikely that the code would carry any legal sanctions, but would have the effect of placing moral pressure on banks to improve the monitoring of their business and to move swiftly in cases of suspected crime.[98]

The OECD initiative

A controversial multilateral step towards controlling tax evasion has been taken by the Council of Europe and seemed likely also to be adopted by the OECD. Comments in the press have ranged from high praise to outrage. *The Observer* (London) called it, 'an ambitious attempt to abolish national boundaries as far as taxes are concerned, and turn tax authorities into an international force pledged to uphold the tax laws of other countries.'[99] The *Wall Street Journal* was less impressed: 'Now this proposal has been brought into the open, we're confident it will be seen for the nuisance it is. But it would also help damp future regulatory zeal if, instead of deferring the proposal to death, someone got up at the next meeting and forthrightly denounced the treaty.'[100] It was perhaps best summed up by the former Chairman of the American Bar Association's white-collar crime committee: 'From the government's perspective, this could become a prosecutor's dream. And from the citizen's, a nightmare.'[101]

In 1977, the OECD Fiscal Affairs Committee began to consider the possibility of increased efforts by its members to combat tax evasion. It recommended that countries strengthen 'their powers of investigation for the detection of tax avoidance and evasion' by, in part, 'making more intensive use of international conventions or instruments in force and by seeking new arrangements of a bilateral and multilateral character.'

Meanwhile the UN, too, was concerned with the tax evasion issue, and in December 1983 presented 'Guidelines for International Co-operation to Combat International Tax Evasion and Avoidance'. Not to be outdone, the Members of the Committee of Experts on Tax Law had been busy within the Council of Europe.

From these various efforts evolved 'The Draft Convention on Mutual Administrative Assistance in Tax Matters',[102] adopted in June 1987 by the 21 nations of the Council of Europe. In order to be implemented, the Convention must be ratified by member governments, and it has been agreed that it will be open for signing on 25 January 1988. The OECD is expected to embark on a similar procedure.[103]

The Convention calls for 'automatic' and 'spontaneous' exchanges of taxpayer data[104] and cooperation between authorities to recover taxes owed in another country, including taxes on income and profits, capital gains, net wealth and compulsory social security contributions.[105] The treaty would grant tax agents unprecedented access to the files of other nations' corporate and individual taxpayers, even where no crime has been alleged. Simply to have chosen to bank, invest, work or carry on business in an area where tax treatment would be more favorable than at home could expose a firm or individual to investigation.[106] Tax agents would be able to share information on a taxpayer without informing him. In addition, a country's tax authority would be empowered to confiscate property owned by a taxpayer who is a resident of another country even if the latter's case is still in dispute in his home country.[107]

The proposed Convention has had a stormy passage, and in some quarters continues to be vigorously fought. The United States favors it, as do the Scandinavian countries, France and the United Kingdom.[108] But Austria, Belgium, Ireland, Italy, Portugal and Liechtenstein have all expressed doubts[109] and Switzerland, West Germany and Luxembourg have categorically refused to lend their support.[110] The International Chamber of Commerce was also profoundly disturbed by the whole matter and announced its determination to work against it. It has warned of 'risks inherent in this convention' that could 'endanger the profitability and confidentiality of trans-border commercial dealings between companies.'[111]

There are undoubtedly flaws in the agreement. Quite apart from the potential for improper disclosure of trade secrets, no distinction is made between tax evasion and avoidance, meaning that quite legal practices, such as transfer pricing, may fall under scrutiny. (Transfer pricing is the means by which multinationals reduce their tax bill by maximizing the profits they earn in low-tax countries.) It may also prove tricky to resolve basic differences in the tax laws of participating countries.

The 1984 decision concerning the conductor Pierre Boulez is a case in point. After cutting an album for a US record company while he was a resident of West Germany, Boulez received a percentage of the proceeds from record sales. West German agents called these payments 'royalties' that were taxable under an existing tax agreement. The US IRS called them 'income for personal services', taxable in the United States. Eventually Boulez lost and both countries taxed him on the same income.[112]

Finally, there appear to be no limits on or redress mechanisms to prevent witch-hunts or fishing expeditions against taxpayers innocent of any illegal act.[113]

The issue of tax evasion also came up during 1988 as a possible stumbling-block in the creation of a unified financial market in the EC by 1992. Under the liberalization, nationals of all Community countries would be able to open bank accounts and borrow anywhere in the EC. Both France and Denmark expressed strong reservations that this could lead to widespread tax evasion, and made a strong case that tax harmonization should precede freeing of capital flows – a long and arduous task. In the end, they were assuaged by agreement that the EC would 'work toward' harmonization of tax systems on investment portfolios and savings accounts, and that a study commission would investigate 'risk of fiscal distortions, evasion and fraud', with a guaranteed ministerial decision on the matter by June 1989.[114]

The UN initiative

On 14 December 1984, the General Assembly of the United Nations requested that the Commission on Narcotic Drugs initiate the 'preparation of a draft convention against illicit traffic in narcotic drugs which considers the various aspects of the problem as a whole and, in particular, those not envisaged in existing international instruments.' As well as relevant studies on the matter, the comments of member governments were considered and in June 1986 the initial draft convention was presented.[115]

This consisted of 14 articles addressing topics such as methods for cooperation among countries to combat production and transportation of narcotics, adequate sanctions for drug offenses, strengthening of extradition procedures, and measures to control the cultivation of narcotic plants. Of particular interest however is that the convention, in addition to considering the production and trafficking of drugs, deals in some depth with the question of the proceeds and their laundering. Proceeds are defined as 'property of every description, whether corporeal or incorporeal, movable or non-movable, tangible or intangible, and deeds and instruments evidencing title to, or interest in, such property.' Laundering is defined as 'the concealment or disguise of the true nature, source, disposition, movement or ownership of proceeds and includes the movement or conversion of proceeds by electronic transmission.' Mexico, in comments, suggested that 'the concept of laundering can be more restrictive . . . and can apply exclusively to the placing in circulation of money obtained from the sale of the illicit product.'[116]

There are number of points relating to laundering in the document that are noteworthy: (1) It is to be established, along with trafficking, as a serious offense under criminal law; (2) It is to be punishable by imprisonment and fines; (3) Countries are to adopt national legislative and administrative measures to facilitate the identification, tracing, freezing, seizure and forfeiture of proceeds, in order to prevent the acquisition, possession, transfer and laundering of such funds. In addition they are in these respects to facilitate effective coordinated action at the national level and provide one another with appropriate assistance; (4) Laundering is to be an extraditable offense; (5) The widest measure of mutual legal assistance is to be employed, which would include provision of relevant documents and records, including bank, financial, corporate and business records; (6) Countries are to cooperate closely to facilitate the sharing of information on, inter alia, the movement of proceeds; and (7) Training programs are to be developed or enhanced dealing, inter alia, with detecting and monitoring the flow of proceeds and methods used in laundering them. Programs for countries to share expertise on such matters are also to be implemented. By the end of September 1988, negotiation of the treaty between over 100 countries, including the United States, was in its final stages with final agreement confidently predicted by US Administration officials.

Despite these moves it must be accepted that all multilateral efforts suffer from the same basic weakness – the fundamental difference of interest among countries in curbing secret money flows. Discontinuities in tax systems, economic policies, political and judicial arrangements, law enforcement and other factors bearing on secrecy demand and supply virtually doom from the outset any efforts to achieve cooperation beyond relatively narrow confines of mutual interest.

A key barrier is the fear that if a country joins a multilateral agreement another will refuse, and business will simply shift there. For tangible results, enforceability on the widest international scale is a prerequisite, otherwise funds will simply flow along the course of least resistance. The requisite worldwide commitment seems a long way off. For many, the words of a senior executive of the Norwegian Central Bank sum it up: 'Money in – good; money out – bad.'[117]

Summary

The problem of controlling secret money is devilishly difficult. People are surely right when they point to secret money as a symptom rather than a cause. But others have an equally valid point when they note that attacking secrecy may do more damage to the underlying illicit transactions than trying to deal with them head-on. Pressuring the 'facilitators' makes their deals more costly, more risky and less attractive, regardless of the kinds of activities that are involved.

Each approach to raise barriers to secret money flows has its problems. Unilateral efforts are necessarily partial and, at least in the United States, implementation has been rather difficult. Pressuring foreign countries to change their policies on financial secrecy runs into extraterritoriality problems, imposes costs on them, and invariably leads to intergovernmental conflict. Bilateral cooperation can make some headway, but is seriously impaired by conflicting views and interests, and by the diversion of secrecy seekers to other, possibly less cooperative suppliers. Multilateral approaches remain well beyond reach.

So, apart from spotty successes against egregious uses of secret money, the countermeasures seem rather ineffectual, taken as a whole. We can expect the flows to change in form, in direction and (from time to time) in size. But unless there are some underlying changes in the motivating forces, business will continue to thrive.

Notes

1 Peter Fuhrman, 'A Time for Change – But Slowly', *Forbes*, 13 June 1988.
2 Richard H. Blum and John Kaplan, 'Offshore Banking: Issues With Respect to Criminal Use', mimeo., The Ford Foundation, 1979, p. 28.
3 'Numbered Accounts: The Feds Get a Peak', *Business Week*, 4 July 1988.
4 William Dullforce, 'Still a Marketable Advantage', *Financial Times*, 11 December 1987.
5 'Pope Reminds Swiss About Ethics', *The Times* (London), 15 June 1984.
6 Richard Evans, 'Forcing Discreet Money Into the Open', *Euromoney*, Nov. 1986.
7 Thomas C. Jefferson and Vassel G. Johnson, 'Cayman Commits Itself to Financial Confidentiality', *Taxes International*, February 1985.
8 Andy Pasztor and Sonia L. Nazario, 'Cayman Islands Grant U.S. Access to Offshore Bank Data', *Wall Street Journal*, 3 July 1986.

9 Robert Taylor, 'Cayman Islands Could be Erased as Haven for Drug Profits Under Pact, U.S. Says', *Wall Street Journal*, 13 September 1984.
10 Martha Brannigan, 'Courts Aid Officials' Efforts to Get Offshore Bank Data of U.S. Firms', *Wall Street Journal*, 24 July 1984.
11 Ian Lyon, 'Paradise Under Pressure', *Investment International*, June 1987.
12 Richard Evans, *op. cit.* (n. 6).
13 Andy Pasztor and Sonia L. Nazario, *op. cit.* (n. 8).
14 Jon Nordheimer, 'Head of Isles near Bahamas Accused of Drug Plot', *New York Times*, 6 March 1985.
15 'U.S. Reaches Pact in Caribbean to Deter Money Laundering', *Wall Street Journal*, 19 September 1986.
16 Ibid.
17 John Moody, 'Dirty Dollars', *Time*, 19 January 1987.
18 Ibid.
19 Richard Evans, *op. cit.* (n. 6).
20 Christopher Stoakes, 'The People vs. Confidentiality', *Euromoney*, August 1986.
21 Ibid.
22 Robert Taylor, 'Bank of Nova Scotia Quietly Complies With US Subpoena of Bahamas Records', *Wall Street Journal*, 22 September 1983.
23 Christopher Stoakes, *op. cit.* (n. 20).
24 Jud Harwood, 'Commentary – Bank of Nova Scotia (Brady Subpoena) – US Government Lawyers Deceive the Courts', *Taxes International*, March 1985.
25 Richard Blum and John Kaplan, *op. cit.* (n. 2).
26 'The Antilles Heel', *Wall Street Journal*, 15 July 1987.
27 Shirley Hobbs Scheibla, 'Where Hot Money Hides', *Barrons*, 11 July 1983.
28 Richard A. Gordon, *Tax Havens and Their Use by U.S. Taxpayers* (Washington, D.C.: Internal Revenue Service, 1981).
29 'Tax Havens and Funk Money', *International Currency Review*, Vol. 15, No. 2, 1983.
30 John M. Fedders, 'Foreign Secrecy: A Key to the Lock', *New York Times*, 16 October 1983.
31 Sarah Bartlett, 'Another Threat to Foreign Bank Secrecy', *Business Week*, 28 January 1985.
32 John M. Fedders, *op. cit.* (n. 30).
33 Scott McMurray, George Anders, E. S. Browning and Bruce Ingersoll, 'As Global 24 Hours Trading Nears, Regulators Warn of Market Abuses', *Wall Street Journal*, 10 February 1985.
34 Nathaniel C. Nash, 'Stretching the SEC's Reach', *New York Times*, 13 July 1986.
35 Ibid.
36 Gordon M. Henry, 'Dark Clouds over Wall Street', *Time*, 26 May 1986.
37 Christopher Stoakes, 'The Insider Trader's Global Guide', *Euromoney*, July 1986.
38 Bruce Ingersoll, 'SEC Hails Ruling by Swiss Court Forcing Banks to Help in Inquiry', *Wall Street Journal*, 18 May 1984.
39 Clive Wolman, 'How Big Fish Escape', *Financial Times*, 4 March 1986.
40 Christopher Stoakes, *op. cit.* (n. 37).
41 Ibid.
42 Thomas W. Netter, 'Swiss Bank Secrecy Laws Are Put to New Test in U.S. Insider Trading Case', *International Herald Tribune*, 20 May 1986.
43 Terry Dodsworth, 'Cutting the Swiss Web', *Financial Times*, 10 April 1986.
44 Bruce Ingersoll, *op. cit.* (n. 38).
45 'Insider Case Guilty Plea', *New York Times*, 19 March 1987.
46 Terry Dodsworth, *op. cit.* (n. 43).
47 Bruce Ingersoll, 'Santa Fe Investors Agree to Give Up Profits from Insider-Trading Case', *European Wall Street Journal*, 27 February 1986.
48 Terry Dodsworth, *op. cit.* (n. 43).
49 James Sterngold, '8 to Repay $7.8 Million in SEC Insider Case', *New York Times*, 28 February 1986.
50 Terry Dodsworth, *op. cit.* (n. 43).
51 Bruce Ingersoll, *op. cit.* (n. 47).
52 Terry Dodsworth, *op. cit.* (n. 43).

53 Chris Welles, John Templeman and Vicky Cahan, 'The Mysterious "Coincidences" in Insider Trading Case', *Business Week*, 9 August 1986.
54 Bruce Ingersoll, *op. cit.* (n. 47).
55 'Swiss Firm Told to Give Papers to U.S.', *International Herald Tribune*, 13 December 1985.
56 Terry Dodsworth, *op. cit.* (n. 43).
57 Chris Welles, John Templeman and Vicky Cahan, *op. cit.* (n. 53).
58 'Swiss Firm Told to Give Papers to U.S.', *op. cit.* (n. 55).
59 Terry Dodsworth, *op. cit.* (n. 43).
60 Chris Welles, John Templeman and Vicky Cahan, *op. cit.* (n. 53).
61 Thomas E. Ricks, 'Foreign Brokerages Appear Frequently in Insider Trading Reports, Study Says', *Wall Street Journal*, 6 June 1988.
62 Richard Blum and John Kaplan, *op. cit.* (n. 2), p. 29.
63 Bruce Ingersoll, *op. cit.* (n. 38).
64 John Templeman, 'The Stone Wall of Swiss Secrecy', *Business Week*, 29 April 1985.
65 'Swiss and US in Insider Pact', *New York Times*, 20 October 1987.
66 Peter Truell, 'Insider Trading Pact Seen Soon for U.S., Britain', *Wall Street Journal*, 4 September 1986.
67 Nathaniel C. Nash, 'Stretching the SEC's Reach', *New York Times*, 13 July 1986.
68 Peter Truell, *op. cit.* (n. 66).
69 John Templeman, 'The Insider Trading Dragnet is Stretching Across the Globe', *Business Week*, 23 March 1987.
70 Gary Putka, 'Insider Trading Raises Fewer Hackles', *Wall Street Journal*, 2 December 1986.
71 Peter Truell, *op. cit.* (n. 66).
72 Nathaniel C. Nash, *op. cit.* (n. 67).
73 Gary Putka, *op. cit.* (n. 70).
74 Peter Gumbel, 'West Germany is Taking a Closer Look at Insider Trading Following AEG Case', *Wall Street Journal*, 21 August 1986.
75 Lynne Curry, 'Opinions Split on Insider Trading', *New York Times*, 24 September 1986.
76 Christopher Stoakes, *op. cit.* (n. 37).
77 Ibid.
78 John Templeman, *op. cit.* (n. 69).
79 Ibid.
80 Gary Putka, *op. cit.* (n. 70).
81 Lynne Curry, *op. cit.* (n. 75).
82 Clive Wolman, *op. cit.* (n. 39).
83 Lynne Curry, *op. cit.* (n. 75).
84 Christopher Stoakes, *op. cit.* (n. 37).
85 Clive Wolman, 'Insider Dealing Rings Operate Offshore Links', *Financial Times*, 4 March 1986.
86 Lynne Curry, *op. cit.* (n. 75).
87 Clive Wolman, *op. cit.* (n. 39).
88 Lynne Curry, *op. cit.* (n. 75).
89 William Dullforce, 'Swiss Insider Trading Law Starts 1 July', *Financial Times*, 3 June 1988. Alan McGregor, 'New Swiss Insider Trading Law on Trial', *The Times*, 20 June 1988.
90 John Templeman, *op. cit.* (n. 69).
91 Christopher Stoakes, *op. cit.* (n. 37).
92 Peter Gumbel, *op. cit.* (n. 74).
93 John Templeman, *op. cit.* (n. 69).
94 Ibid.
95 Ibid.
96 See David Sanger, 'Insider Trading, the Japanese Way', *The New York Times*, 10 August 1988. See also David Sanger, 'Japan Insider Trading: A Tradition is Ending', *New York Times*, 11 August 1988; and Stefan Wafstyl, 'Japanese Take Tough Action on Insider Dealing', *Financial Times*, 21 September 1988.
97 John Mulcahy, 'The Chinese Laundry', *Far Eastern Economic Review*, 20 August 1987.
98 David Lascelles and John Wicks, 'Banking Nations Aim to Crack Down on Fraud', *Financial Times*, 27 April 1988.

99   'Waking Up the OECD', *The Economist*, 29 November 1986.
100 'Tax Man on Hold', *Wall Street Journal*, 9 December 1986.
101 Burr Leonard, 'Tax Deform', *Forbes*, 15 December 1986.
102 H. Anton Keller, 'A Global IRS?', *Wall Street Journal*, 9 May 1986.
103 Axel Krause, 'European Tax Pact Adopted', *International Herald Tribune*, 27 June 1987.
104 H. Anton Keller, *op. cit.* (n. 102).
105 Axel Krause, *op. cit.* (n. 103).
106 'Tax Man on Hold', *op. cit.* (n. 100).
107 Burr Leonard, *op. cit.* (n. 101).
108 Ibid.
109 'Bank Secrecy', *The Banker*, August 1985.
110 Axel Krause, *op. cit.* (n. 103).
111 Ibid.
112 Burr Leonard, *op. cit.* (n. 101).
113 H. Anton Keller, *op. cit.* (n. 102).
114 'EC Agrees on Free Capital Movement', *International Herald Tribune*, 14 June 1988. See also, 'Curbs on Capital Flows Will Test Finance Ministers', *Financial Times*, 14 June 1988.
115 United Nations Economic and Social Council, *Implementation and Development of International Instruments on the Control of Narcotic Drugs and Psychotropic Substances* (New York: UN Economic and Social Council, Commission on Narcotic Drugs, 19 June 1986).
116 Ibid., addendum, 29 January 1987.
117 John Mulcahy, *op. cit.* (n. 97).

11

Consequences

Having toured the subject of international financial secrecy in its various dimensions – its character, its roots in both human behavior and complex external pressures – we now come to the consequences. Does it all really matter? Have we been concerned all along with something that is of trivial importance in the workings of global political, and social and economic systems? Can it be that secret money is indeed nothing more than a symptom – the result of factors that are themselves much more fundamental in nature? If so, the ebb and flow of secret money can give us some useful guidelines about things that cause it, but not much more. Or does secret money itself permit or facilitate behavior that in turn has real and serious consequences for society? If this is the case, then we are dealing with something that is of far greater interest, and that public policy should address directly.

We have emphasized in this book that the desire for financial secrecy – and the willingness to pay for it – is based on an underlying profile of economic, political and social motives, as well as highly individualistic and personal preferences and attitudes. For example, confiscatory tax policies or measures that affect the convertibility of one currency into others (and into physical assets) can have profound effects on the demand for financial secrecy. However, even in a world completely free of such adversity, demand for financial secrecy driven by economic self-interest hardly disappears, since the need always remains for business confidentiality and personal privacy. So do other motives that have nothing whatever to do with onerous government policies and market distortions. Beyond this, political risk, which can be seen as a matter of uncertainty about future government policies, plays a major role in determining the desire for financial secrecy, as do social pressures, envy, and differing concepts of fairness. Combining economic, political and social factors, we can conclude that the demand for international financial secrecy is largely, but certainly not entirely, man-made.

Within this context, the man-made considerations are by no means

300

predictable in terms of their impact on people's desire for secret money. Some people are simply more secretive than others, just as some people are more averse to risk than others. So a particular set of external factors can result in a wide range of responses with respect to the desire for financial secrecy. Yet the external factors do play enough of a role that one can legitimately talk about a 'derived demand' for secrecy – derived from man-made conditions that determine the environment within which the individual tries to operate in his own best interest.

If various factors in the environment affect the demand for financial secrecy, is it also true that the existence of secrecy vehicles or 'products' affects a range of political, social and economic factors? That is, how might the world look if secret money did not exist? This question begins to get at an identification of the effects of international financial secrecy, and the potential consequences of the kinds of anti-secrecy measures described in Chapters 9 and 10.

Economic effects

The economic implications of international financial secrecy are relatively straightforward, but nevertheless highly speculative. There are implications for national income and output, income distribution, savings and investment, fiscal and monetary policies, national balances of payments and exchange rates, and the terms of international trade, among others. And the effects of secret money make themselves felt at the national as well as the international level.

In terms of international payments, we have suggested that there is little doubt that secret money movements are responsible for major inter-country capital transfers – encompassing flight capital, tax evasion and ordinary criminal flows. That these have adverse balance of payments consequences, if a country is trying to maintain a fixed exchange rate, is beyond doubt. Indeed, we have identified overvalued exchange rates brought on by misguided economic policies as a prime cause of international capital flight. A number of countries, including Mexico, Venezuela and the Philippines in the recent past, have found capital flight to be among their most troublesome economic problems. So have their bankers and other creditors, since the capital flight hemorrhage has often been compensated for by massive external borrowing. This, in turn, has certainly exacerbated some of the well-known debt problems that have afflicted developing countries in the 1980s.

In effect, countries borrowed abroad only to see a major part of the proceeds used to feed residents' bank accounts, purchases of real estate, and other asset holdings overseas. It has often been argued that the absence of secret money and its aggressive promotion by bankers and real estate salesmen traveling troubled countries would make their international financial problems a good deal easier to manage. In the words of one US banker embarking on a trip to one of the heavily indebted Latin American countries: 'When I saw my colleagues in the private banking division at the airport and they said they were making a lot of money, I knew that the countries they were coming from were in trouble. When people "vote" with their cash that way you know the end is nigh.'[1] Unable to do anything about the availability of financial havens abroad, governments have tried to clamp down hard on the actual transfers themselves, with mixed success. Tax evasion and criminal transactions involve similar balance of payments 'financing', requiring either a reduction in the country's external reserves or an increase in its external debt if exchange rates are fixed, or a currency devaluation/ depreciation if they are not.

Ultimately, the residents of the country have to pay the piper, through either increased exports or reduced imports of real goods and services, or both, representing a real reduction in levels of living. Those lucky or foresighted enough to have access to foreign assets benefit at the expense of the government and those who have not. According to one authority on the subject:

> There has been an enormous redistribution of wealth from public to private hands. First, these governments sold foreign exchange to the rich. Now that they've run into the external debt problem, they've had to do large depreciations and lower real wages. So Latin American workers are working harder to pay the interest on debts that have enabled the rich either to invest abroad or to consume luxury imports.[2]

The story is somewhat different if the country has maintained a realistic, market-oriented exchange rate from the outset. In that case, the secret money outflows will cause its currency to depreciate in the foreign exchange market and produce an adverse shift in the country's terms of trade – the local-currency price of imports will rise and the foreign-currency price of its exports will fall. In international trade transactions, the country will thus be 'poorer', in the sense that its exports will buy fewer imports. Moreover, the adverse terms of trade shift will tend to trigger changes in international trade flows. Since exports are now cheaper for foreign buyers, they will tend to rise. And since imports are now more expensive for domestic buyers, they will tend to fall. Once again, the secret money outflows will be 'paid for' by more exports and fewer imports, leaving a smaller amount of goods and services available for absorption by domestic residents in their consumption and investment activities.

On the other hand, in economies with substantial unemployment one could even argue (though probably only with tongue in cheek) that, by causing the domestic currency to weaken, secret money outflows may actually stimulate domestic economic activity by causing a favorable swing in the balance of trade and increased production for exports as well as the home market.

In fact, the kinds of effects of secret money flows under flexible exchange rates just described may well apply mainly in the case of tax evasion and criminal flows, since a realistic exchange rate and continued currency convertibility under relatively free-market conditions should help reduce or altogether eliminate the motivation for capital flight. However, this argument was not entirely credible after the 1980 election of President Mitterand in France, where *expectations* of future economic and political conditions played a major role in triggering capital flight.

Beyond balance of payments and exchange-rate effects, there are a number of mainly domestic economic consequences that might be traced to secret money flows. For one thing, capital formation financed by domestic savings is likely to be smaller than would be the case without capital flight – particularly troublesome in countries that are already starved for capital. Consequently, the rate of national economic growth will tend to be slower. There may also be adverse consequences for economic growth in terms of the quality of the labor force (human capital), and for the pace of technological change as skilled manpower and entrepreneurs depart, sending their money abroad ahead of them. Secret money flows associated with tax evasion may sap the government's ability to invest in economic and social infrastructure, thus compromising a prerequisite to economic development in many countries.

Secret money outflows thus appear to be unambiguously adverse to the process of economic growth. But it is too easy to confuse cause and effect. Most probably it is the bleak growth outlook *itself* and the questionable economic policies that are ultimately responsible for the gloomy prospects that may be the source of much of the capital flight. Countries with bright economic prospects based on a solid and consistent record of responsible economic management are rarely hit by capital flight. And there may be a few (perhaps arguable) 'offsets', such as the use of secret money to pay for education or medical treatment abroad for people who will later return home to become more productive citizens.

Then there is the matter of income distribution. Free markets for goods, services, land, labor and capital create a particular market-driven income distribution. In the absence of monopoly power by business firms or labor unions or landlords, this tends to result in an optimum allocation of resources in the national economy. Most of the time, governments do not regard such a market-driven distribution of income as being inherently 'fair', and usually apply some sort of progressive structure of taxation and transfer payments to redress the alleged inequities produced by the free market for capital, labor and land.

Income taxes, welfare payments, death duties, wealth taxes, even confiscation of property are all ways of addressing the fairness issue. People who do not regard the government's definition of 'fairness' as being fair have the option of resorting to international financial secrecy. By being able to do so, they can bring about less equality in the distribution of wealth and income. For some people, indeed, any taxes at all are considered excessive and unfair. Stories circulate discreetly about fleet-footed people who pay no taxes to any political jurisdiction, and even about people who cannot recall any members of their families who have ever paid taxes to anyone for generations.

Regardless of the level or structure of taxation, what is not paid by some must be paid by others, so that tax evasion always redistributes the burden of financing the public sector. The fact that some people are getting away without shouldering a 'fair' share of the tax burden – with 'fairness' defined politically – clearly undermines the willingness of others to go along with a system regarded as grossly inequitable, and can result in a wholesale erosion of tax morality. Once tax evasion becomes a national sport, with or without the use of international financial secrecy, it is extraordinarily difficult to rebuild tax compliance, as a number of countries have found out to their great dismay.

For countries that are the recipients of secret money, the economic consequences, by and large, tend to be far happier ones. Inflows of secret money may have beneficial balance of payments and/or exchange-rate effects, which ultimately permit residents to consume more goods and services than they otherwise would have been able to do. In the case of Colombia, secret money inflows have supported the value of the currency, even to the point that it was sold on the black market at an exchange rate that was *above* the official rate from time to time. The national terms of trade will tend to improve as its currency strengthens, although this may not be regarded as beneficial if it prices domestic products out of local and foreign markets, which may lead to an erosion of competitiveness and increased unemployment. A number of countries on the receiving end of secret money flows, notably Switzerland, have had this problem from time to time and have addressed it by offering negative interest rates, and other disincentives that may themselves produce certain benefits for the secrecy vendor. On the other hand, the influx of funds can promote domestic price stability via its upward pressure on the exchange rate (and reduced prices of imported goods and services), while at the same time making things quite difficult for the central bank in its efforts to 'sterilize' them – that is, prevent these inflows from causing an unwanted expansion of the domestic money supply and exerting inflationary pressures in the national economy. Properly managed, however, secret money flows can certainly lower the cost of credit to borrowers in recipient countries (including US Treasury borrowings) and aid in financing national budgetary deficits, development of infrastructure, as well as private capital formation – hence promoting economic growth.

At the same time, the secret money industry exports a group of financial services whose 'value-added' can itself promote national economic development, both directly and through a variety of linkage effects. Secrecy seekers who want to 'visit' their accounts have to buy airplane tickets, hotel rooms and restaurant meals and may want to take a short holiday in the process. The domestic financial services industry and related sectors may end up significantly larger with the secrecy business than without it, and exports of secrecy services may have multiplier effects that ripple through the national economy with favorable implications for income as well as employment.

So what is an economic and financial plague for some countries is a boon for others. Buyers are poorer and sellers are richer, as the economic consequences of secret money influence national, international and even global economic developments. Unfortunately, in order to quantify its effects one would have to run the world twice – once as it *is* and once as it *would have been* in the absence of secret money. Since this is obviously impossible to accomplish, and since reliable data on the actual secret money flows are virtually non-existent, all we can do is speculate that the economic impact of secret money is indeed rather significant.

Political effects

Beyond economics, secret money can have some important political effects as well. Again, these make themselves felt at both the national and international levels. Secret money may, for example, provide a certain degree of protection from political persecution. Throughout the ages, religious, racial or ethnic groups subjected to popular or government-instigated persecution have had limited options. They could wait it out (if they survived), or they could try to escape to safety abroad.

Political refugees are as much an international fact of life in the modern world as they have been in the past. Many are desperately poor, but others are relatively well-off, having been significant contributors to economic activity back home. The ability to shift funds to havens abroad provides some degree of solace for the victims of political persecution. The trauma of personal flight may be lessened by the availability of start-up capital to begin again somewhere else, and the knowledge that the assets are safe and secure may make political persecution at home a bit easier to bear. Although political refugees often turn out to be long-term economic assets for the host countries that ultimately receive the persecuted, the adjustment burdens are sometimes hard to carry, and may be alleviated by secret money squirreled away abroad before emigration becomes necessary.

However, political conditions do not have to become truly intolerable for secrecy seekers to spring into action, just the prospect of adverse political change may trigger a perceived need for secret money lodged abroad. Nor does political persecution in the conventional sense have to be involved. The mere possibility of political change may raise the specter of higher taxes, wage and price controls, or simply a worsening of the way the economy is managed. Or the imposition of exchange controls may appear to be in the offing, or the nationalization or expropriation of business and private assets, or perhaps the perceived threat of execution for 'profiteering' or 'economic crimes against the people', or re-education in the new political line.

All such prospective events have two characteristics. The first is the expected direction of change, its magnitude, and its prospective consequences. The second is the probability of various potential outcomes actually occurring. People who are risk-averse will react to both of these factors. Since some people are more risk-averse than others (and some are more optimistic or pessimistic than others), their responses to prospective political change will be highly individualized. But respond they will, and the politically triggered capital flight that results can be enormous – sometimes even sufficient to alter the nature of the political outcomes that caused them in the first place.

Whether the country is Argentina, Mexico, Israel, Italy, France, the Philippines or Hong Kong, political flight capital has periodically reached very large proportions indeed. And the knowledge that secret money abroad is a readily available option for some of their more affluent and productive citizens may dissuade politicians from going to extremes. Thus, secret money may actually serve as a source of political stability.

What about the political decision-makers themselves? The newspapers are rife with stories of bribers and bribees, with politicians prominently represented among those with open palms. In many parts of the world, bribery and corruption are a way of life. As noted in Chapter 3, in order to work, bribery requires financial secrecy. Big-time bribery, especially, is greatly facilitated by pots of secret money. Slush funds held abroad provide the wherewithal for the briber, the illicit transaction itself has to be kept secret permanently, and then the bribery proceeds themselves have to be stashed away. Secret money held abroad is clearly more valuable than domestic funds for both sides in the transaction, because it is harder to discover and trace.[3]

So it may well be that the very existence of international secret money promotes bribery and corruption around the world, with possibly serious adverse economic and political consequences – resources are misallocated, income is redistributed to those who haven't earned it, political processes are undermined, and so on. Perhaps more frequently than anyone cares to remember, coups d'état are staged to eject corrupt governments only to install a new management that in short order returns to business as usual. Memories of firing squads are apparently very short. And for those lucky enough to get away, the enjoyment of riches in the fun capitals of the world is tempered by the ever-present threat of sudden retribution by 'hit men' from home.

But is it really justified to blame secret money for the scale of bribery and corruption that appears to exist around the world? There would certainly be a good deal less illicit activity in its absence. But the underlying reasons for bribery and corruption must ultimately be found in government-imposed distortions of market mechanisms, gaps in morality and law enforcement, and imperfections in the political process itself.

Bribery is by definition illegal, but often is considered a 'victimless crime', overlooked by the authorities and the people at large until its consequences have become intolerable and the inevitable crackdown begins. Cleaning house must begin at home, and secret accounts abroad can be viewed more as a symptom than a cause. Countries where secret money is lodged consequently take a rather benign attitude toward the problem – secure in the knowledge that blame cannot rightfully be laid at their doorstep.

Then there is the matter of terrorism. In a world where one man's terrorist is indeed another man's freedom fighter, the use of secret money to support terrorism, insurgency and 'national liberation' movements internationally is probably beyond anyone's control. Again, in the absence of secret money the financing of terrorist movements, the procurement of weapons, and the training and transportation of terrorist cadres would be a great deal more difficult. But the ease of disguising international funds flows and the difficulty of assembling the kind of coordinated effort that is required to ferret out payments destined for terrorists probably means that secret money is a permanent feature of the global terrorist scene.

Finally, there is the issue of international political relations. We know that secret money is used to finance subversive movements, clandestine actions and other political involvements by one country in the affairs of others. It is part and parcel of the cloak and dagger world of international espionage and political intrigue. Occasionally, it can be used to ascertain what the 'other side' is up to, and once the cover is blown the political consequences of disclosure can be quite dramatic, often severely straining diplomatic relations.

We conclude that international financial secrecy plays an important role in the political equation at both the national and international levels. It permits politically sensitive activity of various kinds to go on that would be impossible in its absence. Yet it remains doubtful that secrecy

307

itself is in any sense a causative force in the political affairs in which it is intimately involved. It is a vehicle – a facilitator that makes things possible that would probably go on anyway, though perhaps to a lesser degree.

Social effects

As we have seen in previous chapters, secret money also has a bearing on social phenomena. Most obvious is criminal activity, although it may well be that a certain degree of sophistication has to be reached before international financial secrecy plays a role in fostering crime. Small-time criminals have little need for such services. But when running drugs or guns, where the criminal is sophisticated and the amounts involved can be enormous – and where the long arm of the law can be equally sophisticated – international financial secrecy may be a useful weapon in the criminal's arsenal. The volume of funds movements involved in money laundering, to the extent that guesses can be made, is as enormous as the channels are complex. Would the drugs trade grind to a halt in the absence of secret money laundries? Probably not but it could be restricted. Law enforcement agencies may well be able to proceed more effectively against the launderers than against the drugs runners themselves, simply because bankers are more concerned with the consequences of discovery and prosecution, are more risk-averse, and have more to lose than hardened criminals. If some of the money laundries are closed, the criminal element may be forced into increasingly narrow financial channels that are more costly, more risky, easier to monitor and possibly to choke off.

The importance of the drug problem as a source of secret money and a social cancer cannot be overstated. A variety of solutions have been suggested. In some quarters it has been proposed that drugs be legalized. It is argued that the price would drop dramatically with the elimination of the criminal-risk premium, which would in turn reduce the need of addicts to commit crime to fund their habit. But this runs the serious risk of increasing addiction and, because addicts tend to lack the means of support, the burden on the State. Others suggest that marijuana should be legalized so that users of soft drugs do not come inevitably into contact, as they do now, with more addictive drugs. Marijuana could perhaps be subject to the same age restrictions as alcohol, and even be taxed like cigarettes. It is estimated that in the US this would provide some $11 billion in revenue to be used on hard drug-enforcement and rehabilitation schemes. There would be the added advantage that marijuana is increasingly a homegrown product in the US which could remove it yet further from the elements dealing in hard drugs.

An interesting attempt along legalization lines has been made in this respect in the Netherlands, where since 1976 no prosecutions have been made against anyone holding less than 30 grams of marijuana. Since then, small quantities of the drug have been sold in coffee houses and a blind eye has been turned by the authorities provided the quantities remain small and no hard drugs are made available. There has been no surge in marijuana consumption and heroin addiction appears to have fallen, particularly among the young. In 1981, 14 per cent of heroin addicts were under 22; in 1988 the figure was 4.8 per cent.

Others take the view that even tougher enforcement is the answer. This was the basis of the Zero Tolerance policy, whereby even the smallest pinch of drugs would involve prosecution and seizure of property. It is also felt that more money should be spent on enforcement at street level. New York City officials claim to have made great progress with Operation Pressure Point, which focused manpower on the streets of the Lower East Side of Manhattan. Still others place emphasis on education and drug treatment.

International cooperation remains vital in the war against the drug barons. Until recently only limited cooperation had been forthcoming from the producer nations, who had simply blamed the sources of demand. More recently, however, they are discovering that their own populations are not immune. Colombia has some 500,000 regular cocaine addicts, probably more per capita than the US. Burma has at least 300,000 users of heroin and opium. Thailand has 150,000 heroin addicts. These nations appear to realize that they too must tackle the disease and this is likely to lead to greater international effort.[4]

In addition to drugs as a major social issue in many countries of the world, there is also the social problem of 'white-collar' crime, such as financial fraud or infractions of the securities laws like insider trading. Again, in many cases these need international financial secrecy to work, and for the criminal to escape from the jurisdiction of national law-enforcement authorities. Disclosure and prosecution, as we have seen, require a great deal of cooperation among countries, cooperation that is not always forthcoming.

Besides its link to crime, does international financial secrecy have any other major social consequences? One could argue that privacy and confidentiality are important attributes of any free society, and that privacy indeed can be regarded as an important 'right' in non-totalitarian states. Abrogation or infringement of this right may be viewed as a matter of grave importance for the character of the social order, yet we have seen that the execution of a variety of social functions, such as law enforcement and taxation, requires a certain abridgement of that right. The question is one of balance. Where do the social costs of secrecy begin to exceed the social benefits? Every society has to answer this question for itself, and the answers will differ widely between countries.

This is where international financial secrecy comes in, by allowing non-disclosure to continue that would be prohibited domestically. The 'optimum' degree of disclosure prevailing at home may thus be short-circuited. On the other hand, the actual degree of disclosure permitted may not in fact represent a social optimum, but rather one that is imposed on society by non-democratic means. In such cases, inter-national financial secrecy can actually move society toward an optimum level of financial disclosure. The question of social optima is an exceed-ingly difficult one, and weighing the social costs and benefits of international financial secrecy remains a rather thankless task.

All individual freedoms, of course, have come under attack in various places at various times throughout history. But it may well be true that financial privacy has been more thoroughly and permanently eroded than any of the others. As governments have grown to take successively larger shares of real income and output, the definition of 'abuse' of financial confidentiality has changed. It always was an abuse of financial confidentiality to employ it in the commission of a crime, and society has the right to defend itself against such behavior. The same has tradi-tionally been true of acts of treason and related political offenses aimed at the overthrow of the state or its defeat in time of war. But it has been the encroachment of the public sector on the allocation of resources in society, accompanied by higher tax burdens, that has probably led most dramatically to a redefinition of financial confidentiality. With it has come a commensurate erosion of individual freedom.

Personal effects

We have seen in Chapter 1 (and this will be formalized in economic theory in Annex 1) that individuals value secrecy, and that personal behavior reflects this fact, although the precise value people place on financial secrecy – and the reduced returns or increased risk they are willing to trade-off for it – is a highly personal matter. That is, the value of secret money will differ widely among individuals and over time. Secrecy is certainly critical to the drugs-runner, and without it he would be out of business. But it is marginally important to the middle-income, honest wage-earner who simply wants to keep his financial affairs to himself.

As noted, financial secrecy conveys a certain degree of freedom to the individual and, as such, it could be regarded as a fundamental human right and an important factor in determining the quality of life. Over the centuries this right has been abridged, often virtually supplanted by the supremacy of the state over the individual. Yet people try to hang on to whatever financial secrecy they are able to retain, and are willing to pay for it and sometimes take chances in order to obtain it. If it involves assets held abroad, they are willing to subject themselves to the rules of the game that exist abroad, even in expensive places like Switzerland and risky places like Panama.

They are also willing to put part of their wealth in the hands of agents, which raises principal–agent and moral hazard problems. Is the agent honest? Can he be trusted to carry out the principal's wishes with respect to asset deployment? Can he be trusted to keep his mouth and his ledgers shut? And what recourse is open to the secrecy seeker in the event of serious problems with the agent's execution of his fiduciary responsibilities? Legal redress may have to be sought in foreign courts of law, under foreign rules of the game, and always under threat of disclosure. If the penalty associated with disclosure is sufficiently severe, redress may be impossible to obtain, and this puts an enormous premium on the selection of the agent in the first place – and may be reflected in the price the agent can extract for his services. All this may still be very worthwhile if it retains for the individual his security, safety and mobility, asset values, and personal freedoms that would not otherwise exist.

Summary

We have broken down the effects of international financial secrecy into four more or less distinct but highly interrelated dimensions – economic, political, social and personal. Its implications for the national economy and international economic linkages can be very significant indeed, whether the frame of reference involves the actual level and growth of economic activity, the exchange rate and the balance of payments, or the distribution of income. The political implications are no less important, involving political stability, the integrity of governmental systems and structures, and the ability to carry out political goals at the national and international levels. Bribery and corruption, the abuse of drugs, and erosion of the fabric of society are some of the social dimensions of secret money, while at a personal level there are equally important consequences for the quality of life.

Would the world be better off without international financial secrecy? The issue is so complex that such a question is impossible to answer. Some people, some groups and some countries would clearly be better off, while others would sustain serious damage. And since there is no useful frame of reference for deciding whether the world as a whole would be better or worse off, the highest level on which this question can be addressed is the national state – and even then there are serious problems in reconciling the national interest with the interests of groups and individuals. It is probably best to be selective. Aggressive pursuit of money laundering connected with drugs-running may well lead to

311

improvements in social welfare, but this conclusion is far less clear-cut in the case of tax evasion or capital flight.

Secret money is the product of human nature. People lie. People cheat. People commit crimes. People are driven to protect what they regard as theirs. People elect or tolerate governments that foster political and economic adversity and uncertainty. People take advantage of the misery of others. A true international market for secret money is the inevitable result: a market that itself is appropriately cloaked in secrecy. While it may change form and substance over the years, human nature will insure that this market will continue to thrive.

Notes

1   Lenny Glynn and Peter Koenig, 'The Capital Flight Crisis', *Institutional Investor*, November 1984.
2   Ibid., p. 305.
3   See Thomas N. Gladwin and Ingo Walter, *Multinationals Under Fire* (New York: John Wiley, 1980), Chapter 5.
4   Andrew Kupfer, 'What to do About Drugs', *Fortune*, 20, June 1988.

12

The Outlook

How does the future of international financial secrecy look? Probably very positive. The industry will continue to survive and prosper. It will also change in the years ahead, as it has done in recent decades, with mostly gradual but sometimes abrupt shifts in the underlying demand and supply factors.

On the demand side, for example, only decriminalization of the production, trade and use of drugs will lead to an erosion of the associated secret money flows. Decriminalization did in fact occur in the United States with the lifting of prohibition of alcoholic beverages in 1933, as well as the legalization of off-track betting on horse racing in various localities and the introduction of state-sponsored lotteries in more recent times. Other countries have had similar experiences. But the socially debilitating effects of mind-altering substances like heroin, cocaine, Quaaludes, even marijuana, are unlikely to lead to widespread decriminalization in today's environment. Whereas such a measure would certainly reduce prices, expand consumption and eliminate the need for associated secret money flows, it would also produce an unknown series of social consequences. Some of these, such as under-cutting resources available to organized crime, are fairly certain and undoubtedly positive. Others, like the prospects for reduced vagrancy, muggings, burglaries and other individual criminal activities, as well as the loads they place on the criminal justice system, are much more debatable. Still others, such as the incidence of 'driving while under the influence', labor productivity, military preparedness, and the quality of life for those who refuse to indulge, are almost certainly adverse. And the experience of countries such as the Netherlands that have experimented with decriminalization hardly seems encouraging. So countries will remain highly risk-averse with respect to the issue of decriminalization of drugs, and indeed many have stepped up enforcement efforts, ranging from mandatory death penalties for possession in parts of Southeast Asia to the application of sophisticated military hardware in the war on drugs smuggling in North America.

All of this has implications for the secret money business. On the one hand, demand for secret money vehicles and the willingness to pay for them will remain strong and perhaps grow. On the other, in their war on those who deal in drugs, the authorities will increasingly target people, institutions and countries that handle secret money, forcing greater innovation, greater complexity, and higher costs. They doubtless will achieve some successes, perhaps even some dramatic ones, but as long as the underlying economic motivations exist they will never entirely succeed. People are too ingenious, too quick, too greedy. Difficult as it is to observe this war dispassionately, without cheering for the good guys and booing the social parasites, its collateral damage to financial confidentiality could be substantial as the authorities strip away legal safeguards for ordinary people in their pursuit of culprits.

True criminal demand for secret money in other dimensions will be equally durable in the years ahead. Prostitution, protection, labor racketeering, larceny, fraud, auto theft and the like will continue to be blemishes on the fabric of society, as they have been in the past. All will continue to require secret money. Nobody in these businesses will file tax returns, even if for some reason they feel so moved. The money will stay underground, and through various organizational layers will often find its way from the 'retail' level to the 'wholesale' level of organized crime. This is where international financial secrecy comes in. Again, with a few exceptions (perhaps 'victimless crimes' like prostitution and illegal gambling) decriminalization is out of the question. So the demand for secrecy will remain intact, and again will ebb and flow with the intensity of criminal activities and the exertions of law enforcement authorities motivated by political pressure based on public outrage.

For example, in the wake of the Bank of Boston revelations (discussed in Chapter 5), a coordinated approach to bank fraud was initiated by federal law enforcement and banking regulators in the United States during April 1985. Investigative procedures were altered; uniform enforcement guidelines were adopted; training programs were stepped up, and government-wide sharing of information was initiated, all supported by senior regulatory and enforcement officials including the Attorney General, the FBI, the Federal Reserve Board, the Federal Home Loan Bank Board, and the Controller of the Currency, among others. According to a US House of Representatives report, 'criminal activity by bankers has been a major factor in US bank failures ... Losses to the two major federal deposit insurance funds because of failures linked to fraud were estimated to be more than $1 billion [in 1984].'[1]

Significantly, a major proposal contained in this initiative involved legislative and regulatory changes in US financial privacy laws in order to permit banking authorities to provide prosecutors more easily with confidential information. A side-effect of this initiative against financial secrecy aimed at criminal activities may thus be an erosion of financial confidentiality for ordinary citizens.

With respect to such patently criminal uses of international financial secrecy, one is on relatively safe ground. One can predict that robust demand will continue because the underlying incentives will remain intact, but that the shape and structure of that demand will shift as countries alter the legal and judicial framework and the mechanics of law enforcement. Things get a bit more fuzzy once one moves beyond the realm of unambiguous criminality.

Take the politically motivated demand for secret money involving terrorism, insurgency, illegal political contributions and government-sponsored covert activities. Again, there is no evidence that demand emanating from such sources is ebbing, although periodic crackdowns, domestic political scandals, and restoration of political tranquility in one country or another may change the location and nature of that demand. But the criminal nature of the associated secret money flows is rather ambiguous. Authorities in Luxembourg may be legitimately unconcerned about financial transactions that ultimately are used in support of a particular political party in Algeria despite violations of local laws. Authorities in Switzerland may legitimately feel it is none of their business when funds are routed through local financial institutions in support of technology acquisitions in the United States by operatives acting on behalf of Albania.

So, while crackdowns on secret money flows associated with activities that are unambiguously criminal in nature can expect at least some degree of international cooperation and even coordination, flows related to politically motivated activities cannot. Coordination will continue to have a spotty record at best, and even cooperation and comity among national authorities will (perhaps legitimately) continue to be extraordinarily difficult to achieve. It certainly does not help matters when a government seeks international assistance regarding one type of politically driven flow of secret money, while at the same time initiating, aiding or abetting others. Since political needs for secret money are accompanied by the willingness to pay for them, middlemen quickly emerge and the economic incentive structure falls into place. Unless one is able to predict the dawning of a golden age of domestic and international political tranquility, this source of demand for secret money will continue to be a vibrant one indeed.

Things get even more difficult in prognostications about the use of secret money for purposes like insider trading in the securities markets, smuggling, evasion of exchange controls and taxation.

As discussed in Chapter 3, there is a great deal of controversy about the justification for barriers to insider trading, in terms of their economic and social consequences. Improved information flows should limit opportunities for insider trading, but again will never entirely eliminate them. Political concerns about the inherent fairness of capital markets to all participants will keep markets heavily policed. Perhaps, over time, the two forces together will gradually erode this particular demand for secret money even as the global integration of financial markets enhances the potential significance of this issue. The fact that most financial centers around the world have a vested interest in continued access to all of the world's premier financial markets makes cooperation and coordination all the more likely.

Smuggling and evasion of exchange controls are always the products of market distortions. Trade barriers to protect domestic industry, price controls and unrealistic exchange rates invariably create incentives to evade. There are risks to be taken and money to be made, often staggering amounts, which must subsequently be hidden, preferably abroad. There is some evidence that governments are increasingly convinced of the futility of some of these distortions in terms of their long-range damage to the process of national economic growth. Observed differences in economic performance between countries that have piled on distortions and those that have followed relatively free-market principles have begun to sink in.

The financial difficulties of many countries in the early 1980s have provoked serious thinking about the efficacy of trade and financial distortions, sometimes promoted from the outside by institutions like the International Monetary Fund. It may be that we have entered a period of liberalization of market mechanisms, and with the erosion and dismantling of distortions will come a reduction in this particular source of the demand for secret money. Still, political decisions will continue to dominate market decisions in many cases, and so the incentive to evade and the role of secret money in making evasion possible will hardly disappear. Nor will international coordination and cooperation in combating this type of secret money flow get very far, in some cases perhaps fortunately so from the standpoint of global market efficiency and economic development.

Things get even more difficult with respect to tax evasion, certainly the largest single factor underlying the demand for international financial secrecy. It is easy to predict that secret money demand from this source will remain strong, as governments continue to lay claim to large shares of national income and output and are forced to raise the necessary financial resources in various ways that are more or less easily subject to evasion. Certainly the need to fund defense, infrastructure and social programs will continue to put pressure on fiscal resources, but the size and shape of that pressure will surely continue to change over time.

On the one hand, there has been a powerful movement around the world to reassess the efficacy and efficiency of government expenditure and the claims of various interest groups on the public purse. The need

316

for the public sector to live within its means is increasingly recognized politically, painful as it may be, particularly given the inflationary impact of debt monetization (as an alternative to taxation) on national economic performance. This has placed limits on spending and upward pressure on taxation. It has also run up against equally widespread recognition of the damage that can be done by excessive taxation, which has triggered an effort in many countries to ease tax burdens in order to stimulate economic incentives to work, invest and innovate. The result is an energetic search for public-sector economies, including greater efficiency in the provision of government services, more careful defense procurement, denationalization of government-owned enterprises and the like.

Unfortunately, the restoration of sensible public policies in the tax area is exceedingly difficult. There are too many vested interests built into the existing arrangements, and taxes are too tempting as a tool of social tinkering for politicians. Yet only major tax reform can begin to attack the incentives to evade, and there always remains the question whether tax morality, once lost, can ever be completely restored.

So, in the United States as in other countries, the demand for financial secrecy arising from tax evasion seems destined to continue unabated. The same goes for the underground economy, which itself is driven in part by tax evasion. This includes an enormous volume of cash transactions ranging from skimming of profits by owners of small businesses, to workers engaging in services transactions 'off the books', profits of street vendors, and the like.

To the extent that a commitment to fiscal responsibility can be coupled with a reasonable balance between the claims of the private and public sectors on economic resources, growth of the tax-evasion demand for secret money nevertheless may be eased somewhat. But since there will always be at least *some* incentive to evade taxes, and since countries will differ vastly in terms of the level, structure and incidence of taxation, that demand will persist. Again, not much can be expected in terms of an effectively coordinated attack on tax evasion. Countries differ too much in terms of their perceptions of tax issues. And many are genuinely scornful of what they regard as other countries' dysfunctional tax systems. So the most important single demand for international financial secrecy may enjoy a rosy future.

It is possible, of course, that the increasing integration of financial markets and increasing concerns about political risk will change the nature of secret money flows related to tax evasion. We know from Chapter 6 that the tax-motivated secrecy seeker (or any secrecy seeker, for that matter) is always interested in three things – secrecy, return and risk – and that he is caught in a constant balancing game among these three considerations. Assets held in the United States may be viewed very favorably with respect to returns and risk, but flawed with respect to secrecy. Assets held in Panama may look good from a secrecy and return point of view, yet may be quite risky. Of course, different elements can be put together in order to obtain more of all three elements – assets placed with a good US or British bank in Nassau, for example. But it may be that secrecy seekers' concerns with the rapidly growing flow of financial information and the increasing need to trade actively in volatile financial markets, and increasing worries about political risks, will encourage even the most fleet-footed among tax evaders to establish a tax home in a respectable country and pay at least some taxes. Secrecy seekers, too, need allies, and a legitimate tax home is one way of obtaining them. By paying this price, it should be possible to operate essentially in the open and take advantage of market opportunities as well as assets held in politically secure locations. Individuals may well find that they are much better off. If this realization takes hold, some of the tax-linked demand for secret money may ease, although certainly not for US citizens, who are fully subject to all US taxes (except for an exempt amount) no matter where in the world they establish tax residence. Yet even they get value for money – after all, how many people actually renounce their US citizenship in order legally to escape US taxation?

Things are even more complex with regard to demand for secrecy driven by capital flight. People's expectations and uncertainties about future political or economic conditions, which give rise to flight capital, will continue to emerge from time to time. There is little to suggest that either the political or the economic management of countries will systematically improve or stabilize on a world scale in the years ahead, and so spurts of secret money will continue to flow. More so than even in the case of tax evasion, efforts by countries to stanch those flows will meet with little cooperation abroad, even in anti-secrecy bastions such as the United States.

In short, the things that drive the demand for secret money today will prevail in the years ahead. Some will weaken, while others will strengthen from time to time as the underlying forces change and as government action narrows some options and forces secrecy seekers to use others.

Similar currents will affect the future of secret money on the supply side. The players will be as heterogeneous as the secrecy seekers are complex in their motivations. As we have seen in Chapter 4, individuals, institutions and countries have found that it pays to sell secrecy-oriented products. For individuals and institutions there is money to be made and market niches to be exploited. Crooks will always have their bankers in a rough and furtive game of mutual exploitation against the ever-present backdrop of legally and morally reprehensible behavior; so will tax evaders and those on the run from political and economic adversity around the world.

To serve the needs of capital fleeing from foreign taxation and political instability, up-market institutions around the world will continue to stand ready – usually without moral or ethical burdens to worry about – to serve their needs alongside businesses and individuals who have no need for secrecy. Competition among these institutions is as severe as the potential profits are high, and the players are continually confronted with the need to distinguish between those secrecy seekers whom they wish to attract and those they must avoid like the plague. As the Deak & Co. case discussed in Chapter 5 shows, errors in judgment or wilful misconduct can be exceedingly costly for the institution, and perhaps 'terminal' for the managers involved. Little can be worse for an institution than to be under investigation for involvement with crooks. Ordinary, morally outraged clients will turn to the competition for a cleaner environment, while other secrecy seekers will head for the hills in a scramble to avoid the chance that the spotlight will accidentally fall on their affairs as well. Once contaminated in this way, it seems doubtful that an institution can regain its previous position within any reasonable time-frame.

Indeed, one can argue that this rather severe sanction of the market-place is sufficiently strong to make sure that the major financial institutions that sell financial secrecy remain relatively free of crooked money – with 'crookedness' being defined legally and politically in their home countries and in the host countries in which they operate. Of course, errors do occur, but employees involved in such errors can expect to find themselves in the job market almost immediately.

Down-market institutions and individuals have less to lose and more to gain from contaminated money, so that the niches they seek may be a good deal less scrupulous. Some are smaller financial institutions caught in a web of severe competition with the majors, who feel driven toward more risky business, are poorly managed, or are owned and controlled by investors who are not particularly risk-averse. And some are individual lawyers, accountants and financial advisers who are happy to make hay while the sun shines and then run for cover when foul weather strikes. They are happy to catch whatever funds abandon the up-market institutions. The hapless secrecy seeker, meanwhile, finds that costs and risks alike rise dramatically as he moves successively down-market.

The heterogeneous structure of market supply facing the secrecy seeker will prevail, both within and between countries. Like the auto-mobile market with its Subarus, Nissans, Chevrolets, Buicks, Volvos, BMWs, Jaguars, Mercedes-Benzes and Rolls-Royces, there are different products for different needs. Competition is severe, and the choice is sufficiently wide that an appropriate product selection can usually be made.

We have seen that individuals and firms are not the only secrecy vendors. Countries are too. Their gain comes from the industry itself as well as from linkages to other sectors in the form of jobs, incomes, growth, and foreign exchange earnings. Their role as suppliers of secrecy services is doubly important, because they set the legal and regulatory structures within which the direct vendors of secret money operate and compete with each other. They too face costs and risks, ranging from increased international tension and imported criminal elements and corruption that may accompany the acceptance of tainted funds, to the financial shocks that accompany abrupt runoffs of internationally mobile funds. But for some, especially small, underdeveloped countries with few other resources the potential benefits even of operating close to (or beyond) the edge will often outweigh the risks.

Individuals, institutions and countries will thus continue to stand ready to supply a rich variety of secrecy services into the foreseeable future. Just as secrecy seekers are prepared to pay, the vendors are prepared to profit, and they will.

What can we conclude? On an economic plane it seems clear that international financial secrecy is indeed an important phenomenon that can be and should be examined, interpreted and evaluated in a rational way and that has wide-ranging effects on the performance and structure of national economies as well as the international economy as a whole. It can also have profound effects on the formation and execution of economic and financial policies, and the information on which they are based. Economics permits a relatively value-free examination of these effects, including the external benefits and costs that lie beyond the secrecy business itself.

It is when we move beyond economics into the realm of politics and social values that things become far more complex. The signals are not nearly as clear. There are virtually no absolutes, even with regard to what many regard as blatantly criminal use of secret money. Nor are the social and political costs and benefits easily identifiable or measurable. Consequently, the public policies that emerge are often confused, ambiguous and ineffectual. They will undoubtedly remain so, ensuring lasting prosperity for the secret money industry around the world.

So the international market for financial secrecy promises to continue to thrive, each segment with its own structure of demand, supply and competitive performance. Its costs and benefits form an enormously complex web. But would the world really be better off in its absence? Would governments not be subject to even fewer checks and balances than they already are? As with much of international financial secrecy, the answers to such questions remain shrouded in mystery.

Note

1 Andy Pasztor and Leon E. Wynter, 'US Set War on Bank-Industry Fraud', *Wall Street Journal*, 2 April 1975.

Annex 1

Theory of International Financial Secrecy

The core chapters of this book have attempted to describe, to the extent possible, the phenomenon of international financial secrecy based on bits and pieces of available evidence. The approach has basically been an economic one, presupposing that financial non-disclosure is something that has value and that can be bought and sold. This approach suggests that it ought to be possible to develop a reasonably coherent conceptual framework using conventional tools of economics, which can then be applied to an analysis of observed secrecy phenomena and to predict their causes, course and consequences. This framework can be constructed from models of secrecy-oriented behavior that make it easier to explain what is really going on and perhaps to reach reasoned, defensible judgments about the probable behavior of people and institutions under a wide variety of circumstances.

Economists are fond of developing more or less elegant models of human behavior, intended both to interpret observed events and to suggest the probable course of future change. These models are invariably simplifications, based on assumptions that keep things within reasonable limits of complexity but that can later be relaxed in order to move closer to the real world. They require a focus that is confined to the framework specified, often involving the analysis of a single market but sometimes extending to the behavior of entire economies. Used judiciously, models of economic behavior can be quite instructive in coming to grips with observations that may otherwise be extraordinarily difficult to interpret.

This Annex attempts to lay out such a model by examining the tradeoffs that exist between secrecy, risks and returns, the determinants of the real value of secret money, and the characteristics of markets for financial secrecy.

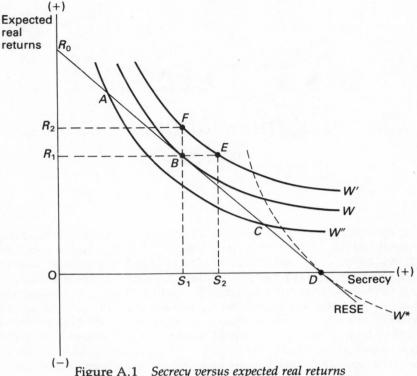

Figure A.1   *Secrecy versus expected real returns*

Secrecy versus expected returns

Secrecy is rarely 'free'. It must be purchased by an individual intent on non-disclosure by putting together a portfolio of assets (or a single asset) that yields the desired level of confidentiality. One 'cost' of secrecy to the individual is thus the difference between the expected yield on his secrecy-oriented portfolio and the yield on a 'benchmark portfolio' put together by the same individual when secrecy is not a consideration. The tradeoff involved is depicted in Figure A.1.

A portfolio of assets that contains no secrecy has an expected market return of R_0 in Figure A.1. This could be a composite of interest or dividend returns, rents and royalties, expected capital gains, and the like, all in real terms. As the secrecy consideration mounts, it is probable that the expected return on successive portfolios displaced from the completely 'open' mix of assets will decline – possibly to zero and perhaps even to negative real values – along line *RESE*, the return/ secrecy relationship depicted in Figure A.1. That relationship may not, of course, be linear. In addition it may not be stable as different secrecy vehicles shift in terms of expected real returns.

322

The preference for expected yield compared to the level of secrecy for an individual is given by the shape of welfare contours W in Figure A.1. Their shape indicates a diminishing marginal rate of substitution of portfolio returns for secrecy. When the secrecy content of the asset portfolio is already very high, for example, the individual would want to add still more secrecy only if the 'price' in terms of further erosion of expected real returns is rather low. As the degree of secrecy *and* expected returns increase from W'' to W to W', the individual is successively better off. The optimum mix of expected yield and secrecy is point B (R_1 and S_1) in Figure A.1. Combinations A (high expected yield, low secrecy) and C (low expected yield, high secrecy) are both inferior because they lie on curve W'', which is lower than W. Similarly, points such as F (S_1 and R_2) as well as E (R_1 and S_2) cannot be attained with the available secrecy-bearing assets, even though curve W' represents a level of welfare that is superior to W.

The optimum level of secrecy the individual would want to purchase is S_1, with an expected real return on the portfolio of assets held being R_1, and a 'cost' of secrecy equal to $R_1 - R_0$. This cost would then have to be balanced against the benefits of secrecy (the probability and disutility of disclosure), which are imbedded in the position and shape of the welfare contours W. For example, if the cost of disclosure in Figure A.1 rises (perhaps, because of increased competitive disadvantages attributable to disclosure), the welfare contours shift to the right perhaps to W^*. As a result, the desired amount of secrecy purchases rises substantially, expected yield in this example drops to zero and the 'cost' of secrecy increases to $0 - R_0$. The cost could, of course, increase still further if the expected real returns on the assets held became negative, as when currency is buried in the ground during a period of inflation, or if intermediaries charge heavily for their services.

Secrecy versus risk

Besides the cost of secrecy imbedded in the expected real returns on assets, there is also the matter of risk. It seems likely that portfolios of assets containing greater degrees of financial secrecy are also more risky. For example, assets may have to be held abroad, resulting in foreign exchange risk and country risk. Or they may be forced into configurations that are susceptible to increased interest-rate risk. Various ways of hedging risk, including the ability to diversify portfolios and shift risk by means of futures and options markets, may not be available to the secrecy seeker. One could argue that the degree of risk (defined in terms of the covariance of expected future returns on the assets contained in the portfolio) tends to increase with the secrecy content of the portfolio. Again, we have a tradeoff line such as SERI in

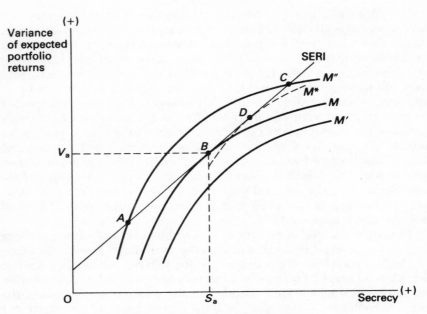

Figure A.2 *Secrecy versus risk*

Figure A.2. As it is drawn, the figure suggests there is some degree of risk associated with *any* conceivable portfolio of assets, no matter how well hedged or diversified – that is, SERI cuts the vertical axis somewhere above zero. As secrecy requirements increase, which in turn may limit asset selection, availability of hedging vehicles, etc., the risk tends to increase as well.

The position and shape of SERI, whether linear or not, can be argued at length. For example, it may be that at very high levels of secrecy the asset-holder is forced into a tightly restricted portfolio selection (perhaps a single type of asset in a single location), and the SERI curve at those secrecy levels may well become increasingly steep.

In conjunction with the tradeoff between the degree of risk embodied in asset portfolios and their built-in level of secrecy, there is an interplay between the preference for risk and the preference for secrecy on the part of the asset-holder. If we assume such individuals are normally risk-averse, then they tend to prefer portfolios that incorporate lower rather than higher covariances in expected future real asset returns, all else equal, although, of course, the attitude towards risk may differ enormously among individuals. Similarly, the assumption of a positive value on secrecy results in welfare contours such as M in Figure A.2. The shape of M indicates how much additional risk the individual is willing to accept in return for additional financial secrecy, yet still be equally well off. The shape of M in Figure A.2 implies that the tolerance for increased risk decreases once very high secrecy levels have already been attained and, conversely, that very substantial reductions in risk would be necessary to induce acceptance of lower financial secrecy once these are already at minimum levels, all under the presumption that the individual is no better and no worse off than before.

If the market makes available a risk/secrecy tradeoff depicted by SERI in Figure A.2 and the individual's risk/secrecy preferences are given by the shape of M, a level of risk indicated by a covariance in expected returns V_a would be accepted in return for level S_a of secrecy. A lower level of risk *and* secrecy, such as A, or a higher level of both (C) would be worse in view of the individual's preferences – it would leave him on welfare level M'', which is clearly inferior to M. In much the same way, while the individual would be better off with risk level V_a *and* greater secrecy than S_a, or with secrecy level S_a *and* lower risk than V_a (for example, a move onto M', which is superior to M), he cannot achieve either one, given the tradeoffs available in the market.

If the individual's desire for secrecy increases, it is logical that he would be willing to take on an increased degree of risk. This might be represented by the new family of preference contours M^* in Figure A.2, which induce the individual to seek greater secrecy *and* accept greater risk at a point such as D.

Risk versus returns with secrecy

Conventional views on the creation of 'efficient' portfolios do not take financial secrecy considerations into account. But they can easily be made to accommodate them. An efficient portfolio is one that maximizes investor returns, subject to a risk constraint, or minimizes risk given a particular target return. Both the individual's attitude toward risk, or risk preference, and the measurement of risks and returns available in asset markets are important elements in the design of efficient portfolios.

Consider Figure A.3, where the horizontal axis measures the expected real return on a portfolio of assets, and the vertical axis measures the covariance of those returns. RR is the risk/return relationship provided by the market. Even at zero risk, there will be some positive return. As the risk rises, so does the expected return. The individual's risk/return preferences are indicated by a family of welfare contours such as N. The way they are drawn assumes the individual is normally risk-averse – that is, he will accept more risk only if he expects to receive a higher return in order not to sacrifice in terms of welfare. More risk with a given expected return means reduced welfare (a move from N to N'' for example). So does a lower expected return with a given level of risk.

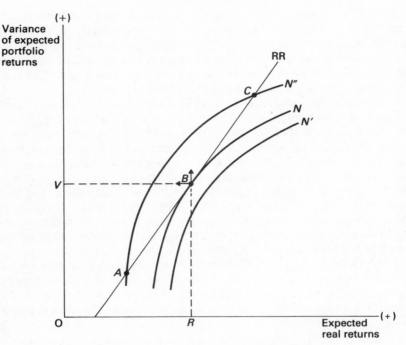

Figure A.3 *Secrecy and the efficient portfolio*

An individual will maximize his welfare with an asset portfolio such as *B*, with a risk level of *V* and a return of *R*. A portfolio characterized by higher expected returns *and* higher risk, such as *C*, would leave the individual on a lower level of welfare *N''*. So would a portfolio that combined a lower level of risk and lower expected returns, such as *A*. The individual would, of course, be better off (*N'*) if he could obtain higher expected returns with a given level of risk, or obtain a lower risk level with given expected real returns. Unfortunately, the market's risk/return tradeoff given by RR in Figure A.3 precludes that.

Now what happens when we incorporate an individual's desire for financial secrecy? From the earlier discussion, he should be willing to accept a reduced rate of return and/or be willing to expose himself to a higher level of risk. Here, it would tend to displace the efficient portfolio represented by point *B* in the direction of the arrows. That is, the individual will have to make do either with a reduced expected return or increased risk, or both. And so, from a risk/return perspective, he will be worse off and the level of welfare attained may shift from *N* to, say *N''*. Does this mean he is really worse off in terms of his total welfare? Certainly not, because the welfare gains from the enhanced secrecy may well outweigh the welfare losses in the risk/return dimension.

An overall view

We now have three different dimensions under discussion – risk, return and secrecy. Between any two of these dimensions, there are clearly tradeoffs presented by the markets for various types of assets – between risk and returns, between returns and secrecy, and between secrecy and risk – as discussed in the preceding sections. At the same time, we have seen that there are tradeoffs between each *pair* of objectives as perceived by the individual asset-holder. In each case, an optimum combination can be defined once the individual's preferences and the market's tradeoffs are known – one that optimizes the individual's welfare under the constraints imposed by the market.

The basic model can be depicted quite neatly in Figure A.4. For convenience, we invert the horizontal 'risk' axis to represent 'safety', with a minimum-risk portfolio represented by point *A* on the axis, and asset covariance rising (safety declining) as one moves to the left on the horizontal scale. We know that asset markets present the individual with a risk/return tradeoff, here line *AC*, showing returns rising with increasing risk, or decreasing safety. We also believe that these markets present a returns/confidentiality tradeoff, here shown as line *CB*, with *C* being the maximum attainable real portfolio returns when confidentiality plays no role whatsoever, and returns declining with increased confidentiality, perhaps eventually resulting in negative net returns to the left of *B*. Finally, we posit a confidentiality/risk tradeoff, under the assumption that the acquisition of greater confidentiality forces the individual into a more risky selection of assets or closes off options for portfolio diversification or risk-shifting. This tradeoff is shown by line *AB* in Figure A.4 – increased confidentiality may have to be 'purchased' by asset portfolios that embody a reduced degree of safety.

If we assume that all three market-determined tradeoffs are linear, we can thus define the plane *ABC* in the three-dimensional space in Figure A.4. The individual involved in capital flight can choose any asset mix yielding a combination of safety, returns and confidentiality that lies on the *ABC* plane. For example, if confidentiality plays no role whatsoever in the individual's objectives, he will want to operate along line *AC* at the 'back edge'of the plane. Similarly, if returns are an immaterial consideration compared with safety and confidentiality, he will want to operate along the *AB* 'edge' of the plane. If all three considerations are to be taken into account, he will want to position himself somewhere on the inside of the *ABC* plane.

The precise 'mix' of the three attributes will be determined by the individual's relative preferences. We can depict the preference for safety versus returns by the shape of a contour (the shaded area in Figure A.4) which in the risk/return plane shows that the individual is willing to accept reduced safety for increased returns, but at a decreasing rate –

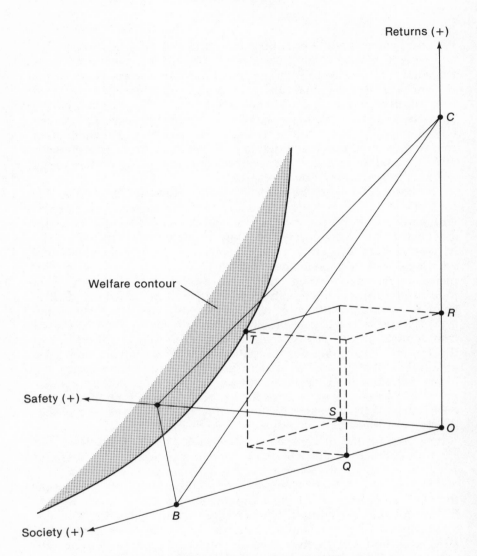

Figure A.4 *Balancing risks, returns, and secrecy*

that is, the individual is normally risk-averse. Similarly, the individual is
willing to trade lower returns for increased confidentiality along the
shaded contour in the secrecy/return plane, again at a decreasing rate.
And he is likewise willing to trade lower levels of safety for higher levels
of confidentiality along the shaded contour in the safety/secrecy plane.
The shape of the three-dimensional contour itself depends on the

328

marginal rates of substitution with the individual's preference set between each pair of objectives. The better any two objectives substitute for one another, the more 'flatter' the contour. The less they are regarded by the individual as substitutes, the more 'convex' the contour will be to the origin at point 0.

We thus have in the shaded area in Figure A.4 a convex 'preference surface' among the three objectives that defines the nature of an individual's relative preferences at a given level of welfare. If the surface lies 'higher' – farther away from the origin – he will obviously be better off by being able to avail himself of more confidentiality *and* safety *and* returns. Conversely, a 'lower' preference surface represents a lower level of personal welfare.

We can now complete the picture by combining the individual's confidentiality/safety/returns preference contour and the market's 'supply' pattern defined by the *ABC* plane. Given the tradeoffs dictated by the market, the individual in this example will want to obtain a level Q of confidentiality, which requires a portfolio of assets yielding S of safety and earns R of net real returns – at point T in Figure A.4, where the demand surface is just tangent to the plane representing the opportunity set. At this point the individual will maximize his welfare, given the alternatives available in the market. Of course, he could also operate with any other mix of confidentiality/safety/returns defined by the *ABC* plane. But any such mix would leave him worse off – i.e., on a *lower* preference contour – and consequently would make no sense. Nor could he reach a higher preference contour under existing market conditions. Point T thus represents the optimum attainable level of welfare.

How can the individual become better off and move to a higher preference contour? One way is for the market to throw off higher returns, as when global credit conditions tighten – point C is moved upward. Another is for the cost of confidentiality to decline, as when there is increased competition among vendors of assets embodying confidentiality – point B moves to the southwest. If new, less risky types of assets become available, or greater opportunities for diversification or risk-shifting present themselves, point A moves to the left. Any of these developments will raise the *ABC* plane and permit an increase in the individual's level of welfare – a move to a higher preference contour. Unless all three increase proportionately, however, the *shape* of the *ABC* plane will change as well, and hence the *mix* of safety, returns and confidentiality will likewise be altered (the relative location of point T). Conversely, factors affecting reduced yields, confidentiality, and port-folio safety will leave the individual worse off, on a lower welfare contour.

Now suppose the *ABC* plane remains unchanged, but the individual's preferences shift. For example, if the asset-holder's government lifts capital controls or grants an amnesty, he may no longer need the same degree of confidentiality. He would therefore operate at the tangency of AC and the preference contour, with point T moving onto line AC – he would end up better off in the risk/return dimension. If, on the other hand, the perceived benefits from confidentiality increase, point T would move to reflect a preference contour that is more 'biased' in that direction than before. Similar changes in the mix would reflect an alteration in the relative preference for safety versus returns.

The acquisition of external assets in the presence of confidentiality, on the part of individuals engaging in capital flight, can thus be thought of as a rational process – one that balances a number of perceived costs against benefits and in which perceived changes are likely to change behavior in rather predictable ways. If we assume that these asset-holders are normally risk-averse, they will tend to prefer portfolios incorporating greater confidentiality together with lower variances in expected future total returns, all else equal. That is, they will prefer a rather conservative portfolio, both because of the reduced probability of disclosure and because they may be heavily and differentially exposed to risk at home.

Marginal costs and benefits

The discussion can be joined by using a cost-benefit framework – always keeping in mind that costs and benefits to the individual need somehow to be established, especially in an incremental sense, for the development of reasonably robust conclusions. In Figure A.5, the vertical axis is intended to measure the incremental cost and benefit associated with the acquisition of one additional unit of financial secrecy, measured along the horizontal axis.

If the marginal benefits associated with acquisition of various levels of financial secrecy are as depicted by curve MB in Figure A.5, then increased secrecy throws off successively lower marginal benefits. We know from Chapter 3 that the MB curve has imbedded in it a set of motives driving the individual's preferences – whether they are related to normal business or financial confidentiality, prospective divorce proceedings, tax or exchange-control evasion, bribery and corruption, or conventional criminal activities ranging from drugs trafficking to securities fraud. These motives will determine both the shape and the position of the MB curve. As we have also discussed earlier, the incremental acquisition of financial secrecy entails incremental costs, either in the form of reduced real expected returns on assets or increased portfolio risk. This is shown in the position and shape of the MC curve in Figure A.5, and is the result of factors prevailing in the market for secrecy that faces the individual concerned – a market that may itself be

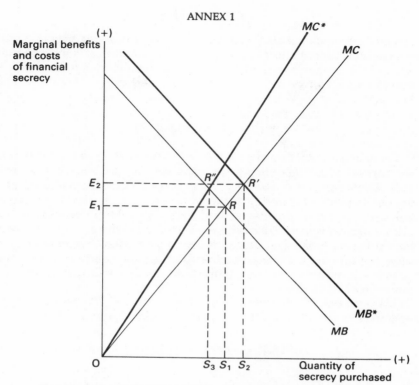

Figure A.5 *Cost–benefit analysis applied to financial secrecy*

highly segmented. The optimum amount of secrecy acquired will be S_1, associated with a marginal cost and benefit level of E_1. Given MB and MC, levels of secrecy lower than S_1 meant that the incremental benefits of increased purchases would exceed the incremental costs, and more should be acquired, while levels in excess of S_1 represent an excessive acquisition of financial secrecy under existing cost–benefit conditions.

Clearly, a shift in benefit or cost factors will alter the behavior of the individual. Increases in tax rates, in political instability or in personal security concerns, for example, will cause a shift in MB to the right – perhaps to MB^*. The individual would then be willing to pay more for the existing level of secrecy, and to acquire more (S_2 in Figure A.5), at a marginal cost of E_2. Similarly, a change in market conditions might increase the marginal cost (MC^*) of secrecy. This might be attributable to government measures to crack down on domestic secrecy vendors, institute tighter exchange controls, reach agreements with foreign governments on access to offshore financial records, and the like – thus forcing the individual into higher-cost vehicles or into vehicles that expose him to greater risk. With unchanged marginal benefits, therefore, he could be expected to acquire less financial secrecy (S_3).

331

The acquisition of financial secrecy can thus be thought of as a rational process, one that balances costs against benefits and in which a change perceived in either one is likely to change behavior of individuals in rather predictable ways.

Value of secret assets

How much are secret assets really worth? As the foregoing discussion has implied, it all depends on the risks and net returns, benefits and costs. The value of any asset depends in part on the returns the asset is expected to generate during future time periods, the costs associated with bringing in those returns, and their variability in relation to the returns variability associated with the market as a whole, as a measure of risk. In the case of secret assets, it also depends on the probability of being found out, the penalties that may be imposed, and the individual's attitude toward risk (both asset-related risk and discovery/ punishment risk).

This can be stated very simply as follows, where NPV_t represents the net present value of a secret asset portfolio to the individual:

$$NPV = \sum_{t=0}^{n} \frac{[ER_t - EC_t]\,[1 - P_t\,a_t^{\cdot}]}{(1 + i^t + B_t)^t} \quad \begin{array}{l} -\infty \leqslant P_t + \leqslant 1 \\ 0 \leqslant_t^{\cdot} \leqslant 1 \end{array}$$

ER_t represents the expected return flows on the assets concerned. Earnings may be zero in the case of domestic currency or demand balances, or positive in the case of interest-bearing assets or equities expected to pay dividends or undergo capital appreciation. Expected returns on assets denominated in foreign currencies, gold, other precious metals and collectables also depend on changing market values anticipated for the future. All values include expectations regarding the return of principal.

EC_t represents the expected costs associated with holding the assets. These might include warehousing and insurance costs (as in the case of gold or other valuables), payments to third parties (e.g. trustees), possible costs of legal or enforcement actions, etc. Consequently, $(ER_t - EC_t)$ represents the *net* expected returns on a portfolio of assets over successive future time periods.

Of course, virtually all assets are subject to certain risks. There are exchange-rate risks, transfer risks, default risks, market risks, and risks of theft. Therefore, the net expected returns have to be discounted appropriately. In the equation above, i^* represents the risk-free rate of return – for a US citizen that might be represented by the Treasury bill rate. Clearly, if i^* rises, the net present value of other assets (e.g.

fixed-rate loans and gold) will tend to decline as reflected either in market prices or in opportunity costs. This loss may be limited if the assets held throw off returns that move in tandem with the risk-free rate, such as floating-rate financial instruments.

The term B_t, represents the risk associated with the assets held. If only one asset is held, that risk is driven by the variability of the expected future net returns on that asset in relation to the variability of all assets in the market. The higher the variability, and the more risk-averse the individual, the larger will be the value of B_t and the lower the net present value of the secret asset to the individual. If a diversified portfolio of assets is held, B_t is affected by the covariance among different assets in the portfolio, in addition to market variability and the attitude of the individual towards risk. The more risky the portfolio of assets, and the more risk-averse the asset-holder, the lower will be the value of those future streams of expected net returns to the individual.

However, risk-adjusted net returns are only part of the story if secrecy is a motivation. It is also important to look at. P_t, which represents the disutility (or pain) of punishment that would befall the secrecy seeker should he get caught. The greater the value of P_t, the smaller will be the present value of the assets. If discovery were sufficiently painful – execution or life imprisonment, for example, the value of those assets in the event of discovery is likely to be low indeed. Lesser punishments might include jail terms of varying durations, back taxes, fines and penalties, a nagging spouse, or loss of control over personal or business affairs.

Of course, it is not at all certain that the individual will be exposed, and the whole purpose of secrecy is to prevent this from happening. The term a_t^* in the equation indicates the probability of getting caught associated with a particular set of secrecy-containing assets, as modified once again by the individual's attitude towards the risk of being found out. The smaller a_t^*, the larger will be NPV_t, either because the chances of getting caught with the assets are smaller, or because the asset-holder has a sanguine view about the likelihood of being found out.

Given a certain attitude of a secrecy seeker toward risk, the equation clearly points to a number of tradeoffs that have been shown diagrammatically earlier. Specifically, a reduction of a_t^* may have to be 'purchased' with an increase in B_t (the risk associated with the secrecy-containing portfolio), a decrease in ER_t (a reduction in expected returns on a secrecy-containing portfolio) or an increase in EC_t (the associated costs). The rational secrecy seeker will obviously want to maximize the net present value of his assets, NPV_t, and this will require that careful attention be paid to these tradeoffs.

One would be tempted to argue that, in terms of their investment behavior, secrecy seekers should be a conservative lot. Since they are already substantially exposed to risk in terms of the origins of their need for secrecy, they ought to have relatively little tolerance for risk in their asset portfolios. One would conclude that they therefore want a high degree of secrecy *and* a high degree of safety. Given the tradeoffs provided by the market, they would thus be willing to pay a high price, in terms of earnings forgone for the dual attributes. This may not be quite so true if taxation is taken into account. Since secrecy seekers may well operate entirely or largely free of tax in the financial markets they use, the after-tax return comparison may not look quite as bad in comparison with those of (taxed) investors not concerned with secrecy. Moreover, the absence of tax on income as well as on assets, estates and capital gains may increase the secrecy seeker's interest in somewhat more risky assets, since the expected returns are effectively higher. In the real world, it appears, a significant proportion of secrecy seekers are not particularly risk-averse at all.

The principal–agent problem

An investor on the open market walks into a brokerage firm or the trust department of a bank and enters into an asset-management relationship with the investment manager. As the 'principal', he explains his interest in capital appreciation, dividend or interest income, tax exemption, or other investment objectives, as well as his attitude toward risk. The investment manager, in turn, takes on a fiduciary responsibility to carry out that mandate as faithfully as possible, in return for commissions and fees that presumably reflect the value of services rendered. He is to manage the portfolio in accordance with the investor's wishes, and in this role he becomes the investor's 'agent'. Interpreting and fulfilling the investor's objectives are an example of what has become known as the 'principal–agent problem'.

An agency relationship exists whenever an asset-holder delegates some decision-making authority to the manager of a discretionary account. If such a relationship exists, there will be positive monitoring and bonding costs, which can be monetary or non-monetary in nature. In addition, there will often be some divergence between the agent's actual decisions and those decisions that would in fact maximize the welfare of the principal. The principal will thus incur a 'residual loss', which is yet another cost of the agency relationship. Usually, contracts between principals and agents provide appropriate incentives for the agent to make decisions that will maximize the principal's welfare, given existing market uncertainties.

Financial secrecy in an international context raises some unique agency issues. Ordinarily, the agent will have to interpret the investor's wishes and carry them out as best he can. But interpretation of these wishes may not be easy, and can lead to serious disputes down the road.

Or the investor's objectives may change, either explicitly or implicitly, with the agent being uninformed or poorly advised. Or the investor may psychologically reposition his objectives after the fact, if the value of his assets has underperformed an alternative portfolio, with undeserved blame assigned to the agent. Or the agent himself may abuse his mandate by 'churning' the portfolio to bolster commission income, for example, or by 'stuffing' it with substandard securities he wants to be rid of. Or he may simply not be very competent. Clearly, if secrecy is added to the agent's mandate, his job becomes very much more complex. He must do all in his power to safeguard secrecy within the limits of (and sometimes outside of) the law. Violation of his fiduciary role, at least in the eyes of the principal, includes violation of his secrecy mandate, triggering potentially serious disputes between the two parties – with possible damage to the agent through erosion in the value of his secrecy-oriented 'product'.

However, the agent has some leverage on his side as well. Ordinarily, agency-related disputes can be taken into court in civil suits, which then supersede other forms of dispute-settlement that have proven unsuccessful. Still, how can the secrecy seeker take the agent to court when a foreign legal jurisdiction is involved, when that jurisdiction is unclear, or when such an action would compromise the very secrecy he is after – that is, when the suit would itself severely erode the real value of his assets? So the agent acquires a certain immunity from the sort of redress usually available to asset-holders confronted by agent misconduct. Could this not tempt him to abuse his agency function, to enrich himself at the expense of the secrecy-seeking investor? Could he not use his fiduciary position and *de facto* immunity from suit to hold himself harmless as well from other forms of redress, like physical violence, by threat of disclosure?

The addition of secrecy to the conventional principal–agent problem obviously has some interesting implications. The real question is whether the shelter attributable to secrecy influences the behavior of the agent. On the one hand, there is a strong incentive for agents to maximize their own welfare, since they are at least partially protected from retribution. In addition, secrecy seekers are fully prepared to pay any normal agency costs that come with secrecy, as long as there are no large unaccountable losses. On the other hand, the competition a secrecy vendor faces from other sellers, as well as traditions of prudence and competence, tend to impose constraints on abusive behavior.

It may be reasonable to assume that there are relatively few cases where agents seek to maximize their own welfare at the expense of asset-holders, and that any such tendency could be checked by competitive and social pressures. Still, this problem puts a real premium on selection of the agent, who must be depended upon to carry out his fiduciary responsibility with great care and sensitivity to client desires –

which themselves are subject to change – yet without succumbing to the temptations that derive from his potential leverage as a 'secret agent'.

Demand and supply

The foregoing discussion implies that the demand for financial secrecy will be a negative function of price. That is, the quality of secrecy-containing assets acquired by the individual will be larger, the lower their assessed cost to the investor. In Figure A.6, a demand curve for secrecy-containing assets is drawn (D) that is relatively inelastic at its upper end and relatively elastic at lower prices. The suggestion here is that the demand for financial secrecy will be relatively insensitive to price for those individuals for whom exposure would be a very serious matter indeed (e.g. drugs traffickers), while less burdened secrecy seekers will tend to have better alternatives available to them or be willing to go without, thus leaving such individuals fairly sensitive to price. Once again, by 'price' we mean the risk-adjusted returns on secrecy-containing assets subtracted from the risk-adjusted returns on non-secret assets of equivalent nominal value.

Various developments could cause the demand curve to shift – changes in income, alterations in asset-related risks, changes in tax rates, increases or decreases in penalties associated with exposure or the probability of getting caught, etc. The curve applies only to residents of a particular country. Both the position and shape of the demand curve may differ substantially among countries.

The provision of secrecy-containing assets is represented by the supply curve S in Figure A.6. The curve starts to the right of 0, meaning that a certain amount of secrecy can be obtained by secrecy seekers at zero cost. This may be rather substantial, with secrecy provided simply by ordinary confidential relationships that are possible in asset port-folios constructed even in the absence of the secrecy objective. However, acquisition of additional secrecy can be undertaken only at successively higher cost (as defined earlier). Once again, the elasticity of curve S is likely to be relatively low at high levels, where the vendors either face substantial incremental costs in shielding their product from prying eyes, or believe that they can extract very high prices for their services.

Once again, a number of things cause the supply curve to shift, including changes in penalties associated with selling secret assets and the probability of being found out, the cost of intermediaries' services, and attractiveness of alternative assets.

Given the demand and supply curves depicted in Figure A.6, the market price of secret assets of a particular type is P_1 and quantity Q_1 will be bought. Some of these assets would have been bought by individuals

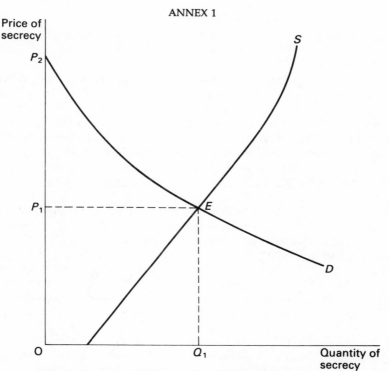

Figure A.6   *Supply, demand and market equilibrium*

willing to pay a much higher price (even P_2), who thus obtain an 'unearned' benefit equal to the amount they *would have been willing to pay* and P_1. This is the 'secrecy seeker's surplus' (SSS), already mentioned in Chapter 1. Here, SSS is given by the area P_1P_2E in the diagram. Similarly, some secrecy vendors would have been willing to sell at a price far less than P_1, and even give it away free. By being able to change the market price of P_1, they therefore receive a 'secrecy vendor's surplus' (SVS) equal to the area of $0P_1EQ_1$ in Figure A.6. Secrecy sales and purchases thus make everyone better off – both buyers and sellers – which is, of course, necessary if exchange in secrecy-containing assets is to take place. What it does to others who are not immediate participants in the secrecy market cannot be determined from this (partial) analysis.

Completing the story, developments that raise the benefits of financial secrecy to purchasers will cause the quantity demanded to rise, while factors that increase the supply of secret assets (e.g. due to the entry of new vendors) will increase the quantity bought and decrease the price. The former will increase SVS, while the latter will increase SSS. Similarly a reduction in the supply of secrecy (e.g. due to a crackdown on vendors by the authorities) will raise the price and reduce

337

quantity (and cut SSS), while a reduction in demand (perhaps due to improved alternatives to secrecy) will reduce both price and quantity (and SVS).

All of this assumes, of course, that secrecy-seekers are a homogeneous group who will all pay the same price. We noted in Chapter 3 that the drugs trafficker may be willing to pay far more for financial secrecy than the father intent on keeping financial information from his children. Secrecy vendors may thus be able to discriminate among groups of secrecy seekers (and even among individuals) on the basis of their respective sensitivity to price – thus draining off part of the SSS and enhancing SVS – as long as the secret assets cannot be resold.

Consider Figure A.7, which depicts a 'market' consisting of two groups with different secrecy preferences. Group A's demand for secrecy (D_A) is clearly less price-sensitive than Group B's (D_B), so it makes sense for secrecy vendors to charge A more than B. M_A and M_B are the corresponding marginal revenue curves associated with sales of secret assets to the two groups. TD and TM are the two groups' respective demand and marginal revenue curves added together, while MC is the marginal cost to the vendor of supplying additional amounts of secret assets. The secrecy seller will want to operate where overall marginal revenue (TM) is just equal to his cost (MC), at point E. Rather than charging both groups the same price, it would make sense to sell Q_A to group A $(MC = M_A)$ at price P_A and Q_B to group B $(MC = M_B)$ at price P_B. That way, vendors can capture a good share of the SSS that the secrecy seekers would obtain if one price applied to all.

Of course, more than two groups of secrecy seekers may exist, and it is possible to set as many prices as there are identifiable groups with different demand characteristics. At the limit, where price discrimination is so perfect that each secrecy seeker has to pay the maximum he is actually willing to pay for a given amount of secrecy, SSS goes to zero. Whether this ever happens in the real world is doubtful. But vendors surely are able to 'hold up' individuals from time to time to extract from them substantial secrecy-related profits – particularly when it is possible for those vendors to collude with one another.

The externality problem

The secrecy business clearly has some extremely wide-ranging effects, many of which bear on people other than those directly involved, and which are not directly captured in the economics of the industry. Secrecy seekers gain from the absence of financial disclosure, and are willing to pay for it. Secrecy vendors have a product from which they can extract economic rents, as long as there aren't too many competitors

338

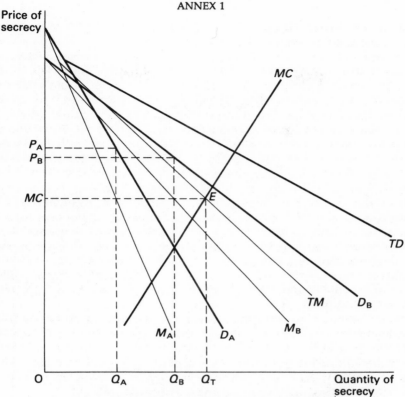

Figure A.7   *Price discrimination among secrecy seekers*

in the game. Both sides win. But others may win or lose as well. International financial secrecy generates 'externalities' that can be both positive (like education) and negative (like pollution).

What about refugees from unjust political or economic persecution around the world, for example? Secrecy offers an opportunity for the oppressed to escape confiscation of assets by capricious or arbitrary actions of governments that may themselves hold power without much claim to political legitimacy. The availability of this avenue may encourage individuals to redouble their economic effort by reducing the risks associated with exposure to possible loss, and others (employees, customers, suppliers, society as a whole) benefit either directly or indirectly. They would, of course, benefit more if the perceived risk were itself lessened and the need for secrecy reduced or eliminated. But half a loaf may be better than none at all. And, if people are ultimately forced to flee, countries in which they seek refuge will be less burdened if some of their financial assets have successfully sought refuge first. Such positive external effects of financial secrecy are magnified whenever human rights, racial and ethnic persecution, and similar non-economic considerations are brought into play.

Positive externalities associated with international financial secrecy have their counterparts on the negative side, of course. The ready availability of secret assets makes possible tax evasion, from which all honest taxpayers suffer. It facilitates bribery and corruption through the maintenance of slush funds and caches for ill-gotten gains. Bribes, in turn, can severely distort resource allocation and income distribution – and the political process itself – to the detriment of individuals and groups around the world. It makes possible organized and unorganized crime ranging from gunrunning and drugs, to rackets and hijacking, to illegal gambling, smuggling, terrorism and espionage, even contract murder, from which millions of ordinary citizens may ultimately suffer. Not least important, it reduces the commitment of political leaders worldwide, who know that a secret nest-egg abroad may save them from the full consequences of their errors of omission or commission. One could even argue that popular uprisings and the emergence of military dictatorships are often linked to financial secrecy, which encourages the kind of endemic official corruption that eventually leads to revolt and the need to 'clean house'.

None of these benefits and costs is reflected in the market for secrecy itself. Do the negative externalities outweigh the positive ones? Nobody knows. In any case, forcing them back into the secrecy markets – much as is done in pollution control, for example – requires concerted efforts in terms of intergovernmental coordination and enforcement that in today's world stand virtually no chance of coming about.

International trade in financial secrecy

We know that secrecy havens exist. Their characteristics have been explored in detail in Chapters 7 and 8. This means that secrecy vendors in some countries supply services that involve value-added to residents of other countries. In other words, there exists a lively international trade in secrecy-related financial services. Why? Obviously, there must be substantial inter-country differences in the demand for, and supply of, financial secrecy. Referring back to Figure A.6, the supply and demand functions that characterize the market for financial secrecy must differ quite substantially among countries. This is depicted in Figure A.8.

In Country X, the demand for financial secrecy looks quite impressive compared to Country Y. Why? Perhaps tax rates are higher. Or the economic or political system is rife with corruption. Or the illegal drug business is thriving. As discussed in Chapter 3, market distortions in general create a fertile environment within which a buoyant demand for

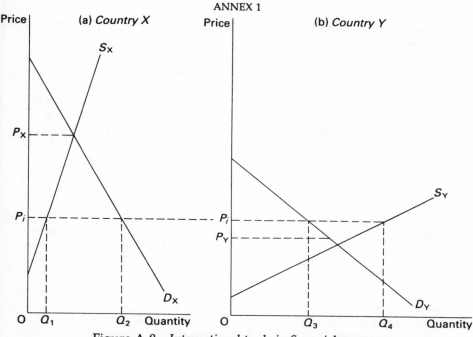

Figure A.8 *International trade in financial secrecy*

financial secrecy usually develops. Meantime, the supply of financial secrecy in X looks rather limited, perhaps owing to various government enforcement actions, lack of effective legal protection against forced disclosure, or similar factors that constrain its availability and make secrecy very expensive at the margin, as discussed in Chapter 4. In Country Y, on the other hand, the demand for financial secrecy seems small, probably because many of the factors that give rise to the need for it in X are absent in Y. At the same time, strict bank secrecy laws, ample financial infrastructure and human resources make the supply of secrecy in that country quite robust. If the two markets for financial secrecy remain in isolation it is not hard to predict the outcome: secret money would be expensive (P_X) in Country X and cheap (P_Y) in Country Y.

A perfect opportunity for international trade! We would predict that Country Y (the secrecy haven) will export Q_3Q_4 of secrecy-related service to Country X (the secrecy hell), whose imports are Q_1Q_2. Purchases of financial secrecy-related services will flow from where they are cheap (Y) to where they are expensive (X). In the process, those services will become more readily available (and cheaper) in Country X, residents will gain substantial SSS, and local secrecy vendors will suffer in competition with their foreign rivals. In the secrecy haven (Country

Y), vendors will benefit substantially with increased output of secrecy-related services and increased SVS, as the price of financial secrecy rises owing to the incremental foreign demand without, however, seriously injuring whatever domestic secrecy seekers are present – price will rise from P_Y to P_i. Moreover, since the production of secrecy-related financial services increases in Country Y, employment, taxation, balance of payments contributions, and various other linked elements – the so-called 'external benefits' – are likely to be quite favorable, and will encourage the continuation of government policies that underlie the country's status as a secrecy haven.

Summary

This chapter has attempted to present, within a consistent structure, the conceptual underpinnings of the international market in financial secrecy. Individuals normally try to maximize their welfare in a more or less rational way. This means they try to maximize the returns on asset portfolios within predetermined risk parameters, or minimize risk subject to some target rate of return. The market for financial assets throws up a tradeoff between risk and returns, and individuals try to maximize their welfare (given the strength of their preferences for returns and their risk aversion) within the constraint. Financial secrecy adds a third variable to the equation. Now individuals must try to maximize their welfare with a portfolio of assets that combines risk, return and secrecy attributes. Again, however, the market throws up tradeoffs between secrecy and risk, and between secrecy and returns, as well as between risks and returns. The strength of the individual's relative preferences for the three objectives, when coupled to the constraints set by the market, determines the structure of an optimum asset portfolio in the presence of a secrecy objective. Clearly, that portfolio may incorporate many different types of real and financial assets, both domestic and offshore. The true value to the individual of such a portfolio depends on expected future returns, portfolio-related risk, the probability of disclosure, the 'disutility' associated with punishment, and the individual's own attitude toward risk.

The 'market' for secrecy-containing assets was described in this chapter as being relatively 'normal'. That is, the demand for such assets is negatively related to their price, while the supply is positively related to their price. This means that an 'equilibrium' can be identified within a given economy, based on factors such as tax rates, extent of criminal activity, law-enforcement activity, and similar factors, all of which can change over time and affect the nature of that market. We know, furthermore, that these conditions may be vastly different between countries, as are factors affecting the supply of secrecy-containing financial services. Consequently, some countries end up exporting financial secrecy services to the residents of other countries, giving rise to a vigorous flow of international trade in those services.

Annex 2

Catalog of US Cases Involving Bank or Commercial Secrecy

Case name	Type of case	Foreign country involved	Date*
I LAUNDERING OR ILLEGALLY SECRETING PROFITS			
In the Matter of Arawak Trust Co.	Laundering kickbacks via foreign corporations	Cayman Islands	1980
Bank Saderat (Iran) v. Marashi	Misappropriating bank funds through foreign trust	Liechtenstein	1982
Dennis Carlson	Laundering drug profits through foreign entities	Cayman Islands, Liechtenstein	N.A.
James Cross	Secreting embezzled funds in foreign accounts	Bermuda	N.A.
Francisco Fernandez & Guillermo Hernandez	Laundering drug profits through foreign accounts	Colombia, Cayman Islands	N.A.
Rogelio A. Fernandez	Concealing source of drug profits through foreign contract	Mexico	N.A.
Firestone Rubber, Inc.	Secreting legal and illegal profits through foreign accounts	Switzerland	N.A.
John D. Fox	Laundering drug profits through foreign accounts	Ecuador	N.A.
Eduardo Garcia & Alfredo Garcia	Secreting illegally obtained funds in foreign accounts	Panama, Puerto Rico	N.A.
Michael J. Grassi	Laundering drug profits through foreign accounts	Cayman Islands	N.A.

344

Hughes Tool Co. v. Meier	Secreting diverted corporate funds in foreign accounts	Netherland Antilles	1977
Ostrer v. US	Laundering embezzled funds through foreign casinos	Bahamas	1977
People v. Wilson	Secreting pornography profits in foreign accounts	Cayman Islands, Switzerland	1982
Carlos R. Porro	Laundering drug profits through foreign accounts	Several offshore countries	N.A.
Derek Price	Laundering drug profits through foreign accounts	Cayman Islands	N.A.
SEC v. Certain Unknown Purchasers of Santa Fe Stock, SEC v. Martin	Secreting securities fraud profits in foreign accounts	Switzerland	1982
SEC v. Zolp	Secreting securities fraud profits in foreign accounts	Bahamas	1982
US v. Beltempo	Laundering drug profits through foreign accounts	Switzerland	1982
US v. Dichne	Secreting embezzled funds in foreign accounts	Switzerland	1980
US v. DiStefano	Laundering kickbacks through foreign accounts	Bahamas	1973
US v. Eimers	Laundering prostitution profits through foreign accounts	Bahamas	1982
US v. Enstam	Laundering drug profits through foreign accounts	Cayman Islands	1980
US v. Erwin	Secreting embezzled funds in foreign accounts	Cayman Islands	1982
US v. Friedland	Secreting kickbacks in foreign accounts	Cayman Islands, Switzerland	1981
US v. Garfield	Laundering drug profits	Bermuda, Panama	1981
US v. Garfield Bank	Laundering drug profits via US accounts	Bermuda, Panama, Liberia	1981
US v. Govern	Laundering drug profits through US accounts	Cayman Islands, Netherland Antilles	1982

US v. The Great American Bank	Laundering drug profits through US accounts, secreting drug profits in foreign accounts	Switzerland, Panama, Peru	1982
US v. Long	Laundering drug profits through foreign accounts	Bahamas	N.A.
US v. Rittenberg	Laundering drug profits through foreign accounts	Lichtenstein, Switzerland, Bahamas	1980
US v. Sand	Laundering drug profits through US accounts	Bahamas	1976
US v. Scotto	Laundering kickbacks through foreign and US accounts	Switzerland	1980
US v. Sonal Corp	Laundering drug profits through US accounts	Colombia	1981
US v. Sterling	Laundering drug profits through foreign accounts	Switzerland, Liechtenstein, Cayman Islands	1982
US v. Toombs	Laundering drug profits through foreign corporations	Cayman Islands, Bahamas	1982
Chester Zabik	Secreting kickbacks in foreign accounts	Switzerland	N.A.

II SECRETING LEGITIMATE ASSETS FOR ILLEGITIMATE PURPOSES

Roy G. Anderson	Secreting funds in foreign accounts to facilitate tax evasion	Bermuda	N.A.
John Berkey and Phillip Weinstein	Diverting corporate receipts to foreign accounts	Belgium	N.A.
Bronston v. United States	Secreting assets from creditors in foreign accounts	Switzerland	1973
CBS Imports, Inc.	Using foreign subsidiary to make illegal payoffs	Hong Kong	N.A.
Victor M. Divivo	Diverting corporate receipts, secreting in foreign accounts	Switzerland	N.A.
Ralph D. Franks	Secreting funds in foreign corporations to facilitate tax evasion	Bermuda	N.A.

Margarito Garza	Concealing unreported receipts through foreign bond purchases	Mexico	N.A.
Don H. Lloyd	Secreting funds in foreign entities to facilitate tax evasion	Cayman Islands	N.A.
Phillips Petroleum, Inc.	Secreting funds for illegal payoffs in foreign accounts	Panama	N.A.
William I. Rials and Stanley E. Galkin	Diverting corporate receipts, secreting in foreign accounts	Cayman Islands	N.A.
Paul L. Rioux	Secreting funds in foreign accounts to facilitate tax evasion	Canada	N.A.
Schlensky v. Dorsey	Secreting corporate funds for illegal campaign contributions in foreign subsidiary's accounts	Bahamas	1978
In the matter of Harry L. Sears	Secreting corporate funds for illegal campaign contributions in foreign accounts	Bahamas	1977
Charles W. Sizemore	Secreting funds in foreign accounts to facilitate tax evasion	Bahamas	N.A.
Frank J. Tuseck	Secreting funds in foreign accounts to facilitate tax evasion	Cayman Islands	
US v. Aita	Secreting funds in US accounts to facilitate tax evasion	Italy	1982
US v. Baskes	Secreting funds in foreign corporations' accounts to facilitate tax evasion	Cayman Islands	1980
US v. Carver	Secreting funds for kickbacks in foreign accounts	Liberia, Switzerland, Liechtenstein, Cayman Islands	N.A.
US v. Crawford	Illegally bribing foreign officials for business purposes through foreign accounts	Mexico	1982
US v. Hajecate	Secreting funds in foreign accounts to facilitate tax evasion	Cayman Islands	1982
US v. McPartlin	Illegally bribing city officials through foreign accounts	Liechtenstein, Switzerland	1979

347

US v. Phillips Petroleum Company	Secreting funds for illegal campaign contributions in foreign bank accounts	Switzerland	1977

III   USE OF OFFSHORE AND FOREIGN ENTITIES AS AN INTEGRAL PART OF AN OVERALL CRIMINAL SCHEME

CFTC v. US Metal Depository	Conducting boiler-room operations through foreign bank	Luxembourg	1979
Oran W. Cotton	Deducting costs, eventually returned through foreign accounts	Cayman Islands	N.A.
Karl L. Dahlstrom	Participating in sham 'double trusts' in foreign countries	Belize, Turks & Caicos Islands	N.A.
Billie Sol Estes	Concealing US transactions through foreign accounts	Liechtenstein	N.A.
Calvin Eisenberg	Deduction costs, eventually returned to foreign accounts through foreign entity	Bahamas	N.A.
Robert Falvo & Richard D. Smith	Taking false deductions involving foreign tax shelters	Colombia	N.A.
Fidenas v. Compagnie International pour L'Informatique, Honeywell Bull, SA	Using foreign corporations to defraud	Bahamas, Switzerland	1979
John S. Howell	Secreting funds in foreign accounts to facilitate tax evasion	Belize, Puerto Rico	N.A.
IIT, an International Investment Trust v. Cornfield	Using foreign subsidiary to defraud	Canada, Panama	1980
Index Fund Inc. v. Hagopian	Using foreign mutual fund to commit securities fraud	Bahamas	1976
Schact v. McCollum	Accepting kickbacks through foreign entities	Lebanon, Mexico	N.A.
Lea J. Marks v. Harold J. Marks	Taking false deductions involving foreign tax shelters	Liechtenstein, Switzerland, Cayman Islands	N.A.

348

James M. Moran	Taking false deductions involving foreign corporations	Bahamas, Cayman Islands	N.A.
Benjamin Mudd	Concealing foreign account	Switzerland	N.A.
New York County v. Firestone	Using foreign account to establish fraudulent tax shelters	Bahamas	1982
Virgil Ogletree	Secreting property ownership in foreign country to evade taxes	Bahamas	N.A.
Gerald Rogers	Participating in fraudulent tax shelters involving foreign country	Panama	N.A.
Leonard Rosen	Secreting funds in foreign accounts to facilitate tax evasion	Bahamas	N.A.
Robert M. Saunders	Taking false deductions involving foreign entity	England	N.A.
SEC v. Bank of Credit and Commerce International, SA	Using foreign entities to violate securities regulations	Kuwait, Saudi Arabia, Luxembourg	1978
SEC v. Banque de Paris et des Pays-Bas (Suisse)	Using foreign banks to violate securities regulations	Switzerland	1977
SEC v. Cayman Islands Reinsurance Corp., Ltd.	Using foreign corporation to violate securities regulations	Cayman Islands	1982
SEC v. Diplomat National Bank	Trading in violation of securities regulations on behalf of foreign nationals	Korea	1977
SEC v. Everest Management Corp.	Using foreign accounts to commit securities fraud	Switzerland	1971
SEC v. General Refractories Co.	Using foreign corporations to commit securities fraud	Several in Europe	1975
SEC v. Kasser	Using foreign corporations to commit securities fraud	Canada, Switzerland	1977
SEC v. Katy Industries	Using foreign subsidiary to commit securities fraud and make illegal payoffs	Cayman Islands	1978

SEC v. Vesco	Using foreign corporations to commit securities fraud	Bahamas, Luxembourg, Costa Rica	1972
State of Arizona v. Williams	Using foreign corporations to commit securities fraud and evade taxes	Panama, Mexico, Montserrat	1981
US v. Becker	Using foreign banks to defraud investors	Bahamas	1978
US v. Brinlee	Using foreign accounts to defraud	Antigua	1981
US v. Courtois	Using foreign accounts to commit securities fraud	Bermuda, Bahamas, Luxembourg, Switzerland	N.A.
US v. Crosby	Using foreign banks to honor worthless checks	St Vincent	1982
US v. Federbush	Using foreign banks to defraud	St Vincent	1980
US v. Firestone Rubber	Using foreign subsidiary to circumvent US regulations	Switzerland	1981
US v. Jaeger	Using foreign accounts to commit currency exchange fraud	Turks & Caicos Islands	1979
US v. Kelly	Using foreign trust to commit securities fraud	Liechtenstein, Switzerland	1965
US v. Kelly	Using foreign fund to defraud	Panama	1978
US v. Kilpatrick	Using foreign banks and corporations to establish fraudulent tax shelters	Cayman Islands	1982
US v. Krown	Using foreign banks to establish fraudulent tax shelters and defraud	St Vincent	1980
US v. McDevitt	Using foreign corporations to establish fraudulent tax shelters and defraud	Anguilla, Bahamas	1982
US v. McDonnell Douglas Corp.	Using foreign corporations to bribe foreign officials	Guernsey, Cayman Islands, Bermuda, Belgium	1979
US v. Newman	Using foreign banks and trusts to commit securities fraud	Bermuda, Bahamas, Luxembourg, Switzerland	1981

US v. Osserman	Using foreign banks to establish fraudulent tax shelters	Cayman Islands	1980
US v. Palm State Bank	Using foreign accounts to defraud and evade taxes	Cayman Islands	1980
US v. Parker	Using foreign corporations to establish fraudulent tax shelters	Switzerland, Cayman Islands, Italy, Germany	N.A.
US v. Rodriguez	Using foreign accounts to defraud	Antigua	1982
US v. Sarault	Using foreign banks to honor worthless checks	Bahamas	1982
US v. Twombly	Using foreign corporations to bribe foreign officials	Bermuda, Puerto Rico	1980
US v. Sindona	Using foreign banks to commit securities fraud	Switzerland, Italy	1980
US v. Vetco, Inc.	Using foreign subsidiary to circumvent US regulations	Switzerland	1981
US v. Whipple	Using foreign corporations to establish fraudulent tax shelters	Cayman Islands, Andorra	N.A.
US v. Wolfson	Using foreign banks to promote worthless checks	Bahamas	1971
US v. Wolfson	Using foreign bank to promote worthless checks	St Vincent	1980
Alfred I. Willett	Concealing commodities fraud through a foreign corporation	Libya	N.A.
Herbert M. Wolstencraft	Aiding in false representations to IRS involving activities in foreign countries	Bahamas	N.A.

IV DISCLOSURE OF FINANCIAL RECORDS IN SUPPORT OF CRIMINAL INVESTIGATIONS

In the matter of Arawak Trust Co.	Complying with grand jury subpoena of foreign bank records	Cayman Islands	1980

Application of Chase Manhattan Bank	Complying with subpoena for bank records in light of possible violation of foreign law	Panama	1962
Ings v. Ferguson	Complying with subpoena for bank records in light of possible foreign law violations	Canada	1960
Ryan v. Commission of Internal Revenue	Complying with subpoena for bank records in light of possible foreign law violation	Switzerland	1975
SEC v. Banca della Svizzera Italiana	Complying with subpoena for bank records in light of possible foreign law violation	Switzerland	1981
SEC v. Minas de Artemisa, SA	Complying with subpoena for bank records in light of possible foreign law violation	Mexico	1945
Société Internationale pour Participation Industrielle v. Rogers	Complying with subpoena for bank records in light of possible foreign law violation	Switzerland	1958
Trade Development Bank v. Continental Insurance Co.	Mandating secrecy waivers at court discretion	Switzerland	1972
US v. Bank of Nova Scotia	Complying with subpoena for bank records in light of possible foreign law violation	Bahamas	1981
In re Grand Jury Proceedings US v. Field	Complying with subpoena for bank records in light of possible foreign law violation	Cayman Islands	1976
US v. Loften	Liability for substantive legal violations of attorneys representing racketeers	Various	1981

US v. Payner	Complying with subpoena of bank records in light of fourth amendment constitutional challenge	Bahamas	1980
US v. Quigg	Complying with subpoena of bank records of possible foreign law violations	Bahamas	1980

* N.A. = Multiple years or not available.

Source: Senate Committee on Governmental Affairs, Permanent Subcommittee on Investigations, *Crime and Secrecy: The Use of Offshore Banks and Companies* (Washington, DC: US Government Printing Office, 1983).

References

Achleitner, Paul M., *Das Bankgeheimnis in Öesterreich, Deutschland und der Schweiz* (Vienna: Österreichisches Forschungsinstitut für Sparkassenwesen, 1981).

Achleitner, Paul M., 'Das Bankgeheimnis in Ausslandischen Staaten', *Öesterreichische Sparkassenzeitung*, 15 October 1981.

Ahmed, Reazuddin, 'While Bangladesh Struggles, its Smugglers Thrive', *International Herald Tribune*, 26 June 1986.

Akst, Daniel, 'Fallen Star', *Wall Street Journal*, 10 July 1987.

Allen, Michael, 'Defense Lawyers Fear Becoming Targets Under Sweeping Money-Laundering Law', *Wall Street Journal*, 2 December 1986.

Anders, George, and Studer, Margaret, 'Stuck on Tradition, Swiss Banks Discover their Role is Waning as a Financial Center', *Wall Street Journal*, 21 March 1985.

Ansberry, Clare, 'Survival Strategy', *Wall Street Journal*, 1 October 1986.

Ayittey, George B. N., 'The Real Foreign Debt Problem', *Wall Street Journal*, 8 April 1986.

Babcock, Charles R., 'Anti-Libya Plan Tied to Iran Slush Fund', *International Herald Tribune*, 20 May 1987.

Bartlett, Sarah, 'Another Threat to Foreign Bank Secrecy', *Business Week*, 28 January 1985.

Bartlett, Sarah, and Elliott, Dorinda, 'The Mess at Deak & Co. is Worse than Anyone Thought', *Business Week*, 11 February 1985.

Bartlett, Sarah, Wallace, G. David, Robbins, Carla Anne, Therrien, Lois, Grover, Ronald, Riemer, Blanca and Rossant, John, 'Money Laundering', *Business Week*, 18 March 1985.

Baum, Dan, 'U.S.–Swiss Accord on Marc Rich Papers is Snarled Over Terms of Pact', *Wall Street Journal*, 3 July 1983.

Beam, Alex, 'Bank of Boston: A Public Relations Nightmare', *Business Week*, 4 March 1985.

Beam, Alex, 'Two Brokerages Get Tangled in the Money Laundering Net', *Business Week*, 11 March 1985.

Bennett, Robert A., 'Two Banks Broke US Cash Rules', *New York Times*, 28 March 1985.

Berg, Eric N., 'Dennis Levine: Study in Contradictions', *International Herald Tribune*, 16 May 1986.

Berg, Eric N., 'Brazil Banking Customs Cited in Morgan Case', *International Herald Tribune*, 24 May 1986.

REFERENCES

Berss, Marcia, 'The Prince That Roared', *Forbes*, 29 April 1985.

Bhagwati, J. N., Krueger, A. and Wibulswasdi, C., *Capital Flight from LDC's: A Statistical Analysis*, (Amsterdam: North Holland Publishing Company, 1974).

Bhagwati, Jagdish, 'On the Underinvoicing of Imports', in J. N. Bhagwati (ed.), *Illegal Transactions in International Trade*, (Amsterdam: North Holland, 1981).

Blum, Richard H., and Kaplan, John, 'Offshore Banking: Issues With Respect to Criminal Use', mimeo., The Ford Foundation, 1979.

Blum, Richard H., *Offshore Haven Banks, Trusts and Companies* (New York: Praeger Publishers, 1984).

Borell, John, 'Bankers With a Bad Case of Nerves', *Time*, 31 August 1987.

Branigin, William, 'Fictitious Name on Account Helped Pay for Shopping', *International Herald Tribune*, 12 March 1986.

Branigin, William, 'Marcos Tied to $1 Billion Sugar Fraud', *International Herald Tribune*, 29, 30 March 1986.

Branigin, William, 'Marcos Control of Mining Firm is Alleged', *International Herald Tribune*, 5, 6 April 1986.

Branigin, William, 'Mexican Anti-Drug Campaign Failing to Stem Flow Into US', *Washington Post*, 4 August 1987.

Brannigan, Martha, 'Courts Aid Officials' Efforts to Get Offshore Bank Data of U.S. Firms', *Wall Street Journal*, 24 July 1984.

Brannigan, Martha, 'Bankers Face Trial Today for Aiding Smugglers in Getting Control of Bank', *Wall Street Journal*, 5 August 1985.

Brauchli, Marcus W., 'Swedish Prosecutor Investigating Bofors Will Seek Access to Swiss Bank Records', *Wall Street Journal*, 15 September 1987.

Bray, Nicholas, 'Rock Solid?', *Wall Street Journal*, 24 March 1987.

Brinkley, Joel, 'Marcos Papers Detail Assets Worth Millions', *International Herald Tribune*, 20 March 1986.

Buder, Leonard, '17 at Colombian Airline Accused of Large-Scale Money Smuggling', *New York Times*, 10 April 1987.

Burnham, David, 'Money-Laundering Bill Seen as Privacy Threat', *New York Times*, 23 June 1985.

Burnham, David, 'Treasury Wants More Foreign Data from Banks', *New York Times*, 3 July 1984.

Butterfield, Fox, 'Statement by Boston Bank Due', *New York Times*, 10 February 1985.

Butterfield, Fox, 'Boston Bank Cites "Systems Failure" ', *New York Times*, 12 February 1985.

Butterfield, Fox, 'Boston Bank Calls Misuse of Cash Unwitting', *New York Times*, 22 February 1985.

Butterfield, Fox, 'U.S. Jury Reported Investigating 2 Ex-Employees of Boston Bank', *New York Times*, 25 February 1985.

Butterfield, Fox, 'US Says Boston Bank Know of Rule on Cash', *New York Times*, 27 February 1985.

Butterfield, Fox, 'Bank of Boston Reiterates Denial on Employees', *New York Times*, 28 February 1985.

Butterfield, Fox, 'A Second Bank in Boston Says It Didn't Report Big Cash Transfers', *New York Times*, 9 March 1985.

Butterfield, Fox, 'Marcos Linked to $80 Million', *International Herald Tribune*, 8 March 1986.

Butterfield, Fox, 'North's $10 Million Mistake: Sultan's Gift Lost in a Mixup', *New York Times*, 14 May 1987.

Butterfield, Fox, 'Courier for North Tells of Carrying Cash for Contras', *New York Times*, 15 May 1987.

Butterfield, Fox, 'Marcos Said to Put Millions in Switzerland', *International Herald Tribune*, 15, 16 March 1986.

Carley, William M., 'Terrorist Group Has Financial Operation at Warsaw Company', *Wall Street Journal*, 16 October 1987.

Carrington, Tim, and Pasztor, Andy, 'Weinberger Says Army Apparently Set Improper Price for CIA on Iran Missiles', *Wall Street Journal*, 7 January 1987.

Cass, Alain, and Senoren, Samuel, 'Aquino Team Seizes Assets of Marcos Regime', *Financial Times*, 5 March 1986.

Chambost, Eduard, *Bank Accounts: A World Guide to Confidentiality* (London: John Wiley, 1983).

Chavira, Ricardo, and Sindayen, Nelly, 'Please Speak Into the Microphone', *Time*, 17 July 1987.

Church, George J., 'The Murky World of Weapons Dealers', *Time*, 19 January 1987.

Cody, Edward, 'US Seeks to Reduce Loss of Revenues in Fiscal Fuzz of Caribbean Tax Havens', *Washington Post*, 15 June 1987.

Cohen, Roger, 'Laundry Service: How the Mob is Using Financial Institutions to Disguise Its Gains', *Wall Street Journal*, 12 March 1985.

Cohn, Gary, 'These Smurfs Aren't Blue, But Some Have Reasons to be Sad', *Wall Street Journal*, 11 July 1985.

Colby, Laura, 'Vatican Bank Played A Central Role in Fall of Banco Ambrosiano', *Wall Street Journal*, 27 April 1987.

Cole, Robert J., 'Witness in US Trading Case Tells of Cover Stories', *New York Times*, 29 May 1986.

Cook, James, 'Everybody's Favorite Laundry Man', *Forbes*, 5 December 1983.

Cornwell, Rupert, *God's Bankers* (London: Victor Gollancz, 1983).

Cornwell, Rupert, 'Virus of the Black Economy is Spreading Fast', *Financial Times*, 16 April 1986.

Cox, Patrick, 'More Laws Won't Hamper Drug-Money Launderers,' *Wall Street Journal*, 14 December 1987.

Crossen, Cynthia, 'Look Not Toward the Havens', *Wall Street Journal*, 18 September 1987.

Cummings, Judith, 'DeLorean's Auditors Under Fire', *International Herald Tribune*, 27 March 1986.

Curry, Lynne, 'Opinions Split on Insider Trading', *New York Times*, 24 September 1986.

Dale, Richard, 'Unrecorded Capital Flows: Is the United States Already a Net Debtor?', *The Banker*, December 1984.

Davidson, William H., *The Amazing Race* (New York: John Wiley, 1983).

Davis, Bob, 'US Says Bank of Boston Unit was Told It Broke Law 2 Years Before Compliance', *Wall Street Journal*, 28 February 1985.

Davis, Bob, 'Bank of Boston Unit's Fine Criticized as Inadequate by House Banking Panel', *Wall Street Journal*, 4 April 1985.

Davis, Bob, 'Bank of Boston Report Criticizes Firm Chief Over Cash-Reporting Violations', *Wall Street Journal*, 5 April 1985.

Davis, Bob, 'Bank of Boston Currency Moves Foundation in Probe', *Wall Street Journal*, 10 February 1985.

DeMott, John S., 'Finger Pointing', *Time*, 14 July 1986.

Dentzer, Susan, 'Greed on Wall Street', *Newsweek*, 26 May 1986.

DeStefano, Anthony M., Hertzberg, Daniel and Putka, Gary, 'False Glitter', *Wall Street Journal*, 20 August 1985.

Diamond, Walter H., and Diamond, Dorothy B., *Tax Havens of the World* (New York: Matthew Bender, 1984).

Dionne, E. J., 'New Hope for Clues in Italian Scandals', *New York Times*, 25 March 1985.

Dionne, Jr, E. J., 'Sindona Dies of Poisoning; Dose's Origin Unknown', *International Herald Tribune*, 24 March 1986.

Dodsworth, Terry, 'Cutting the Swiss Web', *Financial Times*, 10 April 1986.

Dullforce, William, 'Gelli Gives Himself Up to Swiss', *Financial Times*, 23 September 1987.

Dullforce, William, 'Swiss Court Sentences Gelli for Bribery', *Financial Times*, 23 December 1987.

Dullforce, William, 'Swiss Insider Trading Law Starts 1 July', *Financial Times*, 3 June 1988.

Dullforce, William, 'Still a Marketable Advantage', *Financial Times*, 11 December 1987.

Dwyer, Paula, 'Big Brother Wants to See Your Bankbook', *Business Week*, 16 September 1985.

Dwyer, Paula, and Brady, Rose, 'The Questions Surrounding Guinness' US Connection', *Business Week*, 27 April 1987.

Eaton, Jonathan, 'Public Debt Guarantees and Private Capital Flight', *World Bank Economic Review*, May 1987.

Elkin, Larry, 'Levine, 4 Others Plead Guilty in Insider Trading', *International Herald Tribune*, 6 June 1986.

Elmer-DeWitt, Philip, 'ZZZZ Best May Be ZZZZ Worst', *Time*, 20 July 1987.

Evans, Richard, 'Bank Leu – or Pandora's Box', *Euromoney*, April 1987.

Evans, Richard, 'Forcing Discreet Money Into the Open', *Euromoney*, November 1986.

Fallon, Ivan, and Hosenball, Mark, 'Secret World of the Inside Stealer', *Sunday Times*, 23 November 1986.

Fedders, John M., 'Foreign Secrecy: A Key to the Lock', *New York Times*, 16 October 1983.

Feige, Edward L., 'A New Perspective on a Macroeconomic Phenomenon', mimeo., August 1980.

Fialka, John J., 'War Center', *Wall Street Journal*, 30 January 1987.

Finn, Jr, Edwin A. and Pouchine, Tatiana, 'Luxembourg: Colour it Green,' *Forbes*, 28 April 1987.

Fisher, Anne B., 'Money Laundering', *Fortune*, 1 April 1985.

Fitchett, Joseph, 'High-Tech Smuggling Risks are Slight', *International Herald Tribune*, 22 May 1984.

Fitchett, Joseph, 'Technology Bandit Led Ring for Russia', *International Herald Tribune*, 5 February 1985.

Ford, Peter, 'Panama's Bankers Weather Civil Unrest', *Financial Times*, 21 July 1987.

Frank, Allan Dodds, 'New Hub for an Old Web', *Forbes*, 7 April 1986.

Frank, Allan Dodds, 'See No Evil', *Forbes*, 6 October 1986.

Frank, Allan Dodds, and King, Jr, Ralph, 'Greed, Inc', *Fortune*, 29 December 1986.

Frank, Allan Dodds, 'You Can't Keep a Smart Crook Down', *Forbes*, 29 December 1986.

357

Friedland, Jonathan, 'Banking Scandal Down Under', *Institutional Investor*, November 1987.

Friedman, Alan, 'Ambrosiano Settlement Signed by Bankers', *Financial Times*, 26 May 1984.

Friedman, Alan, 'Milan Bank Executives Charged Over 10 Million Secret Fund', *Financial Times*, 15 May 1988.

Fuhrman, Peter, 'A Time for Change – But Slowly', *Forbes*, 13 June 1988.

Gardner, David, 'Mexico Defends Record on Capital Flight', *Financial Times*, 16 May 1986.

Gardner, David, 'General Manuel Antonio Noriega, Master Manipulator in a World of Intrigue', *Financial Times*, 18 March 1988.

Garsson, Robert M., 'Professor Raps Banks' Attitude on Secrecy Act', *American Banker*, 5 December 1985.

Gerth, Jeff, 'Testimony Ties Marcos to New York Property Valued at $300 Million', *International Herald Tribune*, 10 April 1986.

Gerth, Jeff, 'Flight of Mexican Capital Threatens Debt Plan', *International Herald Tribune*, 6 October 1986.

Gerth, Jeff, 'The Iran Money Flow: Tracing the Complex Steps', *Wall Street Journal*, 15 December 1986.

Gerth, Jeff, 'Vast Flow of Cash Threatens Currency, Banks and Economies', *New York Times*, 11 April 1988.

Gilhooley, James, 'Whatever Happened to the Amazing Fortune of Antonio de Segura?', *Royal Bank of Scotland Review*, No. 151, September 1986.

Gilpin, Kenneth N., 'Ex-Broker Indicted in Cash Scheme', *New York Times*, 14 March 1987.

Gladwin, Thomas N., and Walter, Ingo, *Multinationals Under Fire* (New York: John Wiley, 1980).

Glynn, Lenny, and Koenig, Peter, 'The Capital Flight Crisis', *Institutional Investor*, November 1984.

Goleman, Daniel, 'The Tax Cheats: Selfish to the Bottom Line', *New York Times*, 11 April 1988.

Goodman, Ellen, 'Public Service Isn't Meant to be a Rip Off', *International Herald Tribune*, 6 March 1986.

Gordon, Richard A., *Tax Havens and their Use by US Taxpayers – An Overview* (The Gordon Report) (Washington, DC: Internal Revenue Service, 12 January 1981).

Gourley, Richard, 'On the Trail of Yamashita's Treasure', *Financial Times*, 11 July 1987.

Graham, Robert, 'Guerillas Fail to Dent Colombian Economy', *Financial Times*, 23 February 1988.

Grant, Keith, 'Latin-American Nations See Progress in Slowing Capital Flight', *International Herald Tribune*, 29 April 1986.

Gruson, Lindsey, 'The Shearson Case Opens New Ground', *New York Times*, 14 July 1986.

Gumbel, Peter, 'West German Bureaucrat Who Blew Whistle on Flick Scandal Had to Fight His Superiors', *Wall Street Journal*, 27 March 1985.

Gumbel, Peter, 'West Germany is Taking a Closer Look at Insider Trading Following AEG Case', *Wall Street Journal*, 21 August 1986.

Gupte, Pranay, 'Bomb Fuses for the Ayatollah', *Forbes*, 16 May 1988.

Gupte, Pranay, 'Who's Got the $60 million?' *Forbes*, 27 June 1988.

Gutmann, Peter M., 'The Subterranean Economy', *Financial Analysts Journal*, November/December 1977.

REFERENCES

Gwertzman, P. Bernard, 'Philippines Moves to Recover Money Marcos Took Out', *New York Times*, 4 March 1986.

Hagerty, Bob, 'Japanese Snap up the Bulk of Special Treasury Issue', *International Herald Tribune*, 3 June 1985.

Harwood, Jud, 'Commentary – Bank of Nova Scotia (Brady Subpoena) – US Government Lawyers Deceive the Courts', *Taxes International*, March 1985.

Hayes, John, 'Don't Talk to Strangers', *Forbes*, 25 August 1986.

Hector, Gary, 'Nervous Money Keeps on Fleeing', *Fortune*, 23 December 1985.

Helm, Sarah, and Freeman, Simon, 'Banks to be Protected Over Drugs Cash Tip-Off', *Sunday Times*, 4 May 1986.

Hemp, Paul, 'Guinness Alleges Breach of Duty by Former Chief', *Wall Street Journal*, 4 March 1987.

Henry, David, 'America's Hottest Export – Funny Money Stocks', *Forbes*, 23 September 1985.

Henry, Gordon M., 'Dark Clouds over Wall Street', *Time*, 26 May 1986.

Henry, Gordon M., 'Circus Time', *Time*, 23 June 1986.

Henry, James S., 'Fallen Angel', *Manhattan, Inc.*, April 1987.

Hertzberg, Daniel, 'Chemical Bank Says It Failed to Report $25.9 Million in Cash Moves Since 1980', *Wall Street Journal*, 27 March 1985.

Hertzberg, Daniel, and Witcher, S. Karene, 'Banker Quits Drexel Amid Investigation by Former Employer, Morgan Guaranty', *Wall Street Journal*, 21 May 1986.

Hertzberg, Daniel, 'SEC Investigates Schiff Hardin Ex-partner', *Wall Street Journal*, 30 June 1986.

Hewitt, Bill, and Fouquet, David, 'A Diamond in the Rough', *Newsweek*, 24 February 1986.

Hulihan, Maile, 'Swiss Vote on Bank Secrecy Curbs After Battle for Hearts and Minds', *Wall Street Journal*, 18 May 1984.

Ingersoll, Bruce, 'SEC Hails Ruling by Swiss Court Forcing Banks to Help in Inquiry', *Wall Street Journal*, 18 May 1984.

Ingersoll, Bruce, 'Santa Fe Investors Agree to Give Up Profits from Insider-Trading Case', *European Wall Street Journal*, 27 February 1986.

Internal Revenue Service, 'Estimates of Income Unreported on Individual Income Tax Returns', IRS Publication 1103 (9–79).

Jefferson, Thomas C., and Johnson, Vassel G., 'Cayman Commits Itself to Financial Confidentiality', *Taxes International*, February 1985.

Johnson, Haynes, 'Three Months of Hearings Fail to Crack the Case', *Washington Post*, 4 August 1987.

Kamm, Thomas, 'Lost Luster', *Wall Street Journal*, 10 July 1987.

Keller, H. Anton, 'A Global IRS?', *Wall Street Journal*, 9 May 1986.

Kelly, Kevin, 'The Oklahoma Town That Drug Money Bought', *Business Week*, 23 May 1988.

Kempe, Frederick, and Pound, Edward T., 'Tongsun Park Finds an Embattled Client: Panama's Noriega', *New York Times*, 29 January 1988.

Kessler, Felix, 'Legal Tug of War Over Marc Rich & Co. Centers on Small Swiss Town of Zug', *Wall Street Journal*, 15 November 1983.

Kessler, Felix, 'Neutral Switzerland, Without Enemies, Spending Millions on Fallout Shelters', *Wall Street Journal*, 21 December 1983.

Khan, M. S., and Ul Haque, N., 'Capital Flight from Developing Countries', *Finance and Development*, March 1987.

Kilburn, Peter J., 'Global Trade Mystery: A Vanishing $100 Billion', *New York Times*, 30 July 1983.

Kochan, Nick, and Pym, Hugh, 'The Guinness Affair: Anatomy of a Scandal' (Christopher Helm Publishers, 1987).

Koepp, Stephen, 'The Insider Scandal Travels Abroad', *Time*, 23 March 1987.

Kraar, Louis, 'India Bids for Business', *Fortune*, 6 January 1986.

Kraar, Louis, 'The Drug Trade', *Fortune*, 20 June 1988.

Krause, Axel, 'European Tax Pact Adopted', *International Herald Tribune*, 27 June 1987.

Kronholz, June, 'Buried Treasure', *Wall Street Journal*, 11 February 1987.

Kupfer, Andrew, 'What to do About Drugs', *Fortune*, 20 June 1988.

Kwitney, Jonathan, *The Crimes of Patriots* (New York: W. W. Norton, 1987).

Kwitney, Jonathan, 'Nugan Hand Acted in Covert Operations of U.S. Government', *Wall Street Journal*, 21 August 1983.

Labich, Kenneth, 'The Fast Track Ends for One Baby Boomer', *Fortune*, 9 June 1986.

Lacayo, Richard, 'The International Treasure Hunt', *Time*, 21 April 1986.

Langley, Monica, 'Currency Laws Found Violated by 2 Big Banks', *Wall Street Journal*, 26 July 1985.

Langley, Monica, and Cox, Paul, 'Treasury Fines Crocker Unit $2,250,000 for Failing to Report Cash Transactions', *Wall Street Journal*, 28 August 1985.

Langley, Monica, and Hill, G. Christian, 'Crocker and Treasury Clash Sharply in Wake of Fine for Reporting Violations', *Wall Street Journal*, 29 August 1985.

Lardner, Jr, George, 'New Mobs Change Organized Crime', *International Herald Tribune*, 3 April 1986.

Lascelles, David, 'A Hole in the Secret Heart', *Financial Times*, 3 February 1987.

Lascelles, David, and Wicks, John, 'Banking Nations Aim to Crack Down on Fraud', *Financial Times*, 27 April 1988.

Lee, Elliott D., 'Swiss Drug Firm Secures Financing for Sterling Bid', *Wall Street Journal*, 14 January 1988.

Legarda, Benito, 'Small Island Economies', *Finance and Development*, June 1984.

LeMoyne, James, 'Panama Military Leader Denies Allegations of Crime Activities', *International Herald Tribune*, 19 June 1986.

Leonard, Burr, 'Tax Deform', *Forbes*, 15 December 1986.

Lernoux, Penny, 'The Seamy Side of Florida Banking', *New York Times*, 5 February 1984.

Lessard, Donald, and Tschoegl, Adrian, 'Panama's International Banking Center: Where Does it Stand and What Can be Done to Insure Its Continued Viability and Increase Its Contributions to the Panamanian Economy?', *International Business and Banking Discussion Paper Series*, University of Miami, January 1985.

Lessard, Donald, and Williamson, John, *Capital Flight* (Washington, D.C.: Institute for International Economics, 1987).

Lewis, Paul, 'Cracking a Swiss Bank's Code', *New York Times*, 23 September 1983.

Lissakers, Karin, 'Money in Flight: Bankers Drive the Getaway Cars', *International Herald Tribune*, 6 March 1986.

Lohr, Steve, 'Guinness Ousts Head in Scandal', *New York Times*, 14 January 1987.

Lohr, Steve, 'Guinness Thinks Funds Went to Ex-Chairman', *New York Times*, 9 April 1987.

Loomis, Carol J., 'Limited War on White Collar Crime', *Fortune*, 22 July 1985.

Lowenstein, Roger, 'Looking for Loot', *Wall Street Journal*, 2 December 1986.

Lubasch, Arnold H., 'Promoter is Guilty in $445 Million Tax Fraud', *New York Times*, 26 April 1985.

Lubenow, Gerald, 'Swedish Arms Sales: Nothing to Declare?' *Newsweek*, 20 June 1988.

Lyon, Ian, 'Paradise Under Pressure', *Investment International*, June 1987.

Lyon, Ian, 'Why Choose Cayman?', *Investment International*, June 1987.

Maass, Peter, 'Buyers Are Returning to Antwerp', *New York Times*, 10 July 1986.

Magnuson, Ed, 'Tears of Rage', *Time*, 14 March 1988.

Manne, Henry, *Insider Trading and the Stock Market* (New York: John Wiley, 1966).

Maremont, Mark, 'Look Who May Take a Fall in the Guinness Scandal', *Business Week*, 26 October 1987.

Martin, Everett G., 'Lima's Capitalists Usually are Found in the Underground', *Wall Street Journal*, 16 August 1984.

Martin, Everett G., 'Precarious Pesos', *Wall Street Journal*, 13 August 1986.

McCoy, Charles F., 'Netherlands Antilles Minus a Tax Treaty is Tax-Paradise Lost', *Wall Street Journal*, 31 July 1987.

McGregor, Alan, 'New Swiss Insider Trading Law on Trial', *The Times*, 20 June 1988.

McInnes, Genevieve, 'Swiss Private Banks: Bewilderingly Successful', *Banker International*, August 1987.

McMurray, Scott, Anders, George, Browning, E. S., and Ingersoll, Bruce, 'As Global 24 Hour Trading Nears, Regulators Warn of Market Abuses', *Wall Street Journal*, 10 February 1985.

McMurray, Scott, and Hertzberg, Daniel, 'Drexel Official Accused by SEC of Inside Trades', *Wall Street Journal*, 13 May 1986.

Miller, Frederic A., Kessler, Richard, and Ryser, Jefferson, 'Closely Watched Banks: One That Got Away', *Business Week*, 19 October 1987.

Moody, John, 'Dirty Dollars', *Time*, 19 January 1987.

Morais, Richard, 'He Gave Off That Kind of Aura', *Forbes*, 8 February 1988.

Morgan Guaranty Trust Company, *World Financial Markets*, March 1986.

Mossberg, Walter S., 'Most of Iran-Contra Affair Remains a Mystery, Including Israel's Role, Arms-Sales Suspension', *Wall Street Journal*, 7 January 1987.

Mossberg, Walter S., 'Trail of Money from the Iran-Contra Arms Sales Remains Murky Despite 6 Months of Investigation', *Wall Street Journal*, 5 May 1987.

Mufson, Steve, and Cooke, Stephanie, 'Can Pretoria Evade Sanctions? Let us Count the Ways', *Business Week*, 1 September 1986.

Muir, Frederick M., 'Can Investors Get Any of $150 Million Back from J. David & Co.?', *Wall Street Journal*, 21 March 1984.

Mulcahy, John, 'The Chinese Laundry', *Far Eastern Economic Review*, 20 August 1987.

Murray, Alan E., 'We Find it Very Hard to Believe that J. P. Morgan Began this Way', *Wall Street Journal*, 4 April 1985.

Murray, Allen E., 'Cheating Uncle Sam', *Wall Street Journal*, 10 April 1984.

Murray, Allen E., 'How to Catch Tax Cheaters', *Fortune*, 17 March 1986.

Mydans, Seth, 'Marcos Wealth is Estimated in Billions', *International Herald Tribune*, 6 March 1986.

Mydans, Seth, 'Rapid Progress on Marcos Assets', *International Herald Tribune*, 3 April 1986.

Nash, Nathaniel C., 'Bank of Boston Officer Says He Erred on Rule', *New York Times*, 13 March 1985.

Nash, Nathaniel C., 'E. F. Hutton Guilty in Bank Fraud; Penalties Could Top $10 Million', *New York Times*, 3 May 1985.

Nash, Nathaniel C., 'SEC's New Enforcement Chief', *New York Times*, 5 May 1985.

Nash, Nathaniel C., '4 New York Banks Face Fines by US in Cash Violations', *New York Times*, 18 June 1985.

Nash, Nathaniel C., 'Stretching the SEC's Reach', *New York Times*, 13 July 1986.

Nawaz, Shuja, 'Why the World Current Account Does Not Balance', *Finance and Development*, September 1987.

Neher, Jaques, 'Why Secrecy is Crumbling', *International Herald Tribune*, 13 July 1987.

Netter, Thomas W., 'Swiss Bank Secrecy Laws Are Put to New Test in U.S. Insider Trading Case', *International Herald Tribune*, 20 May 1986.

Netter, Thomas W., 'US Seeks More Information from Swiss on the Iran Affair', *New York Times*, 26 February 1987.

Netter, Thomas, 'Sultan Asks for Return of Contra Cash, Interest', *International Herald Tribune*, 13 June 1987.

Netter, Thomas W., 'Italian Wanted in Bank Collapse and Bombing Gives Up in Geneva', *New York Times*, 22 September 1987.

Nisse, Jason, 'Channel Islands – Too Much of a Good Thing?', *The Banker*, August 1987.

Nordheimer, Jon, 'Head of Isles near Bahamas Accused of Drug Plot', *New York Times*, 6 March 1985.

O'Neil, David M., *Growth of the Underground Economy*, 1950–1981. Joint Economic Committee, US Congress (Washington, DC: US Government Printing Office, 1983).

Oppenheimer, Andres, 'In Colombia, It's No Problem to Launder Loot', *The Miami Herald*, 11 March 1986.

Paltrow, Scot J., 'Iran-Contra Inquiry Could be Delayed by Bids to Block Access to Swiss Accounts', *Wall Street Journal*, 21 January 1987.

Pasztor, Andy, and Wynter, Leon E., 'US Set War on Bank-Industry Fraud', *Wall Street Journal*, 2 April 1978.

Pasztor, Andy, and Pound, Edward T., 'Iranian Officials May Have Gotten Kickbacks on US Arms Sales Via Inflated-Price Scheme', *Wall Street Journal*, 5 March 1987.

Pasztor, Andy, 'Only About 50 Banks Seek Restitution From E F Hutton for Illegal Overdrafts', *Wall Street Journal*, 3 June 1987.

Pasztor, Andy, and Nazario, Sonia, 'Cayman Islands Grant U.S. Access to Offshore Bank Data', *Wall Street Journal*, 3 July 1986.

Penn, Stanley, 'Levine Case Has Nassau Buzzing Over Bank Leu Unit's Ex-Officials', *Wall Street Journal*, 30 May 1986.

Penn, Stanley, 'Illicit Trade', *Wall Street Journal*, 5 September 1986.

Penn, Stanley, 'Top Spot to Deposit Illegal Narcotics Profits', *Wall Street Journal*, 16 October 1983.

Penn, Stanley, 'Deadly Policies', *Wall Street Journal*, 4 January 1988.

Penn, Stanley, 'Blemished Picture', *Wall Street Journal*, 26 May 1988.

Permanent Subcommittee on Investigations, Committee on Governmental Affairs, United States Senate, *Crime and Secrecy: The Use of Offshore Banks and Companies* (Washington, DC: US Government Printing Office, 1983).

Perry, James M., 'Drugs is a Big Campaign Issue Only for Jackson, But It's a Hot One That Could Backfire on Bush', *Wall Street Journal*, 21 March 1988.

Preston, Julia, 'In Panama, Turmoil Disturbs Peaceful Haven for International Bankers', *International Herald Tribune*, 11 July 1987.

REFERENCES

Putka, Gary, 'Insider Trading Raises Fewer Hackles', *Wall Street Journal*, 2 December 1986.

Putka, Gary, 'Those Famed Swiss Bank Accounts Aren't Quite as Impenetrable as They Used To Be', *Wall Street Journal*, 15 June 1986.

Putka, Gary, 'Guinness plc Made Secret Payments to Accounts of Swiss Bank Pictet & Cie', *Wall Street Journal*, 26 January 1987.

Putka, Gary, 'Secret Payment from Guinness Routed to Caribbean Firm by Ex-Grenfell Aide', *Wall Street Journal*, 13 February 1987.

Putka, Gary, 'Swiss Freeze Bank Accounts of Defendants in SEC Case', *Wall Street Journal*, 23 March 1987.

Raab, Selwyn, 'Financier Declines to Testify in Cash-Laundering Inquiry', *New York Times*, 15 March 1984.

Ramirez-Rojas, C. L., 'Monetary Substitution in Developing Countries', *Finance and Development*, June 1986.

Reich, Carl, *Financier: The Biography of Andre Meyer* (New York: William Morrow, 1983).

Reiss, Spencer, Strasser, Steve, and Barnathan, Joyce, 'Moonlighting Soviet Style', *Newsweek*, 30 June 1986.

Revsin, Philip, 'Swiss Accounts Don't Match Exotic Image', *Wall Street Journal*, 21 February 1985.

Richpuran, Somchai, 'Measuring Tax Evasion', *Finance and Development*, December 1984.

Ricks, Thomas E., 'Drug Lawyer', *Wall Street Journal*, 25 June 1983.

Ricks, Thomas E., 'Tax Evaders Find Foreign Banks Aren't Havens of Secrecy Anymore', *Wall Street Journal*, 14 August 1985.

Ricks, Thomas E., and Brannigan, Martha, 'Drug Lawyers View Carlos Lehder Case With a Mixture of Lust and Trepidation', *Wall Street Journal*, 10 February 1987.

Ricks, Thomas E., 'Foreign Brokerages Appear Frequently in Insider Trading Reports, Study Says', *Wall Street Journal*, 6 June 1988.

Riemer, Blanca, and Therrien, Lois, 'Money Laundering: The Defense Gets a Star Witness', *Business Week*, 28 March 1985.

Roberts, Steven V., 'Secret Saudi Funding Aids US Policy Goals', *International Herald Tribune*, 22 June 1987.

Rogers, David, 'Panama Records Show Strong Link Between Swiss Firm, Airlift to Contras', *Wall Street Journal*, 30 January 1987.

Rogers, David, 'Contras Helped Fund Military Activities With Panamanian Firms' Bank Accounts', *Wall Street Journal*, 5 March 1987.

Rohter, Larry, 'Bank Uncertainty in Panama', *New York Times*, 10 August 1987.

Rosen, R. Eliot, 'Treasury's Blunder in Paradise', *New York Times*, 4 October 1987.

Rosewicz, Barbara, and Seib, Gerald F., 'Big Business', *Wall Street Journal*, 22 July 1986.

Rowe, James, 'Bank Regulators Track Paper Trails in Search of Laundered Transactions', *Washington Post*, 3 March 1985.

Rupert, James, 'Revelation of Marcos Shareholding Gives Big Lift to 2 Inquiry Panels', *Wall Street Journal*, 24 March 1986.

Ryser, Jeffrey, and Javetski, Bill, 'Can South America's Addict Economies Ever Break Free?', *Business Week*, 22 September 1986.

Saunders, Laura, 'And Then There is Hong Kong', *Forbes*, 23 September 1985.

Scheibla, Shirley Hobbs, 'Where Hot Money Hides', *Barrons*, 11 July 1983.

Schuster, Lynda, 'Argentines Find Tax Avoidance an Untaxing Job', *Wall Street Journal*, 21 August 1984.

Shao, Maria, Templeman, John, and Gaffney, Charles, 'Hot on the Trail of the Marcos Billions', *Business Week*, 17 August 1987.

Shenon, Philip, 'Swiss May Open Files Tied to Iran Case', *New York Times*, 17 September 1987.

Shenon, Philip, 'Swiss Bank Records in Iran-Contra Case Are Released to US', *New York Times*, 4 November 1987.

Sherwell, Chris, 'Indonesia Cleans Up Its Ports and Customs', *Financial Times*, 12 June 1985.

Silk, Leonard, 'Economic Scene – Latin Nations – Capital Flight', *New York Times*, 17 April 1985.

Simons, Marlise, 'Tracking the Flight of Latin American Capital', *International Herald Tribune*, 9 May 1986.

Simons, Marlise, 'The Parallel Economy is Crime, and Crime Pays', *New York Times*, 6 June 1988.

Skousen, Mark, *The Complete Guide to Financial Privacy* (New York: Simon & Schuster, 1983).

Smith, Richard E., 'Swiss Court Indicates Banks Must Refuse Some Business', *Wall Street Journal*, 17 October 1985.

Snitzer, Adam, 'Stash Accounting', *Forbes*, 6 April 1987.

Solis, Dianna, 'Shady Exchanges', *Wall Street Journal*, 19 July 1986.

Stabler, Charles N., 'The Outlook – Underground Economy May Start Shrinking', *Wall Street Journal*, 25 August 1986.

Sterngold, James, 'Boston Bank Cites More Violations', *New York Times*, 29 March 1985.

Sterngold, James, 'Hutton Moves Resulted in Interest Free Loans', *New York Times*, 3 May 1985.

Sterngold, James, 'Bank of Boston Details Its Failures', *New York Times*, 25 July 1985.

Sterngold, James, '8 to Repay $7.8 Million in SEC Insider Case', *New York Times*, 28 February 1986.

Sterngold, James, 'Letter Unravelled Levine Case', *New York Times*, 10 June 1986.

Sterngold, James, 'Goldman Aide Tied to Insiders', *New York Times*, 9 July 1986.

Sterngold, James, 'Security-Conscious Wall Street', *New York Times*, 14 July 1986.

Sterngold, James, 'Wall Street, Hit by Insider Cases, Reviews Security', *International Herald Tribune*, 6 September 1986.

Sterngold, James, 'Merrill Lynch Official Named in $4 million Insider Scheme', *New York Times*, 12 March 1987.

Sterngold, James, 'Merrill Dismisses Accused Official', *New York Times*, 13 March 1987.

Stewart, James B., and Witcher, S. Karene, 'US Attorney Launches an Investigation of Former Banker at Morgan Guaranty', *Wall Street Journal*, 22 May 1986.

Stewart, James B., and Winkler, Matthew, 'Merrill Lynch Aide, Israeli Face Trading Charges', *Wall Street Journal*, 12 March 1987.

Stoakes, Christopher, 'The Insider Trader's Global Guide', *Euromoney*, July 1986.

Stoakes, Christopher, 'The People vs. Confidentiality', *Euromoney*, August 1986.

Stone, Michael, 'Insiders', *New York Times*, 28 July 1986.

Studer, Margaret, 'Swiss Authorities Seize Marcos Funds, Set Plan to Return Them to the Philippines', *Wall Street Journal*, 19 July 1986.

Studer, Margaret, 'Marcos Blocks Transfer to Philippines of Money Deposited in Zurich Bank', *Wall Street Journal*, 22 July 1986.

Studer, Margaret, 'Swiss Agency Seeks Tougher Curbs on Bank Secrecy', *Wall Street Journal*, 24 March 1987.

Subcommittee on Crime, Committee of the Judiciary, U.S. House of Representatives, 99th Congress, *Current Problems of Money Laundering* (Washington, D.C.: U.S. Government Printing Office, 1985).

Symonds, William C., *et al.*, 'The Sicilian Mafia is Still Going Strong', *Business Week*, 18 April 1988.

Tagliabue, John, 'Swiss Banks: As their International Role Grows, Secrecy Laws Bow to Foreign Pressure', *International Herald Tribune*, 3 June 1986.

Tagliabue, John, 'Swiss Company Calls Dealings Legal', *New York Times*, 2 December 1986.

Tagliabue, John, 'Swiss Account Linked to Arms Deal is Frozen', *New York Times*, 8 December 1986.

Tagliabue, John, 'Companies in Switzerland Appear to Have Been Fronts', *New York Times*, 15 December 1986.

Tagliabue, John, 'Accounts at Bank Frozen by Swiss', *New York Times*, 16 December 1986.

Tagliabue, John, 'US Gives Swiss 7 Names in Inquiry in Iran Affair', *New York Times*, 20 December 1986.

Tagliabue, John, 'Swiss to Freeze Iran Arms Accounts', *New York Times*, 31 December 1986.

Tagliabue, John, 'Vatican Prelate Said to Face Arrest in Milan Bank Collapse', *New York Times*, 26 February 1987.

Tanzi, Vito, *The Underground Economy* (Lexington, Mass: D.C. Heath, 1982).

Taylor, Robert E., 'Laundry Service', *Wall Street Journal*, 25 July 1983.

Taylor, Robert, 'Bank of Nova Scotia Quietly Complies With US Subpoena of Bahamas Records', *Wall Street Journal*, 22 September 1983.

Taylor, Robert, 'Cayman Islands Could be Erased as Haven for Drug Profits Under Pact, US Says.' *Wall Street Journal*, 13 September 1984.

Taylor, Robert E., 'Ex-Smuggler Tells of Huge Drug Profits Laundered, Placed at Major US Banks', *Wall Street Journal*, 12 February 1988.

Templeman, John, 'The Stone Wall of Swiss Secrecy', *Business Week*, 29 April 1985.

Templeman, John, 'The Insider Trading Dragnet is Stretching Across the Globe', *Business Week*, 23 March 1987.

Templeman, John, and Glasgall, William, 'A Mouse That's Roaring Into Money Management', *Business Week*, 1 February 1988.

Tolchin, Martin, 'Soviet Tried to Buy 3 US Banks', *Wall Street Journal*, 19 February 1986.

Toman, Barbara, 'Bank Leu Sells Embarrassing Guinness Stake', *Asian Wall Street Journal*, 18 May 1987.

Treatser, Joseph B., 'Panama Offers a Haven for Shadowy Concerns', *New York Times*, 21 December 1986.

Truell, Peter, 'Insider Trading Pact Seen Soon for US, Britain', *Wall Street Journal*, 4 September 1986.

Truell, Peter, and Power, William, 'Morgan Guaranty Ex-Official Gets 3½ Years in Jail, Fine', *Wall Street Journal*, 3 March 1987.

Tully, Shawn, 'The Lifestyle of Rich, the Infamous', *Fortune*, 22 December 1986.

United Nations Economic and Social Council, *Implementation and Development of*

International Instruments on the Control of Narcotic Drugs and Psychotropic Substances (New York, UN Economic and Social Council, Commission on Narcotic Drugs, 19 June 1986).

Vogel, Carol, 'Financier's Absence Deepens $130 Million Mystery', *New York Times*, 27 May 1988.

Wallace, Ellen, 'Swiss Wash Their Laundry', *Euromoney*, April 1987.

Warsh, David, 'The Money Launderers Stay a Step Ahead', *Boston Globe*, 15 June 1986.

Weigel, Russell, Hessing, Richard, and Ellflers, Henk, 'Psychological Profiles of Tax Evaders', *Journal of Personality and Social Psychology*, April 1988.

Welles, Chris, Templeman, John, and Cahan, Vicky, 'The Mysterious "Coincidences" in Insider Trading Case', *Business Week*, 9 August 1986.

Wermiel, Stephen, 'Top Court Lets Boston Bank's Penalty Stand', *Wall Street Journal*, 10 November 1987.

Wessel, David, and Langley, Monica, 'Boston Banks Didn't Report Cash Transfers', *Wall Street Journal*, 11 March 1985.

Wessel, David, 'US Accuses 5 of Using Bank to Defraud Holders of Pesos', *International Herald Tribune*, 5 March 1986.

Wicks, John, 'Swiss Bankers' Code Should Become Law', *Financial Times*, 30 May 1984.

Wicks, John, 'Swiss Banks on the Up and Up', *The Banker*, July 1984.

Wicks, John, 'Dollar Spur for Swiss Bank Assets', *Financial Times*, 26 April 1985.

Winkler, Matthew, 'Switzerland Beat out US in Extradition of Richard Keats in Bogus Securities Case', *Wall Street Journal*, 29 October 1983.

Winkler, Matthew, 'US Change in Rule on Withholding is Reshaping Eurodollar Bond Market', *Wall Street Journal*, 20 June 1985.

Winkler, Matthew, 'Bank Leu is Brushed by Scandals in Its Rush to Expand', *Wall Street Journal*, 26 January 1987.

Witcher, S. Karene, 'Brazil is Seeking Morgan Guaranty Account Names', *Wall Street Journal*, 23 May 1986.

Wolman, Clive, 'Insider Dealing Rings Operate Offshore Links', *Financial Times*, 4 March 1986.

Wolman, Clive, 'The Crime That Can Span a Host of Countries', *Financial Times*, 14 April 1986.

Wolman, Clive, 'How Big Fish Escape', *Financial Times*, 4 October 1986.

Wong, Jan, 'US Attorney Expects to Indict Banks in Boston for Currency-Law Violations', *Wall Street Journal*, 29 August 1985.

Wong, Jesse, 'Hong Kong Kiting Probe Looks at Citibank', *Wall Street Journal*, 13 May 1986.

Woolley, Suzanne, 'Opening a Swiss Account is No Big Secret', *Business Week*, 3 August 1987.

Zuckerman, Laurence, 'Wanted: Noriega', *Time*, 15 February 1988.

Index

Ingo Walter is the Charles Simon Professor of Applied Financial Economics at the Stern School of Business Administration, New York University. He also serves as Director of New York University Salomon Center. He has served as a consultant to various government agencies, banks, and corporations on international economic and financial problems.

Dr Walter is the author of many books, including *Global Financial Services* (1990). He is the editor of the *Handbook of International Business* (1988) and *Handbook of International Management* (1988). He is also the Series Editor of *World Industry Studies* (Unwin Hyman).